SOPHOCLES'

Oedipus Cycle

A Dual Language Edition

Οἰδίπους Τύραννος	*Oedipus the King*
Οἰδίπους ἐπὶ Κολωνῷ	*Oedipus at Colonus*
Ἀντιγόνη	*Antigone*

Greek Text Edited by
Sir Richard Jebb

English Translation and Notes by
Ian Johnston

Edited by
Evan Hayes and Stephen Nimis

FAENUM PUBLISHING
OXFORD, OHIO

Sophocles Oedipus Cycle: *A Dual Language Edition*
First Edition

© 2017 by Faenum Publishing

ISBN-10: 1940997917
ISBN-13: 9781940997919

Published by Faenum Publishing, Ltd.
Cover Design: Evan Hayes

for Geoffrey (1974-1997)

οἵη περ φύλλων γενεὴ τοίη δὲ καὶ ἀνδρῶν.
φύλλα τὰ μέν τ᾽ ἄνεμος χαμάδις χέει, ἄλλα δέ θ᾽ ὕλη
τηλεθόωσα φύει, ἔαρος δ᾽ ἐπιγίγνεται ὥρῃ:
ὣς ἀνδρῶν γενεὴ ἣ μὲν φύει ἣ δ᾽ ἀπολήγει.

Generations of men are like the leaves.
In winter, winds blow them down to earth,
but then, when spring season comes again,
the budding wood grows more. And so with men:
one generation grows, another dies away. (*Iliad* 6)

TABLE OF CONTENTS

EDITORS' NOTE

This volume presents the Ancient Greek text of Sophocles' *Oedipus the King* with a facing English translation. The Greek text is that of Richard Jebb, which is in the public domain and available as a pdf. This text has also been digitized by the Perseus Project (perseus.tufts.edu). The English translation and accompanying notes are those of Ian Johnston of Vancouver Island University, Nanaimo, BC. This translation is available freely online (records.viu.ca/~johnstoi/). We have reset both texts, making a number of very minor corrections and modifications, and placed them on opposing pages. This facing-page format will be useful to those wishing to read the English translation while looking at version of the Greek original, or vice versa.

Occasionally readings from other editions of or commentaries on Sophocles' Greek text are used, accounting for some minor departures from Jebb. Even so, some small discrepancies exist between the Greek text and the English translation.

FATE, FREEDOM, AND THE TRAGIC EXPERIENCE:
An Introductory Lecture on Sophocles' *Oedipus the King*
by Ian Johnston

Introduction

This week we are discussing one of the world's most famous plays, Sophocles's *Oedipus the King*, and my purpose here is to offer a general introduction to this famous and often puzzling work, which, from the time of the Classical Greeks, has set the standard for a form of literature we call *dramatic tragedy*. I shall be addressing that claim in some detail later on, but before getting to that or to the text of the play itself, I would like to clarify a couple of terms which are going to be crucial parts of the interpretative remarks I have to offer. In this preliminary part of the lecture, I shall attempt to link what goes on in this play to other works we have studied (or will be studying).

The lecture thus falls into three parts: first, an initial discussion of some terms I wish to use (particularly the terms *fate* and *hero*), then an application of those terms to what we see going on in *Oedipus the King*, and finally, building on these two concerns, I would like to address the terms *tragedy* and *tragic vision of experience*.

Fate, Fatalism, A Fatalistic World View

In Sophocles's play, as in other works we have read, we encounter an obviously important notion, the role played by *fate* or *the fates*. The emphasis placed on these words (and sometimes the personalities representing them) gives to the stories and the vision of life they hold up something we might call a *fatalistic* quality. What exactly does this mean? What does a text mean when it invokes the concept of *fate*?

Now, almost everyone will offer a definition of this quality, but it's surprising how those definitions can often differ. So let me attempt to clarify what, for the purposes of this lecture and beyond, I understand by these important terms.

To invoke the concept of *fate* or to have a *fatalistic* vision of experience is, simply put, to claim that the most important forces which create, shape, guide, reward, and afflict human life are out of human control. There is something else out there (where exactly varies from one vision to the next) which, in effect, sets and controls the rules of our lives, determining most or all things of particular importance to us: our good and bad fortune, our happiness and sorrow, and, above all, our death. To have a fatalistic sense of life is to hold that in this game of life, the rules, the flow of play, the success or failure of my team (and my contribution to that), and so on are out of the control of any human being or collection of human beings. The outcome and all the various stages of the game are determined from non-human sources.

The terms fate and fatalistic do assert, however, that something or someone is in control, and hence the universe does not operate by *chance*. We may have little to no accurate idea of why fate works the way it does (although differing fatalistic vision will provide different senses of just how much we can know and deal with fate), but at least there is something out there controlling what goes on. To assert that *chance* rules all things (as Jocasta does in the play) is to claim that there is little we can do to control things and nothing we can learn about it, since the concept of chance suggests that what occurs is quite arbitrary, unrelated to any higher system of order or meaning.

All these points are clear enough, but it is important to insist upon them, because (as I shall mention later) such fatalism is, in many ways, profoundly different from what we believe nowadays, and thus books which hold up a fatalistic view of life (and that includes almost all books up until the eighteenth century) can provide difficulties for us, especially since a fatalistic view of life in some ways challenges some of our most cherished beliefs and can make us profoundly uncomfortable (a factor which is, of course, something which can make such books uniquely valuable to us).

If we hold a fatalistic world view or believe in fate, it is not uncommon to give that fate a name or series of names, that is, to provide some way of talking about or picturing such fatal forces. Hence arises (according to many scholars of myth) the entire concept of divinity or a divine family—superhuman personalities (who may or may not have human forms and attributes) who control the rules and the events of our lives according to their own principles, which may or may not be intelligible to us (more about that later).

For instance, it's clear that the visions of life in *Gilgamesh* and the Old Testament, for all their differences, are fatalistic in the sense I have described. Ultimate control over human life is exercised by non-human forces or personalities. The human beings who believe these fatalistic visions have names for such controlling figures. In the Old Testament there is only one such fatal figure; in *Gilgamesh*, as in the Greek epics, there are numerous controlling figures. But the principle is the same: our lives are not in our own hands.

Giving fate a name or series of names is a necessary imaginative act, for it permits the human subject to such fate to understand his situation. Such a symbolic construct makes the most important features of human life emotionally intelligible, allowing us to explain and generally to accept the game we are all in, even if we are conscious that we did not choose it and can imagine a better one. It also permits us in the process to establish a relationship with the controlling forces of our existence. Such a relationship often forms the basis for personal or communal religious practices, especially if I believe that such fatal presences do listen and can sometimes be persuaded by prayer, sacrifice, penitence, and so on.

Let me give you a personal example. A few years my son was killed very unexpectedly. At once, I, like everyone else, searched for an explanation. Why did this disaster have to happen? What in this best of all possible worlds could justify such an unwelcome event? And after reading all the police reports and talking to countless people, I could come up with only one explanation: The Lord giveth and the Lord taketh away. Blessed be the name of the Lord.

Now, I'm not a particularly religious person. But that explanation (as unsatisfactory as many may find it) was enormously consoling. My son died because that's what fate, destiny, the Lord, or whatever one chooses to call it, had so determined. The event was not simply fortuitous, inexplicable. I could put a name and a personality on the disaster. I might not have been able to come up with a clear human reason, but I could at least make that event emotionally intelligible to me within the framework of a supportable belief system.

It's important at this stage to stress what such a fatalistic world view does not mean (or not necessarily mean). To call a world view fatalist or to believe in fate is not necessarily to characterize that fate as having any particular form. So, for example, a fatalistic world view might be extremely pessimistic, seeking in the non-human forces an irrational and often malignant force or personality which has little love for human beings and who takes a great delight in human suffering and death (or who, at least, permits it without much scruple). Alternatively, a fatalistic world view might well hold that the controlling forces or personalities of the cosmos are, on the whole, benevolent and friendly and that, if I attend carefully to what they demand, I may lead a generally satisfying life, perhaps even going on to some eternal happiness in the life hereafter. Such conflicting visions are both equally fatalistic, for they both share the sense that there is no human control over the rules and no method humans can devise for changing such rules. But they differ profoundly on how they view such fatal rules, the first being much more pessimistic than the second.

Another important point to note in discussing fatalism or a fatalistic view of life is that it does not therefore mean that human beings have no freedom. This point is crucial. The fates (or the gods, if I characterize my fatalistic vision in that manner) may indeed control all the rules and determine the good and bad things that happen to me, including my own death. But I am free to adopt towards that fate whatever attitude I choose. In other words, how I confront my fate is my free choice, the way in which I exercise my human freedom.

This point, indeed, should be clear enough after a reading of Exodus or *Gilgamesh*. For the key element in both books is an education in the appropriate stance towards the fatal conditions of life, something over which the people in the stories have complete freedom. God may control the world and the future of the Israelites, but they have freedom whether or not they believe in him. And that story shows us the great difficulty the Israelites, in their freedom in the desert, experience in maintaining the faith. God promises to reward them or their descendants if they believe, He gives them all sorts of demonstrations of His power, He punishes those who break faith and the rules which demonstrate that faith, but He does not determine their belief: they are free not to believe. Similarly in *Gilgamesh*, the hero goes through an extensive education before he freely chooses to accept his fate, return to Uruk, and live his life in the full and free acceptance of how the world operates. Gilgamesh has the freedom not to return, after all.

I stress this point about the importance of free will in a fatalistic universe, because it's the key to understanding most of the ancient stores we read. The quality of being human, in such stories, comes, not from the extent to which the hero controls his own destiny or fate (which is ultimately in the hands of other forces), but from the attitude(s) he adopts in the face of a fatal destiny.

[To appreciate the point one has only to think about a modern sports hero, whose greatness derives not from changing the rules or inventing a new game or whatever, but from operating within the given structure of the game, over which he has no control. What he does control is his own effort and attitude to what is going on. A sports figure who whines all the time about the unfairness of the rules is of little interest.]

For many of you I have been re-stating the obvious. However, for some here this concept of fatalism may seem rather odd or at least strange. For we North Americans (particularly those on the West Coast who are not Natives) are, in many respects the least fatalistic of people, and we spend most of our lives either denying the entire concept of a fatalistic vision of experience or trying hard to forget it. And we do that because we are heirs to a tradition, now about two hundred years old, which has attempted to deny the existence of fate in the old-fashioned sense I have been outlining above and to insist, by contrast, that human beings must be encouraged to take control over their own lives, to make their own rules, and where necessary to fight and conquer the given conditions of life, which are not fatal divine presences but human problems, capable of human solutions. We have all enlisted in the fight against Humbaba, the divine monster in *Gilgamesh* and our most cherished cultural belief is that we can and will eventually win.

We, in other words, have been trying to take control of the game of life, to reshape it to our own purposes, and to deny the existence of some greater powers over which we have no control. We have done this by launching a massive project to assault as much of nature as we can, so as to bring it under human control, so that we are no longer victims of casual changes in climate, bacterial infections, harvest failures, natural disasters. And we have been, in many quarters, so spectacularly successful that we are encouraged to think that we have only a short route to go before we become, as the saying has it, masters of our own fate.

This point is clear enough if you think for a moment about how everyone in here carries a clear fate, and no one has to have a religious sensibility to accept it. That is, each of us carries a biological destiny in our genes, something which, it seems clear, is going to control a great deal of what happens to us, no matter what we do. But most of us here are aware that we are assaulting that genetic destiny with a vengeance, so as to gain control of it, to subsume the mystery of our biological fate under human rational control. And many of us are extremely confident that once that victory is complete, we will have gained a significant victory over fate, putting human life, and perhaps even that strongest reminder of our fate, our death, into our own hands.

This two-hundred year old project has been accompanied by a general hostility to fatalistic ways of looking at the world (religious and otherwise), because any notion of fatalism, the sense that the controlling forces of the world are much more mysterious and powerful than we can imagine is an uncomfortable reminder that we may be deluding ourselves about our own powers, that what we are up against may be a great deal more complex and unknowable than we can imagine. Severe natural disasters or new outbreaks of massive lethal epidemics and similar occurrences are often unpleasant reminders that, even if we don't like to think about fate, we may not have put our fates as much under our control as we might wish. This very play, Sophocles's *Oedipus the King*, some have argued, is making precisely that point (I'll come back to this idea later).

The Hero

If we grasp something about the basic notion of a fatalistic universe (which is, as I say, fundamental to almost all traditional stories), then we can see why the principal character in many traditional stories has a unique importance. It's not simply a matter that the hero is very successful (although he often is) or that he he carries out deeds which no one else can carry out (although he frequently does just that). The hero is more likely to be someone who confronts fate in a very personal manner and whose reaction to that encounter serves to illuminate for us our own particular condition.

Sophocles

Most of us, after all, live in a community where we don't have to think about the implications of a fatalistic vision of the universe very much because our social group has educated us in a particular way of understanding the world and has provided, in addition to that education, all sorts of stories, rituals, institutions, and so on to reinforce our common approach to experience. We are all, to a great degree, creatures of habit in this respect. And so we don't constantly explore the basis for our belief or (if we stay more or less within our community) have to cope with any challenge to it.

The story of a hero who challenges or encounters fate and has to respond (particularly outside the community, physically or psychologically) can force us to confront some basic truths about life and about how what we like to believe rests on some fundamental assumptions. That can happen (and often does happen) even if the vision of fate which the hero has to deal with is quite strange to us. For the basic questions about life which a fatalistic vision of life raises transcend the particular details of that vision.

Let me explain. Many of us no longer believe in the Lord of the Old Testament, and we would be unlikely to sign on with Moses in his journey through the wilderness. But when we read that story, we have to confront a challenge: Who does control our lives? What sort of relationship do we have to that divine force? Does an acknowledgement of a fatal divine presence impose any moral obligations on me relative to my fellow believers? And so on. Moses gives us a vision of a particular answer to such questions. We don't have to share it in order for these questions to register as important and challenging. We may well prefer not to have to think about them most of the time. But if we are reading the Old Testament imaginatively, we can scarcely avoid them. And what comes out of that collision does not depend upon whether or not I share the faith of Moses in the Lord and the Lord's promise to His people's historical destiny (although the reader's evaluation of his response will certainly be different if he is a believer or a non-believer).

Similarly, I don't have to believe in the panoply of gods in *Gilgamesh* to sense that this is a fatalistic universe, that the hero's conduct forces him to confront his awareness of and attitude to the fates which control his destiny, and that his various responses (which go from ignoring fate, to challenging it, to accepting it) raise some serious issues for me.

[Incidentally, to digress for a moment, in this business, there's an important difference between someone we call a hero and someone we call a celebrity. The latter is someone who is very successful within the context of the social group, who has become well known because of his skill in existing within a particular set of rules, without having to question those rules. A hero, by contrast, is someone who confronts issues beyond the social rules, who encounters (often by a long physical journey) the fundamental conditions of life itself and who thus comes to some understanding, as Moses and Gilgamesh do, of the relationship between the way the world runs and the social group which bases itself on a shared community understanding. Celebrities, if you like, show us that our society can produce worldly success; heroes help us understand the reasons why our society works the way it does. Heroes, especially traditional heroes, are usually (often invariably) also celebrities, like Moses, Gilgamesh, and Oedipus. But heroes don't have to be celebrities (like Socrates).

Because heroes explore the roots of their society's beliefs (rather than just exploiting them), their stories will often be particularly illuminating about the particular cultural values of their communities. To understand why Moses is such a great hero (when, for example, he is in many ways unlike heroes from other cultures) is to understand a great deal about why the Israelites behave the way they do. To understand why Gilgamesh is such a great hero is to understand some things that lie at the heart of the vision of fate which *Gilgamesh* illuminates for us. To compare Moses and Gilgamesh as heroic characters is to come to an understanding of some of the fundamental differences between two famous and imaginatively moving fatalistic visions very different from our own understanding of the world.

The most significant feature of a traditional hero in comparison with the others in his community is his willingness to act, to make decisions (usually in response to a crisis of some kind), and to step forward and take risks in the face of fate at a time when such decisions are necessary. In Greek tragedies, nowhere more clearly than in *Oedipus the King*, this quality is what separates the hero from the chorus. The latter typically acknowledge their timidity or bewilderment or anxiety in the face of the crisis and look to the hero for leadership, often placing their hopes in the hero's record of previous successes. They are followers and require someone to step out an assume the risks of making decisions about what the community should do.

Oedipus the King: Some Initial Observations

I would now like to establish some preliminary observations (at first, some very obvious ones) about Oedipus in order to establish, following some of the remarks I have made above, why we can consider him a great hero and what his famous story reveals about the vision of human life which this play illuminates for us.

Oedipus is, we recognize right from the start, a great celebrity, a national leader of a city-state at a moment of crisis. Thebes has been mysteriously attacked by the plague, something which both Oedipus and the citizen see as a manifestation of the fatal forces of the universe in which they live. The citizens are dying, and they want, if possible, to stop the disaster. The future of their city depends upon that. They naturally turn to Oedipus, their firm and popular ruler.

The opening of the play makes at least two things clear to us. First, the citizens have enormous respect, even love, for Oedipus. They acknowledge not only his political power (which they have given him), but also his pre-eminence among all human beings for wisdom, especially in dealing with things they don't understand: "We judge you/ the first of men in what happens in this life/and in our interactions with the gods" (37-39). Second, we see in Oedipus a person of enormous self-assurance and self-confidence, a man who is willing to take on full responsibility for dealing with the crisis, a task which he clearly accepts as his own unique challenge. Oedipus has, we observe right from the opening lines, an enormously powerful sense of his own excellence, of his own worth (the most obvious indication of this point, something worth attending to throughout the entire play, is the frequency of the pronouns *I* and *me* in all of Oedipus's utterances).

The opening also makes clear to us that both the chorus's confidence in Oedipus and his strong sense of his own worth derive from past experience. Oedipus has saved the city before, at a time when many others had tried. And he did it with his mind, his intellect: he solved the riddle of the Sphinx. So the opening speeches clearly establish a harmonious relationship between ruler and ruled, based on past experience. Oedipus's confidence is not, in other words, merely an illusion. He has an exemplary record, the people have come to him because of that quality, and he fully intends to live up to that standard. Yes, he has a high regard for himself, but we are given to understand that that is quite deserved and shared by those over whom he rules.

And his first steps to deal with the crisis, that is, to send to the oracle for some instructions, are entirely appropriate. Given that fate has brought on the plague, what can fate reveal about its origins? Oedipus has, in fact, anticipated the request of the priest: he has already acted on his own initiative to address the crisis. And when the oracle's report is made public, Oedipus immediately and forcefully proclaims his famous curse against the murderer of Laius, the previous king. All this seems very appropriate. And, in fact, it does serve to reassure the people. Their fears are calmed, because Oedipus, their king who saved them before, is taking care of the problem.

At the same time, however, this scene gives us our first sense of what becomes inescapable later on. Oedipus, in accepting the responsibility, has no room for sharing the problem with anyone else. As a measure of his own greatness, he will resolve Thebes's distress, and he will do it openly for all to see. That's why he can dismiss Creon's suggestion that he listen to the report about the oracle privately first and why he can confidently declare "Then I will start afresh, and once again/ shed light on darkness" (159). He is taking on the task as a personal challenge, to be dealt with in his terms, not by delegating it to someone else or, indeed, by discussing the matter with others or, as we shall see, by listening to what others have to say and acting on their suggestions.

Oedipus's Self-Assertion

The quality I have just referred to (Oedipus's determination to deal with the issues himself), hinted at here in the opening scene, becomes increasingly evident as the play progresses. Indeed, it becomes his most obvious characteristic—his will to see this matter through on his own terms, no matter what the cost. And the more we learn about the ironic net of facts which he is uncovering about the murder, the more we see his determination grow. Even as he becomes increasingly aware about his own possible implication in the death of Laius, his commitment to finding an answer by himself remains strong.

This quality is the most puzzling and most important feature of Oedipus's character, and we need to appreciate it in order to understand both certain incidents in the play and the effect the play has on us. For Oedipus is fundamentally different from the heroes we have encountered so far. He is not like Moses, a man with hardly any sense of his own magnificence, a man who sees himself first and foremost as a servant of God charged with bringing religious and political discipline to his community. Nor is he like Gilgamesh, a man capable of learning to listen to others and finally to accept what they tell him about the nature of existence. Oedipus is a fiercely self-assertive man throughout his story. He is, to put the matter simply, a man who answers only to himself, to his image of his own greatness. The fact that he is acting in the interests of Thebes and trying to do the right thing (at least at first) doesn't alter this point at all. Oedipus is trying to live up to a standard, but it is not a standard given to him by God or one taught to him by others: the standard he answers to is the measure he sets of his own greatness. So prominent is this feature of his character, that we cannot separate out clearly Oedipus's desire to help the city from his desire to manifest his own greatness. In his eyes (and those of the chorus), of course, the two are identical.

For that reason, Oedipus has very little political sense, and the play has no political dimension to it at all. Creon seems to be the one with a political sensibility (where caution and a sense of political outcomes matter). Oedipus does everything publicly, as if hiding something would compromise his own greatness. He is Oedipus. He and everyone else recognize his greatness. To practice duplicity or political prudence would be to compromise his own sense of himself.

Sophocles

Oedipus and Teiresias

The most obvious indication of Oedipus's total commitment to himself is the famous quarrel with Teiresias. To some readers Oedipus's conduct here seems very odd, but this quarrel makes perfect sense if we see Oedipus as someone with no sense of ambiguity in life, as a person wedded to the view that his conception of what matters is, in fact, the truth.

By that standard, Oedipus has good reason to be angry with Teiresias and to suspect him. For Teiresias knows the murderer of Laius and will not tell. Oedipus has absolutely no sense that he might be involved at all. And since he has no conception of that as a possibility, it cannot be true. Thus, when Teiresias announces to Oedipus that "the accursed polluter of this land is you" (421), Oedipus's interpretation is clear enough: Teiresias must be lying, and he must have a reason, a secret agenda. A different man might well stop at this point, calm down, and ask Teiresias what he meant. That is to say, a different man might have stopped hanging onto his own certainties, confident that they were the truth, and have listened carefully to what someone else had to say (as Gilgamesh learns to do). But Oedipus is not that sort of person. In fact, rather than listen to Teiresias, Oedipus reminds everyone of his previous triumph over the Sphinx (stressing that Teiresias failed to help Thebes then)—he derives a sense of what is right from who he is based on his past achievements, rather than from any more flexible appreciation for more complex possibilities.

Many first-time readers of the play are quick to criticize Oedipus here, to say that, in effect, he is too hot tempered or proud or whatever. But it's important to remember that Oedipus has every reason to be fully confident that he is not implicated in the murder of Laius, as well as to be confident in his own abilities to get to the truth (after all, he's done it before). True, he might be more cautious and polite here, but if he had those qualities he almost certainly wouldn't be king of Thebes in the first place or, if he were, he would be too prudent to launch the sort of investigation he does.

This last point (to which I shall return) is crucial to grasp. At the heart of Oedipus's greatness is an enormous (and, as we learn, naïve) self-confidence. And we can be quick to criticize that as a failing. But without this self-confidence, this absolute trust in his own power to act decisively, publicly, and quickly, Oedipus would be like the Chorus, impotent in the face of the crisis, looking around for someone to take charge. The very things that we might find lacking in his character are the very things that enable him to step up to the front, make decisions, and act to meet the crisis (and eventually, let us remember, to deal with it, since he does find the murderer of Laius and cleanse the city of plague).

The Chorus and Other Characters

The contrast between Oedipus and the Chorus, very prominent in a stage production, is perhaps less evident to a reader. But it's important to note just how incapable they are of acting decisively. They want something done, but they are all too aware of their own limitations, their fear in the face of the unknown, typically addressing their fates with acknowledgements of their own terror or fearful questions:

> My fearful heart twists on the rack and shakes with fear.
> O Delian healer, for whom we cry aloud
> in holy awe, what obligation
> will you demand from me, a thing unknown
> or now renewed with the revolving years?
> Immortal voice, O child of golden Hope,
> speak to me! (185-191)

The Choral utterances are reminders of what we might call a normal response to experience—hesitation, fears, hopes, questions. They want to believe in the benevolence of their gods, but they know all too well that that may not be there. Confronting their fates with such feelings, naturally they lack the assertive self-confidence to do anything significant at the time of crisis, and they look to Oedipus to take actions because they not only have no idea what to do but lack the self-confidence to do anything.

Oedipus's treatment of Teiresias and Creon concerns the Chorus, and they make some attempt to calm things down, recognizing that Oedipus's quick judgment may be leading him to misjudge what Creon and Teiresias are saying. But they will not abandon or criticize Oedipus because they understand that if some decisive action needs to be taken, he's the only one who can do it.

They certainly cannot expect Creon to tackle the problem head on. After all, he makes it clear to everyone (including the readers) that he's primarily a cautious political operator, happy to play that game as second fiddle, with no desire to manifest his own excellence to the full. One gets the distinct sense that if Creon were in charge of the investigation into the plague, he would (like so many college administrators) appoints a series of committees to meet behind closed doors to talk the problem away if possible.

And Jocasta clearly wants the whole matter just to go away. She has precisely the wrong advice for Oedipus (not that he would listen to anyone's advice anyway) when she advises him to cease his investigation into his fate because there's no such thing, inviting him to live his life for the moment:

> Why should a man whose life seems ruled by chance
> live in fear—a man who never looks ahead,

who has no certain vision of his future.
It's best to live haphazardly, as best one can. (1161-1164)

What she's doing here, of course, is inviting Oedipus to be someone else, someone who has no concern for living up to his reputation for knowledge and courage. And, of course, Oedipus doesn't listen to her, just as he doesn't listen to anyone else.

One needs to measure Oedipus's stature against the other characters in the play, taking into account his capacity for decisive action in comparison to their inaction or unwillingness to think through the need for action. Whatever one might like to say by way of criticizing Oedipus, that point remains.

The Irony of Oedipus's Story: The Interplay of Fate and Free Will

What makes Oedipus's actions in this quarrel with Teiresias and throughout the play so dramatically compelling and increasingly tense is that we, the readers, know the outcome of the story. That is, we are familiar with Oedipus's fate. And yet there's no sense during the story that Oedipus is compelled to act the way he does: he freely chooses to initiate the chain of events which eventually reveals his fate to him. In that sense, the interplay between Oedipus's sense of his own freedom and our sense of his eventual outcome constitutes the main dramatic power in the play (for there's no suspense about the outcome of a story which is so well known to the audience before they arrive at the theatre or pick up the text to read it).

Oedipus has spent all his life dealing with his fate. He has, we learn, been told that he is fated to kill his father and marry his mother. And he has refused to accept that fate. He has spent much of his life moving around, so as to avoid his fate. In other words, he has freely chosen, for reasons which we can surely understand and applaud, to construct a life in which what he has been told will happen will not happen.

And, so far as he can tell, he has been spectacularly successful. In doing what he has done, Oedipus has gained (he thinks) the knowledge that a man does not have to meekly accept an unwelcome fate, and one, moreover, which is morally abhorrent to him and to the play's audience. He can take efforts to change the direction assigned to his life. This fact, once again, gives him powerful reasons for feeling very confident in his own abilities to deal with the mysterious powers which control the world. In his own mind, he is a human being who has thwarted his fate (although he is still very worried that it might eventually happen).

We, of course, know otherwise. So throughout the play there is a powerful sense of irony at work, an irony which manifests itself in the growing discrepancy between what Oedipus thinks is the case and what we know to be the case. We understand why he sees the world and himself the way he does (and we can applaud him for that). At the same time, we know he is wrong. He is deceived about his relationship to the world. In that sense, he is blind (a really important metaphor here).

[As an aside, one might observe that the very name *Oedipus*, which means either swollen foot or knowledge of one's feet or both, is a constant reminder of this ironic tension. Here the greatest of men, famous for his insight into the mysteries of life, is blind to the significance of his own name, an obvious clue to his past.]

The ironic tension builds as the play goes on, of course. The clues about the real murderer accumulate, yet Oedipus persists in believing he cannot be the one, even though he remembers killing a man at a road junction. And so, in his ignorance he redoubles his efforts, resisting all urges from Jocasta, his wife, to abandon the investigation. For Oedipus finding the truth becomes something of an obsession: he has to see this matter through, because that's the sort of man he is. Finding the truth is far more important than what that truth might reveal.

Hence, what we witness here is a strongly pessimistic vision of fate: here we have the best of men, the most knowledgeable, the most successful, and, in many ways, the best intentioned, who sets out to save his own city. And in a very fundamental way Oedipus is entirely *innocent*. He has done nothing by any standard of conventional morality to merit such a fate. But even such a man, for all his excellence and past success, cannot know enough about what fate is really like to recognize what it has in store for him. The truth of what he is and what he has done is even worse than he can possible imagine. And the course of events which leads him to discover the truth about himself has been freely initiated and maintained throughout by himself.

The vision of life here is very mysterious and very cruel. Even the best and most innocent of men, it seems to say, one who has striven to live the best life possible and who endures to find out the truth of who he really is and what his life really amounts to will be horrified to learn the truth. Fate has not established a reasonable covenant here with some clear rules and a happier future (as in Exodus), nor does fate offer a secure and valued life in the community (as in *Gilgamesh*), nor is there any sense that Oedipus's fate is linked to some sin he has committed. Here fate punishes arbitrarily and mercilessly those who choose to confront the mystery.

Oedipus as a Tragic Hero

It is time now to turn to a term which I have deliberately kept out of the discussion until this point, the word *tragedy* and its corollaries *tragic hero* and *tragic vision*. But now, having considered very cursorily some of the major points about *Oedipus the King*, I would like to introduce it in order to amplify the discussion of the play and to place that in a wider context.

Oedipus's story, I have argued, focuses our attention on a very particular heroic character, one who insists upon acting according to his own vision of experience, who persists freely in the course of action he has initiated, brushing aside or shouting down the objections or alternative suggestions of other people. He imposes on his life his own views of what he thinks is right, refusing to attend to what others are saying (he insists on agreement, rather than listening to others and weighing what they tell him). Oedipus, in his freedom, sets in motion a chain of events for which he accepts full responsibility and, even as disaster looms, he continues as before, not flinching or assigning blame or tasks to anyone else.

It's worth noting that, even when he learns the horrific truth of his life, Oedipus himself takes on the full responsibility for his own punishment. First, he stabs out his own eyes and then he insists on banishment. At no time in the play does he compromise: what needs to be done is what he decides needs to be done. And even in the face of the disastrous truth, Oedipus does not bend or break or start asking advice. He will act decisively until the very end.

In this respect, Oedipus stands in marked contrast to Gilgamesh, who, in response to the death of Enkidu is placed in a similar situation and for similar reasons—he thought he knew all there was to know about life. But Gilgamesh learns from that experience and changes. His behaviour towards others undergoes a significant transformation, and he comes back to Uruk at the end of the story a changed personality. Oedipus remains at the end of the play, for all the total reversal of his fortune, still the self-assertive man exercising full free control over his own life. If he is going to suffer, then he will determine what form that suffering will take.

Oedipus, of course, is more than just a particular character: he is also a character type. In fact, his story helps to define a certain heroic response to experience which we call *tragic*, and this play is commonly hailed as our greatest dramatic tragedy. While Sophocles's Oedipus is by no means our first tragic hero, he is certainly the most famous (outside of Shakespeare) and hence has exerted a decisive influence on literature in the West. Thus, I would like to spend a few moments looking at the general characteristics of his character, indicating how these help us to understand what we mean by a tragic hero (as opposed to other kinds of heroes), and then suggesting some observations about the vision of life which such a tragic hero exemplifies.

One major component in Oedipus's personality which helps to define him as a character we label as tragic is his attitude towards fate. Rather than aligning himself with it (as Moses does) or learning through experience to accept the mystery of fate (as Gilgamesh does) Oedipus chooses to defy fate. He will make his own decisions in his own way, and he will live with the consequences those bring. He will answer to his own sense of himself, rather than shape his life in accordance with someone else's set of rules or an awareness of something bigger and more important than himself. That's true of Oedipus at the start of the play, and he's doing the same thing at the end. At no point is he willing to compromise.

He is, if you like, a man totally committed to his own freedom to be what he thinks he must be, to live up to his own conception of heroic greatness. If there is an obstacle in the way (like Teiresias, for example), then that obstacle must be forcibly removed—it interferes with his sense of what's going on. Oedipus makes no effort to conceal what he is feeling or to hesitate about acting on those feelings. Why should he? After all, he is Oedipus, whose greatness manifests itself in being entirely true to itself, without duplicity.

Obviously he has an enormous ego—the central purpose of his life is to assert that sense of himself. With this powerful ego comes a certain narrowness of vision, which has no room for alternative opinions or dissenting views, and often a very powerfully assertive voice (dominated, as I have observed, by the pronouns *I* and *me*). But (and this is crucial) he is also prepared to accept any and all the consequences of his actions. That, too, is a measure of his greatness. The Chorus at the end of the play (like the reader) may blame fate or the gods or the impossible demands of life. Oedipus does not. He remains the master of what happens to him. The responsibility is his, and what happens to him is entirely up to him.

We need to remember that he is always in a sense the chief architect of what is happening to him. What underscores the irony I referred to earlier is that the Oedipus is dealing with a situation in which he is increasingly having to cope with circumstances initiated by his own decisions. This last point is an essential one. What makes Oedipus so compelling is not that he suffers horribly and endures at the end an almost living death (a great many other non-tragic heroes suffer wretchedly). The force of the play comes from the connection between Oedipus's sufferings and his own freely chosen actions, that is, from our awareness of how he himself is bringing upon his own head the dreadful outcome. His freely chosen decisions are (we know) bringing things closer and closer to an inevitable conclusion. Looking forward in the play we can see that Oedipus is free to go in different directions; in that sense he is not compelled to do what he does. Looking back over the action from the conclusion of the play, we can see a link of inevitable consequences arising from the hero's free decisions.

This is an important point because in common language we often use the term *tragic* or *tragedy* as a loose synonym for *terrible, pathetic,* or *horrible* (e.g., a tragic accident). But strictly speaking in a literary sense, true accidents are never tragic, because they are accidents; they occur by chance. What makes Sophoclean tragedy so moving is the step-by-step link between the hero's own decisions throughout the play and the disaster which awaits. As Aristotle points out, Sophoclean tragedy works, in part, through this sense of inevitability. Oedipus is doomed, mainly because he is the sort of person he is. Someone else, someone with a very different character, would not have suffered Oedipus's life. They would have compromised their sense of freedom in the name of prudence, custom, politics, or survival.

Such a powerfully egoistic character is entirely different from someone like, say, Moses, who sees his life in terms of service to the Lord and the community of Israelites (there's little sense that Moses has anything we might call an ego) or like Gilgamesh, who is prepared to wander adrift throughout the world looking for answers and learning from others so that he accepts limitations on own sense of personal freedom. Moses and Gilgamesh both suffer a great deal, but they learn from that suffering and encourage others to do so. Oedipus learns that he has been horribly wrong about life, but that does not induce him to change, or beg forgiveness, or transpose the blame onto someone else or seek to put his life on a different footing.

And the effects of the stories are quite different. Moses's story serves to confirm the validity of the existing social order, to endorse the vision of social order which the Lord has passed down to His people through Moses. Yes, Moses dies, but he has lived a full life and is in sight of the promised land, which his people will reach very soon. And Gilgamesh's story (like the *Odyssey*) confirms the social order of the community (particularly as that is enshrined by relationships with women) as the very centre of the good life.

Oedipus's story has a different effect. Because of what he has done, we have been given a privileged glimpse into the ineluctable mysteriousness and malignancy of fate. Here the social order is not confirmed as an eternal decree of fate: it is, by contrast, exposed as something of an illusion. The story of Oedipus, that is, offers us no consolation that what we believe about the order of the world or the benevolence of the ruling powers or the eternal rightness of our ways of dealing with them bears any relationship to what they are really like. In that sense it is a much more disturbing narrative (more about that later).

Further Observations on the Tragic Hero

If we take a step back from the story of Oedipus for a moment, we might want to ask ourselves this question: What is the point of telling such a story, or, more interestingly perhaps, why would we ever celebrate such a vision of life? This question is all the more compelling for us because the tragic hero and the vision of life his story holds up for us are something unique to the West, an inheritance passed onto us by the Greeks, something profoundly at odds with most of our religious sensibilities.

Put another way, we might wonder what there is to admire in a character like Oedipus, who confronts the world with a heroic self-assertion so strong that he will never compromise with social custom, prudence, or political strategy—not even when his own survival is at stake. Why should we admire a character who is willing to endure so much rather than to swerve from his self-directed course, even when that leads him to disaster?

The answer to such questions is very complex and much contested, and I can offer only a general indication. But I think it has something to do with our cultural obsession with personal freedom and integrity. For Oedipus (and tragic characters based on a similar vision of life) see life primarily in terms of these two qualities: freedom and integrity. So strong is their sense of the importance of these qualities that they simply ignore all the things which most of us do to remain in a stable well-functioning community, that is, to adjust our sense of our integrity and what we demand out of life to the demands of living in a community, limiting our desires and shaping our identity under certain pressures to conform.

Sophocles's play forces us to confront the disturbing reality about such an attitude: this ultimate expression of my own freedom to express myself, to demand from the world that it answer to me rather than the other way around, leads by a step-by-step process to inevitable destruction. For the fates that rule the cosmos are powerful and mysterious, and we have no right to assume that they are friendly. The human being who sets himself up to live life only on his own terms, as the totally free expressions of his own will, is going to come to a self-destructive end. However grand and imaginatively appealing the tragic stance might be, it is essentially an act of defiance against the gods (or whoever rules the cosmos) and will push the tragic hero to an series of actions (which he initiates in the full sense of his own freedom) culminating in destruction. We cannot live life entirely on our own terms for very long. We may think we can, but Oedipus is a reminder of the consequences. Fate is so much more powerful, complex, and hostile than we can possible imagine it, no matter what our consoling social narratives tell us.

By way of underscoring the nature of the tragic hero, consider for a moment some different varieties of heroic conduct. In many narratives, the hero, like Oedipus, faces a critical situation. But he deals with them in a very different manner—by trickery, disguise, cooperative action, for example (Odysseus is the great example from Greek narratives of such flexible conduct). In Moses's case, his actions are determined, not by self-initiated assertions of a powerful ego declaring its own preeminence, but by following instructions of the Lord on behalf the people (and he has to learn to trust the Lord and even go against his own sense of his abilities in order to serve). Gilgamesh becomes a mature leader only because he is capable of learning to move beyond the assertions of his ego, to acquire humility and an acceptance of his community's values.

In all such cases, the emphasis is very strongly on getting back to the community or hanging onto the community at all costs—the hero will do whatever is necessary within the framework of a shared belief system. And his greatness is measured by his success at confirming the importance of that belief system. To do so, the heroes must frequently compromise or hide their identity or undergo humbling experiences or admit they have been wrong, and so on. Once they display these characteristics, such heroes return home to a sense of continuity and happiness (hence, the frequent ending to such stories: "They lived happily ever after"). Such heroes we generally refer to as comic heroes, a term which does not mean necessarily that they are funny but rather that the ending of their stories is a celebration of community values, most often dramatically exemplified in the final dance (the *komos*).

The tragic hero, by contrast, rarely if ever displays such intellectual and emotional flexibility. He doesn't (in his mind) need to, since the purpose of his life is to live it openly on his own terms. And he ends his story with self-destruction, usually a self-chosen death (or suicide) because the only alternative to destruction (or self-destruction) is compromise, something he will not (or cannot) do. True, Oedipus does not die at the end of the story. But in a sense he is dead, moving out into the waste lands, beyond the community where he has created that sense of his own greatness. There is certainly no sense at the end of the play that Oedipus has anything to look forward to except death. In most of the plays we call tragedies the death is physical.

[Parenthetically, we might note here that it's not entirely clear at the end of the play whether Oedipus returns to the palace or stumbles out into the wilderness beyond the city. We know from the full Oedipus story that he eventually wandered out into the wilderness (as he wishes to do), but there are suggestions in the play that Creon is going to wait before allowing him to do that. However, there is no doubt that having Oedipus wander off away from the palace is the more dramatically compelling ending].

The Appeal of Tragedy

Let me try to explore the differences I have briefly referred to above in another way, using the terminology of an interpreter of the comic and tragic experience, Murray Krieger. Krieger observes that most of us live in communities and that these communities are governed by shared rules of conduct, ethical norms. These ethical norms constitute limits beyond which we do not go, for fear of either fracturing the community or endangering ourselves. Thus, we are all in a sense ethical human beings. We usually keep our disputes and desires and assertions of the self within certain limits, resolving differences of opinion in accordance with procedures and institutions we have set up to deal with them. Such rules may be given to us in our traditions, by our religion, or by a shared rational agreement, or by all three. And we set up civic institutions to ratify this shared social code (courts, churches, schools, legislatures). All around us we place reminders so that we recognize them and act on them. And should we be forced, by circumstance, to recognize that we have become somehow displaced from the community (as Odysseus or Gilgamesh is geographically during his adventures), we strive as hard as possible to get back, to recover the communal joy and security of living within the limits.

Now, acting in accordance with these ethical rules always requires, Krieger observes, certain compromises. We cannot be or do all that we might want, simply because the full range of human possibilities includes things which transgress the limits, the ethical norms upon which the community depends. Thus, an important part of being an ethical member of the community is to control ourselves and, if necessary, to educate ourselves, so that we act within the limits set by the community.

Now, it is clear that in this sense Odysseus and the mature Gilgamesh and Moses are ethical human beings. They do not challenge the basic rules set up for the community; in fact, their survival depends upon recognizing and using those rules. Moses and Odysseus get upset when certain life forms, like the Cyclopes, or certain people, like the rebelling Israelites, do not observe the limits of civilized living. Odysseus is constantly battling bad luck and the various challenges that nature is placing in his way, but he never loses faith in, let alone challenges, the most important shared rules of the community. The same is true of Moses. Both Odysseus and Moses may be displaced from society, outside the community or in the business of creating a community, but they want to get back in, because they believe in and endorse what communal living stands for. At the end of the *Odyssey*, for example, Odysseus and his rivals are prepared to compromise (under the orders of Athena), to end their conflict, in order to achieve tranquility on which the community depends. Gilgamesh is willing to move beyond the loss of Enkidu and his earlier identity and to celebrate the walls of Uruk.

But Oedipus is quite different. He is acting in the interests of the community, but his primary motivation does not come from any sense of ethical propriety or accepted norms of behaviour. He answers only to himself, and he is not willing to compromise his quest for the truth in the name of any social principle which others, like Creon or Jocasta, may offer, because to do so would be to violate his sense of himself. In that sense, he is like Job throughout most of Job's story: the only answer he will accept is one from god. Like Job, Oedipus is extraordinarily stubborn, resisting any pleas for moderation or limits on his own desires for life on his terms. The main difference between Job and Oedipus, of course, is that when fate reveals itself, Job bows down before it; Oedipus continues to defy it to the end.

This feature of the tragic hero as exemplified in Oedipus makes the tragic character a great paradox. For unlike most of us, the tragic hero emerges as anything but a social person. He apparently may begin that way, seemingly motivated by a genuine desire to help the community, as Oedipus and Job both do, but what emerges in the course of the action is that he is actually, deep down where it really counts, far more concerned with his own sense of himself, his own demands for justice on his own terms, than in compromising his desires with any awareness of ethical norms. He is, in fact, far less concerned about his own survival in the community than he is about being right, seeing things through to the very end.

What is there about such a character that commands our admiration? Why have we in the West placed such a high value on this sort of behaviour? For from one perspective tragic heroes, like Oedipus, are anything but attractive. They are usually very stubborn, egocentric, humourless, relentlessly convinced of their own rectitude, quick tempered, and unswerving in their pursuit of truth as they see it, with no room for those who would persuade them otherwise. These are not people whom one would, at first sight, like to invite to dinner or have as next-door neighbours or in-laws (Odysseus, Gilgamesh, or Moses, one senses, would be much better candidates for a social occasion).

And it's true that many people find the stance of the tragic hero unacceptable. Obviously, anyone who believes that certain ethical norms are laws of nature will find the tragic hero's stance simply idiotic—an vain egotistical posturing for self-glorification in defiance of the established truth of things. So it's not surprising that people who believe in the rational progress of human society will have no sympathy for tragedy. Walt Whitman, for example, the great democrat, expressed the views that America had no place for Shakespearean tragedy, and the first Commissar for Education in the Soviet Union, Lunacharsky, said much the same about the new communist state.

To admire the tragic character requires, not that we like him particularly, but rather that we see in his response to experience something magnificently heroic, an unwillingness to accept any shared understanding of experience, a refusal to compromise with any one else's answer as to what life is all about, a determination to push life beyond all simple ethical explanations and to discover for himself the full meaning of experience (that may not be his original intention, as I say, but as the story unfolds that becomes increasingly manifest). If that desire leads to self-destruction, as it usually does, then that is the price the hero is willing to pay. It's not that the tragic hero necessarily sets out with that goal in mind. But somewhere in the course of his adventures he is faced with a choice: compromise or continue on your own terms.

The comic hero, I have suggested, is the one who compromises for survival and a safe return. The tragic hero is the one to chooses not to compromise for the sake of continuing on his own terms, even if that means he will soon come to a nasty ending.

The really puzzling question is this: Why do some people make that choice not to compromise. How do we arrive at a sympathetic understanding of such a radically individualistic stance? There is no way to do so, short of witnessing it in some way. For the tragic stance is profoundly irrational. It stems from something deep inside some people, and has to do with the way they feel about themselves and about life. Most of us, I take it, are not tragic by nature. We are ethical citizens, compromising all the time with our desires to push life's envelope in order to achieve a secure cooperative life in the community. But imaginatively we can see in the tragic hero the courage and resolution of someone who is not prepared to compromise and who is prepared to endure terribly through life and to accept an early death as the price one must pay to live life entirely on one's own terms. To the extent that the tragic figure represents some ultimate possibility of human striving and achievement, we honour it, even if we cannot find adequate rational reasons for conferring communal worth upon it. A culture which values personal freedom and integrity will see in the tragic hero the ultimate symbol of those values.

What I am referring to is summed up in the famous dictum of Horace Walpole: Comedy is for the person who thinks, tragedy for the person who feels. A thinking person, wedded to some rational communal understanding of life, will often find no sense to the tragic stance, since it seems to violate all that community life demands from the individual in the name of joy, security, and justice. Only if I feel within me an emotionally imaginative contact with the tragic hero can it "mean" anything to me.

Krieger puts it this way. As human beings, he says, we have two basic urges—first, to survive in the community and to live on in our family and its descendants, and second, to have our individual life mean something, to have our integrity, our sense of ourselves as unique individuals uncontaminated with any compromise, count for something which endures. Comedy, Krieger argues, is the literary form celebrating the first impulse; tragedy the literary form celebrating the second. In comedy we are prepared to compromise our human individuality in order to secure a life in the enduring community. In tragedy the hero is prepared to sacrifice everything in order to guarantee his integrity.

That is one reason perhaps why comedy, for all its celebration and fun at the end, its sense of a community happily restored to a meaningful ethical way of life which will provide purpose to life, often contains within in a sense of defeat. There is something unwelcome to some people about that famous conclusion, "And lived happily ever after." For comedy inevitably involves a turning away from ultimate questions about the full importance of an individual life and settling for a significance provided by the community's shared values, even when we think (as we may do) that those values are not true or do not answer to everything we might like to achieve for ourselves.

That sense of a let down may also be the clue to one of our most intriguing characters in literature: the clown with the broken heart (Pagliacci, Rigoletto, Feste, Red Skelton, Tony Hancock, and others), the figure who has turned away from any final confrontation with the mystery of life and has devoted his energies to celebrating the joys that are possible in the community, in the full awareness of their illusory nature. We celebrate the fun, because the alternative is too dangerous to contemplate or endure.

Tragedy, by contrast, for all the pain and suffering the hero goes through, often brings with it a sense of triumph, at least to the extent that we have witnessed a possibility of the human spirit which is not prepared to define life by the limits imposed by the community and its shared rule-bound expectations. The tragic hero is a reminder that there are those who are prepared to tear apart the comforting illusions of cosmic order and justice by which we live in our communities, who have the courage to demand from life the truth of things, even if that truth is uncomfortable, as it surely is in Sophocles, or devastatingly pessimistic as it is in Euripides.

That sense of triumph is frequently accompanied by a sense of unease. After all, in tragedy we are celebrating the possibility of a human spirit's moving into uncharted territory in which our well loved social values stand revealed for what they may well be: illusions which we like to believe are the truth but which may be quite wrong.

For example, it is common to observe that *Oedipus the King* may well be a prophetic insight into the nature of our human confidence in our ability to confront fate. Perhaps we, in our scientific confidence, in the optimistic spirit with which we think we can deal with fate, may turn out to be like Oedipus, going up against something much more mysterious and complex and malignant than we can imagine. I don't want to push this interpretation here, but such an approach to the play might well help to generate some unease about the self-assertive confidence with which we declare our own superiority over fate and seek to solve all questions with those tools which seem to have served us so well in the past, our intelligence and daring. Do we even fully understand our own swollen feet?

Interpreting Tragedy

The tragic vision is particularly difficult to interpret, partly because it can be so difficult to accept the vision of the cosmos which it reveals. If the story of the tragic hero is a moving artistic reminder of the extent to which the universe is neither comforting nor rationally just, no matter how much we might like to think so, then as viewers or as readers it is striking at some of those things we most like to believe about the world.

Hence, we often try to moralize the tragic experience away. We try to convert the story of Oedipus from that of a supremely gifted and heroic individual who takes on life on his own terms and discovers the full mysterious destructiveness of the cosmos into a comforting morality story which tells us that Oedipus suffers because he sinned. If only he hadn't been so arrogant or so irascible or so egotistical or belligerent when confronted by his father and his entourage, or whatever, he would have been all right.

This approach to Oedipus or to any Sophoclean tragedy is, of course, disastrous, because it entirely misses the point. Of course, if Oedipus had been someone else, he wouldn't have ended up the way he does. But then he would not be the great person he is either. When we interpret the play in that way, we are like Job's comforters, trying to fit a painful and complex human situation into a moral straight jacket where we can understand it easily and without discomfort.

Oedipus suffers because he is a great human being. Yes, he makes an error, but it is his greatness as a human being which leads him into this error. That word error is important. It comes from Aristotle's concept of *hamartia*, that characteristic of the tragic hero which leads to his destruction. This phrase is often translated as "tragic flaw." And that translation has unfortunately encouraged the moralizing tendency, because the word "flaw" suggests some corrigible moral error, some sin, which he shouldn't have done.

The word "error" is more useful, I think, because it is closer to the Sophoclean idea that the tragic hero initiates his own downfall, not because he is somehow a sinner, but rather because he is so excellent, so capable, so confident of his powers, and so brave that he will take on the consequences. His error is inextricably tied up with his human greatness. If he were a lesser human being, like Creon, he would not suffer the way he does. But then he would not have the tragic greatness Oedipus manifests either.

Putting it another way, we can say Oedipus is capable of doing what he does because he is uniquely brave, excellent, and intelligent. But the tragedy reminds us that even the best and the bravest, those famous throughout the world for their knowledge, are doomed if they set themselves up against the mystery of life itself, and if they try to force life to answer to them, they are going to self-destruct. His error, if that is the word we must use, is not sin but *ignorance*, and he is ignorant of what he is up against because he is a human being. Even the very best of us, the ones with most reason to be confident of our powers of understanding, have no idea what fate is really like, what it has in store.

Sophocles

(One might briefly mention at this point that Oedipus is frequently in-
terpreted as an allegory for the Athens Sophocles lived in, a city which, like
Oedipus, is heading for total destruction because of its amazing achievements.
The play is thus not a warning that Athens ought to behave differently but
rather a tragic vision of the inevitability of Athens's decline and self-destruction. Others, as I have mentioned, following the same allegorizing tendency,
have seen in Oedipus the story of western civilization, especially the story
of its confidence in its own powers to shape nature and make it answer to
its own conceptions).

This desire to moralize the tragic experience is understandable perhaps, but
it takes the human mystery out of this complex vision of experience. It's true
there are many stories called tragedies, especially from the middle ages, which
see punishment for sin as the main point of the play. Whether we should call
these tragedies or not I'm not going to discuss. But I want to insist that they
are fundamentally different from what Sophocles is presenting in his play.

That is one reason why so many people find the end of Job something
unsatisfying. For Job's stance throughout most of his story is very close to
that of a Sophoclean tragic hero (comparisons between Job and Oedipus are
frequent). But Job does not push his demands on the cosmos to the limit.
When he comes to his recognition of the truth of the universe, he bows in
acquiescence to it. That experience does not shatter him. Quite the reverse,
it leads to great material and emotional rewards, and thus to a sense of comic
closure. When the chips are down, Job does what Gilgamesh does: he bows
down before the fates which rule the world, aligning his desires with theirs.

For the same reason, the tragic vision evaporates if we believe that there
is some life after death, if, that is, the life of the hero is not over and that
his death is simply the door to a future life in heaven or elsewhere. What
gives the tragic story so much power is the notion that whatever human life
is about, that significance ends with death. To add something about "living
happily or unhappily ever after" is to take away that sense of a final ending
upon which our admiration for tragic heroism depends. If you think about
it, there's a significant difference between someone like Oedipus and, say,
a Christian martyr who suffers horribly in the name of a faith shared by a
community of Christians and who goes onto an eternal reward. The conduct
may be heroic and the suffering just as intense on a physical level, but it is not
in the same Sophoclean sense tragic, since individual existence is not over.
And the promise of the reward in an afterlife clearly endorses rather than
challenges the ethical norms by which the martyr lived and died.. Hence all
traditional orthodox Christian views of life cannot be tragic but are inherently
comic (a divine comedy).

Parenthetically, it's interesting to observe that although most of Shakespeare's comedies take place in a recognizably Christian community, when

he comes to write tragedies, he generally (but not exclusively) prefers to shift the time of the play to a pagan or pre-Christian epoch. Thus, the sense of a Christian afterlife does not enter into the vision of life held up by the play.

The End of the Tragedy

By way of emphasizing some of the points I have been considering, let me briefly mention another point: how dramatic comedies and tragedies end. Dramatic comedies typically end with some communal celebration, especially of those things most closely associated with the survival of the community: betrothals, weddings, christening, a family feast and dance, from which the evil forces have been excluded (either because they have been exiled, killed, punished, or have reformed). The end of the (non-satiric) comedy thus becomes an enthusiastic endorsement of the ethical norms (often newly reconstituted) which ensure community stability.

The tragic drama, in Sophocles especially, tends to end, not with the death of the hero, but with the community's reflections upon the significance of the life which has just come to an end. In this respect Oedipus is unusual, since he is not dead (although his blindness and his expulsion from the human community indicates that his life in Thebes as a leading citizen is, in effect, over). The tragic hero's death (real or living death) also invites a community celebration, but it tends to be something much more muted, the community's attempts to come to terms with what the hero's story reveals about how the cosmos really works.

The carrying out of the corpse, traditionally the final episode in a tragedy, is thus a reconstituting of the community, but not in a way that emphasizes the joyful fun of community standards. Rather, the citizens are united by a new awareness of the mystery of life, something they, in their daily lives, rarely think about and never discover for themselves. It is given only to the greatest of heroes to take on the intense spiritual journey, and the conclusion of the tragedy, especially in Sophocles, typically confers upon this extraordinary individual the awed respect of a community which has benefited from his willingness to live life to the extreme (even if the reasons for that respect are very hard to explain rationally). They may not know exactly what to make of the experience (for the full tragic sense resists easy moral summation), but they are intensely aware of having been given a glimpse into something truly moving, something beyond the veil of more comforting ethical norms.

> So while we wait to see that final day,
> we cannot call a mortal being happy
> before he's passed beyond life free from pain. (1812-1814)

Sophocles

Postscript: Some Observations on the Historical Development of Tragic Drama

In seeking to elucidate the meaning of the term *tragic drama* we might usefully consider a few historical facts, starting with the point that tragic dramas started as those plays the Athenians put on in the Great Festival of Tragic Drama held at the annual religious festival in honour of the god Dionysus. Writers and actors were commissioned to take part in a competition, and prizes were awarded for the first, second, and third prize. Leading citizens were strongly encouraged to pay for the production.

The festival of tragic drama offered works which focused upon the life, suffering, and death of a great hero, usually one associated with the mythological past--Oedipus, Medea, Xerxes, Agamemnon, Ajax, Achilles, and so on. The audience was invited to witness the depiction and the celebration in art of the culminating event in a great hero or heroine's life, usually the struggle that ended with the main character's death and the community's reflection on that death.

Now, historians of literature, from Aristotle onwards, have for a long time been puzzled about why such a form of drama would emerge in the first place. This is all the more curious, since tragedy is not a form of drama found elsewhere. Unlike comedy, which we can see arising in many different cultures often in very similar ways, tragic drama seems to have been unique to Greece, and tragic drama is one of the most distinctively western traditions passed down to us.

So far as we can tell, tragic drama began in Athens sometime in the sixth century with an actor called Thespis. According to Aristotle's account (in the *Poetics*) originally a tragic drama consisted of a single actor and a large chorus. This feature suggests that tragic drama began as a choral celebration in memory of a dead hero in which someone, probably the leader of the chorus, at some point began to act out the exploits of the person being celebrated. That is, the leader of the chorus took on the role of the dead hero (thus making the celebration dramatic, since for drama to occur someone must pretend to be someone else, take on the role of a different character). Gradually, it seems, the number of actors increased. Aristotle tells us that Aeschylus was the first to introduce a second actor, Sophocles the first to introduce the third actor, and by the time of Euripides it is clear that the number of main actors has increased, and the importance of the massive chorus has decreased.

What should have led the Athenians to this unique form of drama is hard to figure out. Some historians have sought a clue in the word tragedy, which seems etymologically to have something to do with *tragos*, a goat. We know that the first actors clothed themselves in a goat's skin and that the goat was associated with Dionysus, the god at whose festival the tragedies were performed. But beyond that, speculation takes over. One critic has observed that tragedies are like goats, all hairy in front and bald behind. I offer that definition for whatever use you can make of it.

I don't propose here to survey the various theories that have been proposed as explaining the origin of this form of drama, except to observe that the celebration of the famous hero at the culminating point of his or her life may well have something to do with the Athenians' central concern with human excellence as it manifests itself in competition. For the tragic figure is, above all else, one who engages in the most dangerous and challenging of competitions, the struggle to assert one's human individuality to the fullest possible extent in the face of the most intractable opponent, the very nature of life itself--a subject first explored in Homer's *Iliad*, a source book for many Greek dramatic tragedies.

It is important to note that from the start the Athenians associated tragic drama with an important religious festival. For them, whatever took place in the experience of witnessing a tragedy was central to the religious life of the community. And the fiercely competitive nature of the contest and the esteem given to the winning playwright also indicate that tragic drama was for them a vital part of the community life.

The later history of tragedy is a complex business. As one can imagine, the tragic vision of experience (as exemplified in Sophocles) is not compatible with the much more optimistic fatalism of Christianity, with its emphasis on the good life as one of faith, hope, and charity within the Christian community and an eternity of joy or punishment afterwards. Many Christian writers used the term tragedy for relatively simple morality plays in which tragic figures were essentially great sinners whose death reinforces Christian doctrine, something very different in emphasis from Sophocles's vision.

In the Renaissance something like the old vision reappears in the great tragedies of Shakespeare (comparisons between *Oedipus* and *King Lear*, for example, are commonplace). But once we reach the eighteenth century and the powerful appeal of the new rational reforms of society and the aggressive agenda of the new science, traditional tragic drama becomes harder to write and to sell to a public which has little taste for such a challenge (for our culture is losing that sense of fate on which classic tragedy depends, except in some new literary forms, like the novel) and, with some important exceptions (notably Ibsen) tragic drama loses its vitality as a continuing literary form or artistic vision.

ΟΙΔΙΠΟΥΣ ΤΥΡΑΝΝΟΣ

OEDIPUS THE KING

ΤΑ ΤΟΥ ΔΡΑΜΑΤΟΣ ΠΡΟΣΩΠΑ

ΟΙΔΙΠΟΥΣ

ΙΕΡΕΥΣ

ΚΡΕΩΝ

ΧΟΡΟΣ

ΤΕΙΡΕΣΙΑΣ

ΪΟΚΑΣΤΗ

ΑΓΓΕΛΟΣ

ΘΕΡΑΠΩΝ

ΕΞΑΓΓΕΛΟΣ

DRAMATIS PERSONAE

OEDIPUS: king of Thebes

PRIEST: the high priest of Thebes

CREON: Oedipus' brother-in-law

CHORUS of Theban elders

TEIRESIAS: an old blind prophet

BOY: attendant on Teiresias

JOCASTA: wife of Oedipus, sister of Creon

MESSENGER: an old man

SERVANT: an old shepherd

SECOND MESSENGER: a servant of Oedipus

ANTIGONE: daughter of Oedipus and Jocasta, a child

ISMENE: daughter of Oedipus and Jocasta, a child

SERVANTS and ATTENDANTS on Oedipus and Jocasta

Οιδίπους Τύραννος

ΟΙΔΙΠΟΥΣ

ὦ τέκνα, Κάδμου τοῦ πάλαι νέα τροφή,
τίνας ποθ᾽ ἕδρας τάσδε μοι θοάζετε
ἱκτηρίοις κλάδοισιν ἐξεστεμμένοι;
πόλις δ᾽ ὁμοῦ μὲν θυμιαμάτων γέμει,
ὁμοῦ δὲ παιάνων τε καὶ στεναγμάτων·   5
ἀγὼ δικαιῶν μὴ παρ᾽ ἀγγέλων, τέκνα,
ἄλλων ἀκούειν αὐτὸς ὧδ᾽ ἐλήλυθα,
ὁ πᾶσι κλεινὸς Οἰδίπους καλούμενος.
ἀλλ᾽ ὦ γεραιέ, φράζ᾽, ἐπεὶ πρέπων ἔφυς
πρὸ τῶνδε φωνεῖν, τίνι τρόπῳ καθέστατε,   10
δείσαντες ἢ στέρξαντες; ὡς θέλοντος ἂν
ἐμοῦ προσαρκεῖν πᾶν· δυσάλγητος γὰρ ἂν
εἴην τοιάνδε μὴ οὐ κατοικτίρων ἕδραν.

ΙΕΡΕΥΣ

ἀλλ᾽ ὦ κρατύνων Οἰδίπους χώρας ἐμῆς,
ὁρᾷς μὲν ἡμᾶς ἡλίκοι προσήμεθα   15
βωμοῖσι τοῖς σοῖς· οἱ μὲν οὐδέπω μακρὰν
πτέσθαι σθένοντες, οἱ δὲ σὺν γήρᾳ βαρεῖς,
ἱερῆς, ἐγὼ μὲν Ζηνός, οἵδε τ᾽ ἠθέων
λεκτοί· τὸ δ᾽ ἄλλο φῦλον ἐξεστεμμένον
ἀγοραῖσι θακεῖ πρός τε Παλλάδος διπλοῖς   20
ναοῖς, ἐπ᾽ Ἰσμηνοῦ τε μαντείᾳ σποδῷ.
πόλις γάρ, ὥσπερ καὐτὸς εἰσορᾷς, ἄγαν

Oedipus the King

[The action takes place in Thebes in front of the royal palace. The main doors are directly facing the audience. There are altars beside the doors. A crowd of citizens carrying laurel branches garlanded with wool and led by the PRIEST has gathered in front of the altars, with some people sitting on the altar steps. OEDIPUS enters through the palace doors]

OEDIPUS
　　My children, latest generation born from Cadmus,
　　why are you sitting here with wreathed sticks
　　in supplication to me, while the city
　　fills with incense, chants, and cries of pain?[1]
　　Children, it would not be appropriate for me
　　to learn of this from any other source,
　　so I have come in person—I, Oedipus,
　　whose fame all men acknowledge. But you there,
　　old man, tell me—you seem to be the one
　　who ought to speak for those assembled here.　　　　　　[10]
　　What feeling brings you to me—fear or desire?
　　You can be confident that I will help.
　　I shall assist you willingly in every way.
　　I would be a hard-hearted man indeed,
　　if I did not pity suppliants like these.

PRIEST
　　Oedipus, ruler of my native land,
　　you see how people here of every age
　　are crouching down around your altars,
　　some fledglings barely strong enough to fly
　　and others bent by age, with priests as well—
　　for I'm priest of Zeus   and these ones here,
　　the pick of all our youth. The other groups
　　sit in the market place with suppliant branches
　　or else in front of Pallas' two shrines,　　　　　　　　[20]
　　or where Ismenus prophesies with fire.[2]
　　For our city, as you yourself can see,

41

ἤδη σαλεύει κἀνακουφίσαι κάρα
βυθῶν ἔτ᾽ οὐχ οἵα τε φοινίου σάλου,
φθίνουσα μὲν κάλυξιν ἐγκάρποις χθονός,   25
φθίνουσα δ᾽ ἀγέλαις βουνόμοις τόκοισί τε
ἀγόνοις γυναικῶν· ἐν δ᾽ ὁ πυρφόρος θεὸς
σκήψας ἐλαύνει, λοιμὸς ἔχθιστος, πόλιν,
ὑφ᾽ οὗ κενοῦται δῶμα Καδμεῖον, μέλας δ᾽
Ἅιδης στεναγμοῖς καὶ γόοις πλουτίζεται.   30
θεοῖσι μέν νυν οὐκ ἰσούμενόν σ᾽ ἐγὼ
οὐδ᾽ οἵδε παῖδες ἑζόμεσθ᾽ ἐφέστιοι,
ἀνδρῶν δὲ πρῶτον ἔν τε συμφοραῖς βίου
κρίνοντες ἔν τε δαιμόνων συναλλαγαῖς·
ὅς γ᾽ ἐξέλυσας ἄστυ Καδμεῖον μολὼν   35
σκληρᾶς ἀοιδοῦ δασμὸν ὃν παρείχομεν,
καὶ ταῦθ᾽ ὑφ᾽ ἡμῶν οὐδὲν ἐξειδὼς πλέον
οὐδ᾽ ἐκδιδαχθείς, ἀλλὰ προσθήκῃ θεοῦ
λέγει νομίζει θ᾽ ἡμὶν ὀρθῶσαι βίον·
νῦν τ᾽, ὦ κράτιστον πᾶσιν οἰδίπου κάρα,   40
ἱκετεύομέν σε πάντες οἵδε πρόστροποι
ἀλκήν τιν᾽ εὑρεῖν ἡμίν, εἴτε του θεῶν
φήμην ἀκούσας εἴτ᾽ ἀπ᾽ ἀνδρὸς οἶσθά του·
ὡς τοῖσιν ἐμπείροισι καὶ τὰς ξυμφορὰς
ζώσας ὁρῶ μάλιστα τῶν βουλευμάτων.   45
ἴθ᾽, ὦ βροτῶν ἄριστ᾽, ἀνόρθωσον πόλιν,
ἴθ᾽, εὐλαβήθηθ᾽· ὡς σὲ νῦν μὲν ἥδε γῆ
σωτῆρα κλῄζει τῆς πάρος προθυμίας·
ἀρχῆς δὲ τῆς σῆς μηδαμῶς μεμνώμεθα
στάντες τ᾽ ἐς ὀρθὸν καὶ πεσόντες ὕστερον.   50
ἀλλ᾽ ἀσφαλείᾳ τήνδ᾽ ἀνόρθωσον πόλιν·
ὄρνιθι γὰρ καὶ τὴν τότ᾽ αἰσίῳ τύχην
παρέσχες ἡμῖν, καὶ τανῦν ἴσος γενοῦ.
ὡς εἴπερ ἄρξεις τῆσδε γῆς, ὥσπερ κρατεῖς,
ξὺν ἀνδράσιν κάλλιον ἢ κενῆς κρατεῖν·   55
ὡς οὐδέν ἐστιν οὔτε πύργος οὔτε ναῦς
ἔρημος ἀνδρῶν μὴ ξυνοικούντων ἔσω.

is badly shaken—she cannot raise her head
above the depths of so much surging death.
Disease infects fruit blossoms in our land,
disease infects our herds of grazing cattle,
makes women in labour lose their children,
and deadly pestilence, that fiery god,
swoops down to blast the city, emptying
the House of Cadmus, and fills black Hades   [30]
with groans and howls. These children and myself
now sit here by your home, not because we think
you're equal to the gods. No. We judge you
the first of men in what happens in this life
and in our interactions with the gods.
For you came here, to our Cadmeian city,
and freed us from the tribute we were paying
to that cruel singer—and yet you knew
no more than we did and had not been taught.[3]
In their stories, the people testify
how, with gods' help, you gave us back our lives.
So now, Oedipus, our king, most powerful   [40]
in all men's eyes, we're here as suppliants,
all begging you to find some help for us,
either by listening to a heavenly voice,
or learning from some other human being.
For, in my view, men of experience
provide advice that gives the best results.
So now, you best of men, raise up our state.
Act to consolidate your fame, for now,
thanks to your eagerness in earlier days,
the city celebrates you as its saviour.
Don't let our memory of your ruling here   [50]
declare that we were first set right again
and later fell. No. Restore our city,
so that it stands secure. In those times past
you brought us joy—and with good omens, too.
Be that same man today. If you're to rule
as you are doing now, better to be king
in a land of men than in a desert.
An empty ship or city wall is nothing
if no men share a life together there.

ΟΙΔΙΠΟΥΣ

ὦ παῖδες οἰκτροί, γνωτὰ κοὐκ ἄγνωτά μοι
προσήλθεθ᾽ ἱμείροντες· εὖ γὰρ οἶδ᾽ ὅτι
νοσεῖτε πάντες, καὶ νοσοῦντες, ὡς ἐγὼ   60
οὐκ ἔστιν ὑμῶν ὅστις ἐξ ἴσου νοσεῖ.
τὸ μὲν γὰρ ὑμῶν ἄλγος εἰς ἕν᾽ ἔρχεται
μόνον καθ᾽ αὑτὸν κοὐδέν᾽ ἄλλον, ἡ δ᾽ ἐμὴ
ψυχὴ πόλιν τε κἀμὲ καὶ σ᾽ ὁμοῦ στένει.
ὥστ᾽ οὐχ ὕπνῳ γ᾽ εὕδοντά μ᾽ ἐξεγείρετε,   65
ἀλλ᾽ ἴστε πολλὰ μέν με δακρύσαντα δή,
πολλὰς δ᾽ ὁδοὺς ἐλθόντα φροντίδος πλάνοις·
ἣν δ᾽ εὖ σκοπῶν ηὕρισκον ἴασιν μόνην,
ταύτην ἔπραξα· παῖδα γὰρ Μενοικέως
Κρέοντ᾽, ἐμαυτοῦ γαμβρόν, ἐς τὰ Πυθικὰ   70
ἔπεμψα Φοίβου δώμαθ᾽, ὡς πύθοιθ᾽ ὅ τι
δρῶν ἢ τί φωνῶν τήνδε ῥυσαίμην πόλιν.
καί μ᾽ ἦμαρ ἤδη ξυμμετρούμενον χρόνῳ
λυπεῖ τί πράσσει· τοῦ γὰρ εἰκότος πέρα
ἄπεστι πλείω τοῦ καθήκοντος χρόνου.   75
ὅταν δ᾽ ἵκηται, τηνικαῦτ᾽ ἐγὼ κακὸς
μὴ δρῶν ἂν εἴην πάνθ᾽ ὅσ᾽ ἂν δηλοῖ θεός.

ΙΕΡΕΥΣ

ἀλλ᾽ εἰς καλὸν σύ τ᾽ εἶπας οἵδε τ᾽ ἀρτίως
Κρέοντα προσστείχοντα σημαίνουσί μοι.

ΟΙΔΙΠΟΥΣ

ὦναξ Ἄπολλον, εἰ γὰρ ἐν τύχῃ γέ τῳ   80
σωτῆρι βαίη λαμπρὸς ὥσπερ ὄμματι.

ΙΕΡΕΥΣ

ἀλλ᾽ εἰκάσαι μέν, ἡδύς· οὐ γὰρ ἂν κάρα
πολυστεφὴς ὧδ᾽ εἷρπε παγκάρπου δάφνης.

44

Oedipus the King

OEDIPUS

My poor children, I know why you have come—
I am not ignorant of what you yearn for.
For I understand that you are ill, and yet,   [60]
sick as you are, there is not one of you
whose illness equals mine. Your agony
comes to each one of you as his alone,
a special pain for him and no one else.
But here in my heart, I sorrow for myself,
and for the city, and for you—all together.
You are not rousing me from a deep sleep.
You must know I've been shedding many tears
and, in my wandering thoughts, exploring
many pathways. After a careful search
I grasped the only help that I could find
and acted on it. So I have sent away
my brother-in-law, son of Menoeceus,
Creon, to Pythian Apollo's shrine,   [70]
to learn from him what I might do or say
to save our city. But when I count the days—
the time he's been away—I now worry
what he's doing. For he's been gone too long,
well past the time he should have taken.
But when he comes, I'll be a wicked man
if I do not act on all the god reveals.

PRIEST

What you have said is most appropriate,
for these men here have just informed me
that Creon is approaching.

OEDIPUS

                              Lord Apollo,   [80]
as he returns may fine shining fortune,
bright as his countenance, attend on him.

PRIEST

It seems the news he brings is good—if not,
he would not wear that wreath around his head,
a laurel thickly packed with berries.[4]

45

ΟΙΔΙΠΟΥΣ

τάχ᾽ εἰσόμεσθα· ξύμμετρος γὰρ ὡς κλύειν.

ἄναξ, ἐμὸν κήδευμα, παῖ Μενοικέως,　　　　85
τίν᾽ ἡμὶν ἥκεις τοῦ θεοῦ φήμην φέρων;

ΚΡΕΩΝ

ἐσθλήν· λέγω γὰρ καὶ τὰ δύσφορ᾽, εἰ τύχοι
κατ᾽ ὀρθὸν ἐξελθόντα, πάντ᾽ ἂν εὐτυχεῖν.

ΟΙΔΙΠΟΥΣ

ἔστιν δὲ ποῖον τοὔπος; οὔτε γὰρ θρασὺς
οὔτ᾽ οὖν προδείσας εἰμὶ τῷ γε νῦν λόγῳ.　　90

ΚΡΕΩΝ

εἰ τῶνδε χρῄζεις πλησιαζόντων κλύειν,
ἕτοιμος εἰπεῖν, εἴτε καὶ στείχειν ἔσω.

ΟΙΔΙΠΟΥΣ

ἐς πάντας αὔδα· τῶνδε γὰρ πλέον φέρω
τὸ πένθος ἢ καὶ τῆς ἐμῆς ψυχῆς πέρι.

ΚΡΕΩΝ

λέγοιμ ἂν οἷ᾽ ἤκουσα τοῦ θεοῦ πάρα.　　95
ἄνωγεν ἡμᾶς Φοῖβος ἐμφανῶς ἄναξ
μίασμα χώρας, ὡς τεθραμμένον χθονὶ
ἐν τῇδ᾽, ἐλαύνειν μηδ᾽ ἀνήκεστον τρέφειν.

ΟΙΔΙΠΟΥΣ

ποίῳ καθαρμῷ; τίς ὁ τρόπος τῆς ξυμφορᾶς;

ΚΡΕΩΝ

ἀνδρηλατοῦντας ἢ φόνῳ φόνον πάλιν　　100
λύοντας, ὡς τόδ᾽ αἷμα χειμάζον πόλιν.

ΟΙΔΙΠΟΥΣ

ποίου γὰρ ἀνδρὸς τήνδε μηνύει τύχην;

46

OEDIPUS
We'll know soon enough—he's within earshot.

[Enter CREON. OEDIPUS calls to him as he approaches]

My royal kinsman, child of Menoeceus,
what message do you bring us from the god?

CREON
Good news, I tell you. If things work out well,
then these troubles, so difficult to bear,
will end up bringing us great benefits.

OEDIPUS
What is the oracle? So far your words
inspire in me no confidence or fear.   [90]

CREON
If you wish to hear the news in public,
I'm prepared to speak. Or we could step inside.

OEDIPUS
Speak out to everyone. The grief I feel
for these citizens is even greater
than any pain I feel for my own life.

CREON
Then let me report what I heard from the god.
Lord Phoebus clearly orders us to drive away
the polluting stain this land has harboured.
It will not be healed if we keep nursing it.

OEDIPUS
What sort of cleansing? And this disaster—
how did it happen?

CREON
                                    By banishment—   [100]
or atone for murder by shedding blood again,
for blood brings on the storm which blasts our state.

OEDIPUS
And the one whose fate the god revealed—
what sort of man is he?

47

ΚΡΕΩΝ

ἦν ἡμίν, ὦναξ, Λάϊός ποθ᾽ ἡγεμὼν
γῆς τῆσδε, πρὶν σὲ τήνδ᾽ ἀπευθύνειν πόλιν.

ΟΙΔΙΠΟΥΣ

ἔξοιδ᾽ ἀκούων· οὐ γὰρ εἰσεῖδόν γέ πω.   105

ΚΡΕΩΝ

τούτου θανόντος νῦν ἐπιστέλλει σαφῶς
τοὺς αὐτοέντας χειρὶ τιμωρεῖν τινας.

ΟΙΔΙΠΟΥΣ

οἳ δ᾽ εἰσὶ ποῦ γῆς; ποῦ τόδ᾽ εὑρεθήσεται
ἴχνος παλαιᾶς δυστέκμαρτον αἰτίας;

ΚΡΕΩΝ

ἐν τῇδ᾽ ἔφασκε γῇ· τὸ δὲ ζητούμενον   110
ἁλωτόν, ἐκφεύγειν δὲ τἀμελούμενον.

ΟΙΔΙΠΟΥΣ

πότερα δ᾽ ἐν οἴκοις ἢ 'ν ἀγροῖς ὁ Λάϊος
ἢ γῆς ἐπ᾽ ἄλλης τῷδε συμπίπτει φόνῳ;

ΚΡΕΩΝ

θεωρός, ὡς ἔφασκεν, ἐκδημῶν, πάλιν
πρὸς οἶκον οὐκέθ᾽ ἵκεθ᾽, ὡς ἀπεστάλη.   115

ΟΙΔΙΠΟΥΣ

οὐδ᾽ ἄγγελός τις οὐδὲ συμπράκτωρ ὁδοῦ
κατεῖδ᾽, ὅτου τις ἐκμαθὼν ἐχρήσατ᾽ ἄν;

ΚΡΕΩΝ

θνῄσκουσι γάρ, πλὴν εἷς τις, ὃς φόβῳ, φυγὼν
ὧν εἶδε πλὴν ἓν οὐδὲν εἶχ᾽ εἰδὼς φράσαι.

48

CREON

                            Before you came, my lord,
to steer our ship of state, Laius ruled this land.

OEDIPUS

I have heard that, but I never saw the man.

CREON

Laius was killed. And now the god is clear:
those murderers, he tells us, must be punished,
whoever they may be.

OEDIPUS

                          And where are they?
In what country? Where am I to find a trace
of this ancient crime? It will be hard to track.

CREON

Here in Thebes, so said the god. What is sought
is found, but what is overlooked escapes.   [110]

OEDIPUS

When Laius fell in bloody death, where was he—
at home, or in his fields, or in another land?

CREON

He was abroad, on his way to Delphi—
that's what he told us. He began the trip,
but did not return.

OEDIPUS

                     Was there no messenger—
no companion who made the journey with him
and witnessed what took place—a person
who might provide some knowledge men could use?

CREON

They all died—except for one who was afraid
and ran away. There was only one thing
he could inform us of with confidence
about the things he saw.

49

ΟΙΔΙΠΟΥΣ
τὸ ποῖον; ἒν γὰρ πόλλ' ἂν ἐξεύροι μαθεῖν,   120
ἀρχὴν βραχεῖαν εἰ λάβοιμεν ἐλπίδος.

ΚΡΕΩΝ
λῃστὰς ἔφασκε συντυχόντας οὐ μιᾷ
ῥώμῃ κτανεῖν νιν, ἀλλὰ σὺν πλήθει χερῶν.

ΟΙΔΙΠΟΥΣ
πῶς οὖν ὁ λῃστής, εἴ τι μὴ ξὺν ἀργύρῳ
ἐπράσσετ' ἐνθένδ', ἐς τόδ' ἂν τόλμης ἔβη;   125

ΚΡΕΩΝ
δοκοῦντα ταῦτ' ἦν· Λαΐου δ' ὀλωλότος
οὐδεὶς ἀρωγὸς ἐν κακοῖς ἐγίγνετο.

ΟΙΔΙΠΟΥΣ
κακὸν δὲ ποῖον ἐμποδών, τυραννίδος
οὕτω πεσούσης, εἶργε τοῦτ' ἐξειδέναι;

ΚΡΕΩΝ
ἡ ποικιλῳδὸς Σφὶγξ τὸ πρὸς ποσὶν σκοπεῖν   130
μεθέντας ἡμᾶς τἀφανῆ προσήγετο.

ΟΙΔΙΠΟΥΣ
ἀλλ' ἐξ ὑπαρχῆς αὖθις αὔτ' ἐγὼ φανῶ·
ἐπαξίως γὰρ Φοῖβος, ἀξίως δὲ σὺ
πρὸ τοῦ θανόντος τήνδ' ἔθεσθ' ἐπιστροφήν·
ὥστ' ἐνδίκως ὄψεσθε κἀμὲ σύμμαχον   135
γῇ τῇδε τιμωροῦντα τῷ θεῷ θ' ἅμα.
ὑπὲρ γὰρ οὐχὶ τῶν ἀπωτέρω φίλων,
ἀλλ' αὐτὸς αὑτοῦ τοῦτ' ἀποσκεδῶ μύσος.
ὅστις γὰρ ἦν ἐκεῖνον ὁ κτανών, τάχ' ἂν
κἄμ' ἂν τοιαύτῃ χειρὶ τιμωροῦνθ' ἕλοι.   140
κείνῳ προσαρκῶν οὖν ἐμαυτὸν ὠφελῶ.

OEDIPUS

What was that?

We might get somewhere if we had one fact—   [120]
we could find many things, if we possessed
some slender hope to get us going.

CREON

He told us it was robbers who attacked them—
not just a single man, a gang of them—
they came on with force and killed him.

OEDIPUS

How would a thief have dared to do this,
unless he had financial help from Thebes?

CREON

That's what we guessed. But once Laius was dead
we were in trouble, so no one sought revenge.

OEDIPUS

When the ruling king had fallen in this way,
what bad trouble blocked your path, preventing you
from looking into it?

CREON

It was the Sphinx—   [130]
she sang her cryptic song and so forced us
to put aside something we found obscure
to look into the problem we now faced.

OEDIPUS

Then I will start afresh, and once again
shed light on darkness. It is most fitting
that Apollo demonstrates his care
for the dead man, and worthy of you, too.
And so you'll see how I will work with you,
as is right, seeking vengeance for this land,
as well as for the god. This polluting stain
I will remove, not for some distant friends,
but for myself. For whoever killed this man
may soon enough desire to turn his hand   [140]
to punish me in the same way, as well.
Thus, in avenging Laius, I serve myself.

Sophocles

ἀλλ' ὡς τάχιστα, παῖδες, ὑμεῖς μὲν βάθρων
ἵστασθε, τούσδ' ἄραντες ἱκτῆρας κλάδους,
ἄλλος δὲ Κάδμου λαὸν ὧδ' ἀθροιζέτω,
ὡς πᾶν ἐμοῦ δράσοντος· ἢ γὰρ εὐτυχεῖς   145
σὺν τῷ θεῷ φανούμεθ' ἢ πεπτωκότες.

ΙΕΡΕΥΣ

ὦ παῖδες, ἱστώμεσθα· τῶνδε γὰρ χάριν
καὶ δεῦρ' ἔβημεν ὧν ὅδ' ἐξαγγέλλεται.
Φοῖβος δ' ὁ πέμψας τάσδε μαντείας ἅμα
σωτήρ δ' ἵκοιτο καὶ νόσου παυστήριος.   150

ΧΟΡΟΣ

ὦ Διὸς ἁδυεπὲς φάτι, τίς ποτε τᾶς πολυχρύσου
Πυθῶνος ἀγλαὰς ἔβας
Θήβας; ἐκτέταμαι φοβερὰν φρένα, δείματι πάλλων,
ἰήιε Δάλιε Παιάν,
ἀμφὶ σοὶ ἁζόμενος τί μοι ἢ νέον   155
ἢ περιτελλομέναις ὥραις πάλιν ἐξανύσεις χρέος.
εἰπέ μοι, ὦ χρυσέας τέκνον Ἐλπίδος, ἄμβροτε Φάμα.
πρῶτα σὲ κεκλόμενος, θύγατερ Διός, ἄμβροτ' Ἀθάνα   160
γαιάοχόν τ' ἀδελφεὰν
Ἄρτεμιν, ἃ κυκλόεντ' ἀγορᾶς θρόνον εὐκλέα θάσσει,
καὶ Φοῖβον ἑκαβόλον, ἰὼ
τρισσοὶ ἀλεξίμοροι προφάνητέ μοι,
εἴ ποτε καὶ προτέρας ἄτας ὕπερ ὀρνυμένας πόλει   165
ἠνύσατ' ἐκτοπίαν φλόγα πήματος, ἔλθετε καὶ νῦν.

52

But now, my children, quickly as you can
stand up from these altar steps and raise
your suppliant branches. Someone must call
the Theban people to assemble here.
I'll do everything I can. With the god's help
this will all come to light successfully,
or else will prove our common ruin.

[OEDIPUS and CREON go into the palace]

PRIEST

Let us get up, children. For this man
has willingly declared just what we came for.
And may Phoebus, who sent this oracle,
come as our saviour and end our sickness.   [150]

[The PRIEST and the CITIZENS leave. Enter the CHORUS OF THEBAN ELDERS]

CHORUS

O sweet speaking voice of Zeus,
you have come to glorious Thebes from golden Pytho—
but what is your intent?
My fearful heart twists on the rack and shakes with fear.
O Delian healer, for whom we cry aloud
in holy awe, what obligation
will you demand from me, a thing unknown
or now renewed with the revolving years?
Immortal voice, O child of golden Hope,
speak to me!

First I call on you, Athena the immortal,
daughter of Zeus, and on your sister, too,   [160]
Artemis, who guards our land and sits
on her glorious round throne in our market place,
and on Phoebus, who shoots from far away.
O you three guardians against death,
appear to me!
If before now you have ever driven off
a fiery plague to keep disaster
from the city and have banished it,
then come to us this time as well!

53

ὦ πόποι, ἀνάριθμα γὰρ φέρω
πήματα· νοσεῖ δέ μοι πρόπας στόλος, οὐδ᾽ ἔνι φροντί-
δος ἔγχος   170
ᾧ τις ἀλέξεται. οὔτε γὰρ ἔκγονα
κλυτᾶς χθονὸς αὔξεται οὔτε τόκοισιν
ἰηίων καμάτων ἀνέχουσι γυναῖκες·
ἄλλον δ᾽ ἂν ἄλλῳ προσίδοις ἅπερ εὔπτερον ὄρνιν   175
κρεῖσσον ἀμαιμακέτου πυρὸς ὄρμενον
ἀκτὰν πρὸς ἑσπέρου θεοῦ.
ὧν πόλις ἀνάριθμος ὄλλυται·
νηλέα δὲ γένεθλα πρὸς πέδῳ θαναταφόρα κεῖται ἀνοίκτως·
ἐν δ᾽ ἄλοχοι πολιαί τ᾽ ἔπι ματέρες   181
ἀχὰν παραβώμιον ἄλλοθεν ἄλλαν
λυγρῶν πόνων ἱκετῆρες ἐπιστενάχουσιν.
παιὰν δὲ λάμπει στονόεσσά τε γῆρυς ὅμαυλος   185
ὧν ὕπερ, ὦ χρυσέα θύγατερ Διός,
εὐῶπα πέμψον ἀλκάν.
Ἄρεά τε τὸν μαλερόν, ὃς νῦν ἄχαλκος ἀσπίδων   190
φλέγει με περιβόατον, ἀντιάζω
παλίσσυτον δράμημα νωτίσαι πάτρας
ἔπουρον, εἴτ᾽ ἐς μέγαν θάλαμον Ἀμφιτρίτας
εἴτ᾽ ἐς τὸν ἀπόξενον ὅρμων   195
Θρήκιον κλύδωνα·
τελεῖν γὰρ εἴ τι νὺξ ἀφῇ,
τοῦτ᾽ ἐπ᾽ ἦμαρ ἔρχεται·
τόν, ὦ τᾶν πυρφόρων
ἀστραπᾶν κράτη νέμων,   200
ὦ Ζεῦ πάτερ, ὑπὸ σῷ φθίσον κεραυνῷ,
Λύκει᾽ ἄναξ, τά τε σὰ χρυσοστρόφων ἀπ᾽ ἀγκυλᾶν
βέλεα θέλοιμ᾽ ἂν ἀδάματ᾽ ἐνδατεῖσθαι
ἀρωγὰ προσταχθέντα τάς τε πυρφόρους   205
Ἀρτέμιδος αἴγλας, ξὺν αἷς Λύκι᾽ ὄρεα διᾴσσει·

Alas, the pains I bear are numberless—
my people now all sick with plague,
our minds can find no weapons   [170]
to help with our defence. Now the offspring
of our splendid earth no longer grow,
nor do our women crying out in labour
get their relief from a living new-born child.
As you can see—one by one they swoop away,
off to the shores of the evening god, like birds
faster than fire which no one can resist.

Our city dies—we've lost count of all the dead.
Her sons lie in the dirt unpitied, unlamented.   [180]
Corpses spread the pestilence, while youthful wives
and grey-haired mothers on the altar steps
wail everywhere and cry in supplication,
seeking to relieve their agonizing pain.
Their solemn chants ring out—
they mingle with the voices of lament.
O Zeus' golden daughter,
send your support and strength,
your lovely countenance!

And that ravenous Ares, god of killing,   [190]
who now consumes me as he charges on
with no bronze shield but howling battle cries,
let him turn his back and quickly leave this land,
with a fair following wind to carry him
to the great chamber of Amphitrite
or inhospitable waves of Thrace.5
For if destruction does not come at night,
then day arrives to see it does its work.
O you who wield that mighty flash of fire,   [200]
O father Zeus, with your lighting blast
let Ares be destroyed!

O Lycean lord, how I wish those arrows
from the golden string of your bent bow
with their all-conquering force would wing out
to champion us against our enemy,
and I pray for those blazing fires of Artemis
with which she races through the Lycian hills.6

τὸν χρυσομίτραν τε κικλήσκω,
τᾶσδ᾽ ἐπώνυμον γᾶς,   210
οἰνῶπα Βάκχον εὔιον,
Μαινάδων ὁμόστολον,
πελασθῆναι φλέγοντ᾽
ἀγλαῶπι ⟨σύμμαχον⟩
πεύκᾳ ᾽πὶ τὸν ἀπότιμον ἐν θεοῖς θεόν.   215

ΟΙΔΙΠΟΥΣ

αἰτεῖς· ἃ δ᾽ αἰτεῖς, τἄμ᾽ ἐὰν θέλῃς ἔπη
κλύων δέχεσθαι τῇ νόσῳ θ᾽ ὑπηρετεῖν,
ἀλκὴν λάβοις ἂν κἀνακούφισιν κακῶν·
ἀγὼ ξένος μὲν τοῦ λόγου τοῦδ᾽ ἐξερῶ,
ξένος δὲ τοῦ πραχθέντος· οὐ γὰρ ἂν μακρὰν   220
ἴχνευον αὐτός, μὴ οὐκ ἔχων τι σύμβολον,
νῦν δ᾽ ὕστερος γὰρ ἀστὸς εἰς ἀστοὺς τελῶ,
ὑμῖν προφωνῶ πᾶσι Καδμείοις τάδε·
ὅστις ποθ᾽ ὑμῶν Λάϊον τὸν Λαβδάκου
κάτοιδεν ἀνδρὸς ἐκ τίνος διώλετο,   225
τοῦτον κελεύω πάντα σημαίνειν ἐμοί·
κεἰ μὲν φοβεῖται, τοὐπίκλημ᾽ ὑπεξελεῖν
αὐτὸν καθ᾽ αὑτοῦ· πείσεται γὰρ ἄλλο μὲν
ἀστεργὲς οὐδέν. γῆς δ᾽ ἄπεισιν ἀσφαλής.
εἰ δ᾽ αὖ τις ἄλλον οἶδεν ἐξ ἄλλης χθονὸς   230
τὸν αὐτόχειρα, μὴ σιωπάτω· τὸ γὰρ
κέρδος τελῶ ᾽γὼ χἠ χάρις προσκείσεται.
εἰ δ᾽ αὖ σιωπήσεσθε, καί τις ἢ φίλου
δείσας ἀπώσει τοὔπος ἢ χαὑτοῦ τόδε,
ἃκ τῶνδε δράσω, ταῦτα χρὴ κλύειν ἐμοῦ.   235
τὸν ἄνδρ᾽ ἀπαυδῶ τοῦτον, ὅστις ἐστί, γῆς
τῆσδ᾽, ἧς ἐγὼ κράτη τε καὶ θρόνους νέμω,
μήτ᾽ εἰσδέχεσθαι μήτε προσφωνεῖν τινα,
μήτ᾽ ἐν θεῶν εὐχαῖσι μήτε θύμασιν
κοινὸν ποεῖσθαι, μήτε χέρνιβας νέμειν·   240

I call the god who binds his hair with gold,
    the one whose name our country shares,   [210]
the one to whom the Maenads shout their cries,
    Dionysus with his radiant face—
may he come to us with his flaming torchlight,
    our ally against Ares,
    a god dishonoured among gods.[7]

[Enter OEDIPUS from the palace]

OEDIPUS
    You pray. But if you listen now to me,
    you'll get your wish. Hear what I have to say
    and treat your own disease—then you may hope
    to find relief from your distress. I speak
    as one who is a stranger to the story,
    a stranger to the crime. If I alone
    were tracking down this act, I'd not get far   [220]
    without a single clue. But as things stand,
    for it was after the event that I became
    a citizen of Thebes, I now proclaim
    the following to all of you Cadmeians:
    Whoever among you knows the man it was
    who murdered Laius, son of Labdacus,
    I order him to reveal it all to me.
    And if the killer is afraid, I tell him
    to avoid the danger of the major charge
    by speaking out against himself. If so,
    he will be sent out from this land unhurt
    and undergo no further punishment.
    If someone knows the killer is a stranger,   [230]
    from some other state, let him not stay mute.
    As well as a reward, he'll earn my thanks.
    But if he remains quiet, if anyone,
    through fear, hides himself or a friend of his
    against my orders, here's what I shall do—
    so listen to my words. For I decree
    that no one in this land, in which I rule
    as your own king, shall give that killer shelter
    or talk to him, whoever he may be,
    or act in concert with him during prayers,
    or sacrifice, or sharing lustral water.[8]   [240]

Sophocles

ὠθεῖν δ' ἀπ' οἴκων πάντας, ὡς μιάσματος
τοῦδ' ἡμὶν ὄντος, ὡς τὸ Πυθικὸν θεοῦ
μαντεῖον ἐξέφηνεν ἀρτίως ἐμοί.
ἐγὼ μὲν οὖν τοιόσδε τῷ τε δαίμονι
τῷ τ' ἀνδρὶ τῷ θανόντι σύμμαχος πέλω·   245
κατεύχομαι δὲ τὸν δεδρακότ', εἴτε τις
εἷς ὢν λέληθεν εἴτε πλειόνων μέτα,
κακὸν κακῶς νιν ἄμορον ἐκτρῖψαι βίον·
ἐπεύχομαι δ', οἴκοισιν εἰ ξυνέστιος
ἐν τοῖς ἐμοῖς γένοιτ' ἐμοῦ συνειδότος,   250
παθεῖν ἅπερ τοῖσδ' ἀρτίως ἠρασάμην.
ὑμῖν δὲ ταῦτα πάντ' ἐπισκήπτω τελεῖν,
ὑπέρ τ' ἐμαυτοῦ τοῦ θεοῦ τε τῆσδέ τε
γῆς ὧδ' ἀκάρπως κἀθέως ἐφθαρμένης.
οὐδ' εἰ γὰρ ἦν τὸ πρᾶγμα μὴ θεήλατον,   255
ἀκάθαρτον ὑμᾶς εἰκὸς ἦν οὕτως ἐᾶν,
ἀνδρός γ' ἀρίστου βασιλέως τ' ὀλωλότος,
ἀλλ' ἐξερευνᾶν· νῦν δ' ἐπεὶ κυρῶ γ' ἐγὼ
ἔχων μὲν ἀρχὰς ἃς ἐκεῖνος εἶχε πρίν,
ἔχων δὲ λέκτρα καὶ γυναῖχ' ὁμόσπορον,   260
κοινῶν τε παίδων κοίν' ἄν, εἰ κείνῳ γένος
μὴ 'δυστύχησεν, ἦν ἂν ἐκπεφυκότα·
νῦν δ' ἐς τὸ κείνου κρᾶτ' ἐνήλαθ' ἡ τύχη·
ἀνθ' ὧν ἐγὼ τάδ', ὡσπερεὶ τοὐμοῦ πατρός,
ὑπερμαχοῦμαι κἀπὶ πᾶν ἀφίξομαι,   265
ζητῶν τὸν αὐτόχειρα τοῦ φόνου λαβεῖν,
τῷ Λαβδακείῳ παιδὶ Πολυδώρου τε καὶ
τοῦ πρόσθε Κάδμου τοῦ πάλαι τ' Ἀγήνορος.
καὶ ταῦτα τοῖς μὴ δρῶσιν εὔχομαι θεοὺς
μήτ' ἄροτον αὐτοῖς γῆς ἀνιέναι τινὰ   270
μήτ' οὖν γυναικῶν παῖδας, ἀλλὰ τῷ πότμῳ
τῷ νῦν φθερεῖσθαι κἄτι τοῦδ' ἐχθίονι·
ὑμῖν δὲ τοῖς ἄλλοισι Καδμείοις, ὅσοις
τάδ' ἔστ' ἀρέσκονθ', ἥ τε σύμμαχος Δίκη
χοἰ πάντες εὖ ξυνεῖεν εἰσαεὶ θεοί.   275

58

Ban him from your homes, every one of you,
for he is our pollution, as the Pythian god
In this, I'm acting as an ally of the god
and also of dead Laius. And I pray
whoever the man is who did this crime,
one unknown person acting on his own
or with companions, the worst of agonies
will wear out his wretched life. I pray, too,
that, if he should become an honoured guest
in my own home and with my knowledge,   [250]
I may suffer all those things I've just called down
upon the killers. And I urge you now
to make sure all these orders take effect,
for my sake, for the sake of the god,
and for our barren, godless, ruined land.
For in this matter, even if a god
were not urging us, it would not be right
for you to simply leave things as they are
and not to purify the murder of a man
who was so noble and who was your king.
You should have looked into it. But now I
possess the ruling power which Laius held
in earlier days. I have his bed and wife—   [260]
she would have borne his children, if his hopes
to have a son had not been disappointed.
Children from a common mother might have linked
Laius and myself. But as it turned out,
Fate swooped down onto his head. So now,
I'll fight on his behalf, as if this matter
concerned my own father, and I will strive
to do everything I can to find him,
the man who spilled his blood, and thus avenge
the son of Labdacus and Polydorus,
of Cadmus and Agenor from old times.[9]
As for those who do not follow what I urge,
I pray the gods send them no fertile land,
no, nor any children in their women's wombs—   [270]
may they all perish in our present fate
or one more hateful still. To you others,
you Cadmeians who support my efforts,
may Justice, our ally, and all the gods
attend on us with kindness all our days.

ΧΟΡΟΣ

ὥσπερ μ' ἀραῖον ἔλαβες, ὧδ', ἄναξ, ἐρῶ.
οὔτ' ἔκτανον γὰρ οὔτε τὸν κτανόντ' ἔχω
δεῖξαι. τὸ δὲ ζήτημα τοῦ πέμψαντος ἦν
Φοίβου τόδ' εἰπεῖν, ὅστις εἴργασταί ποτε.

ΟΙΔΙΠΟΥΣ

δίκαι' ἔλεξας· ἀλλ' ἀναγκάσαι θεοὺς   280
ἂν μὴ θέλωσιν οὐδ' ἂν εἷς δύναιτ' ἀνήρ.

ΧΟΡΟΣ

τὰ δεύτερ' ἐκ τῶνδ' ἂν λέγοιμ' ἁμοὶ δοκεῖ.

ΟΙΔΙΠΟΥΣ

εἰ καὶ τρίτ' ἐστί, μὴ παρῇς τὸ μὴ οὐ φράσαι.

ΧΟΡΟΣ

ἄνακτ' ἄνακτι ταῦθ' ὁρῶντ' ἐπίσταμαι
μάλιστα Φοίβῳ Τειρεσίαν, παρ' οὗ τις ἂν   285
σκοπῶν τάδ', ὦναξ, ἐκμάθοι σαφέστατα.

ΟΙΔΙΠΟΥΣ

ἀλλ' οὐκ ἐν ἀργοῖς οὐδὲ τοῦτ' ἐπραξάμην.
ἔπεμψα γὰρ Κρέοντος εἰπόντος διπλοῦς
πομπούς· πάλαι δὲ μὴ παρὼν θαυμάζεται.

ΧΟΡΟΣ

καὶ μὴν τά γ' ἄλλα κωφὰ καὶ παλαί' ἔπη.   290

ΟΙΔΙΠΟΥΣ

τὰ ποῖα ταῦτα; πάντα γὰρ σκοπῶ λόγον.

ΧΟΡΟΣ

θανεῖν ἐλέχθη πρός τινων ὁδοιπόρων.

CHORUS LEADER

    My lord, since you extend your oath to me,
    I will say this. I am not the murderer,
    nor can I tell you who the killer is.
    As for what you're seeking, it's for Apollo,
    who launched this search, to state who did it.

OEDIPUS

    That is well said. But no man has power   [280]
    to force the gods to speak against their will.

CHORUS LEADER

    May I then suggest what seems to me
    the next best course of action?

OEDIPUS

                      You may indeed,
    and if there is a third course, too, don't hesitate
    to let me know.

CHORUS LEADER

                  Our lord Teiresias,
    I know, can see into things, like lord Apollo.
    From him, my king, a man investigating this
    might well find out clear details of the crime.

OEDIPUS

    I've taken care of that—it's not something
    I could overlook. At Creon's urging,
    I have dispatched two messengers to him
    and have been wondering for some time now
    why he has not come.

CHORUS LEADER

               Apart from that,
    there are rumours—but inconclusive ones   [290]
    from a long time ago.

OEDIPUS

          What kind of rumours?
    I'm looking into every story.

CHORUS LEADER

                   It was said
    that Laius was killed by certain travellers.

ΟΙΔΙΠΟΥΣ

ἤκουσα κἀγώ. τὸν δ᾽ ἰδόντ᾽ οὐδεὶς ὁρᾷ.

ΧΟΡΟΣ

ἀλλ᾽ εἴ τι μὲν δὴ δείματός γ᾽ ἔχει μέρος,
τὰς σὰς ἀκούων οὐ μενεῖ τοιάσδ᾽ ἀράς,   295

ΟΙΔΙΠΟΥΣ

ᾧ μή 'στι δρῶντι τάρβος, οὐδ᾽ ἔπος φοβεῖ.

ΧΟΡΟΣ

ἀλλ᾽ οὐξελέγξων αὐτὸν ἔστιν· οἵδε γὰρ
τὸν θεῖον ἤδη μάντιν ὧδ᾽ ἄγουσιν, ᾧ
τἀληθὲς ἐμπέφυκεν ἀνθρώπων μόνῳ.

ΟΙΔΙΠΟΥΣ

ὦ πάντα νωμῶν Τειρεσία, διδακτά τε   300
ἄρρητά τ᾽, οὐράνιά τε καὶ χθονοστιβῆ,
πόλιν μέν, εἰ καὶ μὴ βλέπεις, φρονεῖς δ᾽ ὅμως
οἵᾳ νόσῳ σύνεστιν· ἧς σὲ προστάτην
σωτῆρά τ᾽, ὦναξ, μοῦνον ἐξευρίσκομεν.
Φοῖβος γάρ, εἴ τι μὴ κλύεις τῶν ἀγγέλων,   305
πέμψασιν ἡμῖν ἀντέπεμψεν, ἔκλυσιν
μόνην ἂν ἐλθεῖν τοῦδε τοῦ νοσήματος,
εἰ τοὺς κτανόντας Λάϊον μαθόντες εὖ
κτείναιμεν ἢ γῆς φυγάδας ἐκπεμψαίμεθα.
σύ νυν φθονήσας μήτ᾽ ἀπ᾽ οἰωνῶν φάτιν   310
μήτ᾽ εἴ τιν᾽ ἄλλην μαντικῆς ἔχεις ὁδόν,
ῥῦσαι σεαυτὸν καὶ πόλιν, ῥῦσαι δ᾽ ἐμέ,
ῥῦσαι δὲ πᾶν μίασμα τοῦ τεθνηκότος.
ἐν σοὶ γὰρ ἐσμέν· ἄνδρα δ᾽ ὠφελεῖν ἀφ᾽ ὧν
ἔχοι τε καὶ δύναιτο, κάλλιστος πόνων.   315

OEDIPUS

  Yes, I heard as much. But no one has seen
  the one who did it.

CHORUS LEADER

                Well, if the killer
  has any fears, once he hears your curses on him,
  he will not hold back, for they are serious.

OEDIPUS

  When a man has no fear of doing the act,
  he's not afraid of words.

CHORUS LEADER

              No, not in the case
  where no one stands there to convict him.
  But at last Teiresias is being guided here,
  our god-like prophet, in whom truth resides
  more so than in all other men.

[Enter TEIRESIAS led by a small BOY]

OEDIPUS

                    Teiresias, [300]
  you who understand all things—what can be taught
  and what cannot be spoken of, what goes on
  in heaven and here on the earth—you know,
  although you cannot see, how sick our state is.
  And so we find in you alone, great seer,
  our shield and saviour. For Phoebus Apollo,
  in case you have not heard the news, has sent us
  an answer to our question: the only cure
  for this infecting pestilence is to find
  the men who murdered Laius and kill them
  or else expel them from this land as exiles.
  So do not withhold from us your prophecies [310]
  from voices of the birds or by some other means.
  Save this city and yourself. Rescue me.
  Deliver us from all pollution by the dead.
  We are in your hands. For a mortal man
  the finest labour he can do is help
  with all his power other human beings.

ΤΕΙΡΕΣΙΑΣ

φεῦ φεῦ, φρονεῖν ὡς δεινὸν ἔνθα μὴ τέλη
λύῃ φρονοῦντι· ταῦτα γὰρ καλῶς ἐγὼ
εἰδὼς διώλεσ'· οὐ γὰρ ἂν δεῦρ' ἱκόμην.

ΟΙΔΙΠΟΥΣ

τί δ' ἔστιν; ὡς ἄθυμος εἰσελήλυθας.

ΤΕΙΡΕΣΙΑΣ

ἄφες μ' ἐς οἴκους· ῥᾷστα γὰρ τὸ σόν τε σὺ   320
κἀγὼ διοίσω τοὐμόν, ἢν ἐμοὶ πίθῃ.

ΟΙΔΙΠΟΥΣ

οὔτ' ἔννομ' εἶπας οὔτε προσφιλῆ πόλει
τῇδ', ἥ σ' ἔθρεψε, τήνδ' ἀποστερῶν φάτιν.

ΤΕΙΡΕΣΙΑΣ

ὁρῶ γὰρ οὐδὲ σοὶ τὸ σὸν φώνημ' ἰὸν
πρὸς καιρόν· ὡς οὖν μηδ' ἐγὼ ταὐτὸν πάθω—   325

ΟΙΔΙΠΟΥΣ

μὴ πρὸς θεῶν φρονῶν γ' ἀποστραφῇς, ἐπεὶ
πάντες σε προσκυνοῦμεν οἵδ' ἱκτήριοι.

ΤΕΙΡΕΣΙΑΣ

πάντες γὰρ οὐ φρονεῖτ'· ἐγὼ δ' οὐ μή ποτε
τἄμ', ὡς ἂν εἴπω μὴ τὰ σ', ἐκφήνω κακά.

ΟΙΔΙΠΟΥΣ

τί φής; ξυνειδὼς οὐ φράσεις, ἀλλ' ἐννοεῖς   330
ἡμᾶς προδοῦναι καὶ καταφθεῖραι πόλιν;

ΤΕΙΡΕΣΙΑΣ

ἐγὼ οὔτ' ἐμαυτὸν οὔτε σ' ἀλγυνῶ. τί ταῦτ'
ἄλλως ἐλέγχεις; οὐ γὰρ ἂν πύθοιό μου.

TEIRESIAS

    Alas, alas! How dreadful it can be
    to have wisdom when it brings no benefit
    to the man possessing it. This I knew,
    but it had slipped my mind. Otherwise,
    I would not have journeyed here.

OEDIPUS

    What is wrong? You have come, but seem distressed.

TEIRESIAS

    Let me go home. You must bear your burden   [320]
    to the very end, and I will carry mine,
    if you'll agree with me.

OEDIPUS

                  What you are saying
    is not customary and shows little love
    toward the city state which nurtured you,
    if you deny us your prophetic voice.

TEIRESIAS

    I see your words are also out of place.
    I do not speak for fear of doing the same.

OEDIPUS

    If you know something, then, by the gods,
    do not turn away. We are your suppliants—
    all of us—we bend our knees to you.

TEIRESIAS

    You are all ignorant. I will not reveal
    the troubling things inside me, nor will I state
    they are your griefs as well.

OEDIPUS

                What are you saying?   [330]
    Do you know and will not say? Do you intend
    to betray me and destroy the city?

TEIRESIAS

    I will cause neither me nor you distress.
    Why do you vainly question me like this?
    You will not learn a thing from me.

ΟΙΔΙΠΟΥΣ

οὐκ, ὦ κακῶν κάκιστε, καὶ γὰρ ἂν πέτρου
φύσιν σύ γ᾽ ὀργάνειας, ἐξερεῖς ποτε,   335
ἀλλ᾽ ὧδ᾽ ἄτεγκτος κἀτελεύτητος φανεῖ;

ΤΕΙΡΕΣΙΑΣ

ὀργὴν ἐμέμψω τὴν ἐμήν, τὴν σὴν δ᾽ ὁμοῦ
ναίουσαν οὐ κατεῖδες, ἀλλ᾽ ἐμὲ ψέγεις.

ΟΙΔΙΠΟΥΣ

τίς γὰρ τοιαῦτ᾽ ἂν οὐκ ἂν ὀργίζοιτ᾽ ἔπη
κλύων, ἃ νῦν σὺ τήνδ᾽ ἀτιμάζεις πόλιν;   340

ΤΕΙΡΕΣΙΑΣ

ἥξει γὰρ αὐτά, κἂν ἐγὼ σιγῇ στέγω.

ΟΙΔΙΠΟΥΣ

οὐκοῦν ἅ γ᾽ ἥξει καὶ σὲ χρὴ λέγειν ἐμοί.

ΤΕΙΡΕΣΙΑΣ

οὐκ ἂν πέρα φράσαιμι. πρὸς τάδ᾽, εἰ θέλεις,
θυμοῦ δι᾽ ὀργῆς ἥτις ἀγριωτάτη.

ΟΙΔΙΠΟΥΣ

καὶ μὴν παρήσω γ᾽ οὐδέν, ὡς ὀργῆς ἔχω,   345
ἅπερ ξυνίημ᾽· ἴσθι γὰρ δοκῶν ἐμοὶ
καὶ ξυμφυτεῦσαι τοὔργον εἰργάσθαι θ᾽, ὅσον
μὴ χερσὶ καίνων· εἰ δ᾽ ἐτύγχανες βλέπων,
καὶ τοὔργον ἂν σοῦ τοῦτ᾽, ἔφην εἶναι μόνου.

ΤΕΙΡΕΣΙΑΣ

ἄληθες; ἐννέπω σὲ τῷ κηρύγματι   350
ᾧπερ προεῖπας ἐμμένειν, κἀφ᾽ ἡμέρας
τῆς νῦν προσαυδᾶν μήτε τούσδε μήτ᾽ ἐμέ,
ὡς ὄντι γῆς τῆσδ᾽ ἀνοσίῳ μιάστορι.

ΟΙΔΙΠΟΥΣ

οὕτως ἀναιδῶς ἐξεκίνησας τόδε
τὸ ῥῆμα; καὶ ποῦ τοῦτο φεύξεσθαι δοκεῖς;   355

OEDIPUS

You most disgraceful of disgraceful men!
You would move something made of stone to rage!
Will you not speak out? Will your stubbornness
never have an end?

TEIRESIAS

You blame my nature,
but do not see the temper you possess.
Instead, you're finding fault with me.

OEDIPUS

What man who listened to these words of yours
would not be enraged—you insult the city!   [340]

TEIRESIAS

Yet events will still unfold, for all my silence.

OEDIPUS

Since they will come, you must inform me.

TEIRESIAS

I will say nothing more. Fume on about it,
if you wish, as fiercely as you can.

OEDIPUS

I will. In my anger I will not conceal
just what I make of this. You should know
I get the feeling you conspired in the act
and played your part, as much as you could do,
short of killing him with your own hands.
If you could use your eyes, I would have said
that you had done this work all by yourself.

TEIRESIAS

Is that so? Then I would ask you to stand by   [350]
the very words which you yourself proclaimed
and from now on not speak to these men or me.
For the accursed polluter of this land is you.

OEDIPUS

You dare to utter shameful words like this?
Do you think you can get away with it?

67

ΤΕΙΡΕΣΙΑΣ

πέφευγα· τἀληθὲς γὰρ ἰσχῦον τρέφω.

ΟΙΔΙΠΟΥΣ

πρὸς τοῦ διδαχθείς; οὐ γὰρ ἔκ γε τῆς τέχνης.

ΤΕΙΡΕΣΙΑΣ

πρὸς σοῦ· σὺ γάρ μ᾽ ἄκοντα προυτρέψω λέγειν.

ΟΙΔΙΠΟΥΣ

ποῖον λόγον; λέγ᾽ αὖθις, ὡς μᾶλλον μάθω.

ΤΕΙΡΕΣΙΑΣ

οὐχὶ ξυνῆκας πρόσθεν; ἢ 'κπειρᾷ λέγων;   360

ΟΙΔΙΠΟΥΣ

οὐχ ὥστε γ᾽ εἰπεῖν γνωστόν· ἀλλ᾽ αὖθις φράσον.

ΤΕΙΡΕΣΙΑΣ

φονέα σε φημὶ τἀνδρὸς οὗ ζητεῖς κυρεῖν.

ΟΙΔΙΠΟΥΣ

ἀλλ᾽ οὔ τι χαίρων δίς γε πημονὰς ἐρεῖς.

ΤΕΙΡΕΣΙΑΣ

εἴπω τι δῆτα κἄλλ᾽, ἵν᾽ ὀργίζῃ πλέον;

ΟΙΔΙΠΟΥΣ

ὅσον γε χρῄζεις· ὡς μάτην εἰρήσεται.   365

ΤΕΙΡΕΣΙΑΣ

λεληθέναι σε φημὶ σὺν τοῖς φιλτάτοις
αἴσχισθ᾽ ὁμιλοῦντ᾽, οὐδ᾽ ὁρᾶν ἵν᾽ εἶ κακοῦ.

TEIRESIAS

I am getting away with it. The truth
within me makes me strong.

OEDIPUS

Who taught you this?
It could not have been your craft.

TEIRESIAS

You did.
I did not want to speak, but you incited me.

OEDIPUS

What do you mean? Speak it again,
so I can understand you more precisely.

TEIRESIAS

Did you not grasp my words before,
or are you trying to test me with your question?   [360]

OEDIPUS

I did not fully understand your words.
Tell me again.

TEIRESIAS

I say that you yourself
are the very man you're looking for.

OEDIPUS

That's twice you've stated that disgraceful lie—
something you'll regret.

TEIRESIAS

Shall I tell you more,
so you can grow even more enraged?

OEDIPUS

As much as you desire. It will be useless.

TEIRESIAS

I say that with your dearest family,
unknown to you, you are living in disgrace.
You have no idea how bad things are.

Sophocles

ΟΙΔΙΠΟΥΣ

ἦ καὶ γεγηθὼς ταῦτ᾽ ἀεὶ λέξειν δοκεῖς;

ΤΕΙΡΕΣΙΑΣ

εἴπερ τί γ᾽ ἐστὶ τῆς ἀληθείας σθένος.

ΟΙΔΙΠΟΥΣ

ἀλλ᾽ ἔστι, πλὴν σοί· σοὶ δὲ τοῦτ᾽ οὐκ ἔστ᾽ ἐπεὶ   370
τυφλὸς τά τ᾽ ὦτα τόν τε νοῦν τά τ᾽ ὄμματ᾽ εἶ.

ΤΕΙΡΕΣΙΑΣ

σὺ δ᾽ ἄθλιός γε ταῦτ᾽ ὀνειδίζων, ἃ σοὶ
οὐδεὶς ὃς οὐχὶ τῶνδ᾽ ὀνειδιεῖ τάχα.

ΟΙΔΙΠΟΥΣ

μιᾶς τρέφει πρὸς νυκτός, ὥστε μήτ᾽ ἐμὲ
μήτ᾽ ἄλλον, ὅστις φῶς ὁρᾷ, βλάψαι ποτ᾽ ἄν.   375

ΤΕΙΡΕΣΙΑΣ

οὐ γάρ σε μοῖρα πρός γ᾽ ἐμοῦ πεσεῖν, ἐπεὶ
ἱκανὸς Ἀπόλλων, ᾧ τάδ᾽ ἐκπρᾶξαι μέλει.

ΟΙΔΙΠΟΥΣ

Κρέοντος ἢ σοῦ ταῦτα τἀξευρήματα;

ΤΕΙΡΕΣΙΑΣ

Κρέων δέ σοι πῆμ᾽ οὐδέν, ἀλλ᾽ αὐτὸς σὺ σοί.

ΟΙΔΙΠΟΥΣ

ὦ πλοῦτε καὶ τυραννὶ καὶ τέχνη τέχνης   380
ὑπερφέρουσα τῷ πολυζήλῳ βίῳ,
ὅσος παρ᾽ ὑμῖν ὁ φθόνος φυλάσσεται,
εἰ τῆσδέ γ᾽ ἀρχῆς οὕνεχ᾽, ἣν ἐμοὶ πόλις
δωρητόν, οὐκ αἰτητόν, εἰσεχείρισεν,
ταύτης Κρέων ὁ πιστός, οὐξ ἀρχῆς φίλος,   385
λάθρᾳ μ᾽ ὑπελθὼν ἐκβαλεῖν ἱμείρεται,
ὑφεὶς μάγον τοιόνδε μηχανορράφον,
δόλιον ἀγύρτην, ὅστις ἐν τοῖς κέρδεσιν
μόνον δέδορκε, τὴν τέχνην δ᾽ ἔφυ τυφλός.

OEDIPUS

Do you really think you can just speak out,
say things like this, and still remain unpunished?

TEIRESIAS

Yes, I can, if the truth has any strength.

OEDIPUS

It does, but not for you. Truth is not in you—   [370]
for your ears, your mind, your eyes are blind!

TEIRESIAS

You are a wretched fool to use harsh words
which all men soon enough will use to curse you.

OEDIPUS

You live in endless darkness of the night,
so you can never injure me or any man
who can glimpse daylight.

TEIRESIAS

                    It is not your fate
to fall because of me. Lord Apollo
will make that happen. He will be enough.

OEDIPUS

Is this something Creon has devised,
or is it your invention?

TEIRESIAS

                    Creon is no threat.
You have made this trouble on your own.

OEDIPUS

O wealth and ruling power, skill after skill   [380]
surpassing all in life's rich rivalries,
how much envy you must carry with you,
if, for this kingly office—which the city
gave me, for I did not seek it out—
Creon, my old trusted family friend,
has secretly conspired to overthrow me
and paid off a double-dealing quack like this,
a crafty bogus priest, who can only see
his own advantage, who in his special art

71

ἐπεί, φέρ' εἰπέ, ποῦ σὺ μάντις εἶ σαφής; 390
πῶς οὐκ, ὅθ' ἡ ῥαψῳδὸς ἐνθάδ' ἦν κύων,
ηὔδας τι τοῖσδ' ἀστοῖσιν ἐκλυτήριον;
καίτοι τό γ' αἴνιγμ' οὐχὶ τοὐπιόντος ἦν
ἀνδρὸς διειπεῖν, ἀλλὰ μαντείας ἔδει·
ἣν οὔτ' ἀπ' οἰωνῶν σὺ προυφάνης ἔχων 395
οὔτ' ἐκ θεῶν του γνωτόν· ἀλλ' ἐγὼ μολών,
ὁ μηδὲν εἰδὼς Οἰδίπους, ἔπαυσά νιν,
γνώμῃ κυρήσας οὐδ' ἀπ', οἰωνῶν μαθών·
ὃν δὴ σὺ πειρᾷς ἐκβαλεῖν, δοκῶν θρόνοις
παραστατήσειν τοῖς Κρεοντείοις πέλας. 400
κλαίων δοκεῖς μοι καὶ σὺ χὠ συνθεὶς τάδε
ἀγηλατήσειν· εἰ δὲ μὴ 'δόκεις γέρων
εἶναι, παθὼν ἔγνως ἂν οἷά περ φρονεῖς.

ΧΟΡΟΣ

ἡμῖν μὲν εἰκάζουσι καὶ τὰ τοῦδ' ἔπη
ὀργῇ λελέχθαι καὶ τά σ', Οἰδίπους, δοκεῖ, 405
δεῖ δ' οὐ τοιούτων, ἀλλ' ὅπως τὰ τοῦ θεοῦ
μαντεῖ' ἄριστα λύσομεν, τόδε σκοπεῖν.

ΤΕΙΡΕΣΙΑΣ

εἰ καὶ τυραννεῖς, ἐξισωτέον τὸ γοῦν
ἴσ' ἀντιλέξαι· τοῦδε γὰρ κἀγὼ κρατῶ.
οὐ γάρ τι σοὶ ζῶ δοῦλος, ἀλλὰ Λοξίᾳ· 410
ὥστ' οὐ κρέοντος προστάτου γεγράψομαι.
λέγω δ', ἐπειδὴ καὶ τυφλόν μ' ὠνείδισας·
σὺ καὶ δέδορκας κοὐ βλέπεις ἵν' εἶ κακοῦ,
οὐδ' ἔνθα ναίεις, οὐδ' ὅτων οἰκεῖς μέτα.
ἆρ' οἶσθ' ἀφ' ὧν εἶ; καὶ λέληθας ἐχθρὸς ὢν 415
τοῖς σοῖσιν αὐτοῦ νέρθε κἀπὶ γῆς ἄνω,
καί σ' ἀμφιπλὴξ μητρός τε καὶ τοῦ σοῦ πατρὸς
ἐλᾷ ποτ' ἐκ γῆς τῆσδε δεινόπους ἀρά,
βλέποντα νῦν μὲν ὄρθ', ἔπειτα δὲ σκότον.

is absolutely blind. Come on, tell me   [390]
how you have ever given evidence
of your wise prophecy. When the Sphinx,
that singing bitch, was here, you said nothing
to set the people free. Why not? Her riddle
was not something the first man to stroll along
could solve—a prophet was required. And there
the people saw your knowledge was no use—
nothing from birds or picked up from the gods.
But then I came, Oedipus, who knew nothing.
Yet I finished her off, using my wits
rather than relying on birds. That's the man
you want to overthrow, hoping, no doubt,
to stand up there with Creon, once he's king.   [400]
But I think you and your conspirator in this
will regret trying to drive me from the state.
If you did not look so old, you'd find out
the punishment your arrogance deserves.

CHORUS LEADER
    To us it sounds as if Teiresias
    has spoken in anger, and, Oedipus,
    you have done so, too. That isn't what we need.
    Instead we should be looking into this:
    How can we best act on the god's decree?

TEIRESIAS
    You may be king, but I do have the right
    to answer you—and I control that right,
    for I am not your slave. I serve Apollo,   [410]
    and thus will never stand with Creon,
    signed up as his man. So I say this to you,
    since you have chosen to insult my blindness—
    you have your eyesight, and you do not see
    how miserable you are, or where you live,
    or who it is who shares your household.
    Do you know the family you come from?
    Without your knowledge you have turned into
    the enemy of your own relatives,
    those in the world below and those up here,
    and the dreadful scourge of that two-edged curse
    of father and mother will one day drive you
    from this land in exile. Those eyes of yours,
    which now can see so clearly, will be dark.

73

βοῆς δὲ τῆς σῆς ποῖος οὐκ ἔσται λιμήν,   420
ποῖος Κιθαιρὼν οὐχὶ σύμφωνος τάχα,
ὅταν καταίσθῃ τὸν ὑμέναιον, ὃν δόμοις
ἄνορμον εἰσέπλευσας, εὐπλοίας τυχών;
ἄλλων δὲ πλῆθος οὐκ ἐπαισθάνει κακῶν,
ἅ σ᾽ ἐξισώσει σοί τε καὶ τοῖς σοῖς τέκνοις.   425
πρὸς ταῦτα καὶ Κρέοντα καὶ τοὐμὸν στόμα
προπηλάκιζε· σοῦ γὰρ οὐκ ἔστιν βροτῶν
κάκιον ὅστις ἐκτριβήσεταί ποτε.

ΟΙΔΙΠΟΥΣ

ἦ ταῦτα δῆτ᾽ ἀνεκτὰ πρὸς τούτου κλύειν;
οὐκ εἰς ὄλεθρον; οὐχὶ θᾶσσον; οὐ πάλιν   430
ἄψορρος οἴκων τῶνδ᾽ ἀποστραφεὶς ἄπει;

ΤΕΙΡΕΣΙΑΣ

οὐδ᾽ ἱκόμην ἔγωγ᾽ ἄν, εἰ σὺ μὴ 'κάλεις.

ΟΙΔΙΠΟΥΣ

οὐ γάρ τί σ᾽ ᾔδη μῶρα φωνήσοντ᾽, ἐπεὶ
σχολῇ σ᾽ ἂν οἴκους τοὺς ἐμοὺς ἐστειλάμην.

ΤΕΙΡΕΣΙΑΣ

ἡμεῖς τοιοίδ᾽ ἔφυμεν, ὡς μὲν σοὶ δοκεῖ,   435
μῶροι, γονεῦσι δ᾽, οἵ σ᾽ ἔφυσαν, ἔμφρονες.

ΟΙΔΙΠΟΥΣ

ποίοισι; μεῖνον, τίς δέ μ᾽ ἐκφύει βροτῶν;

ΤΕΙΡΕΣΙΑΣ

ἥδ᾽ ἡμέρα φύσει σε καὶ διαφθερεῖ.

ΟΙΔΙΠΟΥΣ

ὡς πάντ᾽ ἄγαν αἰνικτὰ κἀσαφῆ λέγεις.

ΤΕΙΡΕΣΙΑΣ

οὔκουν σὺ ταῦτ᾽ ἄριστος εὑρίσκειν ἔφυς;   440

What harbour will not echo with your cries?   [420]
Where on Cithaeron will they not soon be heard,
once you have learned the truth about the wedding
by which you sailed into this royal house—
a lovely voyage, but the harbour's doomed?[10]
You have no notion of the quantity
of other troubles which will render you
and your own children equals. So go on—
keep insulting Creon and my prophecies,
for among all living mortals nobody
will be destroyed more wretchedly than you.

OEDIPUS

Must I tolerate this insolence from him?
Get out, and may the plague get rid of you!   [430]
Off with you! Now! Turn your back and go!
And don't come back here to my home again.

TEIRESIAS

I would not have come, but you summoned me.

OEDIPUS

I did not know you would speak so stupidly.
If I had, you would have waited a long time
before I called you here.

TEIRESIAS

                 I was born like this.
You think I am a fool, but to your parents,
the ones who made you, I was wise enough.

OEDIPUS

Wait! My parents? Who was my father?

TEIRESIAS

This day will reveal that and destroy you.

OEDIPUS

Everything you speak is all so cryptic—
like a riddle.

TEIRESIAS

             Well, in solving riddles,   [440]
are you not the best there is?

ΟΙΔΙΠΟΥΣ

τοιαῦτ᾽ ὀνείδιζ᾽, οἷς ἔμ᾽ εὑρήσεις μέγαν.

ΤΕΙΡΕΣΙΑΣ

αὕτη γε μέντοι σ᾽ ἡ τύχη διώλεσεν.

ΟΙΔΙΠΟΥΣ

ἀλλ᾽ εἰ πόλιν τήνδ᾽ ἐξέσωσ᾽, οὔ μοι μέλει.

ΤΕΙΡΕΣΙΑΣ

ἄπειμι τοίνυν· καὶ σύ, παῖ, κόμιζέ με.

ΟΙΔΙΠΟΥΣ

κομιζέτω δῆθ᾽· ὡς παρὼν σύ γ᾽ ἐμποδὼν   445
ὀχλεῖς, συθείς τ᾽ ἂν οὐκ ἂν ἀλγύνοις πλέον.

ΤΕΙΡΕΣΙΑΣ

εἰπὼν ἄπειμ᾽ ὧν οὕνεκ᾽, ἦλθον, οὐ τὸ σὸν
δείσας πρόσωπον· οὐ γὰρ ἔσθ᾽ ὅπου μ᾽ ὀλεῖς.
λέγω δέ σοι· τὸν ἄνδρα τοῦτον, ὃν πάλαι
ζητεῖς ἀπειλῶν κἀνακηρύσσων φόνον   450
τὸν Λάϊειον, οὗτός ἐστιν ἐνθάδε,
ξένος λόγῳ μέτοικος, εἶτα δ᾽ ἐγγενὴς
φανήσεται Θηβαῖος, οὐδ᾽ ἡσθήσεται
τῇ ξυμφορᾷ· τυφλὸς γὰρ ἐκ δεδορκότος
καὶ πτωχὸς ἀντὶ πλουσίου ξένην ἔπι   455
σκήπτρῳ προδεικνὺς γαῖαν ἐμπορεύσεται.
φανήσεται δὲ παισὶ τοῖς αὑτοῦ ξυνὼν
ἀδελφὸς αὑτὸς καὶ πατήρ, κἀξ ἧς ἔφυ
γυναικὸς υἱὸς καὶ πόσις, καὶ τοῦ πατρὸς
ὁμόσπορός τε καὶ φονεύς. καὶ ταῦτ᾽ ἰὼν   460
εἴσω λογίζου· κἂν λάβῃς ἐψευσμένον,
φάσκειν ἔμ᾽ ἤδη μαντικῇ μηδὲν φρονεῖν.

OEDIPUS
                    Mock my excellence,
but you will find out I am truly great.

TEIRESIAS
That success of yours has been your ruin.

OEDIPUS
I do not care, if I have saved the city.

TEIRESIAS
I will go now. Boy, lead me away.

OEDIPUS
Yes, let him guide you back. You're in the way.
If you stay, you will provoke me. Once you're gone,
you won't annoy me further.

TEIRESIAS
                    I'm going.
But first I shall tell you why I came.
I do not fear the face of your displeasure—
there is no way you can destroy me. I tell you,
the man you have been seeking all this time,
while proclaiming threats and issuing orders   [450]
about the one who murdered Laius—
that man is here. According to reports,
he is a stranger who lives here in Thebes.
But he will prove to be a native Theban.
From that change he will derive no pleasure.
He will be blind, although he now can see.
He will be a poor, although he now is rich.
He will set off for a foreign country,
groping the ground before him with a stick.
And he will turn out to be the brother
of the children in his house—their father, too,
both at once, and the husband and the son
of the very woman who gave birth to him.
He sowed the same womb as his father
and murdered him. Go in and think on this.   [460]
If you discover I have spoken falsely,
you can say I lack all skill in prophecy.

ΧΟΡΟΣ

τίς ὄντιν' ἁ θεσπιέπεια δελφὶς εἶπε πέτρα

ἄρρητ' ἀρρήτων τελέσαντα φοινίαισι χερσίν; 465

ὥρα νιν ἀελλάδων

ἵππων σθεναρώτερον

φυγᾷ πόδα νωμᾶν.

ἔνοπλος γὰρ ἐπ' αὐτὸν ἐπενθρῴσκει

πυρὶ καὶ στεροπαῖς ὁ Διὸς γενέτας, 470

δειναὶ δ' ἅμ' ἕπονται

κῆρες ἀναπλάκητοι

ἔλαμψε γὰρ τοῦ νιφόεντος ἀρτίως φανεῖσα

φάμα Παρνασοῦ τὸν ἄδηλον ἄνδρα πάντ' ἰχνεύειν.

φοιτᾷ γὰρ ὑπ' ἀγρίαν 475

ὕλαν ἀνά τ' ἄντρα καὶ

πέτρας ἰσόταυρος

μέλεος μελέῳ ποδὶ χηρεύων,

τὰ μεσόμφαλα γᾶς ἀπονοσφίζων 480

μαντεῖα· τὰ δ' ἀεὶ

ζῶντα περιποτᾶται.

δεινὰ μὲν οὖν, δεινὰ ταράσσει σοφὸς οἰωνοθέτας

οὔτε δοκοῦντ' οὔτ' ἀποφάσκονθ'· ὅ τι λέξω δ' ἀπορῶ. 485

πέτομαι δ' ἐλπίσιν οὔτ', ἐνθάδ' ὁρῶν οὔτ' ὀπίσω.

τί γὰρ ἢ Λαβδακίδαις

ἢ τῷ Πολύβου νεῖκος ἔκειτ', οὔτε πάροιθέν ποτ' ἔγωγ' 490

ἔμαθον, πρὸς ὅτου δὴ βασανίζων βασάνῳ

ἐπὶ τὰν ἐπίδαμον φάτιν εἶμ' Οἰδιπόδα Λαβδακίδαις

ἐπίκουρος ἀδήλων θανάτων. 495

[Exit TEIRESIAS led off by the BOY. OEDIPUS turns and goes back into the palace]

CHORUS
    Speaking from the Delphic rock
    the oracular voice intoned a name.
    But who is the man, the one
    who with his blood-red hands
    has done unspeakable brutality?
    The time has come for him to flee—
    to move his powerful foot
    more swiftly than those hooves
    of horses riding like a storm.
    Against him Zeus' son now springs,   [470]
    armed with lightning fire and leading on
    the inexorable and terrifying Furies.[11]

    From the snowy peaks of Mount Parnassus
    the message has just flashed, ordering all
    to seek the one whom no one knows.[12]
    Like a wild bull he wanders now,
    hidden in the untamed wood,
    through rocks and caves, alone
    with his despair on joyless feet,
    keeping his distance from that doom
    uttered at earth's central navel stone.   [480]
    But that fatal oracle still lives,
    hovering above his head forever.

    That wise interpreter of prophecies
    stirs up my fears, unsettling dread.
    I cannot approve of what he said
    and I cannot deny it.
    I am confused. What shall I say?
    My hopes are fluttering here and there,
    with no clear glimpse of past or future.
    I have never heard of any quarrelling,
    past or present, between those two,
    the house of Labdacus and Polybus' son,   [490]
    which could give me evidence enough
    to undermine the fame of Oedipus,
    as he seeks vengeance for the unsolved murder
    in the family line of Labdacus.[13]

Sophocles

ἀλλ᾽ ὁ μὲν οὖν Ζεὺς ὅ τ᾽ Ἀπόλλων ξυνετοὶ καὶ τὰ βροτῶν
εἰδότες· ἀνδρῶν δ᾽ ὅτι μάντις πλέον ἢ ᾽γὼ φέρεται,   500
κρίσις οὔκ ἐστιν ἀλαθής· σοφίᾳ δ᾽ ἂν σοφίαν
παραμείψειεν ἀνήρ.
ἀλλ᾽ οὔποτ᾽ ἔγωγ᾽ ἄν, πρὶν ἴδοιμ᾽ ὀρθὸν ἔπος, μεμφομένων
ἂν καταφαίην.   505
φανερὰ γὰρ ἐπ᾽ αὐτῷ, πτερόεσσ᾽ ἦλθε κόρα
ποτέ, καὶ σοφὸς ὤφθη βασάνῳ θ᾽ ἁδύπολις τῷ ἀπ᾽ ἐμᾶς
φρενὸς οὔποτ᾽ ὀφλήσει κακίαν.   510

ΚΡΕΩΝ

ἄνδρες πολῖται, δείν᾽ ἔπη πεπυσμένος
κατηγορεῖν μου τὸν τύραννον Οἰδίπουν,
πάρειμ᾽ ἀτλητῶν. εἰ γὰρ ἐν ταῖς ξυμφοραῖς   515
ταῖς νῦν νομίζει πρός γ᾽ ἐμοῦ πεπονθέναι
λόγοισιν εἴτ᾽ ἔργοισιν εἰς βλάβην φέρον,
οὔτοι βίου μοι τοῦ μακραίωνος πόθος,
φέροντι τήνδε βάξιν. οὐ γὰρ εἰς ἁπλοῦν
ἡ ζημία μοι τοῦ λόγου τούτου φέρει,   520
ἀλλ᾽ ἐς μέγιστον, εἰ κακὸς μὲν ἐν πόλει,
κακὸς δὲ πρὸς σοῦ καὶ φίλων κεκλήσομαι.

ΧΟΡΟΣ

ἀλλ᾽ ἦλθε μὲν δὴ τοῦτο τοὔνειδος τάχ᾽ ἂν
ὀργῇ βιασθὲν μᾶλλον ἢ γνώμῃ φρενῶν.

ΚΡΕΩΝ

τοὔπος δ᾽ ἐφάνθη, ταῖς ἐμαῖς γνώμαις ὅτι   525
πεισθεὶς ὁ μάντις τοὺς λόγους ψευδεῖς λέγοι;

Apollo and Zeus are truly wise—
they understand what humans do.
But there is no sure way to ascertain
if human prophets grasp things any more
than I do, although in wisdom one man   [500]
may leave another far behind.
But until I see the words confirmed,
I will not approve of any man
who censures Oedipus, for it was clear
when that winged Sphinx went after him
he was a wise man then. We witnessed it.
He passed the test and endeared himself
to all the city. So in my thinking now   [510]
he never will be guilty of a crime.

[Enter CREON]

CREON

You citizens, I have just discovered
that Oedipus, our king, has levelled charges
against me, disturbing allegations.
That I cannot bear, so I have come here.
In these present troubles, if he believes
that he has suffered injury from me,
in word or deed, then I have no desire
to keep on living into ripe old age
still bearing his reproach. For me
the injury produced by this report
is not a single isolated matter—   [520]
no, it has the greatest scope of all,
If I end up being called a wicked man
here in the city, a bad citizen,
by you and by my friends.

CHORUS LEADER

                          Perhaps he charged you
spurred on by the rash power of his rage,
rather than his mind's true judgment.

CREON

Was it publicized that my persuasion
convinced Teiresias to utter lies?

Sophocles

ΧΟΡΟΣ

ηὐδᾶτο μὲν τάδ᾽, οἶδα δ᾽ οὐ γνώμῃ τίνι.

ΚΡΕΩΝ

ἐξ ὀμμάτων δ᾽ ὀρθῶν τε κἀξ ὀρθῆς φρενὸς
κατηγορεῖτο τοὐπίκλημα τοῦτό μου;

ΧΟΡΟΣ

οὐκ οἶδ᾽· ἃ γὰρ δρῶσ᾽, οἱ κρατοῦντες οὐχ ὁρῶ.   530
αὐτὸς δ᾽ ὅδ᾽ ἤδη δωμάτων ἔξω περᾷ.

ΟΙΔΙΠΟΥΣ

οὗτος σύ, πῶς δεῦρ᾽ ἦλθες; ἦ τοσόνδ᾽ ἔχεις
τόλμης πρόσωπον ὥστε τὰς ἐμὰς στέγας
ἵκου, φονεὺς ὢν τοῦδε τἀνδρὸς ἐμφανῶς
λῃστής τ᾽ ἐναργὴς τῆς ἐμῆς τυραννίδος;   535
φέρ᾽ εἰπὲ πρὸς θεῶν, δειλίαν ἢ μωρίαν
ἰδών τιν᾽ ἔν μοι ταῦτ᾽ ἐβουλεύσω ποεῖν;
ἢ τοὔργον ὡς οὐ γνωριοῖμί σου τόδε
δόλῳ προσέρπον ἢ οὐκ ἀλεξοίμην μαθών;
ἆρ᾽ οὐχὶ μῶρόν ἐστι τοὐγχείρημά σου,   540
ἄνευ τε πλήθους καὶ φίλων τυραννίδα
θηρᾶν, ὃ πλήθει χρήμασίν θ᾽ ἁλίσκεται;

ΚΡΕΩΝ

οἶσθ᾽ ὡς πόησον; ἀντὶ τῶν εἰρημένων
ἴσ᾽ ἀντάκουσον, κᾆτα κρῖν᾽ αὐτὸς μαθών.

ΟΙΔΙΠΟΥΣ

λέγειν σὺ δεινός, μανθάνειν δ᾽ ἐγὼ κακὸς   545
σοῦ· δυσμενῆ γὰρ καὶ βαρύν σ᾽ ηὕρηκ᾽ ἐμοί.

82

CHORUS LEADER

    That's what was said. I have no idea
    just what that meant.

CREON

                      Did he accuse me
    and announce the charges with a steady gaze,
    in a normal state of mind?

CHORUS LEADER

                  I do not know.   [530]
    What those in power do I do not see.
    But he's approaching from the palace—
    here he comes in person.

[Enter OEDIPUS from the palace]

OEDIPUS

                You! How did you get here?
    Have you grown so bold-faced that you now come
    to my own home—you who are obviously
    the murderer of the man whose house it was,
    a thief who clearly wants to steal my throne?
    Come, in the name of all the gods, tell me this—
    did you plan to do it because you thought
    I was a coward or a fool? Or did you think
    I would not learn about your actions
    as they crept up on me with such deceit—
    or that, if I knew, I could not deflect them?
    This attempt of yours, is it not madness—   [540]
    to chase after the king's place without friends,
    without a horde of men, to seek a goal
    which only gold or factions could attain?

CREON

    Will you listen to me? It's your turn now
    to let me make a suitable response.
    Once you hear that, then judge me for yourself.

OEDIPUS

    You are a clever talker. But from you
    I will learn little. I know you now—
    a troublemaker, an enemy of mine.

ΚΡΕΩΝ

τοῦτ᾿ αὐτὸ νῦν μου πρῶτ᾿ ἄκουσον ὡς ἐρῶ.

ΟΙΔΙΠΟΥΣ

τοῦτ᾿ αὐτὸ μή μοι φράζ᾿, ὅπως οὐκ εἶ κακός.

ΚΡΕΩΝ

εἴ τοι νομίζεις κτῆμα τὴν αὐθαδίαν
εἶναί τι τοῦ νοῦ χωρίς, οὐκ ὀρθῶς φρονεῖς.   550

ΟΙΔΙΠΟΥΣ

εἴ τοι νομίζεις ἄνδρα συγγενῆ κακῶς
δρῶν οὐχ ὑφέξειν τὴν δίκην, οὐκ εὖ φρονεῖς.

ΚΡΕΩΝ

ξύμφημί σοι ταῦτ᾿ ἔνδικ᾿ εἰρῆσθαι· τὸ δὲ
πάθημ᾿ ὁποῖον φὴς παθεῖν, δίδασκέ με.

ΟΙΔΙΠΟΥΣ

ἔπειθες ἢ οὐκ ἔπειθες, ὡς χρείη μ᾿ ἐπὶ   555
τὸν σεμνόμαντιν ἄνδρα πέμψασθαί τινα;

ΚΡΕΩΝ

καὶ νῦν ἔθ᾿ αὐτός εἰμι τῷ βουλεύματι.

ΟΙΔΙΠΟΥΣ

πόσον τιν᾿ ἤδη δῆθ᾿ ὁ Λάϊος χρόνον

ΚΡΕΩΝ

δέδρακε ποῖον ἔργον; οὐ γὰρ ἐννοῶ.

ΟΙΔΙΠΟΥΣ

ἄφαντος ἔρρει θανασίμῳ χειρώματι;   560

ΚΡΕΩΝ

μακροὶ παλαιοί τ᾿ ἂν μετρηθεῖεν χρόνοι.

84

CREON

  At least first listen to what I have to say.

OEDIPUS

  Do not bother trying to convince me
  that you have done no wrong.

CREON

                 If you think being stubborn
  and forgetting common sense is wise,
  then you're not thinking as you should.   [550]

OEDIPUS

  And if you think you can try to harm
  a man who is a relative of yours
  and escape without a penalty
  then you have not been thinking wisely.

CREON

  I agree. What you've just said makes sense.
  So tell me the nature of the damage
  you claim you're suffering because of me.

OEDIPUS

  Did you or did you not persuade me
  to send for Teiresias, that prophet?

CREON

  Yes. And I'd still give you the same advice.

OEDIPUS

  How long is it since Laius . . . *[pauses]*

CREON

                    Did what?
  What's Laius got to do with anything?

OEDIPUS

  . . . since Laius was carried off and disappeared,
  since he was killed so brutally?   [560]

CREON

                    A long time—
  many years have passed since then.

85

Sophocles

ΟΙΔΙΠΟΥΣ

τότ᾽ οὖν ὁ μάντις οὗτος ἦν ἐν τῇ τέχνῃ;

ΚΡΕΩΝ

σοφός γ᾽ ὁμοίως κἀξ ἴσου τιμώμενος.

ΟΙΔΙΠΟΥΣ

ἐμνήσατ᾽ οὖν ἐμοῦ τι τῷ τότ᾽ ἐν χρόνῳ;

ΚΡΕΩΝ

οὔκουν ἐμοῦ γ᾽ ἑστῶτος οὐδαμοῦ πέλας.   565

ΟΙΔΙΠΟΥΣ

ἀλλ᾽ οὐκ ἔρευναν τοῦ κτανόντος ἔσχετε;

ΚΡΕΩΝ

παρέσχομεν, πῶς δ᾽ οὐχί; κοὐκ ἠκούσαμεν.

ΟΙΔΙΠΟΥΣ

πῶς οὖν τόθ᾽ οὗτος ὁ σοφὸς οὐκ ηὔδα τάδε;

ΚΡΕΩΝ

οὐκ οἶδ᾽· ἐφ᾽ οἷς γὰρ μὴ φρονῶ σιγᾶν φιλῶ.

ΟΙΔΙΠΟΥΣ

τοσόνδε γ᾽ οἶσθα καὶ λέγοις ἂν εὖ φρονῶν.   570

ΚΡΕΩΝ

ποῖον τόδ᾽; εἰ γὰρ οἶδά γ᾽, οὐκ ἀρνήσομαι.

ΟΙΔΙΠΟΥΣ

ὁθούνεκ᾽, εἰ μὴ σοὶ ξυνῆλθε, τάσδ᾽ ἐμὰς
οὐκ ἄν ποτ᾽ εἶπε Λαΐου διαφθοράς.

ΚΡΕΩΝ

εἰ μὲν λέγει τάδ᾽, αὐτὸς οἶσθ᾽· ἐγὼ δὲ σοῦ
μαθεῖν δικαιῶ ταῦθ᾽ ἅπερ κἀμοῦ σὺ νῦν.   575

86

OEDIPUS

At that time,
was Teiresias as skilled in prophecy?

CREON

Then, as now, he was honoured for his wisdom.

OEDIPUS

And back then did he ever mention me?

CREON

No, never—not while I was with him.

OEDIPUS

Did you not investigate the killing?

CREON

Yes, of course we did. But we found nothing.

OEDIPUS

Why did this man, this wise man, not speak up?

CREON

I do not know. And when I don't know something,
I like to hold my tongue.

OEDIPUS

You know enough—   [570]
at least you understand enough to say . . .

CREON

What? If I really do know something
I will not deny it.

OEDIPUS

If Teiresias
were not working with you, he would not name me
as the one who murdered Laius.

CREON

If he says this,
well, you're the one who knows. But I think
the time has come for me to question you
the way that you've been questioning me.

Sophocles

ΟΙΔΙΠΟΥΣ
ἐκμάνθαν'· οὐ γὰρ δὴ φονεὺς ἁλώσομαι.

ΚΡΕΩΝ
τί δῆτ'; ἀδελφὴν τὴν ἐμὴν γήμας ἔχεις;

ΟΙΔΙΠΟΥΣ
ἄρνησις οὐκ ἔνεστιν ὧν ἀνιστορεῖς.

ΚΡΕΩΝ
ἄρχεις δ' ἐκείνῃ ταὐτὰ γῆς ἴσον νέμων;

ΟΙΔΙΠΟΥΣ
ἃν ᾗ θέλουσα πάντ' ἐμοῦ κομίζεται.   580

ΚΡΕΩΝ
οὔκουν ἰσοῦμαι σφῷν ἐγὼ δυοῖν τρίτος;

ΟΙΔΙΠΟΥΣ
ἐνταῦθα γὰρ δὴ καὶ κακὸς φαίνει φίλος.

ΚΡΕΩΝ
οὔκ, εἰ διδοίης γ' ὡς ἐγὼ σαυτῷ λόγον.
σκέψαι δὲ τοῦτο πρῶτον, εἴ τιν' ἂν δοκεῖς
ἄρχειν ἑλέσθαι ξὺν φόβοισι μᾶλλον ἢ   585
ἄτρεστον εὕδοντ', εἰ τά γ' αὔθ' ἕξει κράτη.
ἐγὼ μὲν οὖν οὔτ' αὐτὸς ἱμείρων ἔφυν
τύραννος εἶναι μᾶλλον ἢ τύραννα δρᾶν,
οὔτ' ἄλλος ὅστις σωφρονεῖν ἐπίσταται.
νῦν μὲν γὰρ ἐκ σοῦ πάντ' ἄνευ φόβου φέρω,   590
εἰ δ' αὐτὸς ἦρχον, πολλὰ κἂν ἄκων ἔδρων.
πῶς δῆτ' ἐμοὶ τυραννὶς ἡδίων ἔχειν
ἀρχῆς ἀλύπου καὶ δυναστείας ἔφυ;
οὔπω τοσοῦτον ἠπατημένος κυρῶ
ὥστ' ἄλλα χρῄζειν ἢ τὰ σὺν κέρδει καλά.   595
νῦν πᾶσι χαίρω, νῦν με πᾶς ἀσπάζεται,
νῦν οἱ σέθεν χρῄζοντες ἐκκαλοῦσί με·
τὸ γὰρ τυχεῖν αὐτοῖσι πᾶν ἐνταῦθ' ἔνι.
πῶς δῆτ' ἐγὼ κεῖν' ἂν λάβοιμ' ἀφεὶς τάδε;

88

OEDIPUS

Ask whatever you wish. You'll never prove
that I'm the murderer.

CREON

Then tell me this—
are you not married to my sister?

OEDIPUS

Since you ask me, yes. I don't deny that.

CREON

And you two rule this land as equals?

OEDIPUS

Whatever she desires, she gets from me.   [580]

CREON

And am I not third, equal to you both?

OEDIPUS

That's what makes your friendship so deceitful.

CREON

No, not if you think this through, as I do.
First, consider this. In your view, would anyone
prefer to rule and have to cope with fear
rather than live in peace, carefree and safe,
if his powers were the same? I, for one,
have no natural desire to be king
in preference to performing royal acts.
The same is true of any other man
whose understanding grasps things properly.
For now I get everything I want from you,   [590]
but without the fear. If I were king myself,
I'd be doing many things against my will.
So how can being a king be sweeter to me
than royal power without anxiety?
I am not yet so mistaken in my mind
that I want things which bring no benefits.
Now all men are my friends and wish me well,
and those who seek to get something from you
now flatter me, since I'm the one who brings
success in what they want. So why would I
give up such benefits for something else?

οὐκ ἂν γένοιτο νοῦς κακὸς καλῶς φρονῶν.　　600
ἀλλ᾽ οὔτ᾽ ἐραστὴς τῆσδε τῆς γνώμης ἔφυν
οὔτ᾽ ἂν μετ᾽ ἄλλου δρῶντος ἂν τλαίην ποτέ.
καὶ τῶνδ᾽ ἔλεγχον τοῦτο μὲν Πυθώδ᾽ ἰὼν
πεύθου τὰ χρησθέντ᾽ εἰ σαφῶς ἤγγειλά σοι·
τοῦτ᾽ ἄλλ᾽, ἐάν με τῷ τερασκόπῳ λάβῃς　　605
κοινῇ τι βουλεύσαντα, μή μ᾽ ἁπλῇ κτάνῃς
ψήφῳ, διπλῇ δέ, τῇ τ᾽ ἐμῇ καὶ σῇ, λαβών·
γνώμῃ δ᾽ ἀδήλῳ μή με χωρὶς αἰτιῶ.
οὐ γὰρ δίκαιον οὔτε τοὺς κακοὺς μάτην
χρηστοὺς νομίζειν οὔτε τοὺς χρηστοὺς κακούς.　　610
φίλον γὰρ ἐσθλὸν ἐκβαλεῖν ἴσον λέγω
καὶ τὸν παρ᾽ αὑτῷ βίοτον, ὃν πλεῖστον, φιλεῖ.
ἀλλ᾽ ἐν χρόνῳ γνώσει τάδ᾽ ἀσφαλῶς, ἐπεὶ
χρόνος δίκαιον ἄνδρα δείκνυσιν μόνος·
κακὸν δὲ κἂν ἐν ἡμέρᾳ γνοίης μιᾷ.　　615

ΧΟΡΟΣ

καλῶς ἔλεξεν εὐλαβουμένῳ πεσεῖν,
ἄναξ· φρονεῖν γὰρ οἱ ταχεῖς οὐκ ἀσφαλεῖς.

ΟΙΔΙΠΟΥΣ

ὅταν ταχύς τις οὑπιβουλεύων λάθρᾳ
χωρῇ, ταχὺν δεῖ κἀμὲ βουλεύειν πάλιν·
εἰ δ᾽ ἡσυχάζων προσμενῶ, τὰ τοῦδε μὲν　　620
πεπραγμέν᾽ ἔσται, τἀμὰ δ᾽ ἡμαρτημένα.

ΚΡΕΩΝ

τί δῆτα χρῄζεις; ἦ με γῆς ἔξω βαλεῖν;

ΟΙΔΙΠΟΥΣ

ἥκιστα· θνῄσκειν, οὐ φυγεῖν σε βούλομαι.
ὡς ἂν προδείξῃς οἷόν ἐστι τὸ φθονεῖν.

ΚΡΕΩΝ

ὡς οὐχ ὑπείξων οὐδὲ πιστεύσων λέγεις;　　625

A mind that's wise will not turn treacherous.   [600]
It's not my nature to love such policies.
And if another man pursued such things,
I would not work with him. I could not bear to.
If you want proof of this, then go to Delphi.
Ask the prophet if I brought back to you
exactly what was said. At that point,
if you discover I have planned something,
that I've conspired with Teiresias,
then arrest me and have me put to death,
not merely on your own authority,
but on mine as well, a double judgment.
Do not condemn me on an unproved charge.
It's not fair to judge these things by guesswork,
to assume bad men are good or good men bad.   [610]
I say a man who throws away a noble friend
is like a man who parts with his own life,
the thing most dear to him. Give it some time.
Then you will see clearly, since only time
can fully validate a man who's true.
A bad man is exposed in just one day.

CHORUS LEADER
For a man concerned about being killed,
my lord, he has spoken eloquently.
Those who are unreliable give rash advice.

OEDIPUS
If some conspirator moves against me,
in secret and with speed, I must be quick
to make my counter plans. If I just rest
and wait for him to act, then he'll succeed   [620]
in what he wants to do, and I'll be finished.

CREON
What do you want—to exile me from here?

OEDIPUS
No. I want you to die, not just run off—
so I can demonstrate what envy means.

CREON
You are determined not to change your mind
or listen to me?

91

ΟΙΔΙΠΟΥΣ
< . . . >

ΚΡΕΩΝ
οὐ γὰρ φρονοῦντά σ᾽ εὖ βλέπω.

ΟΙΔΙΠΟΥΣ
τὸ γοῦν ἐμόν.

ΚΡΕΩΝ
ἀλλ᾽ ἐξ ἴσου δεῖ κἀμόν.

ΟΙΔΙΠΟΥΣ
ἀλλ᾽ ἔφυς κακός.

ΚΡΕΩΝ
εἰ δὲ ξυνίῃς μηδέν;

ΟΙΔΙΠΟΥΣ
ἀρκτέον γ᾽ ὅμως.

ΚΡΕΩΝ
οὔτοι κακῶς γ᾽ ἄρχοντος.

ΟΙΔΙΠΟΥΣ
ὦ πόλις πόλις.

ΚΡΕΩΝ
κἀμοὶ πόλεως μέτεστιν, οὐχί σοι μόνῳ.   630

ΧΟΡΟΣ
παύσασθ᾽, ἄνακτες· καιρίαν δ᾽ ὑμῖν ὁρῶ
τήνδ᾽ ἐκ δόμων στείχουσαν Ἰοκάστην, μεθ᾽ ἧς
τὸ νῦν παρεστὸς νεῖκος εὖ θέσθαι χρεών.

ΙΟΚΑΣΤΗ
τί τὴν ἄβουλον, ὦ ταλαίπωροι, στάσιν
γλώσσης ἐπήρασθ᾽ οὐδ᾽ ἐπαισχύνεσθε γῆς   635
οὕτω νοσούσης ἴδια κινοῦντες κακά;

92

OEDIPUS

           You'll not convince me,
for there's no way that I can trust you.

CREON

I can see that you've become unbalanced.[14]

OEDIPUS

I'm sane enough to defend my interests.

CREON

You should be protecting mine as well.

OEDIPUS

But you're a treacherous man. It's your nature.

CREON

What if you're wrong?

OEDIPUS

                   I still have to govern.

CREON

Not if you do it badly.

OEDIPUS

                O Thebes—
my city!

CREON

            I, too, have some rights in Thebes—   [630]
it is not yours alone.

[The palace doors open]

CHORUS LEADER

              My lords, an end to this.
I see Jocasta coming from the palace,
and just in time. With her assistance
you should bring this quarrel to a close.

[Enter JOCASTA from the palace]

JOCASTA

You foolish men, why are you arguing
in such a stupid way? With our land so sick,
aren't you ashamed to start a private fight?

Sophocles

οὐκ εἶ σύ τ᾽ οἴκους σύ τε, Κρέων, κατὰ στέγας,
καὶ μὴ τὸ μηδὲν ἄλγος εἰς μέγ᾽ οἴσετε;

ΚΡΕΩΝ

ὅμαιμε, δεινά μ᾽ Οἰδίπους ὁ σὸς πόσις
δρᾶσαι δικαιοῖ δυοῖν ἀποκρίνας κακοῖν   640
ἢ γῆς ἀπῶσαι πατρίδος ἢ κτεῖναι λαβών.

ΟΙΔΙΠΟΥΣ

ξύμφημι· δρῶντα γάρ νιν, ὦ γύναι, κακῶς
εἴληφα τοὐμὸν σῶμα σὺν τέχνῃ κακῇ.

ΚΡΕΩΝ

μή νυν ὀναίμην, ἀλλ᾽ ἀραῖος, εἴ σέ τι
δέδρακ᾽, ὀλοίμην, ὧν ἐπαιτιᾷ με δρᾶν.   645

ΙΟΚΑΣΤΗ

ὦ πρὸς θεῶν πίστευσον, Οἰδίπους, τάδε,
μάλιστα μὲν τόνδ᾽ ὅρκον αἰδεσθεὶς θεῶν,
ἔπειτα κάμὲ τούσδε θ᾽ οἳ πάρεισί σοι.

ΧΟΡΟΣ

πιθοῦ θελήσας φρονήσας τ᾽, ἄναξ, λίσσομαι.

ΟΙΔΙΠΟΥΣ

τί σοι θέλεις δῆτ᾽ εἰκάθω;   650

ΧΟΡΟΣ

τὸν οὔτε πρὶν νήπιον νῦν τ᾽ ἐν ὅρκῳ μέγαν καταίδεσαι.

ΟΙΔΙΠΟΥΣ

οἶσθ᾽ οὖν ἃ χρῄζεις;   655

ΧΟΡΟΣ

οἶδα.

ΟΙΔΙΠΟΥΣ

φράζε δὴ τί φῄς.

94

You, Oedipus, go in the house, and you,
Creon, return to yours. Why inflate
a trivial matter into something huge?

CREON

    Sister, your husband Oedipus intends
to punish me in one of two dreadful ways—   [640]
to banish me from my fathers' country
or arrest me and then have me killed.

OEDIPUS

                      That's right.
Lady, I caught him committing treason,
a vicious crime against me personally.

CREON

    Let me not prosper but die a man accursed,
if I have done what you accuse me of.

JOCASTA

                    Oedipus,
for the sake of the gods, trust him in this.
Respect that oath he made before all heaven—
do it for my sake and for those around you.

CHORUS LEADER

    I beg you, my lord, consent to this—
agree with her.   [650]

OEDIPUS

                What is it then
you're asking me to do?

CHORUS LEADER

                    Pay Creon due respect.
He has not been foolish in the past, and now
that oath he's sworn has power.

OEDIPUS

                  Are you aware
just what you're asking?

CHORUS LEADER

                Yes. I understand.

OEDIPUS

    Then tell me clearly what you mean to say.

ΧΟΡΟΣ

τὸν ἐναγῆ φίλον μήποτ' ἐν αἰτίᾳ
σὺν ἀφανεῖ λόγῳ σ' ἄτιμον βαλεῖν.

ΟΙΔΙΠΟΥΣ

εὖ νυν ἐπίστω, ταῦθ' ὅταν ζητῇς, ἐμοὶ
ζητῶν ὄλεθρον ἢ φυγὴν ἐκ τῆσδε γῆς.

ΧΟΡΟΣ

οὐ τὸν πάντων θεῶν θεὸν πρόμον   660
Ἅλιον· ἐπεὶ ἄθεος ἄφιλος ὅ τι πύματον
ὀλοίμαν, φρόνησιν εἰ τάνδ' ἔχω.
ἀλλά μοι δυσμόρῳ γᾶ φθινὰς   665
τρύχει ψυχάν, τάδ' εἰ κακοῖς κακὰ
προσάψει τοῖς πάλαι τὰ πρὸς σφῷν.

ΟΙΔΙΠΟΥΣ

ὁ δ' οὖν ἴτω, κεἰ χρή με παντελῶς θανεῖν
ἢ γῆς ἄτιμον τῆσδ' ἀπωσθῆναι βίᾳ.   670
τὸ γὰρ σόν, οὐ τὸ τοῦδ', ἐποικτίρω στόμα
ἐλεινόν· οὗτος δ' ἔνθ' ἂν ᾖ στυγήσεται.

ΚΡΕΩΝ

στυγνὸς μὲν εἴκων δῆλος εἶ, βαρὺς δ', ὅταν
θυμοῦ περάσῃς· αἱ δὲ τοιαῦται φύσεις
αὐταῖς δικαίως εἰσὶν ἄλγισται φέρειν.   675

ΟΙΔΙΠΟΥΣ

οὔκουν μ' ἐάσεις κἀκτὸς εἶ;

ΚΡΕΩΝ

                              πορεύσομαι,
σοῦ μὲν τυχὼν ἀγνῶτος, ἐν δὲ τοῖσδ' ἴσος.

96

CHORUS LEADER
You should not accuse a friend of yours
and thus dishonour him with a mere story
which may be false, when he has sworn an oath
and therefore could be subject to a curse.

OEDIPUS
By this point you should clearly understand,
what you are doing when you request this—
seeking to exile me from Thebes or kill me.

CHORUS LEADER
No, no, by sacred Helios, the god   [660]
who stands pre-eminent before the rest!
May I die the most miserable of deaths,
abandoned by the gods and by my friends,
if I have ever harboured such a thought!
But the destruction of our land wears down
my troubled heart—and so does this quarrel,
if you two add new problems to the ones
which have for so long been afflicting us.

OEDIPUS
Let him go, then, even though it means
I must be killed or sent from here in exile,
forced out in disgrace. I have been moved   [670]
to act compassionately by what you said,
not by Creon's words. But if he stays here,
he will be hateful to me.

CREON
                           You are stubborn—
obviously unhappy to concede,
and when you lose your temper, you go too far.
But men like that find it most difficult
to tolerate themselves. In that there's justice.

OEDIPUS
Why not go—just leave me alone?

CREON
                                 I'll leave—
since I see you do not understand me.
But these men here know I'm a reasonable man.

97

Sophocles

ΧΟΡΟΣ
γύναι, τί μέλλεις κομίζειν δόμων τόνδ' ἔσω;

ΙΟΚΑΣΤΗ
μαθοῦσά γ' ἥτις ἡ τύχη.   680

ΧΟΡΟΣ
δόκησις ἀγνὼς λόγων ἦλθε, δάπτει δὲ καὶ τὸ μὴ 'νδικον.

ΙΟΚΑΣΤΗ
ἀμφοῖν ἀπ' αὐτοῖν;

ΧΟΡΟΣ
                    ναίχι.

ΙΟΚΑΣΤΗ
                    καὶ τίς ἦν λόγος;

ΧΟΡΟΣ
ἅλις ἔμοιγ', ἅλις, γᾶς προπονουμένας,   685
φαίνεται ἔνθ' ἔληξεν αὐτοῦ μένειν.

ΟΙΔΙΠΟΥΣ
ὁρᾷς ἵν' ἥκεις, ἀγαθὸς ὢν γνώμην ἀνήρ,
τοὐμὸν παριεὶς καὶ καταμβλύνων κέαρ;

ΧΟΡΟΣ
ὦναξ, εἶπον μὲν οὐχ ἅπαξ μόνον,   690
ἴσθι δὲ παραφρόνιμον, ἄπορον ἐπὶ φρόνιμα
πεφάνθαι μ' ἄν, εἴ σ' ἐνοσφιζόμαν,
ὅς τ' ἐμὰν γᾶν φίλαν ἐν πόνοις
ἀλύουσαν κατ' ὀρθὸν οὔρισας,   695
τανῦν τ' εὔπομπος, ἂν γένοιο.

ΙΟΚΑΣΤΗ
πρὸς θεῶν δίδαξον κἄμ', ἄναξ, ὅτου ποτὲ
μῆνιν τοσήνδε πράγματος στήσας ἔχεις.

98

[Exit CREON away from the palace, leaving OEDIPUS and JOCASTA and the CHORUS on stage]

CHORUS LEADER
Lady, will you escort our king inside?

JOCASTA
Yes, once I have learned what happened here.   [680]

CHORUS LEADER
                                        They talked—
their words gave rise to uninformed suspicions,
but even unjust words inflict sore wounds.

JOCASTA
From both of them?

CHORUS LEADER
                        Yes.

JOCASTA
                                    What caused it?

CHORUS LEADER
With our country already in distress,
it is enough, it seems to me, enough
to leave things as they are.

OEDIPUS
                                    Now do you see
the point you've reached thanks to your noble wish
to dissolve and dull what I felt in my heart?

CHORUS LEADER
My lord, I have declared it more than once,   [690]
so you must know it would have been quite mad
if I abandoned you, who, when this land,
my cherished Thebes, was in great trouble,
set it right again and who, in these harsh times
should prove a trusty and successful guide.

JOCASTA
By all the gods, my king, please let me know
why in this present matter you now feel
such unremitting rage.

Sophocles

ΟΙΔΙΠΟΥΣ

ἐρῶ· σὲ γὰρ τῶνδ᾽ ἐς πλέον, γύναι, σέβω·   700
Κρέοντος, οἷά μοι βεβουλευκὼς ἔχει.

ΙΟΚΑΣΤΗ

λέγ᾽, εἰ σαφῶς τὸ νεῖκος ἐγκαλῶν ἐρεῖς.

ΟΙΔΙΠΟΥΣ

φονέα με φησὶ Λαΐου καθεστάναι.

ΙΟΚΑΣΤΗ

αὐτὸς ξυνειδὼς ἢ μαθὼν ἄλλου πάρα;

ΟΙΔΙΠΟΥΣ

μάντιν μὲν οὖν κακοῦργον εἰσπέμψας, ἐπεὶ   705
τό γ᾽ εἰς ἑαυτὸν πᾶν ἐλευθεροῖ στόμα.

ΙΟΚΑΣΤΗ

σύ νυν ἀφεὶς σεαυτὸν ὧν λέγεις πέρι
ἐμοῦ ᾽πάκουσον, καὶ μάθ᾽ οὕνεκ᾽ ἐστί σοι
βρότειον οὐδὲν μαντικῆς ἔχον τέχνης.
φανῶ δέ σοι σημεῖα τῶνδε σύντομα.   710
χρησμὸς γὰρ ἦλθε Λαΐῳ ποτ᾽, οὐκ ἐρῶ
Φοίβου γ᾽ ἄπ᾽ αὐτοῦ, τῶν δ᾽ ὑπηρετῶν ἄπο,
ὡς αὐτὸν ἕξοι μοῖρα πρὸς παιδὸς θανεῖν,
ὅστις γένοιτ᾽ ἐμοῦ τε κἀκείνου πάρα.
καὶ τὸν μέν, ὥσπερ γ᾽ ἡ φάτις, ξένοι ποτὲ   715
λῃσταὶ φονεύουσ᾽ ἐν τριπλαῖς ἁμαξιτοῖς·
παιδὸς δὲ βλάστας οὐ διέσχον ἡμέραι
τρεῖς, καί νιν ἄρθρα κεῖνος ἐνζεύξας ποδοῖν
ἔρριψεν ἄλλων χερσὶν ἄβατον εἰς ὄρος.
κἀνταῦθ᾽ Ἀπόλλων οὔτ᾽ ἐκεῖνον ἤνυσεν   720
φονέα γενέσθαι πατρὸς οὔτε Λάϊον
τὸ δεινὸν οὐφοβεῖτο πρὸς παιδὸς θανεῖν.
τοιαῦτα φῆμαι μαντικαὶ διώρισαν,

100

OEDIPUS

           To you I'll speak, lady,   [700]
since I respect you more than I do these men.
It's Creon's fault. He conspired against me.

JOCASTA

In this quarrel what was said? Tell me.

OEDIPUS

Creon claims that I'm the murderer—
that I killed Laius.

JOCASTA

           Does he know this first hand,
or has he picked it up from someone else?

OEDIPUS

No. He set up that treasonous prophet.
What he says himself all sounds quite innocent.

JOCASTA

All right, forget about those things you've said.
Listen to me, and ease your mind with this—
no human being has skill in prophecy.
I'll show you why with this example.   [710]
King Laius once received a oracle.
I won't say it came straight from Apollo,
but it was from those who do assist the god.
It said Laius was fated to be killed
by a child of ours, one born to him and me.
Now, at least according to the story,
one day Laius was killed by foreigners,
by robbers, at a place where three roads meet.
Besides, before our child was three days old,
Laius pinned his ankles tight together
and ordered other men to throw him out
on a mountain rock where no one ever goes.
And so Apollo's plan that he'd become   [720]
the one who killed his father didn't work,
and Laius never suffered what he feared,
that his own son would be his murderer,
although that's what the oracle had claimed.

ὧν ἐντρέπου σὺ μηδέν· ὧν γὰρ ἂν θεὸς
χρείαν ἐρευνᾷ, ῥᾳδίως αὐτὸς φανεῖ.　　　725

ΟΙΔΙΠΟΥΣ
οἷόν μ᾽ ἀκούσαντ᾽ ἀρτίως ἔχει, γύναι,
ψυχῆς πλάνημα κἀνακίνησις φρενῶν.

ΙΟΚΑΣΤΗ
ποίας μερίμνης τοῦθ᾽ ὑποστραφεὶς λέγεις;

ΟΙΔΙΠΟΥΣ
ἔδοξ᾽ ἀκοῦσαι σοῦ τόδ᾽, ὡς ὁ Λάϊος
κατασφαγείη πρὸς τριπλαῖς ἁμαξιτοῖς.　　　730

ΙΟΚΑΣΤΗ
ηὐδᾶτο γὰρ ταῦτ᾽ οὐδέ πω λήξαντ᾽ ἔχει.

ΟΙΔΙΠΟΥΣ
καὶ ποῦ 'σθ᾽ ὁ χῶρος οὗτος οὗ τόδ᾽ ἦν πάθος;

ΙΟΚΑΣΤΗ
Φωκὶς μὲν ἡ γῆ κλῄζεται, σχιστὴ δ᾽ ὁδὸς
ἐς ταὐτὸ Δελφῶν κἀπὸ Δαυλίας ἄγει.

ΟΙΔΙΠΟΥΣ
καὶ τίς χρόνος τοῖσδ᾽ ἐστὶν οὑξεληλυθώς;　　　735

ΙΟΚΑΣΤΗ
σχεδόν τι πρόσθεν ἢ σὺ τῆσδ᾽ ἔχων χθονὸς
ἀρχὴν ἐφαίνου, τοῦτ᾽ ἐκηρύχθη πόλει.

ΟΙΔΙΠΟΥΣ
ὦ Ζεῦ, τί μου δρᾶσαι βεβούλευσαι πέρι;

ΙΟΚΑΣΤΗ
τί δ᾽ ἐστί σοι τοῦτ᾽, Οἰδίπους, ἐνθύμιον;

ΟΙΔΙΠΟΥΣ
μήπω μ᾽ ἐρώτα· τὸν δὲ Λάϊον φύσιν　　　740
τίν᾽ ἦλθε φράζε, τίνα δ᾽ ἀκμὴν ἥβης ἔχων.

So don't concern yourself with prophecies.
Whatever gods intend to bring about
they themselves make known quite easily.

OEDIPUS

Lady, as I listen to these words of yours,
my soul is shaken, my mind confused . . .

JOCASTA

Why do you say that? What's worrying you?

OEDIPUS

I thought I heard you say that Laius
was murdered at a place where three roads meet.   [730]

JOCASTA

That's what was said and people still believe.

OEDIPUS

Where is this place? Where did it happen?

JOCASTA

In a land called Phocis. Two roads lead there—
one from Delphi and one from Daulia.

OEDIPUS

How long is it since these events took place?

JOCASTA

The story was reported in the city
just before you took over royal power
here in Thebes.

OEDIPUS

                         O Zeus, what have you done?
What have you planned for me?

JOCASTA

                                              What is it,
Oedipus? Why is your spirit so troubled?

OEDIPUS

                                              Not yet,   [740]
no questions yet. Tell me this—Laius,
how tall was he? How old a man?

103

Sophocles

ΙΟΚΑΣΤΗ
μέγας, χνοάζων ἄρτι λευκανθὲς κάρα,
μορφῆς δὲ τῆς σῆς οὐκ ἀπεστάτει πολύ.

ΟΙΔΙΠΟΥΣ
οἴμοι τάλας· ἔοικ᾽ ἐμαυτὸν εἰς ἀρὰς
δεινὰς προβάλλων ἀρτίως οὐκ εἰδέναι.					745

ΙΟΚΑΣΤΗ
πῶς φῄς; ὀκνῶ τοι πρός σ᾽ ἀποσκοποῦσ᾽, ἄναξ.

ΟΙΔΙΠΟΥΣ
δεινῶς ἀθυμῶ μὴ βλέπων ὁ μάντις ᾖ·
δείξεις δὲ μᾶλλον, ἢν ἓν ἐξείπῃς ἔτι.

ΙΟΚΑΣΤΗ
καὶ μὴν ὀκνῶ μέν, ἃ δ᾽ ἂν ἔρῃ μαθοῦσ᾽ ἐρῶ.

ΟΙΔΙΠΟΥΣ
πότερον ἐχώρει βαιὸς ἢ πολλοὺς ἔχων					750
ἄνδρας λοχίτας, οἷ᾽ ἀνὴρ ἀρχηγέτης;

ΙΟΚΑΣΤΗ
πέντ᾽ ἦσαν οἱ ξύμπαντες, ἐν δ᾽ αὐτοῖσιν ἦν .
κῆρυξ· ἀπήνη δ᾽ ἦγε Λάϊον μία.

ΟΙΔΙΠΟΥΣ
αἰαῖ, τάδ᾽ ἤδη διαφανῆ. τίς ἦν ποτε
ὁ τούσδε λέξας τοὺς λόγους ὑμῖν, γύναι;					755

ΙΟΚΑΣΤΗ
οἰκεύς τις, ὅσπερ ἵκετ᾽ ἐκσωθεὶς μόνος.

ΟΙΔΙΠΟΥΣ
ἦ κἀν δόμοισι τυγχάνει τανῦν παρών;

ΙΟΚΑΣΤΗ
οὐ δῆτ᾽· ἀφ᾽ οὗ γὰρ κεῖθεν ἦλθε καὶ κράτη
σέ τ᾽ εἶδ᾽ ἔχοντα Λάϊόν τ᾽ ὀλωλότα,

JOCASTA

He was big—with hair starting to turn white.
In shape he was not all that unlike you.

OEDIPUS

The worse for me! I may have set myself
under a dreadful curse without my knowledge!

JOCASTA

What do you mean? As I look at you, my king,
I start to tremble.

OEDIPUS

                I am afraid,
full of terrible fears the prophet sees.
But you can reveal this better if you now
will tell me one thing more.

JOCASTA

                I'm shaking,
but if you ask me, I will answer you.

OEDIPUS

Did Laius have a small escort with him   [750]
or a troop of soldiers, like a royal king?

JOCASTA

Five men, including a herald, went with him.
A carriage carried Laius.

OEDIPUS

                Alas! Alas!
It's all too clear! Lady, who told you this?

JOCASTA

A slave—the only one who got away.
He came back here.

OEDIPUS

             Is there any chance
he's in our household now?

JOCASTA

                  No.
Once he returned and understood that you
had now assumed the power of slaughtered Laius,

ἐξικέτευσε τῆς ἐμῆς χειρὸς θιγὼν 760
ἀγρούς σφε πέμψαι κἀπὶ ποιμνίων νομάς,
ὡς πλεῖστον εἴη τοῦδ᾽ ἄποπτος ἄστεως.
κἄπεμψ᾽ ἐγώ νιν· ἄξιος γὰρ οἷ᾽ ἀνὴρ
δοῦλος φέρειν ἦν τῆσδε καὶ μείζω χάριν.

ΟΙΔΙΠΟΥΣ

πῶς ἂν μόλοι δῆθ᾽ ἡμὶν ἐν τάχει πάλιν; 765

ΙΟΚΑΣΤΗ

πάρεστιν· ἀλλὰ πρὸς τί τοῦτ᾽ ἐφίεσαι;

ΟΙΔΙΠΟΥΣ

δέδοικ᾽ ἐμαυτόν, ὦ γύναι, μὴ πόλλ᾽ ἄγαν
εἰρημέν᾽ ᾖ μοι δι᾽ ἅ νιν εἰσιδεῖν θέλω.

ΙΟΚΑΣΤΗ

ἀλλ᾽ ἵξεται μέν· ἀξία δέ που μαθεῖν
κἀγὼ τά γ᾽ ἐν σοὶ δυσφόρως ἔχοντ᾽, ἄναξ. 770

ΟΙΔΙΠΟΥΣ

κοὺ μὴ στερηθῇς γ᾽, ἐς τοσοῦτον ἐλπίδων
ἐμοῦ βεβῶτος. τῷ γὰρ ἂν καὶ μείζονι
λέξαιμ᾽ ἂν ἢ σοί, διὰ τύχης τοιᾶσδ᾽ ἰών;
ἐμοὶ πατὴρ μὲν Πόλυβος ἦν Κορίνθιος,
μήτηρ δὲ Μερόπη Δωρίς. ἠγόμην δ᾽ ἀνὴρ 775
ἀστῶν μέγιστος τῶν ἐκεῖ, πρίν μοι τύχη
τοιάδ᾽ ἐπέστη, θαυμάσαι μὲν ἀξία,
σπουδῆς γε μέντοι τῆς ἐμῆς οὐκ ἀξία.
ἀνὴρ γὰρ ἐν δείπνοις μ᾽ ὑπερπλησθεὶς μέθῃ
καλεῖ παρ᾽ οἴνῳ, πλαστὸς ὡς εἴην πατρί. 780
κἀγὼ βαρυνθεὶς τὴν μὲν οὖσαν ἡμέραν
μόλις κατέσχον, θἀτέρᾳ δ᾽ ἰὼν πέλας
μητρὸς πατρός τ᾽ ἤλεγχον· οἱ δὲ δυσφόρως
τοὔνειδος ἦγον τῷ μεθέντι τὸν λόγον.
κἀγὼ τὰ μὲν κείνοιν ἐτερπόμην, ὅμως δ᾽ 785
ἔκνιζέ μ᾽ ἀεὶ τοῦθ᾽· ὑφεῖρπε γὰρ πολύ.

he clasped my hands, begged me to send him off [760]
to where our animals graze in the fields,
so he could be as far away as possible
from the sight of town. And so I sent him.
He was a slave but he'd earned my gratitude.
He deserved an even greater favour.

OEDIPUS
I'd like him to return back here to us,
and quickly, too.

JOCASTA
                                        That can be arranged—
but why's that something you would want to do?

OEDIPUS
Lady, I'm afraid I may have said too much.
That's why I want to see him here before me.

JOCASTA
Then he will be here. But now, my lord,
I deserve to know why you are so distressed. [770]

OEDIPUS
My forebodings now have grown so great
I will not keep them from you, for who is there
I should confide in rather than in you
about such a twisted turn of fortune.
My father was Polybus of Corinth,
my mother Merope, a Dorian.
There I was regarded as the finest man
in all the city, until, as chance would have it,
something most astonishing took place,
though it was not worth what it made me to do.
At dinner there a man who was quite drunk
from too much wine began to shout at me,
claiming I was not my father's real son. [780]
That troubled me, but for a day at least
I said nothing, though it was difficult.
The next day I went to ask my parents,
my father and mother. They were angry
at the man who had insulted them this way,
so I was reassured. But nonetheless,
the accusation always troubled me—
the story had become known everywhere.

λάθρα δὲ μητρὸς καὶ πατρὸς πορεύομαι
Πυθώδε, καί μ' ὁ Φοῖβος ὧν μὲν ἱκόμην
ἄτιμον ἐξέπεμψεν, ἄλλα δ' ἄθλια
καὶ δεινὰ καὶ δύστηνα προύφηνεν λέγων,   790
ὡς μητρὶ μὲν χρείη με μιχθῆναι, γένος δ'
ἄτλητον ἀνθρώποισι δηλώσοιμ' ὁρᾶν,
φονεὺς δ' ἐσοίμην τοῦ φυτεύσαντος πατρός.
κἀγὼ 'πακούσας ταῦτα τὴν κορινθίαν,
ἄστροις τὸ λοιπὸν ἐκμετρούμενος, χθόνα   795
ἔφευγον, ἔνθα μήποτ' ὀψοίμην κακῶν
χρησμῶν ὀνείδη τῶν ἐμῶν τελούμενα.
στείχων δ' ἱκνοῦμαι τούσδε τοὺς χώρους, ἐν οἷς
σὺ τὸν τύραννον τοῦτον ὄλλυσθαι λέγεις.
καί σοι, γύναι, τἀληθὲς ἐξερῶ. τριπλῆς   800
ὅτ' ἦ κελεύθου τῆσδ' ὁδοιπορῶν πέλας,
ἐνταῦθά μοι κῆρύξ τε κἀπὶ πωλικῆς
ἀνὴρ ἀπήνης ἐμβεβώς, οἷον σὺ φῆς,
ξυνηντίαζον· κἀξ ὁδοῦ μ' ὅ θ' ἡγεμὼν
αὐτός θ' ὁ πρέσβυς πρὸς βίαν ἠλαυνέτην.   805
κἀγὼ τὸν ἐκτρέποντα, τὸν τροχηλάτην,
παίω δι' ὀργῆς· καί μ' ὁ πρέσβυς ὡς ὁρᾷ,
ὄχου παραστείχοντα τηρήσας, μέσον
κάρα διπλοῖς κέντροισί μου καθίκετο.
οὐ μὴν ἴσην γ' ἔτισεν, ἀλλὰ συντόμως   810
σκήπτρῳ τυπεὶς ἐκ τῆσδε χειρὸς ὕπτιος
μέσης ἀπήνης εὐθὺς ἐκκυλίνδεται·
κτείνω δὲ τοὺς ξύμπαντας. εἰ δὲ τῷ ξένῳ
τούτῳ προσήκει Λαΐου τι συγγενές,
τίς τοῦδέ γ' ἀνδρός ἐστιν ἀθλιώτερος;   815
τίς ἐχθροδαίμων μᾶλλον ἂν γένοιτ' ἀνήρ;
ὃν μὴ ξένων ἔξεστι μηδ' ἀστῶν τινι
δόμοις δέχεσθαι μηδὲ προσφωνεῖν τινα,
ὠθεῖν δ' ἀπ' οἴκων. καὶ τάδ' οὔτις ἄλλος ἦν
ἢ 'γὼ 'π' ἐμαυτῷ τάσδ' ἀρὰς ὁ προστιθείς.   820
λέχη δὲ τοῦ θανόντος ἐκ χεροῖν ἐμαῖν
χραίνω, δι' ὧνπερ ὤλετ'· ἆρ' ἔφυν κακός;

And so I went in secret off to Delphi.
I didn't tell my mother or my father.
Apollo sent me back without an answer,
so I didn't learn what I had come to find.
But when he spoke he uttered monstrous things,   [790]
strange terrors and horrific miseries—
my fate was to defile my mother's bed,
to bring forth to men a human family
that people could not bear to look upon,
and slay the father who engendered me.
When I heard that, I ran away from Corinth.
From then on I thought of it just as a place
beneath the stars. I went to other lands,
so I would never see that prophecy fulfilled,
the abomination of my evil fate.
In my travelling I came across that place
in which you say your king was murdered.
And now, lady, I will tell you the truth.   [800]
As I was on the move, I passed close by
a spot where three roads meet, and in that place
I met a herald and a horse-drawn carriage,
with a man inside, just as you described.
The guide there tried to force me off the road—
and the old man, too, got personally involved.
In my rage, I lashed out at the driver,
who was shoving me aside. The old man,
seeing me walking past him in the carriage,
kept his eye on me, and with his double whip
struck me on the head, right here on top.
Well, I retaliated in good measure—   [810]
with the staff I held I hit him a quick blow
and knocked him from his carriage to the road.
He lay there on his back. Then I killed them all.
If that stranger was somehow linked to Laius,
who is now more unfortunate than me?
What man could be more hateful to the gods?
No stranger and no citizen can welcome him
into their lives or speak to him. Instead,
they must keep him from their doors, a curse
I laid upon myself. With these hands of mine,   [820]
these killer's hands, I now contaminate
the dead man's bed. Am I not depraved?

Sophocles

ἆρ' οὐχὶ πᾶς ἄναγνος; εἴ με χρὴ φυγεῖν,
καί μοι φυγόντι μῆστι τοὺς ἐμοὺς ἰδεῖν
μηδ' ἐμβατεύειν πατρίδος, ἢ γάμοις με δεῖ   825
μητρὸς ζυγῆναι καὶ πατέρα κατακτανεῖν
Πόλυβον, ὃς ἐξέφυσε κἀξέθρεψέ με.
ἆρ' οὐκ ἀπ' ὠμοῦ ταῦτα δαίμονός τις ἂν
κρίνων ἐπ' ἀνδρὶ τῷδ' ἂν ὀρθοίη λόγον;
μὴ δῆτα, μὴ δῆτ', ὦ θεῶν ἁγνὸν σέβας,   830
ἴδοιμι ταύτην ἡμέραν, ἀλλ' ἐκ βροτῶν
βαίην ἄφαντος πρόσθεν ἢ τοιάνδ' ἰδεῖν
κηλῖδ' ἐμαυτῷ συμφορᾶς ἀφιγμένην.

ΧΟΡΟΣ
ἡμῖν μέν, ὦναξ, ταῦτ' ὀκνήρ'· ἕως δ' ἂν οὖν
πρὸς τοῦ παρόντος ἐκμάθῃς, ἔχ' ἐλπίδα.   835

ΟΙΔΙΠΟΥΣ
καὶ μὴν τοσοῦτόν γ' ἐστί μοι τῆς ἐλπίδος,
τὸν ἄνδρα τὸν βοτῆρα προσμεῖναι μόνον.

ΙΟΚΑΣΤΗ
πεφασμένου δὲ τίς ποθ' ἡ προθυμία;

ΟΙΔΙΠΟΥΣ
ἐγὼ διδάξω σ'· ἢν γὰρ εὑρεθῇ λέγων
σοὶ ταῦτ', ἔγωγ' ἂν ἐκπεφευγοίην πάθος.   840

ΙΟΚΑΣΤΗ
ποῖον δέ μου περισσὸν ἤκουσας λόγον;

ΟΙΔΙΠΟΥΣ
λῃστὰς ἔφασκες αὐτὸν ἄνδρας ἐννέπειν
ὥς νιν κατακτείνειαν. εἰ μὲν οὖν ἔτι
λέξει τὸν αὐτὸν ἀριθμόν, οὐκ ἐγὼ 'κτανον·
οὐ γὰρ γένοιτ' ἂν εἷς γε τοῖς πολλοῖς ἴσος·   845
εἰ δ' ἄνδρ' ἕν' οἰόζωνον αὐδήσει, σαφῶς
τοῦτ' ἐστὶν ἤδη τοὔργον εἰς ἐμὲ ῥέπον.

Am I not utterly abhorrent?
Now I must fly into exile and there,
a fugitive, never see my people,
never set foot in my native land again—
or else I must get married to my mother
and kill my father, Polybus, who raised me,
the man who gave me life. If anyone
claimed this came from some malevolent god,
would he not be right? O you gods,
you pure, blessed gods, may I not see that day!   [830]
Let me rather vanish from the sight of men,
before I see a fate like that engulf me!

CHORUS LEADER

My lord, to us these things are ominous.
But you must sustain your hope until you hear
the servant who was present at the time.

OEDIPUS

I do have some hope left, at least enough
to wait for the man we've summoned from the fields.

JOCASTA

Once he comes, what do you hope to hear?

OEDIPUS

I'll tell you. If we discover what he says
matches what you say, then I'll escape disaster.   [840]

JOCASTA

What was so remarkable in what I said?

OEDIPUS

You said that in his story the man claimed
Laius was murdered by a band of thieves.
If he still says that there were several men,
then I was not the killer, since one man
could never be mistaken for a crowd.
But if he says it was a single man,
the scales of justice guilt sink down on me.

Sophocles

ΙΟΚΑΣΤΗ

ἀλλ᾽ ὡς φανέν γε τοὔπος ὧδ᾽ ἐπίστασο,
κοὐκ ἔστιν αὐτῷ τοῦτό γ᾽ ἐκβαλεῖν πάλιν·
πόλις γὰρ ἤκουσ᾽, οὐκ ἐγὼ μόνη, τάδε.   850
εἰ δ᾽ οὖν τι κἀκτρέποιτο τοῦ πρόσθεν λόγου,
οὔτοι ποτ᾽, ὦναξ, σόν γε Λαΐου φόνον
φανεῖ δικαίως ὀρθόν, ὅν γε λοξίας
διεῖπε χρῆναι παιδὸς ἐξ ἐμοῦ θανεῖν.
καίτοι νιν οὐ κεῖνός γ᾽ ὁ δύστηνός ποτε   855
κατέκταν᾽, ἀλλ᾽ αὐτὸς πάροιθεν ὤλετο.
ὥστ᾽ οὐχὶ μαντείας γ᾽ ἂν οὔτε τῇδ᾽ ἐγὼ
βλέψαιμ᾽ ἂν εἵνεκ᾽ οὔτε τῇδ᾽ ἂν ὕστερον.

ΟΙΔΙΠΟΥΣ

καλῶς νομίζεις· ἀλλ᾽ ὅμως τὸν ἐργάτην
πέμψον τινὰ στελοῦντα μηδὲ τοῦτ᾽ ἀφῇς.   860

ΙΟΚΑΣΤΗ

πέμψω ταχύνασ᾽· ἀλλ᾽ ἴωμεν ἐς δόμους·
οὐδὲν γὰρ ἂν πράξαιμ᾽ ἂν ὧν οὐ σοὶ φίλον.

ΧΟΡΟΣ

εἴ μοι ξυνείη φέροντι
μοῖρα τὰν εὔσεπτον ἁγνείαν λόγων
ἔργων τε πάντων, ὧν νόμοι πρόκεινται   865
ὑψίποδες, οὐρανίαν
δι᾽ αἰθέρα τεκνωθέντες, ὧν Ὄλυμπος
πατὴρ μόνος, οὐδέ νιν
θνατὰ φύσις ἀνέρων
ἔτικτεν οὐδὲ μή ποτε λάθα κατακοιμάσῃ·   870
μέγας ἐν τούτοις θεὸς οὐδὲ γηράσκει.

ὕβρις φυτεύει τύραννον·
ὕβρις, εἰ πολλῶν ὑπερπλησθῇ μάταν,
ἃ μὴ ᾽πίκαιρα μηδὲ συμφέροντα,   875
ἀκρότατον εἰσαναβᾶσ᾽
αἶπος ἀπότομον ὤρουσεν εἰς ἀνάγκαν,
ἔνθ᾽ οὐ ποδὶ χρησίμῳ

JOCASTA

    Well, that's certainly what he reported then.
    He cannot now withdraw what he once said.
    The whole city heard him, not just me alone.   [850]
    But even if he changes that old news,
    he cannot ever demonstrate, my lord,
    that Laius' murder fits the prophecy.
    For Apollo clearly said the man would die
    at the hands of an infant born from me.
    Now, how did that unhappy son of ours
    kill Laius, when he'd perished long before?
    As far as these predictions go, from now on
    I would not look for confirmation anywhere.

OEDIPUS

    You're right in what you say. But nonetheless,
    send for that peasant. Don't fail to do that.   [860]

JOCASTA

    I'll call him here as quickly as I can.
    Let's go inside. I'll not do anything
    which does not meet with your approval.

[OEDIPUS and JOCASTA go into the palace together]

CHORUS

    I pray fate still finds me worthy,
    demonstrating piety and reverence
    in all I say and do—in everything
    our loftiest traditions consecrate,
    those laws engendered in the heavenly skies,
    whose only father is Olympus.
    They were not born from mortal men,
    nor will they sleep and be forgotten.   [870]
    In them lives an ageless mighty god.

    Insolence gives birth to tyranny—
    that insolence which vainly crams itself
    and overflows with so much wealth
    beyond what's right or beneficial,
    that once it's climbed the highest rooftop,
    it's hurled down by force—such a quick fall
    there's no safe landing on one's feet.

χρῆται. τὸ καλῶς δ' ἔχον   880
πόλει πάλαισμα μήποτε λῦσαι θεὸν αἰτοῦμαι.
θεὸν οὐ λήξω ποτὲ προστάταν ἴσχων.

εἰ δέ τις ὑπέροπτα χερσὶν ἢ λόγῳ πορεύεται,
δίκας ἀφόβητος οὐδὲ δαιμόνων ἔδη σέβων,   885
κακά νιν ἕλοιτο μοῖρα,
δυσπότμου χάριν χλιδᾶς,
εἰ μὴ τὸ κέρδος κερδανεῖ δικαίως
καὶ τῶν ἀσέπτων ἔρξεται   890
ἢ τῶν ἀθίκτων θίξεται ματάζων.
τίς ἔτι ποτ' ἐν τοῖσδ' ἀνὴρ θεῶν βέλη
εὔξεται ψυχᾶς ἀμύνειν;
εἰ γὰρ αἱ τοιαίδε πράξεις τίμιαι,   895
τί δεῖ με χορεύειν;

οὐκέτι τὸν ἄθικτον εἶμι γᾶς ἐπ' ὀμφαλὸν σέβων,
οὐδ' ἐς τὸν Ἀβαῖσι ναὸν οὐδὲ τὰν Ὀλυμπίαν,   900
εἰ μὴ τάδε χειρόδεικτα
πᾶσιν ἁρμόσει βροτοῖς.
ἀλλ', ὦ κρατύνων, εἴπερ ὄρθ' ἀκούεις,   905
Ζεῦ, πάντ' ἀνάσσων, μὴ λάθοι
σὲ τάν τε σὰν ἀθάνατον αἰὲν ἀρχάν.
φθίνοντα γὰρ Λαΐου παλαίφατα
θέσφατ' ἐξαιροῦσιν ἤδη,
κοὐδαμοῦ τιμαῖς Ἀπόλλων ἐμφανής·
ἔρρει δὲ τὰ θεῖα.   910

ΙΟΚΑΣΤΗ

χώρας ἄνακτες, δόξα μοι παρεστάθη
ναοὺς ἱκέσθαι δαιμόνων, τάδ' ἐν χεροῖν
στέφη λαβούσῃ κἀπιθυμιάματα.

But I pray the god never will abolish
the type of rivalry that helps our state.   [880]
That god I will hold onto always,
the one who stands as our protector.[15]

But if a man conducts himself
disdainfully in what he says and does,
and manifests no fear of righteousness,
no reverence for the statues of the gods,
may miserable fate seize such a man
for his disastrous arrogance,
if he does not behave with justice   [890]
when he strives to benefit himself,
appropriates all things impiously,
and, like a fool, profanes the sacred.
What man is there who does such things
who can still claim he will ward off
the arrow of the gods aimed at his heart?
If such actions are considered worthy,
why should we dance to honour god?

No longer will I go in reverence
to the sacred stone, earth's very centre,
or to the temple at Abae or Olympia,   [900]
if these prophecies fail to be fulfilled
and manifest themselves to mortal men.
But you, all-conquering, all-ruling Zeus,
if by right those names belong to you,
let this not evade you and your ageless might.
For ancient oracles which dealt with Laius
are withering—men now set them aside.
Nowhere is Apollo honoured publicly,
and our religious faith is dying away.   [910]

*[JOCASTA enters from the palace and moves to an altar to Apollo which stands
outside the palace doors. She is accompanied by one or two SERVANTS]*

JOCASTA
You leading citizens of Thebes, I think
it is appropriate for me to visit
our gods' sacred shrines, bearing in my hands
this garland and an offering of incense.

Sophocles

ὑψοῦ γὰρ αἴρει θυμὸν Οἰδίπους ἄγαν
λύπαισι παντοίαισιν· οὐδ' ὁποῖ' ἀνὴρ   915
ἔννους τὰ καινὰ τοῖς πάλαι τεκμαίρεται,
ἀλλ' ἐστὶ τοῦ λέγοντος, εἰ φόβους λέγοι.
ὅτ' οὖν παραινοῦσ' οὐδὲν ἐς πλέον ποιῶ,
πρὸς σ', ὦ Λύκει' Ἄπολλον, ἄγχιστος γὰρ εἶ,
ἱκέτις ἀφῖγμαι τοῖσδε σὺν κατεύγμασιν,   920
ὅπως λύσιν τιν' ἡμὶν εὐαγῆ πόρῃς·
ὡς νῦν ὀκνοῦμεν πάντες ἐκπεπληγμένον
κεῖνον βλέποντες ὡς κυβερνήτην νεώς.

ΑΓΓΕΛΟΣ

ἆρ' ἂν παρ' ὑμῶν, ὦ ξένοι, μάθοιμ' ὅπου
τὰ τοῦ τυράννου δώματ' ἐστὶν Οἰδίπου;   925
μάλιστα δ' αὐτὸν εἴπατ', εἰ κάτισθ' ὅπου.

ΧΟΡΟΣ

στέγαι μὲν αἵδε, καὐτὸς ἔνδον, ὦ ξένε·
γυνὴ δὲ μήτηρ ἥδε τῶν κείνου τέκνων.

ΑΓΓΕΛΟΣ

ἀλλ' ὀλβία τε καὶ ξὺν ὀλβίοις ἀεὶ
γένοιτ', ἐκείνου γ' οὖσα παντελὴς δάμαρ.   930

ΙΟΚΑΣΤΗ

αὔτως δὲ καὶ σύ γ', ὦ ξέν'· ἄξιος γὰρ εἶ
τῆς εὐεπείας εἵνεκ'· ἀλλὰ φράζ' ὅτου
χρῄζων ἀφῖξαι χὤ τι σημῆναι θέλων.

ΑΓΓΕΛΟΣ

ἀγαθὰ δόμοις τε καὶ πόσει τῷ σῷ, γύναι.

ΙΟΚΑΣΤΗ

τὰ ποῖα ταῦτα; παρὰ τίνος δ' ἀφιγμένος;   935

116

For Oedipus has let excessive pain
seize on his heart and does not understand
what's happening now by thinking of the past,
like a man with sense. Instead he listens to
whoever speaks to him of dreadful things.
I can do nothing more with my advice,
and so, Lyceian Apollo, I come to you,
who stand here beside us, a suppliant,   [920]
with offerings and prayers for you to find
some way of cleansing what corrupts us.
For now we are afraid, just like those
who on a ship see their helmsman terrified.

[JOCASTA sets her offerings on the altar. A MESSENGER enters, an older man]

MESSENGER

Strangers, can you tell me where I find
the house of Oedipus, your king? Better yet,
if you know, can you tell me where he is?

CHORUS LEADER

His home is here, stranger, and he's inside.
This lady is the mother of his children.

MESSENGER

May her happy home always be blessed,
for she is his queen, true mistress of his house.   [930]

JOCASTA

I wish the same for you, stranger. Your fine words
make you deserve as much. But tell us now
why you have come. Do you seek information,
or do you wish to give us some report?

MESSENGER

Lady, I have good news for your whole house
and for your husband, too.

JOCASTA

                          What news is that?
Where have you come from?

ΑΓΓΕΛΟΣ

ἐκ τῆς Κορίνθου· τὸ δ' ἔπος οὐξερῶ τάχα,

ἥδοιο μέν, πῶς δ' οὐκ ἄν, ἀσχάλλοις δ' ἴσως.

ΙΟΚΑΣΤΗ

τί δ' ἔστι; ποίαν δύναμιν ὧδ' ἔχει διπλῆν;

ΑΓΓΕΛΟΣ

τύραννον αὐτὸν οὐπιχώριοι χθονὸς

τῆς Ἰσθμίας στήσουσιν, ὡς ηὐδᾶτ' ἐκεῖ.   940

ΙΟΚΑΣΤΗ

τί δ'; οὐχ ὁ πρέσβυς πόλυβος ἐγκρατὴς ἔτι;

ΑΓΓΕΛΟΣ

οὐ δῆτ', ἐπεί νιν θάνατος ἐν τάφοις ἔχει.

ΙΟΚΑΣΤΗ

πῶς εἶπας; ἢ τέθνηκε Πόλυβος, ὦ γέρον;

ΑΓΓΕΛΟΣ

εἰ μὴ λέγω τἀληθές, ἀξιῶ θανεῖν.

ΙΟΚΑΣΤΗ

ὦ πρόσπολ', οὐχὶ δεσπότῃ τάδ' ὡς τάχος   945

μολοῦσα λέξεις; ὦ θεῶν μαντεύματα,

ἵν' ἐστέ· τοῦτον Οἰδίπους πάλαι τρέμων

τὸν ἄνδρ' ἔφευγε μὴ κτάνοι, καὶ νῦν ὅδε

πρὸς τῆς τύχης ὄλωλεν οὐδὲ τοῦδ' ὕπο.

MESSENGER

                         I've come from Corinth.
I'll give you my report at once, and then
you will, no doubt, be glad, although perhaps
you will be sad, as well.

JOCASTA

                         What is your news?
How can it have two such effects at once?

MESSENGER

The people who live there, in the lands
beside the Isthmus, will make him their king.[16]
They have announced it.   [940]

JOCASTA

                         What are you saying?
Is old man Polybus no longer king?

MESSENGER

No. He is dead and in his grave.

JOCASTA

                         What?
Has Oedipus' father died?

MESSENGER

                         Yes.
If what I'm telling you is not the truth,
then I deserve to die.

JOCASTA *[to a servant]*

                         You there—
go at once and tell this to your master.

[SERVANT goes into the palace]

O you oracles of the gods, so much for you.
Oedipus has for so long been afraid
that he would murder him. He ran away.
And now Polybus has died, killed by Fate
and not by Oedipus.

[Enter OEDIPUS from the palace]

119

ΟΙΔΙΠΟΥΣ

ὦ φίλτατον γυναικὸς Ἰοκάστης κάρα,   950
τί μ᾽ ἐξεπέμψω δεῦρο τῶνδε δωμάτων;

ΙΟΚΑΣΤΗ

ἄκουε τἀνδρὸς τοῦδε, καὶ σκόπει κλύων
τὰ σέμν᾽ ἵν᾽ ἥκει τοῦ θεοῦ μαντεύματα.

ΟΙΔΙΠΟΥΣ

οὗτος δὲ τίς ποτ᾽ ἐστὶ καὶ τί μοι λέγει;

ΙΟΚΑΣΤΗ

ἐκ τῆς Κορίνθου, πατέρα τὸν σὸν ἀγγελῶν   955
ὡς οὐκέτ᾽ ὄντα Πόλυβον, ἀλλ᾽ ὀλωλότα.

ΟΙΔΙΠΟΥΣ

τί φῄς, ξέν᾽; αὐτός μοι σὺ σημάντωρ γενοῦ.

ΑΓΓΕΛΟΣ

εἰ τοῦτο πρῶτον δεῖ μ᾽ ἀπαγγεῖλαι σαφῶς,
εὖ ἴσθ᾽ ἐκεῖνον θανάσιμον βεβηκότα.

ΟΙΔΙΠΟΥΣ

πότερα δόλοισιν ἢ νόσου ξυναλλαγῇ;   960

ΑΓΓΕΛΟΣ

σμικρὰ παλαιὰ σώματ᾽ εὐνάζει ῥοπή.

ΟΙΔΙΠΟΥΣ

νόσοις ὁ τλήμων, ὡς ἔοικεν, ἔφθιτο.

ΑΓΓΕΛΟΣ

καὶ τῷ μακρῷ γε συμμετρούμενος χρόνῳ.

OEDIPUS

Ah, Jocasta,

my dearest wife, why have you summoned me   [950]
to leave our home and come out here?

JOCASTA

You must hear this man, and as you listen,
decide for yourself what these prophecies,
these solemn proclamations from the gods,
amount to.

OEDIPUS

Who is this man? What report
does he have for me?

JOCASTA

He comes from Corinth,
bringing news that Polybus, your father,
no longer is alive. He's dead.

OEDIPUS

What?
Stranger, let me hear from you in person.

MESSENGER

If I must first report my news quite plainly,
then I should let you know that Polybus
has passed away. He's gone.

OEDIPUS

By treachery,
or was it the result of some disease?   [960]

MESSENGER

With old bodies a slight weight on the scales
brings final peace.

OEDIPUS

Apparently his death
was from an illness?

MESSENGER

Yes, and from old age.

Sophocles

ΟΙΔΙΠΟΥΣ

φεῦ φεῦ, τί δῆτ' ἄν, ὦ γύναι, σκοποῖτό τι
τὴν Πυθόμαντιν ἑστίαν ἢ τοὺς ἄνω   965
κλάζοντας ὄρνεις, ὧν ὑφηγητῶν ἐγὼ
κτενεῖν ἔμελλον πατέρα τὸν ἐμόν; ὁ δὲ θανὼν
κεύθει κάτω δὴ γῆς. ἐγὼ δ' ὅδ' ἐνθάδε
ἄψαυστος ἔγχους· εἴ τι μὴ τὠμῷ πόθῳ
κατέφθιθ'· οὕτω δ' ἂν θανὼν εἴη 'ξ ἐμοῦ.   970
τὰ δ' οὖν παρόντα συλλαβὼν θεσπίσματα
κεῖται παρ' Ἅιδῃ Πόλυβος ἄξι' οὐδενός.

ΙΟΚΑΣΤΗ

οὔκουν ἐγώ σοι ταῦτα προύλεγον πάλαι;

ΟΙΔΙΠΟΥΣ

ηὔδας· ἐγὼ δὲ τῷ φόβῳ παρηγόμην.

ΙΟΚΑΣΤΗ

μὴ νῦν ἔτ' αὐτῶν μηδὲν ἐς θυμὸν βάλῃς.   975

ΟΙΔΙΠΟΥΣ

καὶ πῶς τὸ μητρὸς οὐκ ὀκνεῖν λέχος με δεῖ;

ΙΟΚΑΣΤΗ

τί δ' ἂν φοβοῖτ' ἄνθρωπος ᾧ τὰ τῆς τύχης
κρατεῖ, πρόνοια δ' ἐστὶν οὐδενὸς σαφής;
εἰκῇ κράτιστον ζῆν, ὅπως δύναιτό τις.
σὺ δ' εἰς τὰ μητρὸς μὴ φοβοῦ νυμφεύματα·   980
πολλοὶ γὰρ ἤδη κἀν ὀνείρασιν βροτῶν
μητρὶ ξυνηυνάσθησαν. ἀλλὰ ταῦθ' ὅτῳ
παρ' οὐδέν ἐστι, ῥᾷστα τὸν βίον φέρει.

ΟΙΔΙΠΟΥΣ

καλῶς ἅπαντα ταῦτ' ἂν ἐξείρητό σοι,
εἰ μὴ 'κύρει ζῶσ' ἡ τεκοῦσα· νῦν δ' ἐπεὶ   985
ζῇ, πᾶσ' ἀνάγκη, κεἰ καλῶς λέγεις, ὀκνεῖν.

122

OEDIPUS

Alas! Indeed, lady, why should any man
pay due reverence to Apollo's shrine,
where his prophet lives, or to those birds
which scream out overhead? For they foretold
that I was going to murder my own father.
But now he's dead and lies beneath the earth,
and I am here. I never touched my spear.
Perhaps he died from a desire to see me—
so in that sense I brought about his death. [970]
But as for those prophetic oracles,
they're worthless. Polybus has taken them
to Hades, where he lies.

JOCASTA

                              Was I not the one
who predicted this some time ago?

OEDIPUS

                              You did,
but then I was misguided by my fears.

JOCASTA

You must not keep on filling up your heart
with all these things.

OEDIPUS

                              But my mother's bed—
Surely I should still be afraid of that?

JOCASTA

Why should a man whose life seems ruled by chance
live in fear—a man who never looks ahead,
who has no certain vision of his future?
It's best to live haphazardly, as best one can.
Do not worry you will wed your mother. [980]
It's true that in their dreams a lot of men
have slept with their own mothers, but someone
who ignores all this bears life more easily.

OEDIPUS

Everything you say would be commendable,
if my mother were not still alive.
But since she is, I must remain afraid,
though all that you have said is right.

Sophocles

ΙΟΚΑΣΤΗ

καὶ μὴν μέγας γ᾽ ὀφθαλμὸς οἱ πατρὸς τάφοι.

ΟΙΔΙΠΟΥΣ

μέγας, ξυνίημ᾽· ἀλλὰ τῆς ζώσης φόβος.

ΑΓΓΕΛΟΣ

ποίας δὲ καὶ γυναικὸς ἐκφοβεῖσθ᾽ ὕπερ;

ΟΙΔΙΠΟΥΣ

Μερόπης, γεραιέ, Πόλυβος ἧς ᾤκει μέτα.   990

ΑΓΓΕΛΟΣ

τί δ᾽ ἔστ᾽ ἐκείνης ὑμὶν ἐς φόβον φέρον;

ΟΙΔΙΠΟΥΣ

θεήλατον μάντευμα δεινόν, ὦ ξένε.

ΑΓΓΕΛΟΣ

ἦ ῥητόν; ἦ οὐχὶ θεμιτὸν ἄλλον εἰδέναι;

ΟΙΔΙΠΟΥΣ

μάλιστά γ᾽· εἶπε γάρ με Λοξίας ποτὲ
χρῆναι μιγῆναι μητρὶ τἠμαυτοῦ τό τε   995
πατρῷον αἷμα χερσὶ ταῖς ἐμαῖς ἑλεῖν.
ὧν οὕνεχ᾽ ἡ Κόρινθος ἐξ ἐμοῦ πάλαι
μακρὰν ἀπῳκεῖτ᾽· εὐτυχῶς μέν, ἀλλ᾽ ὅμως
τὰ τῶν τεκόντων ὄμμαθ᾽ ἥδιστον βλέπειν.

ΑΓΓΕΛΟΣ

ἦ γὰρ τάδ᾽ ὀκνῶν κεῖθεν ἦσθ᾽ ἀπόπτολις;   1000

ΟΙΔΙΠΟΥΣ

πατρός τε χρῄζων μὴ φονεὺς εἶναι, γέρον.

124

JOCASTA

But still,
your father's death is a great comfort to us.

OEDIPUS

Yes, it is good, I know. But I do fear
that lady—she is still alive.

MESSENGER

This one you fear,
what kind of woman is she?

OEDIPUS

Old man,
her name is Merope, wife to Polybus.   [990]

MESSENGER

And what in her makes you so fearful?

OEDIPUS

Stranger,
a dreadful prophecy sent from the god.

MESSENGER

Is it well known? Or something private,
which other people have no right to know?

OEDIPUS

No, no. It's public knowledge. Loxias
once said it was my fate that I would marry
my own mother and shed my father's blood
with my own hands.[17] That's why, many years ago,
I left my home in Corinth. Things turned out well,
but nonetheless it gives the sweetest joy
to look into the eyes of one's own parents.

MESSENGER

And because you were afraid of her   [1000]
you stayed away from Corinth?

OEDIPUS

And because
I did not want to be my father's killer.

ΑΓΓΕΛΟΣ
τί δῆτ᾽ ἐγὼ οὐχὶ τοῦδε τοῦ φόβου σ᾽, ἄναξ,
ἐπείπερ εὔνους ἦλθον, ἐξελυσάμην;

ΟΙΔΙΠΟΥΣ
καὶ μὴν χάριν γ᾽ ἂν ἀξίαν λάβοις ἐμοῦ.

ΑΓΓΕΛΟΣ
καὶ μὴν μάλιστα τοῦτ᾽ ἀφικόμην, ὅπως   1005
σοῦ πρὸς δόμους ἐλθόντος εὖ πράξαιμί τι.

ΟΙΔΙΠΟΥΣ
ἀλλ᾽ οὔποτ᾽ εἶμι τοῖς φυτεύσασίν γ᾽ ὁμοῦ.

ΑΓΓΕΛΟΣ
ὦ παῖ, καλῶς εἶ δῆλος οὐκ εἰδὼς τί δρᾷς.

ΟΙΔΙΠΟΥΣ
πῶς, ὦ γεραιέ; πρὸς θεῶν δίδασκέ με.

ΑΓΓΕΛΟΣ
εἰ τῶνδε φεύγεις οὕνεκ᾽ εἰς οἴκους μολεῖν.   1010

ΟΙΔΙΠΟΥΣ
ταρβῶν γε μή μοι Φοῖβος ἐξέλθῃ σαφής.

ΑΓΓΕΛΟΣ
ἦ μὴ μίασμα τῶν φυτευσάντων λάβῃς;

ΟΙΔΙΠΟΥΣ
τοῦτ᾽ αὐτό, πρέσβυ, τοῦτό μ᾽ εἰσαεὶ φοβεῖ.

ΑΓΓΕΛΟΣ
ἆρ᾽ οἶσθα δῆτα πρὸς δίκης οὐδὲν τρέμων;

ΟΙΔΙΠΟΥΣ
πῶς δ᾽ οὐχί, παῖς γ᾽ εἰ τῶνδε γεννητῶν ἔφυν;   1015

ΑΓΓΕΛΟΣ
ὁθούνεκ᾽ ἦν σοι Πόλυβος οὐδὲν ἐν γένει.

MESSENGER

My lord, since I came to make you happy,
why do I not relieve you of this fear?

OEDIPUS

You would receive from me a worthy thanks.

MESSENGER

That's really why I came—so your return
might prove a benefit to me back home.

OEDIPUS

But I will never go back to my parents.

MESSENGER

My son, it is so clear you've no idea
what you are doing . . .

OEDIPUS *[interrupting]*

What do you mean, old man?
In the name of all the gods, tell me.

MESSENGER

. . . if that's the reason you're a fugitive   [1010]
and won't go home.

OEDIPUS

I feared Apollo's prophecy
might reveal itself in me.

MESSENGER

You were afraid
you might become corrupted through your parents?

OEDIPUS

That's right, old man. That was my constant fear.

MESSENGER

Are you aware these fears of yours are groundless?

OEDIPUS

And why is that? If I was born their child . . .

MESSENGER

Because you and Polybus were not related.

Sophocles

ΟΙΔΙΠΟΥΣ

πῶς εἶπας; οὐ γὰρ Πόλυβος ἐξέφυσέ με;

ΑΓΓΕΛΟΣ

οὐ μᾶλλον οὐδὲν τοῦδε τἀνδρός, ἀλλ' ἴσον.

ΟΙΔΙΠΟΥΣ

καὶ πῶς ὁ φύσας ἐξ ἴσου τῷ μηδενί;

ΑΓΓΕΛΟΣ

ἀλλ' οὔ σ' ἐγείνατ' οὔτ' ἐκεῖνος οὔτ' ἐγώ.　　　　1020

ΟΙΔΙΠΟΥΣ

ἀλλ' ἀντὶ τοῦ δὴ παῖδά μ' ὠνομάζετο;

ΑΓΓΕΛΟΣ

δῶρόν ποτ', ἴσθι, τῶν ἐμῶν χειρῶν λαβών.

ΟΙΔΙΠΟΥΣ

κᾆθ' ὧδ' ἀπ' ἄλλης χειρὸς ἔστερξεν μέγα;

ΑΓΓΕΛΟΣ

ἡ γὰρ πρὶν αὐτὸν ἐξέπεισ' ἀπαιδία.

ΟΙΔΙΠΟΥΣ

σὺ δ' ἐμπολήσας ἢ τυχών μ' αὐτῷ δίδως;　　　　1025

ΑΓΓΕΛΟΣ

εὑρὼν ναπαίαις ἐν Κιθαιρῶνος πτυχαῖς.

ΟΙΔΙΠΟΥΣ

ὡδοιπόρεις δὲ πρὸς τί τούσδε τοὺς τόπους;

ΑΓΓΕΛΟΣ

ἐνταῦθ' ὀρείοις ποιμνίοις ἐπεστάτουν.

OEDIPUS
What do you mean? Was not Polybus my father?

MESSENGER
He was as much your father as this man here,
no more, no less.

OEDIPUS
But how can any man
who means nothing to me be just the same
as my own father?

MESSENGER
But Polybus
was not your father, no more than I am.   [1020]

OEDIPUS
Then why did he call me his son?

MESSENGER
If you must know,
he received you as a gift many years ago.
I gave you to him.

OEDIPUS
He really loved me.
How could he if I came from someone else?

MESSENGER
Because before you came, he had no children—
that made him love you.

OEDIPUS
When you gave me to him,
had you bought me or discovered me by chance?

MESSENGER
I found you in Cithaeron's forest valleys.

OEDIPUS
What were you doing wandering up there?

MESSENGER
I was looking after flocks of sheep.

ΟΙΔΙΠΟΥΣ

    ποιμὴν γὰρ ἦσθα κἀπὶ θητείᾳ πλάνης;

ΑΓΓΕΛΟΣ

    σοῦ τ᾽, ὦ τέκνον, σωτήρ γε τῷ τότ᾽ ἐν χρόνῳ.   1030

ΟΙΔΙΠΟΥΣ

    τί δ᾽ ἄλγος ἴσχοντ᾽ ἀγκάλαις με λαμβάνεις;

ΑΓΓΕΛΟΣ

    ποδῶν ἂν ἄρθρα μαρτυρήσειεν τὰ σά·

ΟΙΔΙΠΟΥΣ

    οἴμοι, τί τοῦτ᾽ ἀρχαῖον ἐννέπεις κακόν;

ΑΓΓΕΛΟΣ

    λύω σ᾽ ἔχοντα διατόρους ποδοῖν ἀκμάς.

ΟΙΔΙΠΟΥΣ

    δεινόν γ᾽ ὄνειδος σπαργάνων ἀνειλόμην.   1035

ΑΓΓΕΛΟΣ

    ὥστ᾽ ὠνομάσθης ἐκ τύχης ταύτης ὃς εἶ.

ΟΙΔΙΠΟΥΣ

    ὦ πρὸς θεῶν, πρὸς μητρὸς ἢ πατρός; φράσον.

ΑΓΓΕΛΟΣ

    οὐκ οἶδ᾽· ὁ δοὺς δὲ ταῦτ᾽ ἐμοῦ λῷον φρονεῖ.

ΟΙΔΙΠΟΥΣ

    ἦ γὰρ παρ᾽ ἄλλου μ᾽ ἔλαβες οὐδ᾽ αὐτὸς τυχών;

OEDIPUS

You were a shepherd, just a hired servant
roaming here and there?

MESSENGER

Yes, my son, I was.
But at that time I was the one who saved you. [1030]

OEDIPUS

When you picked me up and took me off,
what sort of suffering did you save me from?

MESSENGER

The ankles on your feet could tell you that.

OEDIPUS

Ah, my old misfortune. Why mention that?

MESSENGER

Your ankles had been pierced and pinned together.
I set them free.

OEDIPUS

My dreadful mark of shame—
I've had that scar there since I was a child.

MESSENGER

That's why fortune gave you your very name,
the one which you still carry.[18]

OEDIPUS

Tell me,
in the name of heaven, did my parents,
my father or my mother, do this to me?

MESSENGER

I don't know. The man who gave you to me
knows more of that than I do.

OEDIPUS

You mean to say
you got me from someone else? It wasn't you
who stumbled on me?

ΑΓΓΕΛΟΣ

οὔκ, ἀλλὰ ποιμὴν ἄλλος ἐκδίδωσί μοι.   1040

ΟΙΔΙΠΟΥΣ

τίς οὗτος; ἦ κάτοισθα δηλῶσαι λόγῳ;

ΑΓΓΕΛΟΣ

τῶν Λαΐου δήπου τις ὠνομάζετο.

ΟΙΔΙΠΟΥΣ

ἦ τοῦ τυράννου τῆσδε γῆς πάλαι ποτέ;

ΑΓΓΕΛΟΣ

μάλιστα· τούτου τἀνδρὸς οὗτος ἦν βοτήρ.

ΟΙΔΙΠΟΥΣ

ἦ κἄστ᾽ ἔτι ζῶν οὗτος, ὥστ᾽ ἰδεῖν ἐμέ;   1045

ΑΓΓΕΛΟΣ

ὑμεῖς γ᾽ ἄριστ᾽ εἰδεῖτ᾽ ἂν οὑπιχώριοι.

ΟΙΔΙΠΟΥΣ

ἔστιν τις ὑμῶν τῶν παρεστώτων πέλας,
ὅστις κάτοιδε τὸν βοτῆρ᾽ ὃν ἐννέπει,
εἴτ᾽ οὖν ἐπ᾽ ἀγρῶν εἴτε κἀνθάδ᾽ εἰσιδών;
σημήναθ᾽, ὡς ὁ καιρὸς ηὑρῆσθαι τάδε.   1050

ΧΟΡΟΣ

οἶμαι μὲν οὐδέν᾽ ἄλλον ἢ τὸν ἐξ ἀγρῶν,
ὃν κἀμάτευες πρόσθεν εἰσιδεῖν· ἀτὰρ
ἥδ᾽ ἂν τάδ᾽ οὐχ ἥκιστ᾽ ἂν Ἰοκάστη λέγοι.

ΟΙΔΙΠΟΥΣ

γύναι, νοεῖς ἐκεῖνον, ὅντιν᾽ ἀρτίως
μολεῖν ἐφιέμεσθα; τόνδ᾽ οὗτος λέγει;   1055

MESSENGER

No, it wasn't me.

Another shepherd gave you to me.   [1040]

OEDIPUS

Who?

Who was he? Do you know? Can you tell me
any details, things you are quite sure of?

MESSENGER

Well, I think he was one of Laius' servants—
that's what people said.

OEDIPUS

You mean king Laius,
the one who ruled this country years ago?

MESSENGER

That's right. He was one of the king's shepherds.

OEDIPUS

Is he still alive? Can I still see him?

MESSENGER

You people live here. You'd best answer that.

OEDIPUS *[turning to the Chorus]*

Do any of you here now know the man,
this shepherd he describes? Have you seen him,
either in the fields or here in Thebes?
Answer me. It's critical, time at last
to find out what this means.   [1050]

CHORUS LEADER

The man he mentioned
is, I think, the very peasant from the fields
you wanted to see earlier. But of this
Jocasta could tell more than anyone.

OEDIPUS

Lady, do you know the man we sent for—
just minutes ago—the one we summoned here?
Is he the one this messenger refers to?

ΙΟΚΑΣΤΗ

τί δ᾽ ὅντιν᾽ εἶπε; μηδὲν ἐντραπῇς· τὰ δὲ
ῥηθέντα βούλου μηδὲ μεμνῆσθαι μάτην.

ΟΙΔΙΠΟΥΣ

οὐκ ἂν γένοιτο τοῦθ᾽ ὅπως ἐγὼ λαβὼν
σημεῖα τοιαῦτ᾽ οὐ φανῶ τοὐμὸν γένος.

ΙΟΚΑΣΤΗ

μὴ πρὸς θεῶν, εἴπερ τι τοῦ σαυτοῦ βίου   1060
κήδει, ματεύσῃς τοῦθ᾽· ἅλις νοσοῦσ᾽ ἐγώ.

ΟΙΔΙΠΟΥΣ

θάρσει· σὺ μὲν γὰρ οὐδ᾽ ἐὰν τρίτης ἐγὼ
μητρὸς φανῶ τρίδουλος, ἐκφανεῖ κακή.

ΙΟΚΑΣΤΗ

ὅμως πιθοῦ μοι, λίσσομαι· μὴ δρᾶ τάδε.

ΟΙΔΙΠΟΥΣ

οὐκ ἂν πιθοίμην μὴ οὐ τάδ᾽ ἐκμαθεῖν σαφῶς.   1065

ΙΟΚΑΣΤΗ

καὶ μὴν φρονοῦσά γ᾽ εὖ τὰ λῷστά σοι λέγω.

ΟΙΔΙΠΟΥΣ

τὰ λῷστα τοίνυν ταῦτά μ᾽ ἀλγύνει πάλαι.

ΙΟΚΑΣΤΗ

ὦ δύσποτμ᾽, εἴθε μήποτε γνοίης ὃς εἶ.

ΟΙΔΙΠΟΥΣ

ἄξει τις ἐλθὼν δεῦρο τὸν βοτῆρά μοι;
ταύτην δ᾽ ἐᾶτε πλουσίῳ χαίρειν γένει.   1070

JOCASTA

> Why ask me what he means? Forget all that.
> There's no point trying to sort out what he said.

OEDIPUS

> With all these indications of the truth
> here in my grasp, I cannot end this now.
> I must reveal the details of my birth.

JOCASTA

> In the name of the gods, no! If you have   [1060]
> some concern for your own life, then stop!
> Do not keep on investigating this.
> I will suffer—that will be enough.

OEDIPUS

> Be brave. Even if I should turn out to be
> born from a shameful mother, whose family
> for three generations have been slaves,
> you will still have your noble lineage.

JOCASTA

> Listen to me, I beg you. Do not do this.

OEDIPUS

> I will not be convinced I should not learn
> the whole truth of what these facts amount to.

JOCASTA

> But I care about your own well being—
> what I tell you is for your benefit.

OEDIPUS

> What you're telling me for my own good
> just brings me more distress.

JOCASTA

>   O you unhappy man!
> May you never find out who you really are!

OEDIPUS *[to Chorus]*

> Go, one of you, and bring that shepherd here.
> Leave the lady to enjoy her noble line.   [1070]

ΙΟΚΑΣΤΗ

ἰοὺ ἰού, δύστηνε· τοῦτο γάρ σ' ἔχω
μόνον προσειπεῖν, ἄλλο δ' οὔποθ' ὕστερον.

ΧΟΡΟΣ

τί ποτε βέβηκεν, Οἰδίπους, ὑπ' ἀγρίας
ᾄξασα λύπης ἡ γυνή; δέδοιχ' ὅπως
μὴ 'κ τῆς σιωπῆς τῆσδ' ἀναρρήξει κακά.   1075

ΟΙΔΙΠΟΥΣ

ὁποῖα χρῄζει ῥηγνύτω· τοὐμὸν δ' ἐγώ,
κεἰ σμικρόν ἐστι, σπέρμ' ἰδεῖν βουλήσομαι.
αὕτη δ' ἴσως, φρονεῖ γὰρ ὡς γυνὴ μέγα,
τὴν δυσγένειαν τὴν ἐμὴν αἰσχύνεται.
ἐγὼ δ' ἐμαυτὸν παῖδα τῆς Τύχης νέμων   1080
τῆς εὖ διδούσης οὐκ ἀτιμασθήσομαι.
τῆς γὰρ πέφυκα μητρός· οἱ δὲ συγγενεῖς
μῆνές με μικρὸν καὶ μέγαν διώρισαν.
τοιόσδε δ' ἐκφὺς οὐκ ἂν ἐξέλθοιμ' ἔτι
ποτ' ἄλλος, ὥστε μὴ 'κμαθεῖν τοὐμὸν γένος.   1085

ΧΟΡΟΣ

εἴπερ ἐγὼ μάντις εἰμὶ καὶ κατὰ γνώμαν ἴδρις,
οὐ τὸν Ὄλυμπον ἀπείρων, ὦ Κιθαιρών,
οὐκ ἔσει τὰν αὔριον   1090
πανσέληνον, μὴ οὐ σέ γε καὶ πατριώταν Οἰδίπουν
καὶ τροφὸν καὶ ματέρ' αὔξειν,
καὶ χορεύεσθαι πρὸς ἡμῶν, ὡς ἐπὶ ἦρα φέροντα τοῖς
    ἐμοῖς τυράννοις.   1095
ἰήϊε Φοῖβε, σοὶ δὲ ταῦτ' ἀρέστ' εἴη.

JOCASTA

> Alas, you poor miserable man!
> There's nothing more that I can say to you.
> I'll never speak another word again.

[JOCASTA runs into the palace]

CHORUS LEADER

> Why has the queen rushed off, Oedipus,
> so full of grief? I fear a disastrous storm
> will soon break through her silence.

OEDIPUS

>   Then let it break,
> whatever it is. As for myself,
> no matter how base born my family,
> I wish to know the seed from where I came.
> Perhaps my queen is now ashamed of me
> and of my insignificant origin—
> she likes to play the noble lady.
> But I will never feel myself dishonoured.   [1080]
> I see myself as a child of Fortune—
> and she is generous, that mother of mine
> from whom I spring, and the months, my siblings,
> have seen me by turns both small and great.
> That's how I was born. I cannot prove false
> to my own nature, nor can I ever cease
> from seeking out the facts of my own birth.

CHORUS

> If I have any power of prophecy
> or skill in knowing things,
> then, by the Olympian deities,
> you, Cithaeron, at tomorrow's moon   [1090]
> will surely know that Oedipus
> pays tribute to you as his native land
> both as his mother and his nurse,
> and that our choral dance and song
> acknowledge you because you are
> so pleasing to our king.
> O Phoebus, we cry out to you—
> may our song fill you with delight!

137

Sophocles

τίς σε, τέκνον, τίς σ' ἔτικτε τᾶν μακραιώνων ἄρα
Πανὸς ὀρεσσιβάτα πατρὸς πελασθεῖσ';   1100
ἢ σέ γ' εὐνάτειρά τις
Λοξίου; τῷ γὰρ πλάκες ἀγρόνομοι πᾶσαι φίλαι·
εἴθ' ὁ Κυλλάνας ἀνάσσων,   1105
εἴθ' ὁ Βακχεῖος θεὸς ναίων ἐπ' ἄκρων ὀρέων σ' εὕρημα
δέξατ' ἔκ του
Νυμφᾶν Ἑλικωνίδων, αἷς πλεῖστα συμπαίζει.

ΟΙΔΙΠΟΥΣ

εἰ χρή τι κἀμὲ μὴ συναλλάξαντά πω,   1110
πρέσβεις, σταθμᾶσθαι, τὸν βοτῆρ' ὁρᾶν δοκῶ,
ὅνπερ πάλαι ζητοῦμεν· ἔν τε γὰρ μακρῷ
γήρᾳ ξυνᾴδει τῷδε τἀνδρὶ σύμμετρος,
ἄλλως τε τοὺς ἄγοντας ὥσπερ οἰκέτας
ἔγνωκ' ἐμαυτοῦ· τῇ δ' ἐπιστήμῃ σύ μου   1115
προύχοις τάχ' ἄν που, τὸν βοτῆρ' ἰδὼν πάρος.

ΧΟΡΟΣ

ἔγνωκα γάρ, σάφ' ἴσθι· Λαΐου γὰρ ἦν
εἴπερ τις ἄλλος πιστὸς ὡς νομεὺς ἀνήρ.

ΟΙΔΙΠΟΥΣ

σὲ πρῶτ' ἐρωτῶ, τὸν Κορίνθιον ξένον,
ἦ τόνδε φράζεις;   1120

ΑΓΓΕΛΟΣ

                    τοῦτον, ὅνπερ εἰσορᾷς.

ΟΙΔΙΠΟΥΣ

οὗτος σύ, πρέσβυ, δεῦρό μοι φώνει βλέπων
ὅσ' ἄν σ' ἐρωτῶ. Λαΐου ποτ' ἦσθα σύ;

138

Who gave birth to you, my child?
Which one of the immortal gods
bore you to your father Pan,   [1100]
who roams the mountainsides?
Was it some bedmate of Apollo,
the god who loves all country fields?
Perhaps Cyllene's royal king?
Or was it the Bacchanalian god
dwelling on the mountain tops
who took you as a new-born joy
from maiden nymphs of Helicon
with whom he often romps and plays?[19]

OEDIPUS *[looking out away from the palace]*
You elders, though I've never seen the man   [1110]
we've been seeking for a long time now,
if I had to guess, I think I see him.
He's coming here. He looks very old—
as is appropriate, if he's the one.
And I know the people coming with him,
servants of mine. But if you've seen him before,
you'll recognize him better than I will.

CHORUS LEADER
Yes, I recognize the man. There's no doubt.
He worked for Laius—a trusty shepherd.

[Enter SERVANT, an old shepherd]

OEDIPUS
Stranger from Corinth, let me first ask you—
is this the man you spoke of?

MESSENGER
                                    Yes, he is—
he's the man you see in front of you.   [1120]

OEDIPUS
You, old man, over here. Look at me.
Now answer what I ask. Some time ago
did you work for Laius?

Sophocles

ΘΕΡΑΠΩΝ

ἢ δοῦλος οὐκ ὠνητός, ἀλλ᾽ οἴκοι τραφείς.

ΟΙΔΙΠΟΥΣ

ἔργον μεριμνῶν ποῖον ἢ βίον τινά;

ΘΕΡΑΠΩΝ

ποίμναις τὰ πλεῖστα τοῦ βίου συνειπόμην.   1125

ΟΙΔΙΠΟΥΣ

χώροις μάλιστα πρὸς τίσι ξύναυλος ὤν;

ΘΕΡΑΠΩΝ

ἦν μὲν Κιθαιρών, ἦν δὲ πρόσχωρος τόπος.

ΟΙΔΙΠΟΥΣ

τὸν ἄνδρα τόνδ᾽ οὖν οἶσθα τῇδέ που μαθών;

ΘΕΡΑΠΩΝ

τί χρῆμα δρῶντα; ποῖον ἄνδρα καὶ λέγεις;

ΟΙΔΙΠΟΥΣ

τόνδ᾽ ὃς πάρεστιν· ἢ ξυναλλάξας τί πω;   1130

ΘΕΡΑΠΩΝ

οὐχ ὥστε γ᾽ εἰπεῖν ἐν τάχει μνήμης ἄπο.

ΑΓΓΕΛΟΣ

κοὐδέν γε θαῦμα, δέσποτ᾽· ἀλλ᾽ ἐγὼ σαφῶς
ἀγνῶτ᾽ ἀναμνήσω νιν. εὖ γὰρ οἶδ᾽ ὅτι
κάτοιδεν, ἦμος τῷ Κιθαιρῶνος τόπῳ,
ὁ μὲν διπλοῖσι ποιμνίοις, ἐγὼ δ᾽ ἑνί,   1135
ἐπλησίαζον τῷδε τἀνδρὶ τρεῖς ὅλους
ἐξ ἦρος εἰς ἀρκτοῦρον ἐκμήνους χρόνους·
χειμῶνα δ᾽ ἤδη τἀμά τ᾽ εἰς ἔπαυλ᾽ ἐγὼ
ἤλαυνον οὗτός τ᾽ εἰς τὰ Λαΐου σταθμά.
λέγω τι τούτων ἢ οὐ λέγω πεπραγμένον;   1140

ΘΕΡΑΠΩΝ

λέγεις ἀληθῆ, καίπερ ἐκ μακροῦ χρόνου.

140

SERVANT

                                    Yes, as a slave.
But I was not bought. I grew up in his house.

OEDIPUS

How did you live? What was the work you did?

SERVANT

Most of my life I've spent looking after sheep.

OEDIPUS

Whereabouts? In what specific places?

SERVANT

On Cithaeron or the neighbouring lands.

OEDIPUS

Do you know if you came across this man
anywhere up there?

SERVANT

                                    Doing what?
What man do you mean?

OEDIPUS

                                The man over here—
this one. Have you ever met him before?   [1130]

SERVANT

Right now I can't say I remember him.

MESSENGER

My lord, that's surely not surprising.
Let me refresh his failing memory.
I think he will remember all too well
the time we spent around Cithaeron.
He had two flocks of sheep and I had one.
I was with him there for six months at a stretch,
from early spring until the autumn season.
In winter I'd drive my sheep down to my folds,
and he'd take his to pens that Laius owned.
Isn't that what happened—what I just said?   [1140]

SERVANT

You spoke the truth. But it was long ago.

ΑΓΓΕΛΟΣ

φέρ' εἰπὲ νῦν, τότ' οἶσθα παῖδά μοί τινα
δούς, ὡς ἐμαυτῷ θρέμμα θρεψαίμην ἐγώ;

ΘΕΡΑΠΩΝ

τί δ' ἔστι; πρὸς τί τοῦτο τοὔπος ἱστορεῖς;

ΑΓΓΕΛΟΣ

ὅδ' ἐστίν, ὦ τᾶν, κεῖνος ὃς τότ' ἦν νέος.　　　　1145

ΘΕΡΑΠΩΝ

οὐκ εἰς ὄλεθρον; οὐ σιωπήσας ἔσει;

ΟΙΔΙΠΟΥΣ

ἆ, μὴ κόλαζε, πρέσβυ, τόνδ', ἐπεὶ τὰ σὰ
δεῖται κολαστοῦ μᾶλλον ἢ τὰ τοῦδ' ἔπη.

ΘΕΡΑΠΩΝ

τί δ', ὦ φέριστε δεσποτῶν, ἁμαρτάνω;

ΟΙΔΙΠΟΥΣ

οὐκ ἐννέπων τὸν παῖδ' ὃν οὗτος ἱστορεῖ.　　　　1150

ΘΕΡΑΠΩΝ

λέγει γὰρ εἰδὼς οὐδέν, ἀλλ' ἄλλως πονεῖ.

ΟΙΔΙΠΟΥΣ

σὺ πρὸς χάριν μὲν οὐκ ἐρεῖς, κλαίων δ' ἐρεῖς.

ΘΕΡΑΠΩΝ

μὴ δῆτα, πρὸς θεῶν, τὸν γέροντά μ' αἰκίσῃ.

ΟΙΔΙΠΟΥΣ

οὐχ ὡς τάχος τις τοῦδ' ἀποστρέψει χέρας;

ΘΕΡΑΠΩΝ

δύστηνος, ἀντὶ τοῦ; τί προσχρῄζων μαθεῖν;　　　　1155

MESSENGER
　All right, then. Now, tell me if you recall
　how you gave me a child, an infant boy,
　for me to raise as my own foster son.

SERVANT
　What? Why ask about that?

MESSENGER
　　　　　　This man here, my friend,
　was that young child back then.

SERVANT
　　　　　　　　　　Damn you!
　Can't you keep quiet about it!

OEDIPUS
　　　　　　　Hold on, old man.
　Don't criticize him. What you have said
　is more objectionable than his account.

SERVANT
　My noble master, what have I done wrong?

OEDIPUS
　You did not tell us of that infant boy,　　　　　[1150]
　the one he asked about.

SERVANT
　　　　　　　　That's what he says,
　but he knows nothing—a useless busybody.

OEDIPUS
　If you won't tell us of your own free will,
　once we start to hurt you, you will talk.

SERVANT
　By all the gods, don't torture an old man!

OEDIPUS
　One of you there, tie up this fellow's hands.

SERVANT
　Why are you doing this? It's too much for me!
　What is it you want to know?

Sophocles

ΟΙΔΙΠΟΥΣ

τὸν παῖδ᾽ ἔδωκας τῷδ᾽ ὃν οὗτος ἱστορεῖ;

ΘΕΡΑΠΩΝ

ἔδωκ᾽· ὀλέσθαι δ᾽ ὤφελον τῇδ᾽ ἡμέρᾳ.

ΟΙΔΙΠΟΥΣ

ἀλλ᾽ εἰς τόδ᾽ ἥξεις μὴ λέγων γε τοὐνδικον.

ΘΕΡΑΠΩΝ

πολλῷ γε μᾶλλον, ἢν φράσω, διόλλυμαι.

ΟΙΔΙΠΟΥΣ

ἀνὴρ ὅδ᾽, ὡς ἔοικεν, ἐς τριβὰς ἐλᾷ.   1160

ΘΕΡΑΠΩΝ

οὐ δῆτ᾽ ἔγωγ᾽, ἀλλ᾽ εἶπον, ὡς δοίην, πάλαι.

ΟΙΔΙΠΟΥΣ

πόθεν λαβών; οἰκεῖον ἢ ᾽ξ ἄλλου τινός;

ΘΕΡΑΠΩΝ

ἐμὸν μὲν οὐκ ἔγωγ᾽, ἐδεξάμην δέ του.

ΟΙΔΙΠΟΥΣ

τίνος πολιτῶν τῶνδε κἀκ ποίας στέγης;

ΘΕΡΑΠΩΝ

μὴ πρὸς θεῶν, μή, δέσποθ᾽, ἱστόρει πλέον.   1165

ΟΙΔΙΠΟΥΣ

ὄλωλας, εἴ σε ταῦτ᾽ ἐρήσομαι πάλιν.

ΘΕΡΑΠΩΝ

τῶν Λαΐου τοίνυν τις ἦν γεννημάτων.

ΟΙΔΙΠΟΥΣ

ἦ δοῦλος ἢ κείνου τις ἐγγενὴς γεγώς;

144

OEDIPUS
                    That child he mentioned—
did you give it to him?

SERVANT
                    I did. How I wish
I'd died that day!

OEDIPUS
                    Well, you are going to die
if you don't speak the truth.

SERVANT
                    And if I do,
the death I suffer will be even worse.

OEDIPUS
It seems to me the man is trying to stall.   [1160]

SERVANT
No, no, I'm not. I've already told you—
I did give him the child.

OEDIPUS
                    Where did you get it?
Did it come from your home or somewhere else?

SERVANT
It was not mine—I got it from someone.

OEDIPUS
Which of our citizens? Whose home was it?

SERVANT
In the name of the gods, my lord, don't ask!
Please, no more questions!

OEDIPUS
                    If I have to ask again,
then you will die.

SERVANT
                    The child was born in Laius' house.

OEDIPUS
From a slave or from some relative of his?

ΘΕΡΑΠΩΝ
οἴμοι, πρὸς αὐτῷ γ᾽ εἰμὶ τῷ δεινῷ λέγειν.

ΟΙΔΙΠΟΥΣ
κἄγωγ᾽ ἀκούειν· ἀλλ᾽ ὅμως ἀκουστέον.　　　　1170

ΘΕΡΑΠΩΝ
κείνου γέ τοι δὴ παῖς ἐκλῄζεθ᾽· ἡ δ᾽ ἔσω
κάλλιστ᾽ ἂν εἴποι σὴ γυνὴ τάδ᾽ ὡς ἔχει.

ΟΙΔΙΠΟΥΣ
ἦ γὰρ δίδωσιν ἥδε σοι;

ΘΕΡΑΠΩΝ
　　　　　　　μάλιστ᾽, ἄναξ.

ΟΙΔΙΠΟΥΣ
ὡς πρὸς τί χρείας;

ΘΕΡΑΠΩΝ
　　　　　　ὡς ἀναλώσαιμί νιν.

ΟΙΔΙΠΟΥΣ
τεκοῦσα τλήμων;　　　　　　　　　　　　1175

ΘΕΡΑΠΩΝ
　　　　　　θεσφάτων γ᾽ ὄκνῳ κακῶν.

ΟΙΔΙΠΟΥΣ
ποίων;

ΘΕΡΑΠΩΝ
　　　　κτενεῖν νιν τοὺς τεκόντας ἦν λόγος.

ΟΙΔΙΠΟΥΣ
πῶς δῆτ᾽ ἀφῆκας τῷ γέροντι τῷδε σύ;

ΘΕΡΑΠΩΝ
κατοικτίσας, ὦ δέσποθ᾽, ὡς ἄλλην χθόνα
δοκῶν ἀποίσειν, αὐτὸς ἔνθεν ἦν· ὁ δὲ

146

SERVANT

    Alas, what I'm about to say now . . .
it's horrible.

OEDIPUS

                    It may be horrible,   [1170]
but nonetheless I have to hear it.

SERVANT

    If you must know, they said the child was his.
But your wife inside the palace is the one
who could best tell you what was going on.

OEDIPUS

    You mean she gave the child to you?

SERVANT

                    Yes, my lord.

OEDIPUS

    Why did she do that?

SERVANT

               So I would kill it.

OEDIPUS

    That wretched woman was the mother?

SERVANT

                         Yes.

She was afraid of dreadful prophecies.

OEDIPUS

    What sort of prophecies?

SERVANT

                 The story went
that he would kill his father.

OEDIPUS

                  If that was true,
why did you give the child to this old man?

SERVANT

    I pitied the boy, master, and I thought
he'd take the child off to a foreign land
where he was from. But he rescued him,

κἄκ' εἰς μέγιστ' ἔσωσεν. εἰ γὰρ οὗτος εἶ 1180
ὅν φησιν οὗτος, ἴσθι δύσποτμος γεγώς.

ΟΙΔΙΠΟΥΣ

ἰοὺ ἰού· τὰ πάντ' ἂν ἐξήκοι σαφῆ.
ὦ φῶς, τελευταῖόν σε προσβλέψαιμι νῦν,
ὅστις πέφασμαι φύς τ' ἀφ' ὧν οὐ χρῆν, ξὺν οἷς τ'
οὐ χρῆν ὁμιλῶν, οὕς τέ μ' οὐκ ἔδει κτανών. 1185

ΧΟΡΟΣ

ἰὼ γενεαὶ βροτῶν,
ὡς ὑμᾶς ἴσα καὶ τὸ μηδὲν ζώσας ἐναριθμῶ.
τίς γάρ, τίς ἀνὴρ πλέον
τᾶς εὐδαιμονίας φέρει 1190
ἢ τοσοῦτον ὅσον δοκεῖν
καὶ δόξαντ' ἀποκλῖναι;
τὸν σόν τοι παράδειγμ' ἔχων,
τὸν σὸν δαίμονα, τὸν σόν, ὦ τλᾶμον Οἰδιπόδα, βροτῶν
οὐδὲν μακαρίζω· 1195

ὅστις καθ' ὑπερβολὰν
τοξεύσας ἐκράτησε τοῦ πάντ' εὐδαίμονος ὄλβου,
ὦ Ζεῦ, κατὰ μὲν φθίσας
τὰν γαμψώνυχα παρθένον
χρησμῳδόν, θανάτων δ' ἐμᾷ 1200
χώρᾳ πύργος ἀνέστα·
ἐξ οὗ καὶ βασιλεὺς καλεῖ
ἐμὸς καὶ τὰ μέγιστ' ἐτιμάθης, ταῖς μεγάλαισιν ἐν
Θήβαισιν ἀνάσσων.

τανῦν δ' ἀκούειν τίς ἀθλιώτερος;
τίς ἄταις ἀγρίαις, τίς ἐν πόνοις 1205
ξύνοικος ἀλλαγᾷ βίου;
ἰὼ κλεινὸν Οἰδίπου κάρα,
ᾗ στέγας λιμὴν
αὑτὸς ἤρκεσεν
παιδὶ καὶ πατρὶ θαλαμηπόλῳ πεσεῖν;

only to save him for the greatest grief of all.   [1180]
For if you are who this man says you are
you know your birth carried an awful fate.

OEDIPUS

Ah, so it all came true. It's so clear now.
O light, let me look at you one final time,
a man who stands revealed as cursed by birth,
cursed by my own family, and cursed
by murder where I should not kill.

[OEDIPUS moves into the palace]

CHORUS

O generations of mortal men,
how I count your life as scarcely living.
What man is there, what human being,
who attains a greater happiness   [1190]
than mere appearances, a joy
which seems to fade away to nothing?
Poor wretched Oedipus, your fate
stands here to demonstrate for me
how no mortal man is ever blessed.

Here was a man who fired his arrows well—
his skill was matchless—and he won
the highest happiness in everything.
For, Zeus, he slaughtered the hook-taloned Sphinx
and stilled her cryptic song. For our state,
he stood there like a tower against death,   [1200]
and from that moment, Oedipus,
we have called you our king
and honoured you above all other men,
the one who rules in mighty Thebes.

But now who is there whose story
is more terrible to hear? Whose life
has been so changed by trouble,
by such ferocious agonies?
Alas for celebrated Oedipus,
the same spacious place of refuge
served you both as child and father,
the place you entered as a new bridegroom.   [1210]

πῶς ποτε πῶς ποθ᾽ αἱ πατρῷαί σ᾽ ἄλοκες φέρειν,
τάλας,   1210
σῖγ᾽ ἐδυνάθησαν ἐς τοσόνδε;

ἐφηῦρέ σ᾽ ἄκονθ᾽ ὁ πάνθ᾽ ὁρῶν χρόνος,
δικάζει τ᾽ ἄγαμον γάμον πάλαι
τεκνοῦντα καὶ τεκνούμενον.   1215
ἰώ, Λαΐειον ὦ τέκνον,
εἴθε σ᾽ εἴθε σε
μήποτ᾽ εἰδόμαν.
δύρομαι γὰρ ὥσπερ ἰάλεμον χέων
ἐκ στομάτων. τὸ δ᾽ ὀρθὸν εἰπεῖν, ἀνέπνευσά τ᾽ ἐκ
σέθεν   1220
καὶ κατεκοίμασα τοὐμὸν ὄμμα.

ΕΞΑΓΓΕΛΟΣ
ὦ γῆς μέγιστα τῆσδ᾽ ἀεὶ τιμώμενοι,
οἷ᾽, ἔργ᾽ ἀκούσεσθ᾽, οἷα δ᾽ εἰσόψεσθ᾽, ὅσον δ᾽
ἀρεῖσθε πένθος, εἴπερ ἐγγενῶς ἔτι   1225
τῶν Λαβδακείων ἐντρέπεσθε δωμάτων.
οἶμαι γὰρ οὔτ᾽ ἂν Ἴστρον οὔτε Φᾶσιν ἂν
νίψαι καθαρμῷ τήνδε τὴν στέγην, ὅσα
κεύθει, τὰ δ᾽ αὐτίκ᾽ εἰς τὸ φῶς φανεῖ κακὰ
ἑκόντα κοὐκ ἄκοντα. τῶν δὲ πημονῶν   1230
μάλιστα λυποῦσ᾽ αἳ φανῶσ᾽ αὐθαίρετοι.

ΧΟΡΟΣ
λείπει μὲν οὐδ᾽ ἃ πρόσθεν εἴδομεν τὸ μὴ οὐ
βαρύστον᾽ εἶναι· πρὸς δ᾽ ἐκείνοισιν τί φῄς;

ΕΞΑΓΓΕΛΟΣ
ὁ μὲν τάχιστος τῶν λόγων εἰπεῖν τε καὶ
μαθεῖν, τέθνηκε θεῖον Ἰοκάστης κάρα.   1235

ΧΟΡΟΣ
ὦ δυστάλαινα, πρὸς τίνος ποτ᾽ αἰτίας;

ΕΞΑΓΓΕΛΟΣ
αὐτὴ πρὸς αὑτῆς. τῶν δὲ πραχθέντων τὰ μὲν
ἄλγιστ᾽ ἄπεστιν· ἡ γὰρ ὄψις οὐ πάρα.

How could the furrow where your father planted,
poor wretched man, have tolerated you
in such silence for so long?

Time, which watches everything
and uncovered you against your will,
now sits in judgment of that fatal marriage,
where child and parent have been joined so long.
O child of Laius, how I wish
I'd never seen you—now I wail
like one whose mouth pours forth laments.   [1220]
To tell it right, it was through you
I found my life and breathed again,
and then through you the darkness veils my eyes.

[The Second Messenger enters from the palace]

SECOND MESSENGER
O you most honoured citizens of Thebes,
what actions you will hear about and see,
what sorrows you will bear, if, as natives here,
you are still loyal to the house of Labdacus!
I do not think the Ister or the Phasis rivers
could cleanse this house. It conceals too much
and soon will bring to light the vilest things,
brought on by choice and not by accident.[20]   [1230]
What we do to ourselves brings us most pain.

CHORUS LEADER
The calamities we knew about before
were hard enough to bear. What can you say
to make them worse?

SECOND MESSENGER
                                         I'll waste no words—
know this—noble Jocasta, our queen, is dead.

CHORUS LEADER
That poor unhappy lady! How did she die?

SECOND MESSENGER
She killed herself. You did not witness it,
so you'll be spared the worst of what went on.

ὅμως δ’, ὅσον γε κἂν ἐμοὶ μνήμης ἔνι,
πεύσει τὰ κείνης ἀθλίας παθήματα.　　　　1240
ὅπως γὰρ ὀργῇ χρωμένη παρῆλθ’ ἔσω
θυρῶνος, ἵετ’ εὐθὺ πρὸς τὰ νυμφικὰ
λέχη, κόμην σπῶσ’ ἀμφιδεξίοις ἀκμαῖς.
πύλας δ’, ὅπως εἰσῆλθ’, ἐπιρράξασ’ ἔσω
καλεῖ τὸν ἤδη Λάϊον πάλαι νεκρόν,　　　　1245
μνήμην παλαιῶν σπερμάτων ἔχουσ’, ὑφ’ ὧν
θάνοι μὲν αὐτός, τὴν δὲ τίκτουσαν λίποι
τοῖς οἷσιν αὐτοῦ δύστεκνον παιδουργίαν.
γοᾶτο δ’ εὐνάς, ἔνθα δύστηνος διπλοῦς
ἐξ ἀνδρὸς ἄνδρα καὶ τέκν’ ἐκ τέκνων τέκοι.　　1250
χὤπως μὲν ἐκ τῶνδ’ οὐκέτ’ οἶδ’ ἀπόλλυται·
βοῶν γὰρ εἰσέπαισεν Οἰδίπους, ὑφ’ οὗ
οὐκ ἦν τὸ κείνης ἐκθεάσασθαι κακόν,
ἀλλ’ εἰς ἐκεῖνον περιπολοῦντ’ ἐλεύσσομεν.
φοιτᾷ γὰρ ἡμᾶς ἔγχος ἐξαιτῶν πορεῖν,　　　1255
γυναῖκά τ’ οὐ γυναῖκα, μητρῴαν δ’ ὅπου
κίχοι διπλῆν ἄρουραν οὗ τε καὶ τέκνων.
λυσσῶντι δ’ αὐτῷ δαιμόνων δείκνυσί τις·
οὐδεὶς γὰρ ἀνδρῶν, οἳ παρῆμεν ἐγγύθεν.
δεινὸν δ’ ἀύσας ὡς ὑφηγητοῦ τινος　　　　1260
πύλαις διπλαῖς ἐνήλατ’, ἐκ δὲ πυθμένων
ἔκλινε κοῖλα κλῇθρα κἀμπίπτει στέγῃ.
οὗ δὴ κρεμαστὴν τὴν γυναῖκ’ ἐσείδομεν,
πλεκταῖσιν αἰώραισιν ἐμπεπλεγμένην.
ὁ δ’ ὡς ὁρᾷ νιν, δεινὰ βρυχηθεὶς τάλας　　　1265
χαλᾷ κρεμαστὴν ἀρτάνην. ἐπεὶ δὲ γῇ
ἔκειτο τλήμων, δεινὰ δ’ ἦν τἀνθένδ’ ὁρᾶν.
ἀποσπάσας γὰρ εἱμάτων χρυσηλάτους
περόνας ἀπ’ αὐτῆς, αἷσιν ἐξεστέλλετο,
ἄρας ἔπαισεν ἄρθρα τῶν αὑτοῦ κύκλων,　　　1270
αὐδῶν τοιαῦθ’, ὁθούνεκ’ οὐκ ὄψοιντό νιν
οὔθ’ οἷ’ ἔπασχεν οὔθ’ ὁποῖ’ ἔδρα κακά,
ἀλλ’ ἐν σκότῳ τὸ λοιπὸν οὓς μὲν οὐκ ἔδει
ὀψοίαθ’, οὓς δ’ ἔχρῃζεν οὐ γνωσοίατο.

But from what I recall of what I saw
you'll learn how that poor woman suffered.   [1240]
She left here frantic and rushed inside,
the fingers of both hands clenched in her hair.
She ran through the hall straight to her marriage bed.
She went in, slamming both doors shut behind her
and crying out to Laius, who's been a corpse
a long time now. She was remembering
that child of theirs born many years ago—
the one who killed his father, who left her
to conceive cursed children with that son.
She lay moaning beside the bed, where she,
poor woman, had given birth twice over—
a husband from a husband, children from a child.   [1250]
How she died after that I don't fully know.
With a scream Oedipus came bursting in.
He would not let us see her suffering,
her final pain. We watched him charge around,
back and forth. As he moved, he kept asking us
to give him a sword, as he tried to find
that wife who was no wife—whose mother's womb
had given birth to him and to his children.
As he raved, some immortal power led him on—
no human in the room came close to him.
With a dreadful howl, as if someone   [1260]
had pushed him, he leapt at the double doors,
bent the bolts by force out of their sockets,
and burst into the room. Then we saw her.
She was hanging there, swaying, with twisted cords
roped round her neck. When Oedipus saw her,
with a dreadful groan he took her body
from the noose in which she hung, and then,
when the poor woman was lying on the ground—
what happened next was a horrific sight—
from her clothes he ripped the golden brooches
she wore as ornaments, raised them high,
and drove them deep into his eyeballs,   [1270]
crying as he did so: "You will no longer see
all those atrocious things I suffered,
the dreadful things I did! No. You have seen
what you never should have looked upon,
and what I wished to know you did not see.

Sophocles

τοιαῦτ᾽ ἐφυμνῶν πολλάκις τε κοὐχ ἅπαξ   1275
ἤρασσ᾽ ἐπαίρων βλέφαρα. φοίνιαι δ᾽ ὁμοῦ
γλῆναι γένει᾽ ἔτελλον, οὐδ᾽ ἀνίεσαν
φόνου μυδώσας σταγόνας, ἀλλ᾽ ὁμοῦ μέλας
ὄμβρος χαλάζης αἱματοῦς ἐτέγγετο.
τάδ᾽ ἐκ δυοῖν ἔρρωγεν, οὐ μόνου κάτα,   1280
ἀλλ᾽ ἀνδρὶ καὶ γυναικὶ συμμιγῆ κακά.
ὁ πρὶν παλαιὸς δ᾽ ὄλβος ἦν πάροιθε μὲν
ὄλβος δικαίως· νῦν δὲ τῆδε θἠμέρᾳ
στεναγμός, ἄτη, θάνατος, αἰσχύνη, κακῶν
ὅσ᾽ ἐστὶ πάντων ὀνόματ᾽, οὐδέν ἐστ᾽ ἀπόν.   1285

ΧΟΡΟΣ
νῦν δ᾽ ἔσθ᾽ ὁ τλήμων ἐν τίνι σχολῇ κακοῦ;

ΕΞΑΓΓΕΛΟΣ
βοᾷ διοίγειν κλῇθρα καὶ δηλοῦν τινα
τοῖς πᾶσι Καδμείοισι τὸν πατροκτόνον,
τὸν μητέρ᾽—αὐδῶν ἀνόσι᾽ οὐδὲ ῥητά μοι,
ὡς ἐκ χθονὸς ῥίψων ἑαυτὸν οὐδ᾽ ἔτι   1290
μενῶν δόμοις ἀραῖος, ὡς ἠράσατο.
ῥώμης γε μέντοι καὶ προηγητοῦ τινος
δεῖται· τὸ γὰρ νόσημα μεῖζον ἢ φέρειν.
δείξει δὲ καὶ σοί· κλῇθρα γὰρ πυλῶν τάδε
διοίγεται· θέαμα δ᾽ εἰσόψει τάχα   1295
τοιοῦτον οἷον καὶ στυγοῦντ᾽ ἐποικτίσαι.

ΧΟΡΟΣ
ὦ δεινὸν ἰδεῖν πάθος ἀνθρώποις,
ὦ δεινότατον πάντων ὅσ᾽ ἐγὼ
προσέκυρσ᾽ ἤδη. τίς σ᾽, ὦ τλῆμον,
προσέβη μανία; τίς ὁ πηδήσας   1300
μείζονα δαίμων τῶν μακίστων
πρὸς σῇ δυσδαίμονι μοίρᾳ;
φεῦ φεῦ, δύσταν᾽·
ἀλλ᾽ οὐδ᾽ ἐσιδεῖν δύναμαί σε, θέλων

154

So now and for all future time be dark!"
With these words he raised his hand and struck,
not once, but many times, right in the sockets.
With every blow blood spurted from his eyes
down on his beard, and not in single drops,
but showers of dark blood spattering like hail.   [1280]
So what these two have done has overwhelmed
not one alone—this disaster swallows up
a man and wife together. That old happiness
they had before in their rich ancestry
was truly joy, but now lament and ruin,
death and shame, and all calamities
which men can name are theirs to keep.

CHORUS LEADER
    And has that suffering man found some relief
    to ease his pain?

SECOND MESSENGER
                    He shouts at everyone
    to open up the gates and thus reveal
    to all Cadmeians his father's killer,
    his mother's . . . but I must not say those words.
    He wants them to cast him out of Thebes,   [1290]
    so the curse he laid will not come on this house
    if he still lives inside. But he is weak
    and needs someone to lead him on his way.
    His agony is more than he can bear—
    as he will show you—for on the palace doors
    the bolts are being pulled back. Soon you will see
    a sight which even a man filled with disgust
    would have to pity.

[OEDIPUS enters through the palace doors]

CHORUS LEADER
    An awful fate for human eyes to witness,
    an appalling sight—the worst I've ever seen.
    O you poor man, what madness came on you?
    What eternal force pounced on your life   [1300]
    and, springing further than the longest leap,
    brought you this fearful doom? Alas! Alas!
    You unhappy man! I cannot look at you.

πόλλ' ἀνερέσθαι, πολλὰ πυθέσθαι,
πολλὰ δ' ἀθρῆσαι·   1305
τοίαν φρίκην παρέχεις μοι.

ΟΙΔΙΠΟΥΣ
αἰαῖ αἰαῖ, δύστανος ἐγώ,
ποῖ γᾶς φέρομαι τλάμων; πᾷ μοι
φθογγὰ διαπωτᾶται φοράδην;   1310
ἰὼ δαῖμον, ἵν' ἐξήλλου.

ΧΟΡΟΣ
ἐς δεινὸν οὐδ' ἀκουστὸν οὐδ' ἐπόψιμον.

ΟΙΔΙΠΟΥΣ
ἰὼ σκότου
νέφος ἐμὸν ἀπότροπον, ἐπιπλόμενον ἄφατον,
ἀδάματόν τε καὶ δυσούριστον ὄν.   1315
οἴμοι,
οἴμοι μάλ' αὖθις· οἷον εἰσέδυ μ' ἅμα
κέντρων τε τῶνδ' οἴστρημα καὶ μνήμη κακῶν.

ΧΟΡΟΣ
καὶ θαῦμά γ' οὐδὲν ἐν τοσοῖσδε πήμασιν
διπλᾶ σε πενθεῖν καὶ διπλᾶ φορεῖν κακά.   1320

ΟΙΔΙΠΟΥΣ
ἰὼ φίλος,
σὺ μὲν ἐμὸς ἐπίπολος ἔτι μόνιμος· ἔτι γὰρ
ὑπομένεις με τὸν τυφλὸν κηδεύων.
φεῦ φεῦ.
οὐ γάρ με λήθεις, ἀλλὰ γιγνώσκω σαφῶς,   1325
καίπερ σκοτεινός, τήν γε σὴν αὐδὴν ὅμως.

ΧΟΡΟΣ
ὦ δεινὰ δράσας, πῶς ἔτλης τοιαῦτα σὰς
ὄψεις μαρᾶναι; τίς σ' ἐπῆρε δαιμόνων;

ΟΙΔΙΠΟΥΣ
Ἀπόλλων τάδ' ἦν, Ἀπόλλων, φίλοι,
ὁ κακὰ κακὰ τελῶν ἐμὰ τάδ' ἐμὰ πάθεα.   1330

I want to ask you many things—there's much
I wish to learn. You fill me with such horror,
yet there is so much I must see.

OEDIPUS

Aaaiiii, aaaiii . . . Alas! Alas!
How miserable I am . . . such wretchedness . . .
Where do I go? How can the wings of air   [1310]
sweep up my voice? O my destiny,
how far you have sprung now!

CHORUS LEADER

To a fearful place from which men turn away,
a place they hate to look upon.

OEDIPUS

O the dark horror engulfing me,
this nameless visitor I can't resist
swept here by fair and fatal winds.
Alas for me! And yet again, alas for me!
The pain of stabbing brooches pierces me!
The memory of agonizing shame!

CHORUS LEADER

In your distress it's not astonishing
you bear a double load of suffering,   [1320]
a double load of pain.

OEDIPUS

                              Ah, my friend,
so you still care for me, as always,
and with patience nurse me now I'm blind.
Alas! Alas! You are not hidden from me—
I recognize you all too clearly.
Though I am blind, I know that voice so well.

CHORUS LEADER

You have carried out such dreadful things—
how could you dare to blind yourself this way?
What god drove you to it?

OEDIPUS

                              It was Apollo, friends.
It was Apollo. He brought on these troubles—   [1330]
the awful things I suffer. But the hand

157

ἔπαισε δ᾽ αὐτόχειρ νιν οὖτις, ἀλλ᾽ ἐγὼ τλάμων.
τί γὰρ ἔδει μ᾽ ὁρᾶν,
ὅτῳ γ᾽ ὁρῶντι μηδὲν ἦν ἰδεῖν γλυκύ;   1335

ΧΟΡΟΣ
ἦν τᾷδ᾽ ὅπωσπερ καὶ σύ φῄς.

ΟΙΔΙΠΟΥΣ
τί δῆτ᾽ ἐμοὶ βλεπτὸν ἢ
στερκτὸν ἢ προσήγορον
ἔτ᾽ ἔστ᾽ ἀκούειν ἡδονᾷ φίλοι;
ἀπάγετ᾽ ἐκτόπιον ὅ τι τάχιστά με,   1340
ἀπάγετ᾽, ὦ φίλοι, τὸν μέγ᾽ ὀλέθριον
τὸν καταρατότατον, ἔτι δὲ καὶ θεοῖς
ἐχθρότατον βροτῶν.   1345

ΧΟΡΟΣ
δείλαιε τοῦ νοῦ τῆς τε συμφορᾶς ἴσον,
ὡς σ᾽ ἠθέλησα μηδέ γ᾽ ἂν γνῶναί ποτε.

ΟΙΔΙΠΟΥΣ
ὄλοιθ᾽ ὅστις ἦν, ὃς ἀγρίας πέδας
μονάδ᾽ ἐπιποδίας ἔλυσ᾽ μ᾽ ἀπό τε φόνου   1350
ἔρυτο κἀνέσωσεν, οὐδὲν εἰς χάριν πράσσων.
τότε γὰρ ἂν θανὼν
οὐκ ἦ φίλοισιν οὐδ᾽ ἐμοὶ τοσόνδ᾽ ἄχος.   1355

ΧΟΡΟΣ
θέλοντι κἀμοὶ τοῦτ᾽ ἂν ἦν.

ΟΙΔΙΠΟΥΣ
οὔκουν πατρός γ᾽ ἂν φονεὺς
ἦλθον οὐδὲ νυμφίος
βροτοῖς ἐκλήθην ὧν ἔφυν ἄπο.
νῦν δ᾽ ἄθεος μέν εἰμ᾽, ἀνοσίων δὲ παῖς,   1360
ὁμολεχὴς δ᾽ ἀφ᾽ ὧν αὐτὸς ἔφυν τάλας.
εἰ δέ τι πρεσβύτερον ἔτι κακοῦ κακόν,   1365
τοῦτ᾽ ἔλαχ᾽ Οἰδίπους.

which stabbed out my eyes was mine alone.
In my wretched life, why should I have eyes
when there was nothing sweet for me to see?

CHORUS LEADER
What you have said is true enough.

OEDIPUS
What is there for me to see, my friends?
What can I love? Whose greeting can I hear
and feel delight? Hurry now, my friends,   [1340]
lead me away from Thebes—take me somewhere,
a man completely lost, utterly accursed,
the mortal man the gods despise the most.

CHORUS LEADER
Unhappy in your fate and in your mind
which now knows all. Would I had never known you!

OEDIPUS
WHOEVER the man is who freed my feet,
who released me from that cruel shackle   [1350]
and rescued me from death, may that man die!
It was a thankless act. Had I perished then,
I would not have brought such agony
to myself or to my friends.

CHORUS LEADER
                                                    I agree—
I, too, would have preferred if you had died.

OEDIPUS
I would not have come to kill my father,
and men would not see in me the husband
of the woman who gave birth to me.
Now I am abandoned by the gods,   [1360]
the son of a corrupted mother,
conceiving children with the woman
who gave me my own miserable life.
If there is some horrific suffering
worse than all the rest, then it too belongs
in the fate of Oedipus.

159

Sophocles

ΧΟΡΟΣ

οὐκ οἶδ᾽ ὅπως σε φῶ βεβουλεῦσθαι καλῶς·
κρείσσων γὰρ ἦσθα μηκέτ᾽ ὢν ἢ ζῶν τυφλός.

ΟΙΔΙΠΟΥΣ

ὡς μὲν τάδ᾽ οὐχ ὧδ᾽ ἔστ᾽ ἄριστ᾽ εἰργασμένα,
μή μ᾽ ἐκδίδασκε, μηδὲ συμβούλευ᾽ ἔτι.   1370
ἐγὼ γὰρ οὐκ οἶδ᾽ ὄμμασιν ποίοις βλέπων
πατέρα ποτ᾽ ἂν προσεῖδον εἰς Ἅιδου μολὼν
οὐδ᾽ αὖ τάλαιναν μητέρ᾽, οἶν ἐμοὶ δυοῖν
ἔργ᾽ ἐστὶ κρείσσον᾽ ἀγχόνης εἰργασμένα.
ἀλλ᾽ ἡ τέκνων δῆτ᾽ ὄψις ἦν ἐφίμερος,   1375
βλαστοῦσ᾽ ὅπως ἔβλαστε, προσλεύσσειν ἐμοί;
οὐ δῆτα τοῖς γ᾽ ἐμοῖσιν ὀφθαλμοῖς ποτε·
οὐδ᾽ ἄστυ γ᾽ οὐδὲ πύργος οὐδὲ δαιμόνων
ἀγάλμαθ᾽ ἱερά, τῶν ὁ παντλήμων ἐγὼ
κάλλιστ᾽ ἀνὴρ εἷς ἔν γε ταῖς θήβαις τραφεὶς   1380
ἀπεστέρησ᾽ ἐμαυτόν, αὐτὸς ἐννέπων
ὠθεῖν ἅπαντας τὸν ἀσεβῆ, τὸν ἐκ θεῶν
φανέντ᾽ ἄναγνον καὶ γένους τοῦ Λαΐου.
τοιάνδ᾽ ἐγὼ κηλῖδα μηνύσας ἐμὴν
ὀρθοῖς ἔμελλον ὄμμασιν τούτους ὁρᾶν;   1385
ἥκιστά γ᾽· ἀλλ᾽ εἰ τῆς ἀκουούσης ἔτ᾽ ἦν
πηγῆς δι᾽ ὤτων φραγμός, οὐκ ἂν ἐσχόμην
τὸ μὴ ἀποκλῇσαι τοὐμὸν ἄθλιον δέμας,
ἵν᾽ ἦ τυφλός τε καὶ κλύων μηδέν· τὸ γὰρ
τὴν φροντίδ᾽ ἔξω τῶν κακῶν οἰκεῖν γλυκύ.   1390
ἰὼ Κιθαιρών, τί μ᾽ ἐδέχου; τί μ᾽ οὐ λαβὼν
ἔκτεινας εὐθύς, ὡς ἔδειξα μήποτε
ἐμαυτὸν ἀνθρώποισιν ἔνθεν ἦ γεγώς;
ὦ Πόλυβε καὶ Κόρινθε καὶ τὰ πάτρια
λόγῳ παλαιὰ δώμαθ᾽, οἷον ἆρά με   1395
κάλλος κακῶν ὕπουλον ἐξεθρέψατε·

CHORUS LEADER

                              I do not believe
what you did to yourself is for the best.
Better to be dead than alive and blind.

OEDIPUS

Don't tell me what I've done is not the best.
And from now on spare me your advice.   [1370]
If I could see, I don't know how my eyes
could look at my own father when I come
to Hades or at my wretched mother.
Against those two I have committed acts
so vile that even if I hanged myself
that would not be sufficient punishment.
Perhaps you think the sight of my own children
might give me joy? No! Look how they were born!
They could never bring delight to eyes of mine.
Nor could the city or its massive walls,
or the sacred images of its gods.
I am the most abhorred of men, I,
the finest man of all those bred in Thebes,   [1380]
I have condemned myself, telling everyone
they had to banish for impiety
the man the gods have now exposed
as sacrilegious—a son of Laius, too.
With such polluting stains upon me,
could I set eyes on you and hold your gaze?
No. And if I could somehow block my ears
and kill my hearing, I would not hold back.
I'd make a dungeon of this wretched body,
so I would never see or hear again.
For there is joy in isolated thought,
completely sealed off from a world of pain.   [1390]
O Cithaeron, why did you shelter me?
Why, when I was handed over to you,
did you not do away with me at once,
so I would never then reveal to men
the nature of my birth? Ah Polybus
and Corinth, the place men called my home,
my father's ancient house, you raised me well—
so fine to look at, so corrupt inside!

νῦν γὰρ κακός τ᾽ ὢν κἀκ κακῶν εὑρίσκομαι.
ὦ τρεῖς κέλευθοι καὶ κεκρυμμένη νάπη
δρυμός τε καὶ στενωπὸς ἐν τριπλαῖς ὁδοῖς,
αἳ τοὐμὸν αἷμα τῶν ἐμῶν χειρῶν ἄπο   1400
ἐπίετε πατρός, ἀρά μου μέμνησθ᾽ ἔτι
οἷ᾽ ἔργα δράσας ὑμὶν εἶτα δεῦρ᾽ ἰὼν
ὁποῖ᾽ ἔπρασσον αὖθις; ὦ γάμοι γάμοι,
ἐφύσαθ᾽ ἡμᾶς, καὶ φυτεύσαντες πάλιν
ἀνεῖτε ταὐτοῦ σπέρμα, κἀπεδείξατε   1405
πατέρας, ἀδελφούς, παῖδας, αἷμ᾽ ἐμφύλιον,
νύμφας, γυναῖκας μητέρας τε, χὠπόσα
αἴσχιστ᾽ ἐν ἀνθρώποισιν ἔργα γίγνεται.
ἀλλ᾽ οὐ γὰρ αὐδᾶν ἔσθ᾽ ἃ μηδὲ δρᾶν καλόν,
ὅπως τάχιστα πρὸς θεῶν ἔξω μέ που   1410
καλύψατ᾽ ἢ φονεύσατ᾽ ἢ θαλάσσιον
ἐκρίψατ᾽, ἔνθα μήποτ᾽ εἰσόψεσθ᾽ ἔτι.
ἴτ᾽, ἀξιώσατ᾽ ἀνδρὸς ἀθλίου θιγεῖν.
πίθεσθε, μὴ δείσητε· τἀμὰ γὰρ κακὰ
οὐδεὶς οἷός τε πλὴν ἐμοῦ φέρειν βροτῶν.   1415

ΧΟΡΟΣ

ἀλλ᾽ ὧν ἐπαιτεῖς εἰς δέον πάρεσθ᾽ ὅδε
Κρέων τὸ πράσσειν καὶ τὸ βουλεύειν, ἐπεὶ
χώρας λέλειπται μοῦνος ἀντὶ σοῦ φύλαξ.

ΟΙΔΙΠΟΥΣ

οἴμοι, τί δῆτα λέξομεν πρὸς τόνδ᾽ ἔπος;
τίς μοι φανεῖται πίστις ἔνδικος; τὰ γὰρ   1420
πάρος πρὸς αὐτὸν πάντ᾽ ἐφεύρημαι κακός.

ΚΡΕΩΝ

οὐχ ὡς γελαστής, Οἰδίπους, ἐλήλυθα,
οὐδ᾽ ὡς ὀνειδιῶν τι τῶν πάρος κακῶν.
ἀλλ᾽ εἰ τὰ θνητῶν μὴ καταισχύνεσθ᾽ ἔτι
γένεθλα, τὴν γοῦν πάντα βόσκουσαν φλόγα   1425
αἰδεῖσθ᾽ ἄνακτος Ἡλίου, τοιόνδ᾽ ἄγος

Now I've been exposed as something gross,
contaminated in my origins.
O you three roads and hidden forest grove,
you thicket and defile where three paths meet,
you who swallowed down my father's blood   [1400]
from my own hands, do you remember me,
what I did there in front of you and then
what else I did when I came here to Thebes?
Ah, you marriage rites—you gave birth to me,
and when I was born, you gave birth again,
children from the child of that same womb,
creating an incestuous blood family
of fathers, brothers, children, brides,
wives and mothers—the most atrocious act
that human beings commit! But it is wrong
to talk about what it is wrong to do,
so in the name of all the gods, act quickly—
hide me somewhere far from the land of Thebes,   [1410]
or slaughter me, or hurl me in the sea,
where you will never gaze on me again.
Come, allow yourself to touch a wretched man.
Listen to me, and do not be afraid—
for this disease infects no one but me.

CHORUS LEADER
    Creon is coming. He is just in time
    to plan and carry out what you propose.
    With you gone he's the only one still left
    to act as guardian of Thebes.

OEDIPUS
                                                    Alas,
    how will I talk to him? How can I ask him
    to put his trust in me? Not long ago   [1420]
    I showed I had no faith in him at all.

[Enter Creon]

CREON
    Oedipus, I have not come here to mock
    or blame you for disasters in the past.
    But if you can no longer value human beings,
    at least respect our lord the Sun, whose light
    makes all things grow, and do not put on show

ἀκάλυπτον οὕτω δεικνύναι, τὸ μήτε γῆ
μήτ᾽ ὄμβρος ἱερὸς μήτε φῶς προσδέξεται.
ἀλλ᾽ ὡς τάχιστ᾽ ἐς οἶκον ἐσκομίζετε·
τοῖς ἐν γένει γὰρ τἀγγενῆ μάλισθ᾽ ὁρᾶν   1430
μόνοις τ᾽ ἀκούειν εὐσεβῶς ἔχει κακά.

ΟΙΔΙΠΟΥΣ

πρὸς θεῶν, ἐπείπερ ἐλπίδος μ᾽ ἀπέσπασας,
ἄριστος ἐλθὼν πρὸς κάκιστον ἄνδρ᾽ ἐμέ,
πιθοῦ τί μοι· πρὸς σοῦ γὰρ οὐδ᾽ ἐμοῦ φράσω.

ΚΡΕΩΝ

καὶ τοῦ με χρείας ὧδε λιπαρεῖς τυχεῖν;   1435

ΟΙΔΙΠΟΥΣ

ῥῖψόν με γῆς ἐκ τῆσδ᾽ ὅσον τάχισθ᾽, ὅπου
θνητῶν φανοῦμαι μηδενὸς προσήγορος.

ΚΡΕΩΝ

ἔδρασ᾽ ἂν εὖ τοῦτ᾽ ἴσθ᾽ ἄν, εἰ μὴ τοῦ θεοῦ
πρώτιστ᾽ ἔχρῃζον ἐκμαθεῖν τί πρακτέαν.

ΟΙΔΙΠΟΥΣ

ἀλλ᾽ ἥ γ᾽ ἐκείνου πᾶσ᾽ ἐδηλώθη φάτις,   1440
τὸν πατροφόντην, τὸν ἀσεβῆ μ᾽ ἀπολλύναι.

ΚΡΕΩΝ

οὕτως ἐλέχθη ταῦθ᾽· ὅμως δ᾽ ἵν᾽ ἕσταμεν
χρείας, ἄμεινον ἐκμαθεῖν τι δραστέον.

ΟΙΔΙΠΟΥΣ

οὕτως ἄρ᾽ ἀνδρὸς ἀθλίου πεύσεσθ᾽ ὕπερ;

ΚΡΕΩΝ

καὶ γὰρ σὺ νῦν τἂν τῷ θεῷ πίστιν φέροις.   1445

pollution of this kind in such a public way,
for neither earth nor light nor sacred rain
can welcome such a sight.

[Creon speaks to the attending servants]

                    Take him inside the house
as quickly as you can. The kindest thing
would be for members of his family   [1430]
to be the only ones to see and hear him.

OEDIPUS

By all the gods, since you are acting now
so differently from what I would expect
and have come here to treat me graciously,
the very worst of men, do what I ask.
I will speak for your own benefit, not mine.

CREON

What are you so keen to get from me?

OEDIPUS

Cast me out as quickly as you can,
away from Thebes, to a place where no one,
no living human being, will cross my path.

CREON

That is something I could do, of course,
but first I wish to know what the god says
about what I should do.

OEDIPUS

                    But what he said   [1440]
was all so clear—the man who killed his father
must be destroyed. And that corrupted man
is me.

CREON

                    Yes, that is what was said. But now,
with things the way they are, the wisest thing
is to ascertain quite clearly what to do.

OEDIPUS

Will you then be making a request
on my behalf when I am so depraved?

CREON

I will. For even you must now trust in the gods.

ΟΙΔΙΠΟΥΣ

καὶ σοί γ' ἐπισκήπτω τε καὶ προστέψομαι,
τῆς μὲν κατ' οἴκους αὐτὸς ὃν θέλεις τάφον
θοῦ· καὶ γὰρ ὀρθῶς τῶν γε σῶν τελεῖς ὕπερ·
ἐμοῦ δὲ μήποτ' ἀξιωθήτω τόδε
πατρῷον ἄστυ ζῶντος οἰκητοῦ τυχεῖν,   1450
ἀλλ' ἔα με ναίειν ὄρεσιν, ἔνθα κλῄζεται
οὑμὸς Κιθαιρὼν οὗτος, ὃν μήτηρ τέ μοι
πατήρ τ' ἐθέσθην ζῶντε κύριον τάφον,
ἵν' ἐξ ἐκείνων, οἵ μ' ἀπωλλύτην, θάνω.
καίτοι τοσοῦτόν γ' οἶδα, μήτε μ' ἂν νόσον   1455
μήτ' ἄλλο πέρσαι μηδέν· οὐ γὰρ ἄν ποτε
θνῄσκων ἐσώθην, μὴ 'πί τῳ δεινῷ κακῷ.
ἀλλ' ἡ μὲν ἡμῶν μοῖρ', ὅποιπερ εἶσ', ἴτω·
παίδων δὲ τῶν μὲν ἀρσένων μή μοι, Κρέων,
προσθῇ μέριμναν· ἄνδρες εἰσίν, ὥστε μὴ   1460
σπάνιν ποτὲ σχεῖν, ἔνθ' ἂν ὦσι, τοῦ βίου·
ταῖν δ' ἀθλίαιν οἰκτραῖν τε παρθένοιν ἐμαῖν,
αἷν οὔποθ' ἡμὴ χωρὶς ἐστάθη βορᾶς
τράπεζ' ἄνευ τοῦδ' ἀνδρός, ἀλλ' ὅσων ἐγὼ
ψαύοιμι, πάντων τῶνδ' ἀεὶ μετειχέτην·   1465
αἷν μοι μέλεσθαι· καὶ μάλιστα μὲν χεροῖν
ψαῦσαί μ' ἔασον κἀποκλαύσασθαι κακά.
ἴθ' ὦναξ,
ἴθ' ὦ γονῇ γενναῖε· χερσί τὰν θιγὼν
δοκοῖμ' ἔχειν σφᾶς, ὥσπερ ἡνίκ' ἔβλεπον.   1470
τί φημί;
οὐ δὴ κλύω που πρὸς θεῶν τοῖν μοι φίλοιν
δακρυρροούντοιν, καί μ' ἐποικτίρας Κρέων
ἔπεμψέ μοι τὰ φίλτατ' ἐκγόνοιν ἐμοῖν;
λέγω τι;   1475

ΚΡΕΩΝ

λέγεις· ἐγὼ γὰρ εἰμ' ὁ πορσύνας τάδε,
γνοὺς τὴν παροῦσαν τέρψιν, ἥ σ' εἶχεν πάλαι.

OEDIPUS

    Yes, I do. And I have a task for you
    as I make this plea—that woman in the house,
    please bury her as you see fit. You are the one
    to give your own the proper funeral rites.
    But never let my father's city be condemned
    to have me living here while I still live.   [1450]
    Let me make my home up in the mountains
    by Cithaeron, whose fame is now my own.
    When my father and mother were alive,
    they chose it as my special burying place—
    and thus, when I die, I shall be following
    the orders of the ones who tried to kill me.
    And yet I know this much—no disease
    nor any other suffering can kill me—
    for I would never have been saved from death
    unless I was to suffer a strange destiny.
    But wherever my fate leads, just let it go.
    As for my two sons, Creon, there's no need
    for you to care for them on my behalf.
    They are men, and, no matter where they are,   [1460]
    they'll always have enough to live on.[21]
    But my two poor daughters have never known
    my dining table placed away from them
    or lacked their father's presence. They shared
    everything I touched—so it has always been.
    So take care of them for me. But first let me
    feel them with my hands and then I'll grieve.
    O my lord, you noble heart, let me do that—
    if my hands could touch them it would seem
    as if I were with them when I still could see.   [1470]

[Some SERVANTS lead ANTIGONE and ISMENE out of the palace]

    What's this? By all the gods I hear something—
    is it my two dear children crying . . . ?
    Has Creon taken pity on me
    and sent out the children, my dear treasures?
    Is that what's happening?

CREON

                   Yes. I sent for them.
    I know the joy they've always given you—
    the joy which you feel now.

ΟΙΔΙΠΟΥΣ

ἀλλ' εὐτυχοίης, καί σε τῆσδε τῆσδε τῆς ὁδοῦ
δαίμων ἄμεινον ἢ 'μὲ φρουρήσας τύχοι.
ὦ τέκνα, ποῦ ποτ' ἐστέ; δεῦρ' ἴτ', ἔλθετε   1480
ὡς τὰς ἀδελφὰς τάσδε τὰς ἐμὰς χέρας,
αἳ τοῦ φυτουργοῦ πατρὸς ὑμὶν ὧδ' ὁρᾶν
τὰ πρόσθε λαμπρὰ προυξένησαν ὄμματα·
ὃς ὑμίν, ὦ τέκν', οὔθ' ὁρῶν οὔθ' ἱστορῶν
πατὴρ ἐφάνθην ἔνθεν αὐτὸς ἠρόθην.   1485
καὶ σφὼ δακρύω· προσβλέπειν γὰρ οὐ σθένω·
νοούμενος τὰ λοιπὰ τοῦ πικροῦ βίου,
οἷον βιῶναι σφὼ πρὸς ἀνθρώπων χρεών.
ποίας γὰρ ἀστῶν ἥξετ' εἰς ὁμιλίας,
ποίας δ' ἑορτάς, ἔνθεν οὐ κεκλαυμέναι   1490
πρὸς οἶκον ἴξεσθ' ἀντὶ τῆς θεωρίας;
ἀλλ' ἡνίκ' ἂν δὴ πρὸς γάμων ἥκητ' ἀκμάς,
τίς οὗτος ἔσται, τίς παραρρίψει, τέκνα,
τοιαῦτ' ὀνείδη λαμβάνων, ἃ ταῖς ἐμαῖς
γοναῖσιν ἔσται σφῷν θ' ὁμοῦ δηλήματα;   1495
τί γὰρ κακῶν ἄπεστι; τὸν πατέρα πατὴρ
ὑμῶν ἔπεφνε· τὴν τεκοῦσαν ἤροσεν,
ὅθεν περ αὐτὸς ἐσπάρη, κἀκ τῶν ἴσων
ἐκτήσαθ' ὑμᾶς, ὧνπερ αὐτὸς ἐξέφυ.
τοιαῦτ' ὀνειδιεῖσθε· κᾆτα τίς γαμεῖ;   1500
οὐκ ἔστιν οὐδείς, ὦ τέκν', ἀλλὰ δηλαδὴ
χέρσους φθαρῆναι κἀγάμους ὑμᾶς χρεών.
ὦ παῖ Μενοικέως, ἀλλ' ἐπεὶ μόνος πατὴρ
ταύταιν λέλειψαι, νὼ γάρ, ὣ 'φυτεύσαμεν,
ὀλώλαμεν δύ' ὄντε, μή σφε περιίδῃς   1505
πτωχὰς ἀνάνδρους ἐκγενεῖς ἀλωμένας,
μηδ' ἐξισώσῃς τάσδε τοῖς ἐμοῖς κακοῖς.
ἀλλ' οἴκτισόν σφας, ὧδε τηλικάσδ' ὁρῶν
πάντων ἐρήμους, πλὴν ὅσον τὸ σὸν μέρος.
ξύννευσον, ὦ γενναῖε, σῇ ψαύσας χερί.   1510
πόλλ' ἂν παρῄνουν· νῦν δὲ τοῦτ' εὔχεσθέ μοι,
οὗ καιρὸς ἐᾷ ζῆν, τοῦ βίου δὲ λῴονος
ὑμᾶς κυρῆσαι τοῦ φυτεύσαντος πατρός.

OEDIPUS
I wish you well.
And for this act, may the god watch over you
and treat you better than he treated me.
Ah, my children, where are you? Come here,   [1480]
come into my arms—you are my sisters now—
feel these hands which turned your father's eyes,
once so bright, into what you see now,
these empty sockets. He was a man who,
seeing nothing, knowing nothing, fathered you
with the woman who had given birth to him.
I weep for you. Although I cannot see,
I think about your life in days to come,
the bitter life which men will force on you.
What citizens will associate with you?
What feasts will you attend and not come home
in tears, with no share in the rejoicing?   [1490]
When you're mature enough for marriage,
who will be there for you, my children,
what husband ready to assume the shame
tainting my children and their children, too?
What perversion is not manifest in us?
Your father killed his father, and then ploughed
his mother's womb—where he himself was born—
conceiving you where he, too, was conceived.
Those are the insults they will hurl at you.   [1500]
Who, then, will marry you? No one, my children.
You must wither, barren and unmarried.
Son of Menoeceus, with both parents gone,
you alone remain these children's father.
Do not let them live as vagrant paupers,
wandering around unmarried. You are
a relative of theirs—don't let them sink
to lives of desperation like my own.
Have pity. You see them now at their young age
deprived of everything except a share
in what you are. Promise me, you noble soul,
you will extend your hand to them. And you,   [1510]
my children, if your minds were now mature,
there's so much I could say. But I urge you—
pray that you may live as best you can
and lead your destined life more happily
than your own father.

ΚΡΕΩΝ

ἅλις ἵν' ἐξήκεις δακρύων· ἀλλ' ἴθι στέγης ἔσω.   1515

ΟΙΔΙΠΟΥΣ

πειστέον, κεἰ μηδὲν ἡδύ.

ΚΡΕΩΝ

πάντα γὰρ καιρῷ καλά.

ΟΙΔΙΠΟΥΣ

οἶσθ' ἐφ' οἷς οὖν εἶμι;

ΚΡΕΩΝ

λέξεις, καὶ τότ' εἴσομαι κλύων.

ΟΙΔΙΠΟΥΣ

γῆς μ' ὅπως πέμψεις ἄποικον.

ΚΡΕΩΝ

τοῦ θεοῦ μ' αἰτεῖς δόσιν.

ΟΙΔΙΠΟΥΣ

ἀλλὰ θεοῖς γ' ἔχθιστος ἥκω.

ΚΡΕΩΝ

τοιγαροῦν τεύξει τάχα.

ΟΙΔΙΠΟΥΣ

φῂς τάδ' οὖν;   1520

ΚΡΕΩΝ

ἃ μὴ φρονῶ γὰρ οὐ φιλῶ λέγειν μάτην.

ΟΙΔΙΠΟΥΣ

ἄπαγέ νύν μ' ἐντεῦθεν ἤδη.

ΚΡΕΩΝ

στεῖχέ νυν, τέκνων δ' ἀφοῦ.

CREON

                               You have grieved enough.
Now go into the house.

OEDIPUS

                               I must obey,
although that's not what I desire.

CREON

                               In due time
all things will work out for the best.

OEDIPUS

                               I will go.
But you know there are conditions.

CREON

                               Tell me.
Once I hear them, I'll know what they are.

OEDIPUS

Send me away to live outside of Thebes.

CREON

Only the god can give you what you ask.

OEDIPUS

But I've become abhorrent to the gods.

CREON

Then you should quickly get what you desire.

OEDIPUS

So you agree?   [1520]

CREON

                               I don't like to speak
thoughtlessly and say what I don't mean.

OEDIPUS

Come then, lead me off.

CREON

                               All right,
but let go of the children.

ΟΙΔΙΠΟΥΣ

μηδαμῶς ταύτας γ' ἕλῃ μου.

ΚΡΕΩΝ

πάντα μὴ βούλου κρατεῖν·
καὶ γὰρ ἁκράτησας οὔ σοι τῷ βίῳ ξυνέσπετο.

ΧΟΡΟΣ

ὦ πάτρας Θήβης ἔνοικοι, λεύσσετ', Οἰδίπους ὅδε,

ὃς τὰ κλείν' αἰνίγματ' ᾔδει καὶ κράτιστος ἦν ἀνήρ,   1525

οὗ τίς οὐ ζήλῳ πολιτῶν ἦν τύχαις ἐπιβλέπων,

εἰς ὅσον κλύδωνα δεινῆς συμφορᾶς ἐλήλυθεν.

ὥστε θνητὸν ὄντα κείνην τὴν τελευταίαν ἰδεῖν

ἡμέραν ἐπισκοποῦντα μηδέν' ὀλβίζειν, πρὶν ἂν

τέρμα τοῦ βίου περάσῃ μηδὲν ἀλγεινὸν παθών.   1530

OEDIPUS

                        No, no!

    Do not take them away from me.

CREON

    Don't try to keep control of everything.
    You have lost the power your life once had.

[CREON, OEDIPUS, ANTIGONE, ISMENE, and ATTENDANTS all enter the palace] [22]

CHORUS

    You residents of Thebes, our native land,
    look on this man, this Oedipus, the one
    who understood that celebrated riddle.
    He was the most powerful of men.
    All citizens who witnessed this man's wealth
    were envious. Now what a surging tide
    of terrible disaster sweeps around him.
    So while we wait to see that final day,
    we cannot call a mortal being happy
    before he's passed beyond life free from pain.   [1530]

NOTES

1. *Cadmus*: legendary founder of Thebes. Hence, the citizens of Thebes were often called children of Cadmus or Cadmeians.

2. *Pallas*: Pallas Athena. There were two shrines to her in Thebes. *Ismenus*: A temple to Apollo Ismenios where burnt offerings were the basis for the priest's divination.

3. *cruel singer*: a reference to the Sphinx, a monster with the body of a lion, wings, and the head and torso of a woman. After the death of king Laius, the Sphinx tyrannized Thebes by not letting anyone into or out of the city, unless the person could answer the following riddle: "What walks on four legs in the morning, on two legs at noon, and three legs in the evening?" Those who could not answer were killed and eaten. Oedipus provided the answer (a human being), and thus saved the city. The Sphinx then committed suicide.

4. *berries*: a suppliant to Apollo's shrine characteristically wore such a garland if he received favourable news.

5. *Ares*, god of war and killing, was often disapproved of by the major Olympian deities. *Amphitrite*: was a goddess of the sea, married to Poseidon.

6. *Lyceian Lord*: a reference to Apollo, god of light.

7. *. . . among gods*: Dionysus was also called Bacchus, and Thebes was sometimes called Baccheia (belonging to Bacchus). The *Maenads* are the followers of Dionysus.

8. *lustral water*: water purified in a communal religious ritual.

9. *Agenor*: King of Tyre in Phoenicia; his son *Cadmus* moved from Tyre to Greece and founded Thebes. *Polydorus*: son of Cadmus, father of Labdacus, and hence grandfather of Laius.

10. *Cithaeron*: the sacred mountain outside Thebes.

11. *Zeus' son*: a reference to Apollo. The *Furies* are the goddesses of blood revenge.

12. *Parnassus*: a famous mountain some distance from Thebes, but visible from the city.

13. *Polybus*: ruler of Corinth, who raised Oedipus and was thus believed to be his father. The house of Labdacus is the Theban royal family (i.e., Laius, Jocasta, and Creon).

14. There is some argument about who speaks which lines in 622-626 of the Greek text. I follow Jebb's suggestions, ascribing 625 to Creon, to whom it seems clearly to belong (in spite of the manuscripts) and adding a line to indicate Oedipus' response.

15. This part of the choral song makes an important distinction between two forms of self-assertive action: the first breeds self-aggrandizement and greed; the second is necessary for the protection of the state.

16. *Isthmus*: The city of Corinth stood on the narrow stretch of land (the Isthmus) connecting the Peloponnese with mainland Greece, a very strategic position.

17. *Loxias*: a common name for Apollo.

18. . . . *still carry*: the name *Oedipus* can be construed to mean either "swollen feet" or "knowledge of one's feet." Both terms evoke a strongly ironic sense of how Oedipus, for all his fame as a man of knowledge, is ignorant about his origin.

19. Cyllene's king is the god Hermes, who was born on Mount Cyllene; the Bacchanalian god is Dionysus.

20. This line refers, not to the entire story, but to what Jocasta and Oedipus have just done to themselves.

21. Oedipus' two sons, Eteocles and Polyneices, would probably be fifteen or sixteen years old at this time, not old enough to succeed Oedipus.

22. It is not entirely clear from these final lines whether Oedipus now leaves Thebes or not. According to Jebb's commentary (line 1519), in the traditional story on which Sophocles is relying, Oedipus was involuntarily held at Thebes for some time before the citizens and Creon expelled him from the city. Creon's lines suggest he is going to wait to hear from the oracle before deciding about Oedipus. However, there is a powerful dramatic logic in having Oedipus stumble off away from the palace. In Book 23 of the *Iliad*, Homer indicates that

Oedipus died at Thebes, and there were funeral games held in his honour in that city.

ΟΙΔΙΠΟΥΣ ΕΠΙ ΚΟΛΩΝΩ

OEDIPUS AT COLONUS

ΤΑ ΤΟΥ ΔΡΑΜΑΤΟΣ ΠΡΟΣΩΠΑ

ΟΙΔΙΠΟΥΣ

ΑΝΤΙΓΟΝΕ

ΙΣΜΗΝΗ

ΘΗΣΕΥΣ

ΚΡΕΩΝ

ΠΟΛΥΝΕΙΚΗΣ

ΞΕΝΟΣ

ΑΓΓΕΛΟΣ

ΧΟΡΟΣ

DRAMATIS PERSONAE

OEDIPUS: exiled king of Thebes, an old blind wanderer

ANTIGONE: daughter of Oedipus

ISMENE: daughter of Oedipus

THESEUS: king of Athens

CREON: regent at Thebes, brother of Oedipus' dead wife, Jocasta

POLYNEICES: elder son of Oedipus

STRANGER: a citizen of Colonus

MESSENGER: a servant of Theseus

CHORUS: elderly citizens of Colonus.

Οἰδίπους ἐπὶ Κολωνῷ

ΟΙΔΙΠΟΥΣ

τέκνον τυφλοῦ γέροντος Ἀντιγόνη, τίνας
χώρους ἀφίγμεθ᾽ ἢ τίνων ἀνδρῶν πόλιν;
τίς τὸν πλανήτην Οἰδίπουν καθ᾽ ἡμέραν
τὴν νῦν σπανιστοῖς δέξεται δωρήμασιν;
σμικρὸν μὲν ἐξαιτοῦντα, τοῦ σμικροῦ δ᾽ ἔτι   5
μεῖον φέροντα, καὶ τόδ᾽ ἐξαρκοῦν ἐμοί·
στέργειν γὰρ αἱ πάθαι με χὠ χρόνος ξυνὼν
μακρὸς διδάσκει καὶ τὸ γενναῖον τρίτον.
ἀλλ᾽, ὦ τέκνον, θάκησιν εἴ τινα βλέπεις
ἢ πρὸς βεβήλοις ἢ πρὸς ἄλσεσιν θεῶν,   10
στῆσόν με κἀξίδρυσον, ὡς πυθώμεθα
ὅπου ποτ᾽ ἐσμέν· μανθάνειν γὰρ ἤκομεν
ξένοι πρὸς ἀστῶν, ἃν δ᾽ ἀκούσωμεν τελεῖν.

ΑΝΤΙΓΟΝΗ

πάτερ ταλαίπωρ᾽ Οἰδίπους, πύργοι μέν, οἳ
πόλιν στέγουσιν, ὡς ἀπ᾽ ὀμμάτων, πρόσω·   15
χῶρος δ᾽ ὅδ᾽ ἱερός, ὡς ἀπεικάσαι, βρύων
δάφνης, ἐλαίας, ἀμπέλου· πυκνόπτεροι δ᾽
εἴσω κατ᾽ αὐτὸν εὐστομοῦσ᾽ ἀηδόνες·
οὗ κῶλα κάμψον τοῦδ᾽ ἐπ᾽ ἀξέστου πέτρου·
μακρὰν γὰρ ὡς γέροντι προύστάλης ὁδόν.   20

ΟΙΔΙΠΟΥΣ

κάθιζέ νύν με καὶ φύλασσε τὸν τυφλόν.

ΑΝΤΙΓΟΝΗ

χρόνου μὲν οὕνεκ᾽ οὐ μαθεῖν με δεῖ τόδε.

Oedipus at Colonus

[The action takes place in front of a grove sacred to the Furies (the Eumenides) in Colonus, a short distance from Athens. Enter OEDIPUS, led on by ANTIGONE]

OEDIPUS

>Antigone, you child of an blind old man,
>what country have we reached? Whose city state?
>What man will welcome wandering Oedipus
>with meagre gifts today? I don't need much,
>and I get even less than that small pittance.
>But that's sufficient for me. My suffering,
>all the long years I have been living through,
>and my own noble origins have taught me
>to be content with that. So, my daughter,
>if you can see a place to rest somewhere
>on public land or by a sacred grove,   [10]
>you must lead me there and let me sit,
>so we can find out where we are. We've come
>as foreigners to learn from people here
>and carry out whatever they may say.

ANTIGONE

>O father, poor tormented Oedipus,
>my eyes can glimpse, off in the distance,
>walls around the city. This place, it seems,
>is sacred ground clustered thick with grapevines,
>with laurel and olive trees. Inside the grove
>many feathered nightingales are chanting
>their sweet songs. Sit down and rest your limbs
>on this rough stone. For a man advanced in years   [20]
>you have come a long, long way.

OEDIPUS

>   All right, set me there,
>A man who cannot see requires help.

ANTIGONE *[helping Oedipus move]*

>That is a task I do not need to learn—
>not after all this time.

ΟΙΔΙΠΟΥΣ

ἔχεις διδάξαι δή μ' ὅποι καθέσταμεν;

ΑΝΤΙΓΟΝΗ

τὰς γοῦν Ἀθήνας οἶδα, τὸν δὲ χῶρον οὔ.

ΟΙΔΙΠΟΥΣ

πᾶς γάρ τις ηὔδα τοῦτό γ' ἡμὶν ἐμπόρων.   25

ΑΝΤΙΓΟΝΗ

ἀλλ' ὅστις ὁ τόπος ἦ μάθω μολοῦσά ποι;

ΟΙΔΙΠΟΥΣ

ναί, τέκνον, εἴπερ ἐστί γ' ἐξοικήσιμος.

ΑΝΤΙΓΟΝΗ

ἀλλ' ἐστὶ μὴν οἰκητός· οἴομαι δὲ δεῖν
οὐδέν· πέλας γὰρ ἄνδρα τόνδε νῷν ὁρῶ.

ΟΙΔΙΠΟΥΣ

ἦ δεῦρο προσστείχοντα κἀξορμώμενον;   30

ΑΝΤΙΓΟΝΗ

καὶ δὴ μὲν οὖν παρόντα· χὦ τί σοι λέγειν
εὔκαιρόν ἐστιν, ἔννεφ', ὡς ἀνὴρ ὅδε.

ΟΙΔΙΠΟΥΣ

ὦ ξεῖν', ἀκούων τῆσδε τῆς ὑπέρ τ' ἐμοῦ
αὐτῆς θ' ὁρώσης, οὕνεχ' ἡμὶν αἴσιος
σκοπὸς προσήκεις ὧν ἀδηλοῦμεν φράσαι—   35

ΞΕΝΟΣ

πρὶν νῦν τὰ πλείον' ἱστορεῖν, ἐκ τῆσδ' ἕδρας
ἔξελθ'· ἔχεις γὰρ χῶρον οὐχ ἁγνὸν πατεῖν.

ΟΙΔΙΠΟΥΣ

τίς δ' ἔσθ' ὁ χῶρος; τοῦ θεῶν νομίζεται;

OEDIPUS *[sitting down]*
                              Where are we?
    Can you tell me that?

ANTIGONE
                              I recognize Athens,
    but not this place.

OEDIPUS
                        Well, every traveller
    we met with on the road has told us that.

ANTIGONE
    Shall I go and find out what this place is called?

OEDIPUS
    Yes, my child—if there is anyone here.

ANTIGONE
    Well, there are houses. But I don't need to leave.
    I see someone nearby.

OEDIPUS
                        Is he coming here?   [30]
    Approaching us?

ANTIGONE
                        He's already come. Ask him
    whatever seems appropriate. He's here.

[Enter the STRANGER, a citizen of Colonus]

OEDIPUS
    O stranger, from this girl whose eyes must serve
    herself and me I learn that you have come
    as an auspicious messenger to us
    to tell us what we do not understand.

STRANGER
    Before you question me at any length,
    move from where you sit—it's a sacrilege
    to walk upon that ground.

OEDIPUS
                        What is this place?
    To which of the gods is it held sacred?

ΞΕΝΟΣ

ἄθικτος οὐδ' οἰκητός· αἱ γὰρ ἔμφοβοι
θεαί σφ' ἔχουσι, Γῆς τε καὶ Σκότου κόραι.   40

ΟΙΔΙΠΟΥΣ

τίνων τὸ σεμνὸν ὄνομ' ἂν εὐξαίμην κλύων;

ΞΕΝΟΣ

τὰς πάνθ' ὁρώσας Εὐμενίδας ὅ γ' ἐνθάδ' ἂν
εἴποι λεώς νιν· ἄλλα δ' ἀλλαχοῦ καλά.

ΟΙΔΙΠΟΥΣ

ἀλλ' ἵλεῳ μὲν τὸν ἱκέτην δεξαίατο·
ὡς οὐχ ἕδρας γῆς τῆσδ' ἂν ἐξέλθοιμ' ἔτι.   45

ΞΕΝΟΣ

τί δ' ἐστὶ τοῦτο;

ΟΙΔΙΠΟΥΣ

                    ξυμφορᾶς ξύνθημ' ἐμῆς.

ΞΕΝΟΣ

ἀλλ' οὐδ' ἐμοί τοι τοὐξανιστάναι πόλεως
δίχ' ἐστὶ θάρσος, πρίν γ' ἂν ἐνδείξω τί δρῶ.

ΟΙΔΙΠΟΥΣ

πρός νυν θεῶν, ὦ ξεῖνε, μή μ' ἀτιμάσῃς,
τοιόνδ' ἀλήτην, ὧν σε προστρέπω φράσαι.   50

ΞΕΝΟΣ

σήμαινε, κοὐκ' ἄτιμος ἔκ γ' ἐμοῦ φανεῖ.

ΟΙΔΙΠΟΥΣ

τίς ἔσθ' ὁ χῶρος δῆτ', ἐν ᾧ βεβήκαμεν;

ΞΕΝΟΣ

ὅσ' οἶδα κἀγὼ πάντ' ἐπιστήσει κλύων·
χῶρος μὲν ἱερὸς πᾶς ὅδ' ἔστ'· ἔχει δέ νιν

STRANGER
It's a holy place, where no man may stay—
a sanctuary of goddesses, daughters   [40]
of Darkness and of Earth.

OEDIPUS
                    Tell me their revered names,
so once I hear that I may pray to them.

STRANGER
The people here would call these goddesses
the Eumenides, the all-seeing Kindly Ones.[1]
But elsewhere other names serve just as well.

OEDIPUS
Then I pray they may receive their suppliant
with kindness, for from this sacred refuge,
here in this land, I never will depart.

STRANGER
What do you mean?

OEDIPUS
                                        It has been prearranged—
this is my destiny.[2]

STRANGER
                                        I do not dare
drive you away from here, until I tell
the city what I'm doing and receive
their sanction.

OEDIPUS
                            By the gods, stranger,
do not dishonour me, a poor wanderer.
I beg you—tell me what I wish to know.   [50]

STRANGER
Then speak up. I will not dishonour you.

OEDIPUS
This country we've just reached, what is it called?

STRANGER
Listen. I will tell you everything I know.
This entire place is consecrated ground,

σεμνὸς Ποσειδῶν· ἐν δ' ὁ πυρφόρος θεὸς   55
Τιτὰν Προμηθεύς· ὃν δ' ἐπιστείβεις τόπον,
χθονὸς καλεῖται τῆσδε χαλκόπους ὁδός,
ἔρεισμ' Ἀθηνῶν· οἱ δὲ πλησίοι γύαι
τόνδ' ἱππότην Κολωνὸν εὔχονται σφίσιν
ἀρχηγὸν εἶναι καὶ φέρουσι τοὔνομα   60
τὸ τοῦδε κοινὸν πάντες ὠνομασμένοι.
τοιαῦτά σοι ταῦτ' ἐστίν, ὦ ξέν', οὐ λόγοις
τιμώμεν', ἀλλὰ τῇ ξυνουσίᾳ πλέον.

ΟΙΔΙΠΟΥΣ
    ἦ γάρ τινες ναίουσι τούσδε τοὺς τόπους;

ΞΕΝΟΣ
    καὶ κάρτα, τοῦδε τοῦ θεοῦ γ' ἐπώνυμοι.   65

ΟΙΔΙΠΟΥΣ
    ἄρχει τις αὐτῶν ἢ 'πὶ τῷ πλήθει λόγος;

ΞΕΝΟΣ
    ἐκ τοῦ κατ' ἄστυ βασιλέως τάδ' ἄρχεται.

ΟΙΔΙΠΟΥΣ
    οὗτος δὲ τίς λόγῳ τε καὶ σθένει κρατεῖ;

ΞΕΝΟΣ
    Θησεὺς καλεῖται, τοῦ πρὶν Αἰγέως τόκος.

ΟΙΔΙΠΟΥΣ
    ἆρ' ἄν τις αὐτῷ πομπὸς ἐξ ὑμῶν μόλοι;   70

ΞΕΝΟΣ
    ὡς πρὸς τί λέξων ἢ καταρτύσων μολεῖν;

ΟΙΔΙΠΟΥΣ
    ὡς ἂν προσαρκῶν σμικρὰ κερδάνῃ μέγα.

ΞΕΝΟΣ
    καὶ τίς πρὸς ἀνδρὸς μὴ βλέποντος ἄρκεσις;

owned by divine Poseidon. In it, too,
dwells the Titan god, the fire bearer,
Prometheus.[3] That spot where you now sit
is called this land's bronze threshold, a place
that safeguards Athens.[4] The neighbouring lands
claim horseman Colonus was their ruler
in ancient times, and they all bear his name   [60]
in common. That's what these holy places are,
stranger. We do not honour them in story
but rather by living here among them.

OEDIPUS
So this land truly has inhabitants.

STRANGER *[pointing to a statue nearby]*
Indeed it does. And they derive their name
from that hero over there, from Colonus.[5]

OEDIPUS
Who governs them? Do they have a king,
or is there a popular assembly?

STRANGER
The king of Athens rules the people here.

OEDIPUS
What man now speaks and acts with royal power?

STRANGER
His name is Theseus, son of Aegeus,
who was king before him.

OEDIPUS
                                    Is it possible   [70]
for one of you to reach him with a message?

STRANGER
With what in mind? To tell him something
or encourage him to come in person?

OEDIPUS
To inform him that a trifling service
will garner him great reward.

STRANGER
                        What assistance
can a man who does not see provide?

Sophocles

ΟΙΔΙΠΟΥΣ

ὅσ' ἂν λέγωμεν πάνθ' ὁρῶντα λέξομεν.

ΞΕΝΟΣ

οἶσθ', ὦ ξέν', ὡς νῦν μὴ σφαλῇς; ἐπείπερ εἰ   75
γενναῖος, ὡς ἰδόντι, πλὴν τοῦ δαίμονος,
αὐτοῦ μέν' οὗπερ κἀφάνης, ἕως ἐγὼ
τοῖς ἐνθάδ' αὐτοῦ μὴ κατ' ἄστυ δημόταις
λέξω τάδ' ἐλθών· οἵδε γὰρ κρινοῦσί σοι
εἰ χρή σε μίμνειν ἢ πορεύεσθαι πάλιν.   80

ΟΙΔΙΠΟΥΣ

ὦ τέκνον, ἦ βέβηκεν ἡμὶν ὁ ξένος;

ΑΝΤΙΓΟΝΗ

βέβηκεν, ὥστε πᾶν ἐν ἡσύχῳ, πάτερ,
ἔξεστι φωνεῖν, ὡς ἐμοῦ μόνης πέλας.

ΟΙΔΙΠΟΥΣ

ὦ πότνιαι δεινῶπες, εὖτε νῦν ἕδρας
πρώτων ἐφ' ὑμῶν τῆσδε γῆς ἔκαμψ' ἐγώ,   85
Φοίβῳ τε κἀμοὶ μὴ γένησθ' ἀγνώμονες,
ὅς μοι, τὰ πόλλ' ἐκεῖν' ὅτ' ἐξέχρη κακά,
ταύτην ἔλεξε παῦλαν ἐν χρόνῳ μακρῷ,
ἐλθόντι χώραν τερμίαν, ὅπου θεῶν
σεμνῶν ἕδραν λάβοιμι καὶ ξενόστασιν,   90
ἐνταῦθα κάμψειν τὸν ταλαίπωρον βίον,
κέρδη μὲν οἰκήσαντα τοῖς δεδεγμένοις,
ἄτην δὲ τοῖς πέμψασιν, οἵ μ' ἀπήλασαν·
σημεῖα δ' ἥξειν τῶνδέ μοι παρηγγύα,
ἢ σεισμὸν ἢ βροντήν τιν' ἢ Διὸς σέλας,   95
ἔγνωκα μέν νυν ὥς με τήνδε τὴν ὁδὸν
οὐκ ἔσθ' ὅπως οὐ πιστὸν ἐξ ὑμῶν πτερὸν
ἐξήγαγ' εἰς τόδ' ἄλσος· οὐ γὰρ ἄν ποτε

OEDIPUS
The words I say have visionary power.

STRANGER
Be careful, stranger, not to come to grief.
For, quite apart from your unlucky fate,
I see you have a true nobility.
Wait where you are. I am going to go
and tell the people what is happening—
those in this district, not the city folk.
They will determine whether you should stay   [80]
or travel back again.

[The STRANGER leaves]

OEDIPUS
                              Tell me, my child,
has that stranger left us?

ANTIGONE
                              He has, father.
You are free to say whatever you wish.
I am the only person close to you.

OEDIPUS
O you fierce-eyed, reverend divinities,
since here at Athens it was at your shrine
I first sought refuge, may you not be ungracious
to Phoebus and to me. When he prophesied
the many evils I would undergo,
he said eventually I would find rest,
once I reached my final goal in a place
where I would find a sacred sanctuary
of dreadful goddesses, shelter for strangers,   [90]
and there my life of suffering would end.
By remaining in that land I would bring
advantages to those who welcomed me
and ruin to the ones who drove me out,
who exiled me from Thebes. Apollo said
that signs of this would come to me—earthquakes
and thunder or a lightning flash from Zeus.
I now recognize it surely must have been
some trusty omen sent from you that led me
on my journey to this consecrated ground.

πρώταισιν ὑμῖν ἀντέκυρσ' ὁδοιπορῶν,
νήφων ἀοίνοις, κἀπὶ σεμνὸν ἑζόμην   100
βάθρον τόδ' ἀσκέπαρνον. ἀλλά μοι, θεαί,
βίου κατ' ὀμφὰς τὰς Ἀπόλλωνος δότε
πέρασιν ἤδη καὶ καταστροφήν τινα,
εἰ μὴ δοκῶ τι μειόνως ἔχειν, ἀεὶ
μόχθοις λατρεύων τοῖς ὑπερτάτοις βροτῶν.   105
ἴτ', ὦ γλυκεῖαι παῖδες ἀρχαίου Σκότου,
ἴτ', ὦ μεγίστης Παλλάδος καλούμεναι
πασῶν Ἀθῆναι τιμιωτάτη πόλις,
οἰκτίρατ' ἀνδρὸς Οἰδίπου τόδ' ἄθλιον
εἴδωλον· οὐ γὰρ δὴ τόδ' ἀρχαῖον δέμας.   110

ΑΝΤΙΓΟΝΗ

σίγα· πορεύονται γὰρ οἵδε δή τινες
χρόνῳ παλαιοί, σῆς ἕδρας ἐπίσκοποι.

ΟΙΔΙΠΟΥΣ

σιγήσομαί τε καὶ σύ μ' ἐξ ὁδοῦ πόδα
κρύψον κατ' ἄλσος, τῶνδ' ἕως ἂν ἐκμάθω
τίνας λόγους ἐροῦσιν· ἐν γὰρ τῷ μαθεῖν   115
ἔνεστιν ηὐλάβεια τῶν ποιουμένων.

ΧΟΡΟΣ

ὅρα. τίς ἄρ' ἦν; ποῦ ναίει;
ποῦ κυρεῖ ἐκτόπιος συθεὶς ὁ πάντων
ὁ πάντων ἀκορέστατος;   120
προσδέρκου λεῦσσέ νιν,
προσπεύθου πανταχῇ.
πλανάτας πλανάτας τις ὁ πρέσβυς οὐδ'
ἔγχωρος· προσέβα γὰρ οὐκ   125
ἄν ποτ' ἀστιβὲς ἄλσος ἐς
τᾶνδ' ἀμαιμακετᾶν κορᾶν,
ἃς τρέμομεν λέγειν
καὶ παραμειβόμεσθ' ἀδέρκτως,   130

How otherwise, in my wandering around,
would I, a temperate man, first have met
you austere goddesses, who touch no wine,   [100]
or sat down on this sacred rough-hewn rock.[6]
O you deities, I pray you let me
follow what Apollo's oracle decreed
and end my life at last, unless perhaps
I seem unworthy, enslaved to misery
far worse than any other mortal man.[7]
Hear me, sweet daughters of eternal Darkness!
Hear me, city named for mighty Pallas,
O Athens, most honoured of all cities,
pity the poor ghost of that man Oedipus,
for now his old living body is no more.   [110]

ANTIGONE

You should stop talking. Some old men are coming
to check out the place where you are sitting.

OEDIPUS

I will be quiet. Hide me in the grove
some distance from the road, until I learn
what these men are saying. That is something
we must find out in order to act safely.

*[ANTIGONE leads OEDIPUS to a hiding place. Enter the CHORUS,
elderly citizens of Colonus]*

CHORUS

Look around. Who was that man,
that most presumptuous of mortals?
Where did he go when he left here?   [120]
Keep a sharp look out. Search the place.
Hunt everywhere. That old man
must be a wandering vagabond,
and not a local citizen,
for otherwise he'd never dare
to set foot in the sacred grove
dedicated to those goddesses
no one can resist—whose very names
we cannot utter without trembling,
and from whose gaze when we walk past   [130]
we avert our eyes and look away,

193

ἀφώνως, ἀλόγως τὸ τᾶς.
εὐφάμου στόμα φροντίδος
ἱέντες, τὰ δὲ νῦν τιν᾽ ἥκειν
λόγος οὐδὲν ἄζονθ᾽,
ὃν ἐγὼ λεύσσων περὶ πᾶν οὔπω   135
δύναμαι τέμενος
γνῶναι ποῦ μοί ποτε ναίει.

ΟΙΔΙΠΟΥΣ

ὅδ᾽ ἐκεῖνος ἐγώ· φωνῇ γὰρ ὁρῶ,
τὸ φατιζόμενον.

ΧΟΡΟΣ

ἰὼ ἰώ,   140
δεινὸς μὲν ὁρᾶν, δεινὸς δὲ κλύειν.

ΟΙΔΙΠΟΥΣ

μή μ᾽, ἱκετεύω, προσίδητ᾽ ἄνομον.

ΧΟΡΟΣ

Ζεῦ ἀλεξῆτορ, τίς ποθ᾽ ὁ πρέσβυς;

ΟΙΔΙΠΟΥΣ

οὐ πάνυ μοίρας εὐδαιμονίσαι
πρώτης, ὦ τῆσδ᾽ ἔφοροι χώρας.   145
δηλῶ δ᾽· οὐ γὰρ ἂν ὧδ᾽ ἀλλοτρίοις
ὄμμασιν εἷρπον
κἀπὶ σμικροῖς μέγας ὥρμουν.

ΧΟΡΟΣ

ἐή, ἀλαῶν ὀμμάτων
ἆρα καὶ ἦσθα φυτάλμιος; δυσαίων   150
μακραίων γ᾽, ὅσ᾽ ἐπεικάσαι.
ἀλλ᾽ οὐ μὰν ἔν γ᾽ ἐμοὶ
προσθήσει τάσδ᾽ ἀράς.
περᾷς γάρ, περᾷς· ἀλλ᾽ ἵνα τῷδ᾽ ἐν ἀ-   155
φθέγκτῳ μὴ προπέσῃς νάπει
ποιάεντι, κάθυδρος οὖ

without a word, our voices mute,
mouthing pious thoughts in silence.
Now, so they say, someone has come,
who has no reverence for these deities.
We've searched this sacred shrine
and caught no glimpse of him.
I do not know where he is hiding.

[OEDIPUS and ANTIGONE leave their hiding place and move forward]

OEDIPUS

    I am the one you seek. The sounds you make
    serve me instead of sight, as people say
    of men who cannot see.

CHORUS *[horrified]*

                        Aaaiii, Aaaiii!   [140]
    What a horrific sight! And that fearful voice!

OEDIPUS

    Do not consider me outside the law—
    I'm begging you!

CHORUS

                By our defender Zeus,
    who could this old man be?

OEDIPUS

                       You citizens,
    guardians of this land, I am a man whose fate
    no one could call happy. That much is clear,
    for otherwise I would not creep around
    requiring help from someone else's eyes,
    my great age propped up by this weak young girl.

CHORUS

    Ah, have you been blind since you were born?
    It looks as if a long and wretched life
    has been your lot. But if I can stop you,   [150]
    in this place you will bring no more curses
    down on yourself. You go too far—too far!
    O you most wretched of all strangers,
    do not stumble into this grassy shrine
    where no one is allowed to speak,

κρατὴρ μειλιχίων ποτῶν
ῥεύματι συντρέχει,   160
τόν, ξένε πάμμορ᾽, εὖ φύλαξαι·
μετάσταθ᾽ ἀπόβαθι. πολ-
λὰ κέλευθος ἐρατύει·
κλύεις, ὦ πολύμοχθ᾽ ἀλᾶτα;   165
λόγον εἴ τιν᾽ οἴσεις
πρὸς ἐμὰν λέσχαν, ἀβάτων ἀποβάς,
ἵνα πᾶσι νόμος,
φώνει· πρόσθεν δ᾽ ἀπερύκου.

ΟΙΔΙΠΟΥΣ
θύγατερ, ποῖ τις φροντίδος ἔλθῃ;   170

ΑΝΤΙΓΟΝΗ
ὦ πάτερ, ἀστοῖς ἴσα χρὴ μελετᾶν,
εἴκοντας ἃ δεῖ κἀκούοντας.

ΟΙΔΙΠΟΥΣ
πρόσθιγέ νύν μου.

ΑΝΤΙΓΟΝΗ
ψαύω καὶ δή.

ΟΙΔΙΠΟΥΣ
ὦ ξένε, μὴ δῆτ᾽ ἀδικηθῶ σοὶ
πιστεύσας καὶ μεταναστάς.   175

ΧΟΡΟΣ
οὔ τοι μήποτέ σ᾽ ἐκ τῶνδ᾽ ἑδράνων,
ὦ γέρον, ἄκοντά τις ἄξει.

ΟΙΔΙΠΟΥΣ
ἔτ᾽ οὖν;

ΧΟΡΟΣ
ἔτι βαῖνε πόρσω.

ΟΙΔΙΠΟΥΣ
ἔτι;   180

where honey offerings and sweet water
pour from the mixing bowl.[8]   [160]
I am giving you fair warning.
Move back from there. Withdraw,
and keep your distance. You hear me,
you long-suffering wanderer?
If you have anything to say to us,
leave that forbidden ground.
Talk where people are allowed to speak.
Until that time, be silent.

OEDIPUS
Daughter, what course of action should we choose?   [170]

ANTIGONE
We must obey the customs here, father,
act as the locals do. We must listen
and where we have no choice do what they say.

OEDIPUS
Then take my hand.

ANTIGONE
                            I have it.

OEDIPUS
                                            Strangers,
if I trust you and leave this sanctuary,
do not harm me.

CHORUS
                            Old man, no one will ever
take you from your refuge here against your will.

[OEDIPUS starts to move out of his hiding place]

OEDIPUS
Is this far enough?

CHORUS
                            Move on a little more.

OEDIPUS
Further still?

ΧΟΡΟΣ

προβίβαζε, κούρα,
πόρσω· σὺ γὰρ ἀΐεις.

ΑΝΤΙΓΟΝΗ

⟨ ... ⟩

ΟΙΔΙΠΟΥΣ

⟨ ... ⟩

ΑΝΤΙΓΟΝΗ

⟨ ... ⟩
ἕπεο μάν, ἕπε᾽ ὧδ᾽ ἀμαυρῷ   182
κώλῳ, πάτερ, σ᾽ ἄγω.

ΧΟΡΟΣ

τόλμα ξεῖνος ἐπὶ ξένης,   184
ὦ τλάμων, ὅ τι καὶ πόλις   185
τέτροφεν ἄφιλον ἀποστυγεῖν
καὶ τὸ φίλον σέβεσθαι.

ΟΙΔΙΠΟΥΣ

ἄγε νυν σύ με, παῖ,
ἵν᾽ ἂν εὐσεβίας ἐπιβαίνοντες
τὸ μὲν εἴποιμεν, τὸ δ᾽ ἀκούσαιμεν,   190
καὶ μὴ χρείᾳ πολεμῶμεν.

ΧΟΡΟΣ

αὐτοῦ· μηκέτι τοῦδ᾽ αὐτοπέτρου
βήματος ἔξω πόδα κλίνῃς.

ΟΙΔΙΠΟΥΣ

οὕτως;

ΧΟΡΟΣ

ἅλις, ὡς ἀκούεις.

ΟΙΔΙΠΟΥΣ

ἦ ἑσθῶ;   195

CHORUS

     You know what me mean, young girl—
lead him out this way.

[. . . . .]9

ANTIGONE

 Come, father, let your dark steps follow me.
 I'll lead you out.

CHORUS

     Stranger in a foreign land,
 you ill-fated man, you must have courage
 to hate what the city here has grown to hate
 and to love what it holds dear.

OEDIPUS

        Lead me out,
 my child, to where we may speak and listen,
 treading a path of pious righteousness,
 not waging war against necessity.

CHORUS

 There! Do not step beyond that rocky ledge!

OEDIPUS

 Right here?

CHORUS

    That's far enough. Are you listening?

OEDIPUS

 Should I sit down?

ΧΟΡΟΣ
>   λέχριός γ᾽ ἐπ᾽ ἄκρου
λᾶος βραχὺς ὀκλάσας.

ΑΝΤΙΓΟΝΗ
>   πάτερ, ἐμὸν τόδ᾽· ἐν ἀσυχαίᾳ

ΟΙΔΙΠΟΥΣ
>   ἰώ μοί μοι.

ΑΝΤΙΓΟΝΗ
>   βάσει βάσιν ἅρμοσαι,
γεραὸν ἐς χέρα σῶμα σὸν   200
προκλίνας φιλίαν ἐμάν.

ΟΙΔΙΠΟΥΣ
>   ὤμοι δύσφρονος ἄτας.

ΧΟΡΟΣ
>   ὦ τλάμων, ὅτε νῦν χαλᾷς,
αὔδασον, τίς ἔφυς βροτῶν;
τίς ὁ πολύπονος ἄγει; τίν᾽ ἂν   205
σοῦ πατρίδ᾽ ἐκπυθοίμαν;

ΟΙΔΙΠΟΥΣ
>   ὦ ξένοι, ἀπόπτολις· ἀλλὰ μὴ

ΧΟΡΟΣ
>   τί τόδ᾽ ἀπεννέπεις, γέρον;

ΟΙΔΙΠΟΥΣ
>   μὴ μὴ μή μ᾽ ἀνέρῃ τίς εἰμι, μηδ᾽ ἐξετάσῃς πέρα
ματεύων.   210

ΧΟΡΟΣ
>   τί τόδ᾽;

ΟΙΔΙΠΟΥΣ
>   αἰνὰ φύσις.

CHORUS

                  Move sideways and crouch there—
down on the edge of that low rock.

ANTIGONE

                                 Father,
let me do it. Gently now . . .

OEDIPUS

                         Alas for me!

ANTIGONE *[helping OEDIPUS sit down]*
    . . . match me step for step. Lean your ancient frame   [200]
here on my loving arm.

Oedipus

                             Ah, my dreadful fate!

CHORUS

    Now you are seated, you unfortunate man,
    speak to us. From what line of mortal men
    do you descend? Who are you to be led like this
    in such distress? What land do you call home?

OEDIPUS

    Strangers, I am a man who has been banished.
    I have no home. But do not . . .

CHORUS

                        What is it, old man,
    you would not have us do?

OEDIPUS

                  You must not ask . . .
you must not ask me who I am.   [210]

CHORUS

                    Why not?

OEDIPUS

    My origin is dreadful.

ΧΟΡΟΣ

αὔδα.

ΟΙΔΙΠΟΥΣ

τέκνον, ὤμοι, τί γεγώνω;

ΧΟΡΟΣ

τίνος εἶ σπέρματος, ὦ ξένε, φώνει, πατρόθεν.   215

ΟΙΔΙΠΟΥΣ

ὤμοι ἐγώ, τί πάθω, τέκνον ἐμόν;

ΑΝΤΙΓΟΝΗ

λέγ᾽, ἐπείπερ ἐπ᾽ ἔσχατα βαίνεις.

ΟΙΔΙΠΟΥΣ

ἀλλ᾽ ἐρῶ· οὐ γὰρ ἔχω κατακρυφάν.

ΧΟΡΟΣ

μακρὰ μέλλετον, ἀλλὰ τάχυνε.

ΟΙΔΙΠΟΥΣ

Λαΐου ἴστε τιν᾽;   220

ΧΟΡΟΣ

ὢ ἰοὺ ἰού.

ΟΙΔΙΠΟΥΣ

τό τε Λαβδακιδᾶν γένος;

ΧΟΡΟΣ

ὦ Ζεῦ.

ΟΙΔΙΠΟΥΣ

ἄθλιον Οἰδιπόδαν;

ΧΟΡΟΣ

σὺ γὰρ ὅδ᾽ εἶ;

ΟΙΔΙΠΟΥΣ

δέος ἴσχετε μηδὲν ὅσ᾽ αὐδῶ.

CHORUS

Tell us more.

OEDIPUS

Alas, my child! What do I say?

CHORUS

Stranger,
tell us your lineage, your father's name.

OEDIPUS

Alas my child, what will become of me?

ANTIGONE

You've come as far as you can go. You must speak.

OEDIPUS

I will speak. I cannot conceal the truth.

CHORUS

You two have been delaying for some time.
Get to the point.

OEDIPUS

Are you familiar with
the son of Laius . . .   [220]

CHORUS

O no!

OEDIPUS

. . . the race of Labdacus . . .

CHORUS

O Zeus!

OEDIPUS

. . . and the pitiful Oedipus?[10]

CHORUS

That's who you are?

OEDIPUS

You must not be afraid
of anything I say.

ΧΟΡΟΣ
　　ἰὼ ὢ ὤ.

ΟΙΔΙΠΟΥΣ
　　　　δύσμορος.

ΧΟΡΟΣ
　　　　　　ὢ ὤ.

ΟΙΔΙΠΟΥΣ
　　θύγατερ, τί ποτ᾽ αὐτίκα κύρσει;　　　　　　　　　　225

ΧΟΡΟΣ
　　ἔξω πόρσω βαίνετε χώρας.

ΟΙΔΙΠΟΥΣ
　　ἃ δ᾽ ὑπέσχεο ποῖ καταθήσεις,

ΧΟΡΟΣ
　　οὐδενὶ μοιριδία τίσις ἔρχεται
　　ἃν προπάθῃ τὸ τίνειν·
　　ἀπάτα δ᾽ ἀπάταις ἑτέραις ἑτέρα　　　　　　　　　　230
　　παραβαλλομένα πόνον, οὐ χάριν, ἀντιδίδωσιν ἔχειν.
　　σὺ δὲ τῶνδ᾽ ἑδράνων πάλιν ἔκτοπος αὖθις ἄφορμος ἐμᾶς
　　χθονὸς ἔκθορε, μή τι πέρα χρέος　　　　　　　　　　235
　　ἐμᾷ πόλει προσάψῃς.

ΑΝΤΙΓΟΝΗ
　　ὦ ξένοι αἰδόφρονες,
　　ἀλλ᾽ ἐπεὶ γεραὸν πατέρα
　　τόνδ᾽ ἐμὸν οὐκ ἀνέτλατ᾽, ἔργων
　　ἀκόντων ἀΐοντες αὐδάν,　　　　　　　　　　　　　240
　　ἀλλ᾽ ἐμὲ τὰν μελέαν, ἱκετεύομεν,
　　ὦ ξένοι, οἰκτίραθ᾽, ἃ
　　πατρὸς ὑπὲρ τοὐμοῦ μόνου
　　ἄντομαι οὐκ ἀλαοῖς προσορωμένα
　　ὄμμα σὸν ὄμμασιν, ὥς τις ἀφ᾽ αἵματος　　　　　　　245
　　ὑμετέρου προφανεῖσα, τὸν ἄθλιον
　　αἰδοῦς κῦρσαι· ἐν ὕμμι γὰρ ὡς θεῷ
　　κείμεθα τλάμονες. ἀλλ᾽ ἴτε, νεύσατε
　　τὰν ἀδόκητον χάριν·

CHORUS
                    O no! No! No!

OEDIPUS
    I am so wretched!

CHORUS
                    No! No!

OEDIPUS
                                My daughter,
    what will happen now?

CHORUS
                    You must leave this land.
    Go away!

OEDIPUS
            What about those words you swore?
    How will you keep your promises to me?[11]

CHORUS
    A man incurs no punishment from Fate
    when he responds to evils done to him.   [230]
    You deceived us—now we are doing the same.
    Such actions bring no gratifying reward
    but merely pain.[12] So you must go away,
    leave where you are sitting, set off again,
    and hurry out of Athens without delay,
    in case you bring pollution to our state.

ANTIGONE
    You reverend strangers, you do not accept
    my aged father. You have heard the stories
    and know what he did without intending to.
    But, strangers, at least pity me, a poor girl,
    I beg you, as I plead for him alone,
    my father. I implore you with these eyes,
    which can still gaze into your own, like one
    who shares your blood, let this suffering man
    win your compassion. In our wretched state
    you are like gods—we are in your power.
    Grant us this unexpected benefit!

πρός σ' ὅ τι σοι φίλον ἐκ σέθεν ἄντομαι,   250
ἢ τέκνον ἢ λέχος ἢ χρέος ἢ θεός·
οὐ γὰρ ἴδοις ἂν ἀθρῶν βροτὸν
ὅστις ἄν, εἰ θεὸς ἄγοι,
ἐκφυγεῖν δύναιτο.

ΧΟΡΟΣ

ἀλλ' ἴσθι, τέκνον Οἰδίπου, σέ τ' ἐξ ἴσου
οἰκτίρομεν καὶ τόνδε συμφορᾶς χάριν·   255
τὰ δ' ἐκ θεῶν τρέμοντες οὐ σθένοιμεν ἂν
φωνεῖν πέρα τῶν πρὸς σὲ νῦν εἰρημένων.

ΟΙΔΙΠΟΥΣ

τί δῆτα δόξης ἢ τί κληδόνος καλῆς
μάτην ῥεούσης ὠφέλημα γίγνεται,
εἰ τάς γ' Ἀθήνας φασὶ θεοσεβεστάτας   260
εἶναι, μόνας δὲ τὸν κακούμενον ξένον
σῴζειν οἵας τε καὶ μόνας ἀρκεῖν ἔχειν;
κἄμοιγε ποῦ τοῦτ' ἐστίν, οἵτινες βάθρων
ἐκ τῶνδέ μ' ἐξάραντες εἶτ' ἐλαύνετε,
ὄνομα μόνον δείσαντες; οὐ γὰρ δὴ τό γε   265
σῶμ' οὐδὲ τἄργα τἄμ'· ἐπεὶ τά γ' ἔργα μου
πεπονθότ' ἐστὶ μᾶλλον ἢ δεδρακότα,
εἴ σοι τὰ μητρὸς καὶ πατρὸς χρείη λέγειν,
ὧν οὕνεκ' ἐκφοβεῖ με· τοῦτ' ἐγὼ καλῶς
ἔξοιδα. καίτοι πῶς ἐγὼ κακὸς φύσιν,   270
ὅστις παθὼν μὲν ἀντέδρων, ὥστ' εἰ φρονῶν
ἔπρασσον, οὐδ' ἂν ὧδ' ἐγιγνόμην κακός;
νῦν δ' οὐδὲν εἰδὼς ἱκόμην ἵν' ἱκόμην,
ὑφ' ὧν δ' ἔπασχον, εἰδότων ἀπωλλύμην.
ἀνθ' ὧν ἱκνοῦμαι πρὸς θεῶν ὑμᾶς, ξένοι,   275
ὥσπερ με κἀνεστήσαθ', ὧδε σώσατε,
καὶ μὴ θεοὺς τιμῶντες εἶτα τοὺς θεοὺς
μοίρας ποιεῖσθε μηδαμῶς· ἡγεῖσθε δὲ

I'm begging you by all the things you love,   [250]
your child, your wife, your property, your gods!
No matter where you search, you will not find
a mortal man who can escape the gods
when they lead him to disaster.

CHORUS

                         Know this,
child of Oedipus, we do have pity
for you and him alike in your ordeal.
But we fear what the gods may do to us
and lack the power to say anything
other than what we have said already.

OEDIPUS

What use is a fine reputation then
or glory, if what it turns out to be
is empty breath? People claim that Athens,   [260]
more than any other place, reveres the gods
and is the only city with the strength
to save a stranger in distress—it alone
can rescue him. Yet in my situation
where are these qualities? You have made me
rise from that rock ledge and will drive me out
only because my name makes you afraid.
For surely you cannot fear my presence
or my actions, because, if I must tell
the story of my father and my mother—
which is why you fear me—then what matters
is not what I did but what I suffered.
I know that well. So how am I by birth   [270]
an evil man, when I was reacting
to others who had harmed me? Even if
I had fully known what I was doing,
you would not allege that I was evil.[13]
But as it was, when I went where I did
I knew nothing, while those who injured me
in full knowledge of what they were doing
sought my destruction.[14] And therefore, strangers,
I'm begging you, in the name of the gods,
just as you made me leave my refuge,
rescue me. While you pay tribute to the gods,
do not, at any moment, act impiously.

βλέπειν μὲν αὐτοὺς πρὸς τὸν εὐσεβῆ βροτῶν,
βλέπειν δὲ πρὸς τοὺς δυσσεβεῖς, φυγὴν δέ του   280
μήπω γενέσθαι φωτὸς ἀνοσίου βροτῶν.
ξὺν οἷς σὺ μὴ κάλυπτε τὰς εὐδαίμονας
ἔργοις Ἀθήνας ἀνοσίοις ὑπηρετῶν,
ἀλλ᾽ ὥσπερ ἔλαβες τὸν ἱκέτην ἐχέγγυον,
ῥύου με κἀκφύλασσε· μηδέ μου κάρα   285
τὸ δυσπρόσοπτον εἰσορῶν ἀτιμάσῃς,
ἥκω γὰρ ἱερὸς εὐσεβής τε καὶ φέρων
ὄνησιν ἀστοῖς τοῖσδ᾽· ὅταν δ᾽ ὁ κύριος
παρῇ τις, ὑμῶν ὅστις ἐστὶν ἡγεμών,
τότ᾽ εἰσακούων πάντ᾽ ἐπιστήσει· τὰ δὲ   290
μεταξὺ τούτου μηδαμῶς γίγνου κακός.

ΧΟΡΟΣ

τἀρβεῖν μέν, ὦ γεραιέ, τἀνθυμήματα
πολλή 'στ᾽ ἀνάγκη τἀπὸ σοῦ· λόγοισι γὰρ
οὐκ ὠνόμασται βραχέσι· τοὺς δὲ τῆσδε γῆς
ἄνακτας ἀρκεῖ ταῦτά μοι διειδέναι.   295

ΟΙΔΙΠΟΥΣ

καὶ ποῦ 'σθ᾽ ὁ κραίνων τῆσδε τῆς χώρας, ξένοι;

ΧΟΡΟΣ

πατρῷον ἄστυ γῆς ἔχει· σκοπὸς δέ νιν,
ὃς κἀμὲ δεῦρ᾽ ἔπεμψεν, οἴχεται στελῶν.

ΟΙΔΙΠΟΥΣ

ἦ καὶ δοκεῖτε τοῦ τυφλοῦ τιν᾽ ἐντροπὴν
ἢ φροντίδ᾽, ἕξειν, αὐτὸν ὥστ᾽ ἐλθεῖν πέλας;   300

ΧΟΡΟΣ

καὶ κάρθ᾽, ὅταν περ τοὔνομ᾽ αἴσθηται τὸ σόν.

ΟΙΔΙΠΟΥΣ

τίς δ᾽ ἔσθ᾽ ὁ κείνῳ τοῦτο τοὔπος ἀγγελῶν;

ΧΟΡΟΣ

μακρὰ κέλευθος· πολλὰ δ᾽ ἐμπόρων ἔπη

Consider this: they watch those who believe
as well as those who show them no respect, [280]
and never yet has any godless man
escaped them. Strangers, seek help from the gods,
and do not shame the good name of Athens
by lowering yourselves to profane deeds.
You have given this suppliant your pledge,
so take me in, protect me to the end.
This face of mine is horrible to look at,
but when you do, do not dishonour me,
for I have come, a pious, holy man,
bringing benefits to all the citizens.
Once your ruler comes, whoever he is
who is your leader, he will hear all things [290]
and understand. Meanwhile, do not harm me.

CHORUS
The argument you have just made, old man,
in words that carry weight, we must respect.
In my view this issue must be resolved
by those who rule this land.

OEDIPUS
                              And where, strangers,
is the ruler of this state?

CHORUS
                                        In the city
of his ancestors, here in this land. The scout
who sent us out has gone to summon him.

OEDIPUS
Do you think he will be concerned enough
about a blind man to come in person? [300]

CHORUS
Of course he will, once he finds out your name.

OEDIPUS
Who will tell him that?

CHORUS
                    It's a long distance,
and many things that travellers report

φιλεῖ πλανᾶσθαι, τῶν ἐκεῖνος ἄϊων,
θάρσει, παρέσται. πολὺ γάρ, ὦ γέρον, τὸ σὸν   305
ὄνομα διήκει πάντας, ὥστε κεἰ βραδὺς
εὕδει, κλύων σοῦ δεῦρ᾽ ἀφίξεται ταχύς.

ΟΙΔΙΠΟΥΣ

ἀλλ᾽ εὐτυχὴς ἵκοιτο τῇ θ᾽ αὑτοῦ πόλει
ἐμοί τε· τίς γὰρ ἐσθλὸς οὐχ αὑτῷ φίλος;

ΑΝΤΙΓΟΝΗ

ὦ Ζεῦ, τί λέξω; ποῖ φρενῶν ἔλθω, πάτερ;   310

ΟΙΔΙΠΟΥΣ

τί δ᾽ ἔστι, τέκνον Ἀντιγόνη;

ΑΝΤΙΓΟΝΗ

                         γυναῖχ᾽ ὁρῶ
στείχουσαν ἡμῶν ἆσσον, Αἰτναίας ἐπὶ
πώλου βεβῶσαν· κρατὶ δ᾽ ἡλιοστεγὴς
κυνῇ πρόσωπα Θεσσαλίς νιν ἀμπέχει.
τί φῶ;   315
ἆρ᾽ ἔστιν; ἆρ᾽ οὐκ ἔστιν; ἢ γνώμη πλανᾷ;
καὶ φημὶ κἀπόφημι κοὐκ ἔχω τί φῶ.
τάλαινα.
οὐκ ἔστιν ἄλλη· φαιδρὰ γοῦν ἀπ᾽ ὀμμάτων
σαίνει με προσστείχουσα· σημαίνει δ᾽ ὅτι   320
μόνης τόδ᾽ ἐστὶ δῆλον Ἰσμήνης κάρα.

ΟΙΔΙΠΟΥΣ

πῶς εἶπας, ὦ παῖ;

ΑΝΤΙΓΟΝΗ

                    παῖδα σήν, ἐμὴν δ᾽ ὁρᾶν
ὅμαιμον· αὐδῇ δ᾽ αὐτίκ᾽ ἔξεστιν μαθεῖν.

get passed around. There is no need to worry.
Once he hears the news, he will come to us.
We are all familiar with your name, old man,
so even if the king is tired and resting,
when he learns of you he'll soon be here.

OEDIPUS

    May he get here quickly and bring good fortune
    to me and to his city. What decent man
    does not help himself by helping others?

ANTIGONE

    O Zeus! What am I going to say, father?   [310]
    What should I think?

OEDIPUS

                        Antigone my child,
    what is it?

ANTIGONE

                I see a woman coming here
    riding a pony—a young Sicilian horse.
    She's wearing a Thessalian cloth hat
    to keep her face protected from the sun.
    What am I to say? Is it her or not?
    My mind keeps changing! Should I say it's her
    or someone else? What a wretched business!
    Yes, it must be her. As she gets closer,
    the brightness in her eyes is welcoming me.
    She's giving me a signal! It's obvious—   [320]
    the rider has to be Ismene.

OEDIPUS

                     My child,
    what are you saying?

ANTIGONE

                       I see my sister,
    your daughter! You'll recognize her soon enough,
    once you hear her voice.

[Enter ISMENE] [15]

ΙΣΜΗΝΗ
ὦ δισσὰ πατρὸς καὶ κασιγνήτης ἐμοὶ
ἥδιστα προσφωνήμαθ᾽, ὡς ὑμᾶς μόλις   325
εὑροῦσα λύπῃ δεύτερον μόλις βλέπω.

ΟΙΔΙΠΟΥΣ
ὦ τέκνον, ἥκεις;

ΙΣΜΗΝΗ
                    ὦ πάτερ δύσμοιρ᾽ ὁρᾶν.

ΟΙΔΙΠΟΥΣ
τέκνον, πέφηνας;

ΙΣΜΗΝΗ
                    οὐκ ἄνευ μόχθου γέ μοι.

ΟΙΔΙΠΟΥΣ
πρόσψαυσον, ὦ παῖ.

ΙΣΜΗΝΗ
                    θιγγάνω δυοῖν ὁμοῦ.

ΟΙΔΙΠΟΥΣ
ὦ σπέρμ᾽ ὅμαιμον.   330

ΙΣΜΗΝΗ
                    ὦ δυσάθλιαι τροφαί.

ΟΙΔΙΠΟΥΣ
ἦ τῆσδε κἀμοῦ;

ΙΣΜΗΝΗ
                    δυσμόρου τ᾽ ἐμοῦ τρίτης.

ΟΙΔΙΠΟΥΣ
τέκνον, τί δ᾽ ἦλθες;

ΙΣΜΗΝΗ
                    σῇ, πάτερ, προμηθίᾳ.

ISMENE

> Ah, there you are, you two,
my father and my sister, a double joy
to utter those two words. How difficult
it was to find you—and now how painful
it is to look at you!

OEDIPUS

> Are you here, my child?

ISMENE

O father, your fate is sad to witness!

OEDIPUS

O Ismene, have you really come?

ISMENE

> Yes I have.
But travelling here was not easy for me.

OEDIPUS

Touch me, my child.

ISMENE

> I'll hold you both at once.

OEDIPUS

O children of my blood!

ISMENE

> What wretched lives!

OEDIPUS

Antigone's and mine?

ISMENE

> And mine as well.
I am the third whose life is miserable.

OEDIPUS

Child, why have you come?

ISMENE

> I came for your sake—
I'm concerned about you.

ΟΙΔΙΠΟΥΣ

πότερα πόθοισι;

ΙΣΜΗΝΗ

καὶ λόγων γ᾽ αὐτάγγελος,
ξὺν ᾧπερ εἶχον οἰκετῶν πιστῷ μόνῳ.

ΟΙΔΙΠΟΥΣ

οἱ δ᾽ αὐθόμαιμοι ποῦ νεανίαι πονεῖν;   335

ΙΣΜΗΝΗ

εἴσ᾽ οὗπέρ εἰσι· δεινὰ τἀν κείνοις τανῦν.

ΟΙΔΙΠΟΥΣ

ὦ πάντ᾽ ἐκείνω τοῖς ἐν Αἰγύπτῳ νόμοις
φύσιν κατεικασθέντε καὶ βίου τροφάς·
ἐκεῖ γὰρ οἱ μὲν ἄρσενες κατὰ στέγας
θακοῦσιν ἱστουργοῦντες, αἱ δὲ σύννομοι   340
τἄξω βίου τροφεῖα πορσύνουσ᾽ ἀεί.
σφῷν δ᾽, ὦ τέκν᾽, οὓς μὲν εἰκὸς ἦν πονεῖν τάδε,
κατ᾽ οἶκον οἰκουροῦσιν ὥστε παρθένοι,
σφὼ δ᾽ ἀντ᾽ ἐκείνων τἀμὰ δυστήνου κακὰ
ὑπερπονεῖτον. ἡ μὲν ἐξ ὅτου νέας   345
τροφῆς ἔληξε καὶ κατίσχυσεν δέμας,
ἀεὶ μεθ᾽ ἡμῶν δύσμορος πλανωμένη
γερονταγωγεῖ, πολλὰ μὲν κατ᾽ ἀγρίαν
ὕλην ἄσιτος νηλίπους τ᾽ ἀλωμένη,
πολλοῖσι δ᾽ ὄμβροις ἡλίου τε καύμασιν   350
μοχθοῦσα τλήμων δεύτερ᾽ ἡγεῖται τὰ τῆς
οἴκοι διαίτης, εἰ πατὴρ τροφὴν ἔχοι.
σὺ δ᾽, ὦ τέκνον, πρόσθεν μὲν ἐξίκου πατρὶ
μαντεῖ᾽ ἄγουσα πάντα, Καδμείων λάθρα,
ἃ τοῦδ᾽ ἐχρήσθη σώματος, φύλαξ τέ μου   355
πιστὴ κατέστης, γῆς ὅτ᾽ ἐξηλαυνόμην·
νῦν δ᾽ αὖ τίν᾽ ἥκεις μῦθον, Ἰσμήνη, πατρὶ
φέρουσα; τίς σ᾽ ἐξῆρεν οἴκοθεν στόλος;
ἥκεις γὰρ οὐ κενή γε, τοῦτ᾽ ἐγὼ σαφῶς
ἔξοιδα, μὴ οὐχὶ δεῖμ᾽ ἐμοὶ φέρουσά τι.   360

OEDIPUS

Did you miss me?

ISMENE

Yes . . . and I came in person to bring news
with the only trusty servant I possess.

OEDIPUS

Where are your young brothers? They should help you.

ISMENE

They are where they are. Their situation
at the present time is dreadful.

OEDIPUS

Those two!
In their style of life and dispositions,
they always seem to like Egyptian ways,
for in that land men sit around the house
working the loom, while women leave the home
all the time to bring back what they live on.   [340]
And in your case, my daughters, those two sons,
who should be doing the work, remain at home,
like girls, while you two assume the burden
of your poor father's pain, instead of them.
This one here, since she stopped being a child
and had sufficient strength, has constantly
been an old man's guide on his harsh journeys,
often wandering barefoot and famished
through savage woods and often beaten down   [350]
by storms or the sun's unrelenting heat.
She resolutely sets aside the comforts
home provides, so her father can have food.
And you too, my child, in earlier days,
without the knowledge of those men in Thebes,
came to your father, bringing him reports
of all the oracles concerning Oedipus.
When I was exiled, driven from that land,
you became a faithful sentry for me.
And now here you are again, Ismene.
What recent news have you brought your father?
Why have you made this journey from your home?
You've not come empty handed—that I know—
not without bringing me some new concern.   [360]

ΙΣΜΗΝΗ

ἐγὼ τὰ μὲν παθήμαθ' ἅπαθον, πάτερ,
ζητοῦσα τὴν σὴν ποῦ κατοικοίης τροφήν,
παρεῖσ' ἐάσω· δὶς γὰρ οὐχὶ βούλομαι
πονοῦσά τ' ἀλγεῖν καὶ λέγουσ' αὖθις πάλιν.
ἃ δ' ἀμφὶ τοῖν σοῖν δυσμόροιν παίδοιν κακὰ   365
νῦν ἐστι, ταῦτα σημανοῦσ' ἐλήλυθα.
πρὶν μὲν γὰρ αὐτοῖς ἦν ἔρως Κρέοντί τε
θρόνους ἐᾶσθαι μηδὲ χραίνεσθαι πόλιν,
λόγῳ σκοποῦσι τὴν πάλαι γένους φθοράν,
οἵα κατέσχε τὸν σὸν ἄθλιον δόμον·   370
νῦν δ' ἐκ θεῶν του κἀλιτηρίου φρενὸς
εἰσῆλθε τοῖν τρὶς ἀθλίοιν ἔρις κακή,
ἀρχῆς λαβέσθαι καὶ κράτους τυραννικοῦ.
χὠ μὲν νεάζων καὶ χρόνῳ μείων γεγὼς
τὸν πρόσθε γεννηθέντα Πολυνείκη θρόνων   375
ἀποστερίσκει, κἀξελήλακεν πάτρας.
ὁ δ', ὡς καθ' ἡμᾶς ἔσθ' ὁ πληθύων λόγος,
τὸ κοῖλον Ἄργος βὰς φυγὰς προσλαμβάνει
κῆδός τε καινὸν καὶ ξυνασπιστὰς φίλους
ὡς αὐτίκ' Ἄργος ἢ τὸ Καδμείων πέδον   380
τιμῇ καθέξον ἢ πρὸς οὐρανὸν βιβῶν.
ταῦτ' οὐκ ἀριθμός ἐστιν, ὦ πάτερ, λόγων,
ἀλλ' ἔργα δεινά· τοὺς δὲ σοὺς ὅπου θεοὶ
πόνους κατοικτιοῦσιν οὐκ ἔχω μαθεῖν.

ΟΙΔΙΠΟΥΣ

ἤδη γὰρ ἔσχες ἐλπίδ' ὡς ἐμοῦ θεοὺς   385
ὥραν τιν' ἕξειν, ὥστε σωθῆναί ποτε;

ΙΣΜΗΝΗ

ἔγωγε τοῖς νῦν γ', ὦ πάτερ, μαντεύμασιν.

ΟΙΔΙΠΟΥΣ

ποίοισι τούτοις; τί δὲ τεθέσπισται, τέκνον;

ISMENE

    Father, I will not speak of what I suffered
in my attempts to find out where you live.
I do not wish to undergo that pain
a second time by telling you the story.
I came to talk about the fearful things
happening with your two ill-fated sons.
At first, being reasonable, they thought
about that old curse on the family,
how it has clung to your unlucky race,
and to make sure the city did not suffer
from pollution, they both wanted Creon   [370]
to be given the throne.[16] But now, urged on
by some god or their own corrupted minds,
these triply-wretched men are now engaged
in vicious war, trying to seize the throne
and win a tyrant's power. The younger one
has stripped his older brother, Polyneices,
of power and expelled him from his home.[17]
So Polyneices, according to what people say
throughout the city, has fled for refuge
to the Argos valley and is taking
a new wife there, a foreigner.[18] His friends
are now comrades in arms, and they intend
that Argos will soon seize Cadmean land   [380]
and win great honour or else sing their praise,
exalting them up to the heavens.[19] Father,
what I have said is not just idle chat!
No! These are desperate acts. At what point
the gods will pity you in your distress
I do not know.

OEDIPUS

          Do you have some sudden hope
the gods will ever care enough about me
to grant me my salvation?

ISMENE

                    Yes, father,
that's what I think from recent oracles.

OEDIPUS

    What are they? My child, what has been foretold?

ΙΣΜΗΝΗ

 σὲ τοῖς ἐκεῖ ζητητὸν ἀνθρώποις ποτὲ

 θανόντ᾽ ἔσεσθαι ζῶντά τ᾽ εὐσοίας χάριν.   390

ΟΙΔΙΠΟΥΣ

 τίς δ᾽ ἂν τοιοῦδ᾽ ὑπ᾽ ἀνδρὸς εὖ πράξειεν ἄν;

ΙΣΜΗΝΗ

 ἐν σοὶ τὰ κείνων φασὶ γίγνεσθαι κράτη.

ΟΙΔΙΠΟΥΣ

 ὅτ᾽ οὐκέτ᾽ εἰμί, τηνικαῦτ᾽ ἄρ᾽ εἴμ᾽ ἀνήρ;

ΙΣΜΗΝΗ

 νῦν γὰρ θεοί σ᾽ ὀρθοῦσι, πρόσθε δ᾽ ὤλλυσαν.

ΟΙΔΙΠΟΥΣ

 γέροντα δ᾽ ὀρθοῦν φλαῦρον ὃς νέος πέσῃ.   395

ΙΣΜΗΝΗ

 καὶ μὴν Κρέοντά γ᾽ ἴσθι σοι τούτων χάριν

 ἥξοντα βαιοῦ κοὐχὶ μυρίου χρόνου.

ΟΙΔΙΠΟΥΣ

 ὅπως τί δράσῃ, θύγατερ; ἑρμήνευέ μοι.

ΙΣΜΗΝΗ

 ὥς σ᾽ ἄγχι γῆς στήσωσι Καδμείας, ὅπως

 κρατῶσι μὲν σοῦ, γῆς δὲ μὴ ᾽μβαίνῃς ὅρων.   400

ΟΙΔΙΠΟΥΣ

 ἡ δ᾽ ὠφέλησις τίς θύρασι κειμένου;

ΙΣΜΗΝΗ

 κείνοις ὁ τύμβος δυστυχῶν ὁ σὸς βαρύς.

ΟΙΔΙΠΟΥΣ

 κἄνευ θεοῦ τις τοῦτό γ᾽ ἂν γνώμῃ μάθοι.

ISMENE

    The people of Thebes will soon seek you out,

    alive or dead, for their own security. [390]

OEDIPUS

    Who might benefit from a man like me?

ISMENE

    People say their power depends on you.

OEDIPUS

    And so when I am no longer living,

    at that point I truly become someone?

ISMENE

    Yes. For the gods are now supporting you.

    Earlier they were set on your destruction.

OEDIPUS

    That is mean-spirited—to restore power

    to an old man who in his youth was crushed.

ISMENE

    Whatever the cause, you should think of this:

    Creon will be coming here to deal with you—

    and soon. It will not take him long.

OEDIPUS

                          What for?

    Tell me why he would do that, my daughter.

ISMENE

    To set you up near Theban territory,

    so they can use their power to control you,

    without you setting foot inside the state. [400]

OEDIPUS

    What help am I to them if I'm lying there

    outside their borders?

ISMENE

                         They face disaster

    should someone fail to pay your tomb due honours.

OEDIPUS

    This I could assume without help from the gods.

ΙΣΜΗΝΗ

τούτου χάριν τοίνυν σε προσθέσθαι πέλας
χώρας θέλουσι, μηδ᾽ ἵν᾽ ἂν σαυτοῦ κρατοῖς.   405

ΟΙΔΙΠΟΥΣ

ἢ καὶ κατασκιῶσι Θηβαίᾳ κόνει;

ΙΣΜΗΝΗ

ἀλλ᾽ οὐκ ἐᾷ τοὔμφυλον αἷμά σ᾽, ὦ πάτερ.

ΟΙΔΙΠΟΥΣ

οὐκ ἄρ᾽ ἐμοῦ γε μὴ κρατήσωσίν ποτε.

ΙΣΜΗΝΗ

ἔσται ποτ᾽ ἆρα τοῦτο Καδμείοις βάρος.

ΟΙΔΙΠΟΥΣ

ποίας φανείσης, ὦ τέκνον, συναλλαγῆς;   410

ΙΣΜΗΝΗ

τῆς σῆς ὑπ᾽ ὀργῆς, σοῖς ὅταν στῶσιν τάφοις.

ΟΙΔΙΠΟΥΣ

ἃ δ᾽ ἐννέπεις, κλύουσα τοῦ λέγεις, τέκνον;

ΙΣΜΗΝΗ

ἀνδρῶν θεωρῶν Δελφικῆς ἀφ᾽ ἑστίας.

ΟΙΔΙΠΟΥΣ

καὶ ταῦτ᾽ ἐφ᾽ ἡμῖν Φοῖβος εἰρηκὼς κυρεῖ;

ΙΣΜΗΝΗ

ὥς φασιν οἱ μολόντες εἰς Θήβης πέδον.   415

ΟΙΔΙΠΟΥΣ

παίδων τις οὖν ἤκουσε τῶν ἐμῶν τάδε;

ISMENE

    That's why they want to keep you near their land,
    but not where you might live by your own rules.

OEDIPUS

    Will they bury me in Theban soil?

ISMENE

                             No.

    That's not allowed, father. You are guilty
    of killing one of your own blood.

OEDIPUS

                 In that case
    they will never get their hands on me!

ISMENE

    At some point that will be calamitous
    for citizens of Thebes.

OEDIPUS

            How will that happen,   [410]
    my child? Under what conditions?

ISMENE

             From your anger,
    when they stand beside your tomb.

OEDIPUS

             Tell me, Ismene,
    where did you hear these things you're saying?

ISMENE

    From sacred messengers when they returned
    from the shrine at Delphi.

OEDIPUS

             Has Phoebus uttered
    all these things about me?

ISMENE

            So those men said
    when they came back to Thebes.

OEDIPUS

         What about my sons—
    has either of them heard this prophecy?

Sophocles

ΙΣΜΗΝΗ

ἄμφω γ' ὁμοίως, κἀξεπίστασθον καλῶς.

ΟΙΔΙΠΟΥΣ

κᾆθ' οἱ κάκιστοι τῶνδ' ἀκούσαντες, πάρος
τοὐμοῦ πόθου προύθεντο τὴν τυραννίδα;

ΙΣΜΗΝΗ

ἀλγῶ κλύουσα ταῦτ' ἐγώ, φέρω δ' ὅμως.   420

ΟΙΔΙΠΟΥΣ

ἀλλ' οἱ θεοί σφιν μήτε τὴν πεπρωμένην
ἔριν κατασβέσειαν, ἔν τ' ἐμοὶ τέλος
αὐτοῖν γένοιτο τῆσδε τῆς μάχης πέρι,
ἧς νῦν ἔχονται κἀπαναίρονται δόρυ·
ὡς οὔτ' ἂν ὃς νῦν σκῆπτρα καὶ θρόνους ἔχει   425
μείνειεν οὔτ' ἂν οὑξεληλυθὼς πάλιν
ἔλθοι ποτ' αὖθις· οἵ γε τὸν φύσαντ' ἐμὲ
οὕτως ἀτίμως πατρίδος ἐξωθούμενον
οὐκ ἔσχον οὐδ' ἤμυναν, ἀλλ' ἀνάστατος
αὐτοῖς ἐπέμφθην κἀξεκηρύχθην φυγάς.   430
εἴποις ἂν ὡς θέλοντι τοῦτ' ἐμοὶ τότε
πόλις τὸ δῶρον εἰκότως κατήνεσεν.
οὐ δῆτ', ἐπεί τοι τὴν μὲν αὐτίχ' ἡμέραν,
ὁπηνίκ' ἔζει θυμός, ἥδιστον δέ μοι
τὸ κατθανεῖν ἦν καὶ τὸ λευσθῆναι πέτροις,   435
οὐδεὶς ἔρωτ' ἐς τόνδ' ἐφαίνετ' ὠφελῶν·
χρόνῳ δ', ὅτ' ἤδη πᾶς ὁ μόχθος ἦν πέπων,
κἀμάνθανον τὸν θυμὸν ἐκδραμόντα μοι
μείζω κολαστὴν τῶν πρὶν ἡμαρτημένων,
τὸ τηνίκ' ἤδη τοῦτο μὲν πόλις βίᾳ   440
ἤλαυνέ μ' ἐκ γῆς χρόνιον, οἱ δ' ἐπωφελεῖν,
οἱ τοῦ πατρός, τῷ πατρὶ δυνάμενοι, τὸ δρᾶν
οὐκ ἠθέλησαν, ἀλλ' ἔπους σμικροῦ χάριν
φυγάς σφιν ἔξω πτωχὸς ἠλώμην ἀεί.

ISMENE
    Yes, both of them. They know all about it.

OEDIPUS
    So those two sons, the very worst of men,
    heard of this, and instead of loving me,
    preferred to seek the throne.[20]

ISMENE
                      To listen to this   [420]
    is difficult, but it's the painful truth.

OEDIPUS
    Well then, I pray the gods will not prevent
    the predestined quarrel of these two sons.
    I wish I could be the final arbiter
    of this battle they are about to fight,
    levelling spears against each other. For then
    the one who holds the sceptre and the throne
    would not survive, and the one in exile
    would not be coming back. I am their father,
    but when the Thebans drove me from my home
    in great disgrace, they did not intervene.
    Nor did they defend me. Those two looked on,
    as I was exiled and the herald cried   [430]
    the edict of my banishment. You might say
    that that was what I wanted at the time
    and thus the city did the proper thing
    in granting me that gift. That is not true!
    For on the very day when my heart burned
    and my sweetest wish was death by stoning,
    no one appeared to grant what I desired.
    Later on, once all my anger ebbed away,
    I thought my passionate heart had sought
    a punishment too great for past mistakes,
    but then the city, after all that time,   [440]
    forced me out of Thebes and into exile.[21]
    At that point those two sons could well have helped—
    two children taking care of their own father.
    But they refused! They did not say a thing,
    not even one small word! By doing that,
    those two abandoned me, let me wander
    for all eternity an exiled beggar!

ἐκ ταῖνδε δ', οὔσαιν παρθένοιν, ὅσον φύσις 445
δίδωσιν αὐταῖν, καὶ τροφὰς ἔχω βίου
καὶ γῆς ἄδειαν καὶ γένους ἐπάρκεσιν·
τὼ δ' ἀντὶ τοῦ φύσαντος εἱλέσθην θρόνους
καὶ σκῆπτρα κραίνειν καὶ τυραννεύειν χθονός.
ἀλλ' οὔ τι μὴ λάχωσι τοῦδε συμμάχου, 450
οὐδέ σφιν ἀρχῆς τῆσδε Καδμείας ποτὲ
ὄνησις ἥξει· τοῦτ' ἐγῷδα, τῆσδέ τε
μαντεῖ' ἀκούων συννοῶν τε τἀξ ἐμοῦ
παλαίφαθ' ἁμοὶ Φοῖβος ἤνυσέν ποτε.
πρὸς ταῦτα καὶ Κρέοντα πεμπόντων ἐμοῦ 455
μαστῆρα, κεἴ τις ἄλλος ἐν πόλει σθένει.
ἐὰν γὰρ ὑμεῖς, ὦ ξένοι, θέληθ' ὁμοῦ
προστάτισι ταῖς σεμναῖσι δημούχοις θεαῖς
ἀλκὴν ποεῖσθαι, τῇδε τῇ πόλει μέγαν
σωτῆρ' ἀρεῖσθε, τοῖς δ' ἐμοῖς ἐχθροῖς πόνους. 460

ΧΟΡΟΣ
ἐπάξιος μέν, Οἰδίπους, κατοικτίσαι,
αὐτός τε παῖδές θ' αἵδ'· ἐπεὶ δὲ τῆσδε γῆς
σωτῆρα σαυτὸν τῷδ' ἐπεμβάλλεις λόγῳ,
παραινέσαι σοι βούλομαι τὰ σύμφορα.

ΟΙΔΙΠΟΥΣ
ὦ φίλταθ', ὡς νῦν πᾶν τελοῦντι προξένει. 465

ΧΟΡΟΣ
θοῦ νῦν καθαρμὸν τῶνδε δαιμόνων, ἐφ' ἃς
τὸ πρῶτον ἵκου καὶ κατέστειψας πέδον.

ΟΙΔΙΠΟΥΣ
τρόποισι ποίοις; ὦ ξένοι, διδάσκετε.

ΧΟΡΟΣ
πρῶτον μὲν ἱερὰς ἐξ ἀειρύτου χοὰς
κρήνης ἐνεγκοῦ, δι' ὁσίων χειρῶν θιγών. 470

It is from these two here, these girls, I get
my daily food, a secure resting place,
and family care, as much as nature
enables them to give. But their brothers
betrayed their father for throne and sceptre
and power to rule the land. Those sons of mine
will never win me as an ally—never!   [450]
And they will derive no benefits at all
from ruling Thebes as king. All this I know
from listening to this girl's prophecies
and thinking about those I remember
from long ago, which Phoebus Apollo
is now at last bringing to fruition.[22]
So let them dispatch Creon to find me,
or anyone else with power in Thebes.
If you, strangers, are willing to protect me,
assisted by these revered goddesses
who guard your people, then you will receive
a powerful saviour for the city
and cause my enemies distress.   [460]

CHORUS
                                           Oedipus,
you have earned our sympathy, you and these girls,
and since, in addition to your story,
you offer yourself as this land's saviour,
I would like now, for your own benefit,
to offer some advice.

OEDIPUS
                         My dearest friends,
give me your help, and I will carry out
everything you say.

CHORUS
                         You must cleanse yourself
before these goddesses you first approached
and on whose grounds you trampled.

OEDIPUS
                                          Tell me how—
instruct me, strangers, what I should perform.

CHORUS
First of all, once you have purified your hands,
bring sacred water from the ever-flowing spring.   [470]

225

ΟΙΔΙΠΟΥΣ

    ὅταν δὲ τοῦτο χεῦμ᾽ ἀκήρατον λάβω;

ΧΟΡΟΣ

    κρατῆρές εἰσιν, ἀνδρὸς εὔχειρος τέχνη,
    ὧν κρᾶτ᾽ ἔρεψον καὶ λαβὰς ἀμφιστόμους.

ΟΙΔΙΠΟΥΣ

    θαλλοῖσιν ἢ κρόκαισιν, ἢ ποίῳ τρόπῳ;

ΧΟΡΟΣ

    οἰός γε νεαρᾶς νεοπόκῳ μαλλῷ λαβών.   475

ΟΙΔΙΠΟΥΣ

    εἶεν· τὸ δ᾽ ἔνθεν ποῖ τελευτῆσαί με χρή;

ΧΟΡΟΣ

    χοὰς χέασθαι στάντα πρὸς πρώτην ἕω.

ΟΙΔΙΠΟΥΣ

    ἦ τοῖσδε κρωσσοῖς οἷς λέγεις χέω τάδε;

ΧΟΡΟΣ

    τρισσάς γε πηγάς· τὸν τελευταῖον δ᾽ ὅλον.

ΟΙΔΙΠΟΥΣ

    τοῦ τόνδε πλήσας θῶ; δίδασκε καὶ τόδε.   480

ΧΟΡΟΣ

    ὕδατος, μελίσσης· μηδὲ προσφέρειν μέθυ.

ΟΙΔΙΠΟΥΣ

    ὅταν δὲ τούτων γῆ μελάμφυλλος τύχῃ;

ΧΟΡΟΣ

    τρὶς ἐννέ᾽ αὐτῇ κλῶνας ἐξ ἀμφοῖν χεροῖν
    τιθεὶς ἐλαίας τάσδ᾽ ἐπεύχεσθαι λιτάς.

ΟΙΔΙΠΟΥΣ

    τούτων ἀκοῦσαι βούλομαι· μέγιστα γάρ.   485

OEDIPUS

When I bring this pure water back, what then?

CHORUS

There are bowls, the work of skilful craftsmen—
cover the rims and handles on both sides.

OEDIPUS

Cover them with what? Wool or olive twigs?

CHORUS

Use wool freshly shorn from a female lamb.

OEDIPUS

All right. What next? How do I end the rite?

CHORUS

Pour your libations facing early dawn.

OEDIPUS

I pour them from the mixing bowls you mentioned?

CHORUS

Yes, from two bowls pour three separate streams,
but with the last one pour it all at once.

OEDIPUS

Before I set the third bowl with the others,   [480]
what do I fill it with? Tell me that.

CHORUS

With water and honey, but add no wine.

OEDIPUS

And when the dark leaf-covered earth has drunk,
what then?

CHORUS

            With both hands set down olive twigs—
three sets of nine—while you recite this prayer . . .

OEDIPUS

I need to hear the prayer—that's most important.

Sophocles

ΧΟΡΟΣ

ὥς σφας καλοῦμεν Εὐμενίδας, ἐξ εὐμενῶν
στέρνων δέχεσθαι τὸν ἱκέτην σωτήριον,
αἰτοῦ σύ τ᾽ αὐτὸς κεἴ τις ἄλλος ἀντὶ σοῦ,
ἄπυστα φωνῶν μηδὲ μηκύνων βοήν·
ἔπειτ᾽ ἀφέρπειν ἄστροφος. καὶ ταῦτά σοι   490
δράσαντι θαρσῶν ἂν παρασταίην ἐγώ·
ἄλλως δὲ δειμαίνοιμ᾽ ἄν, ὦ ξέν᾽, ἀμφὶ σοι.

ΟΙΔΙΠΟΥΣ

ὦ παῖδε, κλύετον τῶνδε προσχώρων ξένων;

ΑΝΤΙΓΟΝΗ

ἠκούσαμέν τε χὤ τι δεῖ πρόστασσε δρᾶν.

ΟΙΔΙΠΟΥΣ

ἐμοὶ μὲν οὐχ ὁδωτά· λείπομαι γὰρ ἐν   495
τῷ μὴ δύνασθαι μήδ᾽ ὁρᾶν, δυοῖν κακοῖν·
σφῷν δ᾽ ἀτέρα μολοῦσα πραξάτω τάδε.
ἀρκεῖν γὰρ οἶμαι κἀντὶ μυρίων μίαν
ψυχὴν τάδ᾽ ἐκτίνουσαν, ἢν εὔνους παρῇ.
ἀλλ᾽ ἐν τάχει τι πράσσετον· μόνον δέ με   500
μὴ λείπετ᾽· οὐ γὰρ ἂν σθένοι τοὐμὸν δέμας
ἔρημον ἕρπειν οὐδ᾽ ὑφηγητοῦ δίχα.

ΙΣΜΗΝΗ

ἀλλ᾽ εἶμ᾽ ἐγὼ τελοῦσα· τὸν τόπον δ᾽ ἵνα
χρῆσταί μ᾽ ἐφευρεῖν, τοῦτο βούλομαι μαθεῖν.

ΧΟΡΟΣ

τοὐκεῖθεν ἄλσους, ὦ ξένη, τοῦδ᾽· ἢν δέ του   505
σπάνιν τιν᾽ ἴσχῃς, ἔστ᾽ ἔποικος ὃς φράσει.

ΙΣΜΗΝΗ

χωροῖμ᾽ ἂν ἐς τόδ᾽· Ἀντιγόνη, σὺ δ᾽ ἐνθάδε
φύλασσε πατέρα τόνδε· τοῖς τεκοῦσι γὰρ
οὐδ᾽ εἰ πονεῖ τις, δεῖ πόνου μνήμην ἔχειν.

228

CHORUS

> Pray that, since we call them the Kindly Ones,
> they will graciously receive a suppliant
> and save him. You must make this prayer yourself
> or have someone recite it in your place.
> Speak so no one hears you. Don't pray out loud.
> Then leave the place, and do not turn around.   [490]
> If you do this, then I will have the strength
> to stand beside you as your friend. If not,
> then, stranger, I would be afraid for you.

OEDIPUS

> Children, did you hear what the strangers said?
> They live here.

ANTIGONE

>   We heard. Tell us what we must do.

OEDIPUS

> It is not possible for me to do it,
> since two afflictions render me unfit:
> I am not strong enough, and I am blind.
> One of you go in and perform this rite.
> For I believe one heart can intercede
> and atone in full for tens of thousands,
> if that heart is pure. But you must hurry.
> Do not leave me by myself—my body   [500]
> cannot shuffle along all on its own,
> not without somebody there to guide me.

ISMENE

> I will go and carry out the ritual,
> but where is the place? I need to know that.

CHORUS

> It's over there, stranger, beyond the grove.
> If you need anything, there's someone there.
> He will direct you.

ISMENE

>   I'll go and do it.
> Antigone, look after our father here.
> If helping out our parents requires work,
> we should not consider that a burden.

[Exit ISMENE]

ΧΟΡΟΣ
δεινὸν μὲν τὸ πάλαι κείμενον ἤδη κακόν, ὦ ξεῖν',
    ἐπεγείρειν·   510
ὅμως δ' ἔραμαι πυθέσθαι

ΟΙΔΙΠΟΥΣ
τί τοῦτο;

ΧΟΡΟΣ
τᾶς δειλαίας ἀπόρου φανείσας
ἀλγηδόνος, ξυνέστας.

ΟΙΔΙΠΟΥΣ
μὴ πρὸς ξενίας ἀνοίξῃς   515
τᾶς σᾶς ἃ πέπονθ' ἀναιδῆ.

ΧΟΡΟΣ
τό τοι πολὺ καὶ μηδαμὰ λῆγον
χρῄζω, ξεῖν', ὀρθὸν ἄκουσμ' ἀκοῦσαι.

ΟΙΔΙΠΟΥΣ
ὤμοι.

ΧΟΡΟΣ
στέρξον, ἱκετεύω.

ΟΙΔΙΠΟΥΣ
φεῦ φεῦ.

ΧΟΡΟΣ
πείθου· κἀγὼ γὰρ ὅσον σὺ προσχρῄζεις.   520

ΟΙΔΙΠΟΥΣ
ἤνεγκ' οὖν κακότατ', ὦ ξένοι, ἤνεγκ' ἀέκων μέν,
θεὸς ἴστω,
τούτων δ' αὐθαίρετον οὐδέν.

ΧΟΡΟΣ
ἀλλ' ἐς τί;

ΟΙΔΙΠΟΥΣ
κακᾷ μ' εὐνᾷ πόλις οὐδὲν ἴδριν   525
γάμων ἐνέδησεν ἄτᾳ.

CHORUS

    Stranger, to stir up ancient suffering   [510]
    that for a long time has been lying dormant
    is a dreadful thing, but I would like to know . . .

OEDIPUS

    What it is?

CHORUS

           . . . about those torment you endured—
    the painful, inescapable regrets.

OEDIPUS

    By all the laws of hospitality,
    do not bring up the shame I have been through.

CHORUS

    But the story is well known, and people
    talk about it still. My friend, I'd like to hear
    the truth about what really happened.

OEDIPUS

    No, no.

CHORUS

           Please tell me. I am begging you.

OEDIPUS

    Alas! Alas!

CHORUS

           You should grant me this request.   [520]
    I have done everything you asked of me.

OEDIPUS

    O my friends, I have suffered agonies,
    the worst there are, but the things I did—
    and may the gods be witness to my words!—
    were unintentional. I did not choose
    to do any of them of my own free will.

CHORUS

    How did that happen?

OEDIPUS

           Without my knowledge,
    the city entangled me in ruin
    with a disastrous marriage.

Sophocles

ΧΟΡΟΣ
η ματρόθεν, ὡς ἀκούω,
δυσώνυμα λέκτρ' ἐπλήσω;

ΟΙΔΙΠΟΥΣ
ὤμοι θάνατος μὲν τάδ' ἀκούειν,
ὦ ξεῖν· αὗται δὲ δύ' ἐξ ἐμοῦ μὲν   530

ΧΟΡΟΣ
πῶς φῄς;

ΟΙΔΙΠΟΥΣ
παῖδε, δύο δ' ἄτα

ΧΟΡΟΣ
ὦ Ζεῦ.

ΟΙΔΙΠΟΥΣ
ματρὸς κοινᾶς ἀπέβλαστον ὠδῖνος.

ΧΟΡΟΣ
σαί τ' εἴσ' ἄρ' ἀπόγονοί τε καὶ

ΟΙΔΙΠΟΥΣ
κοιναί γε πατρὸς ἀδελφεαί.   535

ΧΟΡΟΣ
ἰώ.

ΟΙΔΙΠΟΥΣ
ἰὼ δῆτα μυρίων γ' ἐπιστροφαὶ κακῶν.

ΧΟΡΟΣ
ἔπαθες

ΟΙΔΙΠΟΥΣ
ἔπαθον ἄλαστ' ἔχειν.

ΧΟΡΟΣ
ἔρεξας

ΟΙΔΙΠΟΥΣ
οὐκ ἔρεξα.

CHORUS

Is it true
you shamed the marriage bed by sharing it
with your own mother? That's what people say.

OEDIPUS

Alas for me! Those are deadly words to hear!
Friends, those two girls of mine . . .   [530]

CHORUS

What are you saying?

OEDIPUS

Those two daughters—they are abominations!

CHORUS

O Zeus!

OEDIPUS

Born from their mother's agony—
the very mother who bore me as well!

CHORUS

So these young girls here are your daughters and . . .

OEDIPUS

Yes, and their father's sisters, too.

CHORUS

O god!²³

OEDIPUS

Alas! Countless torments return once more,
wheeling to attack me!

CHORUS

You have suffered . . .

OEDIPUS

What I have been through I cannot forget!

CHORUS

You have committed . . .

OEDIPUS

I have committed nothing!

233

Sophocles

ΧΟΡΟΣ
τί γάρ;

ΟΙΔΙΠΟΥΣ
ἐδεξάμην

δῶρον, ὃ μήποτ᾽ ἐγὼ ταλακάρδιος   540
ἐπωφέλησας πόλεος ἐξελέσθαι.

ΧΟΡΟΣ
δύστανε, τί γάρ; ἔθου φόνον

ΟΙΔΙΠΟΥΣ
τί τοῦτο; τί δ᾽ ἐθέλεις μαθεῖν;

ΧΟΡΟΣ
πατρός;

ΟΙΔΙΠΟΥΣ
παπαῖ. δευτέραν ἔπαισας, ἐπὶ νόσῳ νόσον,

ΧΟΡΟΣ
ἔκανες

ΟΙΔΙΠΟΥΣ
ἔκανον. ἔχει δέ μοι   545

ΧΟΡΟΣ
τί τοῦτο;

ΟΙΔΙΠΟΥΣ
πρὸς δίκας τι.

ΧΟΡΟΣ
τί γάρ;

ΟΙΔΙΠΟΥΣ
ἐγὼ φράσω.

καὶ γὰρ ἄν, οὓς ἐφόνευσ᾽, ἔμ᾽ ἀπώλεσαν·
νόμῳ δὲ καθαρός, ἄϊδρις εἰς τόδ᾽ ἦλθον.

234

CHORUS

What do you mean?

OEDIPUS

I received her as a gift.   [540]
How I wish, in my miserable state,
I had not taken her as my reward
for rescuing the city.[24]

CHORUS

You poor man!
What then? Did you murder . . .

OEDIPUS

What is it now?
What do you wish to know?

CHORUS

Did you kill your father?

OEDIPUS

O no, not that! You stab me once again,
wound piled on wound!

CHORUS

So then you did kill him.

OEDIPUS

I killed him. But in my defence there is . . .

CHORUS

What?

OEDIPUS

. . . something to justify my action.

CHORUS

What is that?

OEDIPUS

I will tell you. I killed men
who would have slaughtered me, and I did so
in ignorance. By law I'm innocent,
and yet I've come to this.[25]

235

Sophocles

ΧΟΡΟΣ

καὶ μὴν ἄναξ ὅδ᾽ ἡμὶν Αἰγέως γόνος
Θησεὺς κατ᾽ ὀμφὴν σὴν ἐφ᾽ ἀστάλη πάρα.   550

ΘΗΣΕΥΣ

πολλῶν ἀκούων ἔν τε τῷ πάρος χρόνῳ
τὰς αἱματηρὰς ὀμμάτων διαφθορὰς
ἔγνωκά σ᾽, ὦ παῖ Λαΐου, τανῦν θ᾽ ὁδοῖς   555
ἐν ταῖσδ᾽ ἀκούων μᾶλλον ἐξεπίσταμαι.
σκευή τε γάρ σε καὶ τὸ δύστηνον κάρα
δηλοῦτον ἡμῖν ὄνθ᾽ ὃς εἶ, καί σ᾽ οἰκτίσας
θέλω ᾽περέσθαι, δύσμορ᾽ Οἰδίπους, τίνα
πόλεως ἐπέστης προστροπὴν ἐμοῦ τ᾽ ἔχων,   560
αὐτός τε χἠ σὴ δύσμορος παραστάτις.
δίδασκε· δεινὴν γάρ τιν᾽ ἂν πρᾶξιν τύχοις
λέξας ὁποίας ἐξαφισταίμην ἐγώ,
ὃς οἶδα καὐτὸς ὡς ἐπαιδεύθην ξένος,
ὥσπερ σύ, χὠς εἷς πλεῖστ᾽ ἀνὴρ ἐπὶ ξένης
ἤθλησα κινδυνεύματ᾽ ἐν τὠμῷ κάρᾳ·   565
ὥστε ξένον γ᾽ ἂν οὐδέν᾽ ὄνθ᾽, ὥσπερ σὺ νῦν,
ὑπεκτραποίμην μὴ οὐ συνεκσῴζειν· ἐπεὶ
ἔξοιδ᾽ ἀνὴρ ὢν χὤτι τῆς εἰς αὔριον
οὐδὲν πλέον μοι σοῦ μέτεστιν ἡμέρας.

ΟΙΔΙΠΟΥΣ

Θησεῦ, τὸ σὸν γενναῖον ἐν σμικρῷ λόγῳ
παρῆκεν, ὥστε βραχέα μοι δεῖσθαι φράσαι.   570
σὺ γάρ μ᾽ ὅς εἰμι κἀφ᾽ ὅτου πατρὸς γεγὼς
καὶ γῆς ὁποίας ἦλθον, εἰρηκὼς κυρεῖς·
ὥστ᾽ ἐστί μοι τὸ λοιπὸν οὐδὲν ἄλλο πλὴν
εἰπεῖν ἃ χρῄζω, χὠ λόγος διοίχεται.

ΘΗΣΕΥΣ

τοῦτ᾽ αὐτὸ νῦν δίδασχ᾽, ὅπως ἂν ἐκμάθω.   575

236

CHORUS

Look over there!
Here comes Theseus, son of Aegeus,
our ruler, responding to your summons
and prepared to help.

[Enter THESEUS and ATTENDANTS]

THESEUS

In the past many men
have told me of the bloody mutilation
of your eyes, son of Laius, and what I heard
while on my way here makes me more certain
I truly recognize just who you are.
Your clothing and your ravaged features, too,
both confirm your identity for us.
I pity you, ill-fated Oedipus,
and I would like to know what petition
to me and to the city brings you here,   [560]
you and that unlucky girl beside you.
Let me hear it. You would have to mention
something outrageous for me to stand aside.
I know I myself was raised in exile,
just as you were, and in foreign countries
I struggled against many mortal dangers,
more so than any other man.[26] And thus
I would not turn away any stranger
in your position or refuse to help.
For I know well I am a mortal man,
and thus my share of what tomorrow brings
is no greater than your own.

OEDIPUS

Theseus,
the nobleness in those few words you spoke
is such that I require no long reply.   [570]
You mentioned who I am, who my father was,
and the land I come from. So there remains
nothing for me to say except to state
what I would like, and then my speech is done.

THESEUS

Well, then, say what it is, so that I know.

237

ΟΙΔΙΠΟΥΣ

    δώσων ἱκάνω τοὐμὸν ἄθλιον δέμας

    σοὶ δῶρον, οὐ σπουδαῖον εἰς ὄψιν· τὰ δὲ

    κέρδη παρ' αὐτοῦ κρείσσον' ἢ μορφὴ καλή.

ΘΗΣΕΥΣ

    ποῖον δὲ κέρδος ἀξιοῖς ἥκειν φέρων;

ΟΙΔΙΠΟΥΣ

    χρόνῳ μάθοις ἄν, οὐχὶ τῷ παρόντι που.   580

ΘΗΣΕΥΣ

    ποίῳ γὰρ ἡ σὴ προσφορὰ δηλώσεται;

ΟΙΔΙΠΟΥΣ

    ὅταν θάνω 'γὼ καὶ σύ μου ταφεὺς γένῃ

ΘΗΣΕΥΣ

    τὰ λοίσθι' αἰτεῖ τοῦ βίου, τὰ δ' ἐν μέσῳ

    ἢ λῆστιν ἴσχεις ἢ δι' οὐδενὸς ποεῖ.

ΟΙΔΙΠΟΥΣ

    ἐνταῦθα γάρ μοι κεῖνα συγκομίζεται.   585

ΘΗΣΕΥΣ

    ἀλλ' ἐν βραχεῖ δὴ τήνδε μ' ἐξαιτεῖ χάριν.

ΟΙΔΙΠΟΥΣ

    ὅρα γε μήν· οὐ σμικρός, οὔχ, ἀγὼν ὅδε.

ΘΗΣΕΥΣ

    πότερα τὰ τῶν σῶν ἐκγόνων κἀμοῦ λέγεις;

ΟΙΔΙΠΟΥΣ

    κεῖνοι κομίζειν κεῖσ' ἄναξ, χρῄζουσί με.

OEDIPUS

> I have come here to offer you a gift,
> this wretched body of mine. To look at,
> it has little value, but the benefits
> it confers surpass a pleasing shape.

THESEUS

> You claim you bring us a great advantages.
> What are they?

OEDIPUS

> You may find out later on,   [580]
> but not right now.

THESEUS

> Well then, at what point
> will this gift of yours reveal itself to us?

OEDIPUS

> When I am dead and you have buried me.

THESEUS

> You ask for your life's final ritual
> but ignore what happens before you die,
> or else you do not care.

OEDIPUS

> It does not matter.
> All those other things are part of my request.[27]

THESEUS

> The favour you request from me is small.

OEDIPUS

> But take care. This is no trivial matter—
> the struggle over me will not be small.

THESEUS

> Are you referring to your sons and me?

OEDIPUS

> My lord, they will be seeking to force you
> to send me back to Thebes.

ΘΗΣΕΥΣ

ἀλλ' εἰ θέλοντά γ' οὐδὲ σοὶ φεύγειν καλόν.   590

ΟΙΔΙΠΟΥΣ

ἀλλ' οὐδ', ὅτ' αὐτὸς ἤθελον, παρίεσαν.

ΘΗΣΕΥΣ

ὦ μῶρε, θυμὸς δ' ἐν κακοῖς οὐ ξύμφορον.

ΟΙΔΙΠΟΥΣ

ὅταν μάθῃς μου, νουθέτει, τανῦν δ' ἔα.

ΘΗΣΕΥΣ

δίδασκ'· ἄνευ γνώμης γὰρ οὔ με χρὴ λέγειν.

ΟΙΔΙΠΟΥΣ

πέπονθα, Θησεῦ, δεινὰ πρὸς κακοῖς κακά.   595

ΘΗΣΕΥΣ

ἦ τὴν παλαιὰν ξυμφορὰν γένους ἐρεῖς;

ΟΙΔΙΠΟΥΣ

οὐ δῆτ', ἐπεὶ πᾶς τοῦτό γ' Ἑλλήνων θροεῖ.

ΘΗΣΕΥΣ

τί γὰρ τὸ μεῖζον ἢ κατ' ἄνθρωπον νοσεῖς;

ΟΙΔΙΠΟΥΣ

οὕτως ἔχει μοι. γῆς ἐμῆς ἀπηλάθην
πρὸς τῶν ἐμαυτοῦ σπερμάτων· ἔστιν δέ μοι   600
πάλιν κατελθεῖν μήποθ', ὡς πατροκτόνῳ.

ΘΗΣΕΥΣ

πῶς δῆτα σ' ἂν πεμψαίαθ', ὥστ' οἰκεῖν δίχα;

ΟΙΔΙΠΟΥΣ

τὸ θεῖον αὐτοὺς ἐξαναγκάσει στόμα.

THESEUS

                          If that is what you wish,   [590]
   then your banishment is not appropriate.

OEDIPUS

   No! When I wanted to remain in Thebes
   they would not agree!

THESEUS

                               You are foolish.
   In times of trouble anger does not help.

OEDIPUS

   Give me advice once you have heard my story.
   Until then, spare me.

THESEUS

                           Then tell it to me.
   I should not speak until I know the facts.

OEDIPUS

   I have suffered dreadfully, Theseus,
   evil after evil—horrific things!

THESEUS

   Do you mean that ancient family curse
   placed on your race?

OEDIPUS

                           No, not that at all.
   That's something the whole of Greece talks about.

THESEUS

   Then are you sick with more than mortal grief?
   What it is?

OEDIPUS

                    My situation is this.
   I was driven away from my own land
   by my two sons, and I cannot return   [600]
   because I killed my father.

THESEUS

                        But why then,
   if you cannot live there, will they summon you?

OEDIPUS

   The oracle of the god will force them to.

Sophocles

ΘΗΣΕΥΣ

ποῖον πάθος δείσαντας ἐκ χρηστηρίων;

ΟΙΔΙΠΟΥΣ

ὅτι σφ᾽ ἀνάγκη τῇδε πληγῆναι χθονί.   605

ΘΗΣΕΥΣ

καὶ πῶς γένοιτ᾽ ἂν τἀμὰ κἀκείνων πικρά;

ΟΙΔΙΠΟΥΣ

ὦ φίλτατ᾽ Αἰγέως παῖ, μόνοις οὐ γίγνεται
θεοῖσι γῆρας οὐδὲ κατθανεῖν ποτε.
τὰ δ᾽ ἄλλα συγχεῖ πάνθ᾽ ὁ παγκρατὴς χρόνος.
φθίνει μὲν ἰσχὺς γῆς, φθίνει δὲ σώματος,   610
θνῄσκει δὲ πίστις, βλαστάνει δ᾽ ἀπιστία,
καὶ πνεῦμα ταὐτὸν οὔποτ᾽ οὔτ᾽ ἐν ἀνδράσιν
φίλοις βέβηκεν οὔτε πρὸς πόλιν πόλει.
τοῖς μὲν γὰρ ἤδη, τοῖς δ᾽ ἐν ὑστέρῳ χρόνῳ
τὰ τερπνὰ πικρὰ γίγνεται καὖθις φίλα.   615
καὶ ταῖσι Θήβαις εἰ τανῦν εὐημερεῖ
καλῶς τὰ πρὸς σέ, μυρίας ὁ μυρίος
χρόνος τεκνοῦται νύκτας ἡμέρας τ᾽ ἰών,
ἐν αἷς τὰ νῦν ξύμφωνα δεξιώματα
δόρει διασκεδῶσιν ἐκ σμικροῦ λόγου·   620
ἵν᾽ οὑμὸς εὕδων καὶ κεκρυμμένος νέκυς
ψυχρός ποτ᾽ αὐτῶν θερμὸν αἷμα πίεται,
εἰ Ζεὺς ἔτι Ζεὺς χὠ Διὸς Φοῖβος σαφής.
ἀλλ᾽ οὐ γὰρ αὐδᾶν ἡδὺ τἀκίνητ᾽ ἔπη,
ἔα μ᾽ ἐν οἷσιν ἠρξάμην, τὸ σὸν μόνον   625
πιστὸν φυλάσσων, κοὔποτ᾽ Οἰδίπουν ἐρεῖς
ἀχρεῖον οἰκητῆρα δέξασθαι τόπων
τῶν ἐνθάδ᾽, εἴπερ μὴ θεοὶ ψεύσουσί με.

ΧΟΡΟΣ

ἄναξ, πάλαι καὶ ταῦτα καὶ τοιαῦτ᾽ ἔπη
γῇ τῇδ᾽ ὅδ᾽ ἀνὴρ ὡς τελῶν ἐφαίνετο.   630

THESEUS

> What evil has the oracle declared
> that makes them so afraid?

OEDIPUS

>   It prophesied
> that in your country they will be defeated.

THESEUS

> And how will they become my enemies?

OEDIPUS

> Dearest son of Aegeus, only gods
> are never troubled by old age and death.
> All other things are finally destroyed
> by all-conquering Time. The power of Earth
> passes away, the body's strength withers,   [610]
> loyalty perishes, distrust appears,
> and between one city and another,
> just as between good friends, relationships
> never remain the same. Sooner or later
> pleasant concord turns to bitter hatred
> and then hatred, once again, to friendship.
> So if today between yourself and Thebes
> the sun is shining bright and all is well,
> the endless passage of infinite Time
> engenders innumerable days and nights,
> and in that time some trivial reason
> will persuade them to shatter with their spears   [620]
> whatever treaties you now have between you.
> And then, if Zeus is, at that time, still Zeus
> and if his son Apollo speaks the truth,
> my frigid, slumbering, and buried corpse
> will drink hot Theban blood. I will not speak
> of secrets that should remain unspoken,
> so let me end my speech where I began:
> if you will only do what you have pledged,
> and if the gods are not deceiving me,
> you will never say you sheltered Oedipus
> here in your land and reaped no benefits.

CHORUS

> My lord, this man has, from the very start,
> made it clear to us he would accomplish
> these and similar good things for our state.   [630]

243

ΘΗΣΕΥΣ

τίς δῆτ᾽ ἂν ἀνδρὸς εὐμένειαν ἐκβάλοι
τοιοῦδ᾽, ὅτῳ πρῶτον μὲν ἡ δορύξενος
κοινὴ παρ᾽ ἡμῖν αἰέν ἐστιν ἑστία;
ἔπειτα δ᾽ ἱκέτης δαιμόνων ἀφιγμένος
γῇ τῇδε κἀμοὶ δασμὸν οὐ σμικρὸν τίνει. 635
ἀγὼ σεβισθεὶς οὔποτ᾽ ἐκβαλῶ χάριν
τὴν τοῦδε, χώρᾳ δ᾽ ἔμπολιν κατοικιῶ.
εἰ δ᾽ ἐνθάδ᾽ ἡδὺ τῷ ξένῳ μίμνειν, σέ νιν
τάξω φυλάσσειν, εἴτ᾽ ἐμοῦ στείχειν μέτα,
τόδ᾽ ἡδύ, τούτων, Οἰδίπους, δίδωμί σοι 640
κρίναντι χρῆσθαι· τῇδε γὰρ ξυνοίσομαι.

ΟΙΔΙΠΟΥΣ

ὦ Ζεῦ, διδοίης τοῖσι τοιούτοισιν εὖ.

ΘΗΣΕΥΣ

τί δῆτα χρήζεις; ἦ δόμους στείχειν ἐμούς;

ΟΙΔΙΠΟΥΣ

εἴ μοι θέμις γ᾽ ἦν· ἀλλ᾽ ὁ χῶρός ἐσθ᾽ ὅδε,

ΘΗΣΕΥΣ

ἐν ᾧ τί πράξεις; οὐ γὰρ ἀντιστήσομαι. 645

ΟΙΔΙΠΟΥΣ

ἐν ᾧ κρατήσω τῶν ἔμ᾽ ἐκβεβληκότων.

ΘΗΣΕΥΣ

μέγ᾽ ἂν λέγοις δώρημα τῆς συνουσίας.

ΟΙΔΙΠΟΥΣ

εἰ σοί γ᾽ ἅπερ φὴς ἐμμενεῖ τελοῦντί μοι.

ΘΗΣΕΥΣ

θάρσει τὸ τοῦδέ γ᾽ ἀνδρός· οὔ σε μὴ προδῶ.

ΟΙΔΙΠΟΥΣ

οὔτοι σ᾽ ὑφ᾽ ὅρκου γ᾽ ὡς κακὸν πιστώσομαι. 650

THESEUS

    Who then would repudiate the friendship
    of a man like this, one for whom, first of all,
    an ally's hearth, by mutual agreement,
    is always welcoming? Then he has come
    as a suppliant to our gods and offers
    no small reward to this land and to me.
    I respect these things—I will never spurn
    the favours of this man. I will establish
    a place here he may live as a citizen.
    If the stranger wishes to remain here,
    I will appoint you his protectors. But if
    he would prefer to, he can come with me.
    Choose the option you think best, Oedipus.   [640]
    Whatever choice you make will be my own.

OEDIPUS

    O Zeus, be gracious to such men as these!

THESEUS

    What would you like? To come back to my home?

OEDIPUS

    I would, if that had been ordained for me.
    But this is the place . . .

THESEUS

                       What will you do here?
    Speak up. I will not countermand your choice.

OEDIPUS

    . . . where I will conquer those who drove me out.

THESEUS

    If so, your presence here would prove to be
    a major benefit for us.

OEDIPUS

                       It will,
    if you fulfil your promises to me.

THESEUS

    Have faith in me. I will not let you down.

OEDIPUS

    I will not ask you to confirm your pledge
    with an oath, as one does with wicked men.   [650]

ΘΗΣΕΥΣ
οὔκουν πέρα γ᾽ ἂν οὐδὲν ἢ λόγῳ φέροις.

ΟΙΔΙΠΟΥΣ
πῶς οὖν ποήσεις;

ΘΗΣΕΥΣ
τοῦ μάλιστ᾽ ὄκνος σ᾽ ἔχει;

ΟΙΔΙΠΟΥΣ
ἥξουσιν ἄνδρες

ΘΗΣΕΥΣ
ἀλλὰ τοῖσδ᾽ ἔσται μέλον.

ΟΙΔΙΠΟΥΣ
ὅρα με λείπων

ΘΗΣΕΥΣ
μὴ δίδασχ᾽ ἃ χρή με δρᾶν.

ΟΙΔΙΠΟΥΣ
ὀκνοῦντ᾽ ἀνάγκη.   655

ΘΗΣΕΥΣ
τοὐμὸν οὐκ ὀκνεῖ κέαρ.

ΟΙΔΙΠΟΥΣ
οὐκ οἶσθ᾽ ἀπειλὰς

ΘΗΣΕΥΣ
οἶδ᾽ ἐγώ σε μή τινα
ἐνθένδ᾽ ἀπάξοντ᾽ ἄνδρα πρὸς βίαν ἐμοῦ.
πολλαὶ δ᾽ ἀπειλαὶ πολλὰ δὴ μάτην ἔπη
θυμῷ κατηπείλησαν, ἀλλ᾽ ὁ νοῦς ὅταν
αὑτοῦ γένηται, φροῦδα τἀπειλήματα.   660
κείνοις δ᾽ ἴσως κεἰ δείν᾽ ἐπερρώσθη λέγειν
τῆς σῆς ἀγωγῆς, οἶδ᾽ ἐγώ, φανήσεται
μακρὸν τὸ δεῦρο πέλαγος οὐδὲ πλώσιμον.
θαρσεῖν μὲν οὖν ἔγωγε κἂν ἐμῆς ἄνευ
γνώμης ἐπαινῶ, Φοῖβος εἰ προὔπεμψέ σε·   665

246

THESEUS
> An oath would be no more reliable
> than giving you my word.

OEDIPUS
>   What will you do?

THESEUS
> What precisely do you fear?

OEDIPUS
>   Men will come . . .

THESEUS
> But these people here will deal with them.

OEDIPUS
> Be careful when you leave me.

THESEUS
>   There is no need
> to instruct me in what I have to do.

OEDIPUS
> My fear drives me to do it.

THESEUS
>   But my heart
> has no fear.

OEDIPUS
>   You know nothing of their threats.

THESEUS
> But I do know this: no one will carry you
> away from here without permission from me.
> Often men utter threats from angry hearts
> in loud and empty words, but when their minds
> regain control once more, their threats are gone.   [660]
> And if those men are bold enough to act
> on threats they made to take you back by force,
> they will, I tell you, sail into rough seas
> on their harsh journey here. You must take heart.
> That's my advice—even without my pledge—
> if Phoebus was the one who led you here.

ὅμως δὲ κἀμοῦ μὴ παρόντος οἶδ᾽ ὅτι
τοὐμὸν φυλάξει σ᾽ ὄνομα μὴ πάσχειν κακῶς.

ΧΟΡΟΣ
εὐίππου, ξένε, τᾶσδε χώρας
ἵκου τὰ κράτιστα γᾶς ἔπαυλα,
τὸν ἀργῆτα Κολωνόν, ἔνθ᾽   670
ἁ λίγεια μινύρεται
θαμίζουσα μάλιστ᾽ ἀηδὼν
χλωραῖς ὑπὸ βάσσαις,
τὸν οἰνωπὸν ἔχουσα κισσὸν
καὶ τὰν ἄβατον θεοῦ   675
φυλλάδα μυριόκαρπον ἀνήλιον
ἀνήνεμόν τε πάντων
χειμώνων· ἵν᾽ ὁ βακχιώτας
ἀεὶ Διόνυσος ἐμβατεύει
θεαῖς ἀμφιπολῶν τιθήναις.   680

θάλλει δ᾽ οὐρανίας ὑπ᾽ ἄχνας
ὁ καλλίβοτρυς κατ᾽ ἦμαρ ἀεὶ
νάρκισσος, μεγάλαιν θεαῖν
ἀρχαῖον στεφάνωμ᾽, ὅ τε
χρυσαυγὴς κρόκος· οὐδ᾽ ἄϋπνοι   685
κρῆναι μινύθουσιν
Κηφισοῦ νομάδες ῥεέθρων,
ἀλλ᾽ αἰὲν ἐπ᾽ ἤματι
ὠκυτόκος πεδίων ἐπινίσσεται
ἀκηράτῳ σὺν ὄμβρῳ   690
στερνούχου χθονός· οὐδὲ Μουσᾶν
χοροί νιν ἀπεστύγησαν οὐδ᾽ ἁ
χρυσάνιος Ἀφροδίτα.

ἔστιν δ᾽ οἷον ἐγὼ γᾶς Ἀσίας οὐκ ἐπακούω   695
οὐδ᾽ ἐν τᾷ μεγάλᾳ Δωρίδι νάσῳ Πέλοπος πώποτε βλαστὸν
φύτευμ᾽ ἀχείρωτον αὐτόποιον,
ἐγχέων φόβημα δαΐων,
ὃ τᾷδε θάλλει μέγιστα χώρᾳ,   700
γλαυκᾶς παιδοτρόφου φύλλον ἐλαίας·

And though I am elsewhere, I know my name
will nonetheless protect you from all harm.

[Exit THESEUS]

CHORUS
    Stranger, in this land famed for horses
    you have reached bright Colonus,
    earth's finest home. Here the nightingale,   [670]
    always chants her sweet, sharp melodies,
    from deep within green forest groves,
    living among the wine-dark ivy vines,
    fruit-rich foliage of the god, a place
    where no sun penetrates, no winds blow
    in any storm, and no man ever treads.
    Here Dionysus, the Bacchic reveller,
    always roams with his companions,
    the nymphs who nursed him as a child.[28]   [680]

    And every day narcissus flowers bloom
    in lovely clusters fed on heavenly dew,
    the ancient crown of two great goddesses,
    as does the glistening gold crocus, too.[29]
    The sleepless fountains never fail to feed
    the wandering waters of the Cephisus,
    whose pure, clear stream flows every day   [690]
    across the ample bosom of the land,
    bringing rich nourishment to the plain.
    Nor do the Muses' dancing choruses
    or Aphrodite of the golden reins
    fail to grant their favours to this land.

    And here we have a certain kind of plant—
    I have not heard of it in Asian lands,
    nor does it thrive in that great Dorian isle
    of Pelops. It grows without man's help,
    renews itself, and terrifies our foes.
    This plant truly flourishes in our land,   [700]
    the gray-leafed olive tree, nurturing
    our country's youth.[30] No young person here

Sophocles

τὸ μέν τις οὐ νεαρὸς οὐδὲ γήρᾳ
συνναίων ἁλιώσει χερὶ πέρσας· ὁ γὰρ αἰὲν ὁρῶν κύκλος
λεύσσει νιν μορίου Διὸς   705
χἀ γλαυκῶπις Ἀθάνα.

ἄλλον δ᾽ αἶνον ἔχω ματροπόλει τᾷδε κράτιστον
δῶρον τοῦ μεγάλου δαίμονος, εἰπεῖν, χθονὸς αὔχημα
    μέγιστον,   710
εὔιππον, εὔπωλον, εὐθάλασσον.
ὦ παῖ Κρόνου, σὺ γάρ νιν εἰς
τόδ᾽ εἷσας αὔχημ᾽, ἄναξ Ποσειδάν,
ἵπποισιν τὸν ἀκεστῆρα χαλινὸν   715
πρώταισι ταῖσδε κτίσας ἀγυιαῖς.
ἁ δ᾽ εὐήρετμος ἔκπαγλ᾽ ἁλία χερσὶ παραπτομένα πλάτα
θρῴσκει, τῶν ἑκατομπόδων
Νηρῄδων ἀκόλουθος.

ΑΝΤΙΓΟΝΗ
ὦ πλεῖστ᾽ ἐπαίνοις εὐλογούμενον πέδον,   720
νῦν σὸν τὰ λαμπρὰ ταῦτα δὴ φαίνειν ἔπη.

ΟΙΔΙΠΟΥΣ
τί δ᾽ ἔστιν, ὦ παῖ, καινόν;

ΑΝΤΙΓΟΝΗ
                          ἆσσον ἔρχεται
Κρέων ὅδ᾽ ἡμῖν οὐκ ἄνευ πομπῶν, πάτερ.

ΟΙΔΙΠΟΥΣ
ὦ φίλτατοι γέροντες, ἐξ ὑμῶν ἐμοὶ
φαίνοιτ᾽ ἂν ἤδη τέρμα τῆς σωτηρίας.   725

ΧΟΡΟΣ
θάρσει, παρέσται· καὶ γὰρ εἰ γέρων ἐγώ,
τὸ τῆσδε χώρας οὐ γεγήρακεν σθένος.

ΚΡΕΩΝ
ἄνδρες χθονὸς τῆσδ᾽ εὐγενεῖς οἰκήτορες,
ὁρῶ τιν᾽ ὑμᾶς ὀμμάτων εἰληφότας
φόβον νεώρη τῆς ἐμῆς ἐπεισόδου,   730

250

will lift a hand to damage or destroy it,
nor any citizen living with old age,
for it guarded by the ever-watchful gaze
of grey-eyed Athena and protector Zeus.[31]

I have more praises for our mother state,
a tribute to those most glorious gifts   [710]
from a mighty god, our country's proudest boast—
the great strength of our colts and stallions
and the great power of the sea. For you,
my lord Poseidon, Cronos' son, placed her
on that proud throne and first introduced
into our roads the bridle and the bit
that curb the wildness in our horses.
You trained our hands to ply the flashing oar
and race in wonder over open seas,
chasing sea nymphs dancing in the waves,
the fifty daughters of Nereus.[32]

ANTIGONE
O Athens, land praised more than any other,   [720]
now is the time to show in how you act
just what such splendid commendations mean.

OEDIPUS
What's happening, my child?

ANTIGONE
It's Creon, father.
He's coming towards us—and with an escort.

OEDIPUS
O you old men, my dearest friends, may you now
make good that final pledge of yours and save me!

CHORUS
Take heart—our pledge still stands. We may have aged,
but still our country's strength has not grown old.

[Enter CREON with an escort]

CREON
You men, noble inhabitants of this land,
from your eyes I see that my arrival
has gripped you all with unexpected fear.   [730]

ὃν μήτ᾽ ὀκνεῖτε μήτ᾽ ἀφῆτ᾽ ἔπος κακόν.
ἥκω γὰρ οὐχ ὡς δρᾶν τι βουληθείς, ἐπεὶ
γέρων μέν εἰμι, πρὸς πόλιν δ᾽ ἐπίσταμαι
σθένουσαν ἥκων, εἴ τιν᾽ Ἑλλάδος, μέγα.
ἀλλ᾽ ἄνδρα τόνδε τηλικόσδ᾽ ἀπεστάλην   735
πείσων ἕπεσθαι πρὸς τὸ Καδμείων πέδον,
οὐκ ἐξ ἑνὸς στείλαντος, ἀλλ᾽ ἀνδρῶν ὕπο
πάντων κελευσθείς, οὕνεχ᾽ ἧκέ μοι γένει
τὰ τοῦδε πενθεῖν πήματ᾽ εἰς πλεῖστον πόλεως.
ἀλλ᾽ ὦ ταλαίπωρ᾽ Οἰδίπους, κλύων ἐμοῦ   740
ἱκοῦ πρὸς οἴκους. πᾶς σε Καδμείων λεὼς
καλεῖ δικαίως, ἐκ δὲ τῶν μάλιστ᾽ ἐγώ,
ὅσῳπερ, εἰ μὴ πλεῖστον ἀνθρώπων ἔφυν
κάκιστος, ἀλγῶ τοῖσι σοῖς κακοῖς, γέρον,
ὁρῶν σε τὸν δύστηνον ὄντα μὲν ξένον,   745
ἀεὶ δ᾽ ἀλήτην κἀπὶ προσπόλου μιᾶς
βιοστερῆ χωροῦντα· τὴν ἐγὼ τάλας
οὐκ ἄν ποτ᾽ ἐς τοσοῦτον αἰκίας πεσεῖν
ἔδοξ᾽, ὅσον πέπτωκεν ἥδε δύσμορος,
ἀεί σε κηδεύουσα καὶ τὸ σὸν κάρα   750
πτωχῷ διαίτῃ, τηλικοῦτος, οὐ γάμων
ἔμπειρος, ἀλλὰ τοὐπιόντος ἁρπάσαι.
ἆρ᾽ ἄθλιον τοὔνειδος, ὦ τάλας ἐγώ,
ὠνείδισ᾽ εἰς σὲ κἀμὲ καὶ τὸ πᾶν γένος;
ἀλλ᾽ οὐ γὰρ ἔστι τἀμφανῆ κρύπτειν, σύ νιν   755
πρὸς θεῶν πατρῴων, Οἰδίπους, πεισθεὶς ἐμοὶ
κρύψον, θελήσας ἄστυ καὶ δόμους μολεῖν
τοὺς σοὺς πατρῴους, τήνδε τὴν πόλιν φίλως
εἰπών· ἐπαξία γάρ· ἡ δ᾽ οἴκοι πλέον
δίκῃ σέβοιτ᾽ ἄν, οὖσα σὴ πάλαι τροφός.   760

ΟΙΔΙΠΟΥΣ

  ὦ πάντα τολμῶν κἀπὸ παντὸς ἂν φέρων
  λόγου δικαίου μηχάνημα ποικίλον,

Do not shrink back or utter hostile words,
for I do not come intending to use force.
I am an old man, and I understand
that if any state in Greece is truly strong
it is the powerful city I have reached.
No. I have been sent here, old though I am,
to convince this man to return to Thebes.
I was not dispatched by just one person,
but by the wish of all the citizens,
and more than any other man in Thebes
it falls on me to grieve for his misfortune,
because he is a relative of mine.[33]
O you, poor miserable Oedipus,   [740]
hear what I have to say and come back home!
Cadmeans are all summoning you back—
and justly so—I more than all the rest.[34]
I would be the very worst of all men born
if I did not find your suffering painful,
seeing you, old man, a wretched outcast,
an eternal wanderer and beggar,
stumbling around with one young girl for help.
Alas, I never thought that she would fall
into such degrading misery as this—
the poor creature, living like a vagrant,
always nursing you in your condition.   [750]
She's of marriageable age, but unwed,
there for some passing man to violate.
In pointing out all these misfortunes,
am I not casting a disgraceful slur
on you and me and our whole family line?
But no one can conceal a public shame.
So, Oedipus, by our ancestral gods,
listen to what I say—hide our disgrace
by agreeing to return to Thebes, the home
of your own ancestors. Bid this place here
a fond farewell—these men have earned your thanks.
But your own homeland merits more respect,
because she nursed you all those years ago.   [760]

OEDIPUS
    You are crass enough to try anything,
    even to base your devious intent

τί ταῦτα πειρᾷ κἀμὲ δεύτερον θέλεις

ἑλεῖν ἐν οἷς μάλιστ' ἂν ἀλγοίην ἁλούς;

πρόσθεν τε γάρ με τοῖσιν οἰκείοις κακοῖς   765

νοσοῦνθ', ὅτ' ἦν μοι τέρψις ἐκπεσεῖν χθονός,

οὐκ ἤθελες θέλοντι προσθέσθαι χάριν·

ἀλλ' ἡνίκ' ἤδη μεστὸς ἦ θυμούμενος

καὶ τοὐν δόμοισιν ἦν διαιτᾶσθαι γλυκύ,

τότ' ἐξεώθεις κἀξέβαλλες, οὐδέ σοι   770

τὸ συγγενὲς τοῦτ' οὐδαμῶς τότ' ἦν φίλον·

νῦν τ' αὖθις ἡνίκ' εἰσορᾷς πόλιν τέ μοι

ξυνοῦσαν εὔνουν τήνδε καὶ γένος τὸ πᾶν,

πειρᾷ μετασπᾶν, σκληρὰ μαλθακῶς λέγων.

καίτοι τίς αὕτη τέρψις ἄκοντας φιλεῖν;   775

ὥσπερ τις εἴ σοι λιπαροῦντι μὲν τυχεῖν

μηδὲν διδοίη μηδ' ἐπαρκέσαι θέλοι,

πλήρη δ' ἔχοντι θυμὸν ὧν χρῄζοις, τότε

δωροῖθ', ὅτ' οὐδὲν ἡ χάρις χάριν φέροι·

ἆρ' ἂν ματαίου τῆσδ' ἂν ἡδονῆς τύχοις;   780

τοιαῦτα μέντοι καὶ σὺ προσφέρεις ἐμοί,

λόγῳ μὲν ἐσθλά. τοῖσι δ' ἔργοισιν κακά.

φράσω δὲ καὶ τοῖσδ', ὥς σε δηλώσω κακόν.

ἥκεις ἔμ' ἄξων, οὐχ ἵν' ἐς δόμους ἄγῃς,

ἀλλ' ὡς πάραυλον οἰκίσῃς, πόλις δέ σοι   785

κακῶν ἄνατος τῆσδ' ἀπαλλαχθῇ χθονός.

οὐκ ἔστι σοι ταῦτ', ἀλλά σοι τάδ' ἔστ', ἐκεῖ

χώρας ἀλάστωρ οὑμὸς ἐνναίων ἀεί·

ἔστιν δὲ παισὶ τοῖς ἐμοῖσι τῆς ἐμῆς

χθονὸς λαχεῖν τοσοῦτον, ἐνθανεῖν μόνον.   790

ἆρ' οὐκ ἄμεινον ἢ σὺ τὰν Θήβαις φρονῶ;

on pleas for justice! Why are you doing this?
Why do you wish to catch me once again
in a snare that will bring me still more grief?
Back when I was suffering from the pain
I brought upon myself, I yearned to leave,
to be driven from Thebes, but you refused!
That favour you were not prepared to grant.
Later, once my anger had run its course
and I desired to live in my own home,
you cast me out, forced me into exile.   [770]
At that time you were not concerned at all
with those common kinship ties you mention.
Now here we are again. When you can see
how this city and its inhabitants
are all offering me their hospitality,
you try to snatch me back once more, voicing
your vicious wish in a sweet-sounding speech.
And yet what pleasure do you get from this,
welcoming me as a guest against my will?
It's as if you kept pleading with someone
to grant a favour but he was unwilling
and refused to help, and then later on,
once your spirit had everything you wished,
he granted your request, when such kindness
would not be kind at all. In such a case,   [780]
would not your joy be empty? Nonetheless,
that is what you are offering me now—
noble-sounding speeches and deceitful acts.
I will explain that to these people here
to show what a dishonest man you are.
You have not come to lead me to my home,
but to take me into custody, to set me
near your borders, so the city of Thebes
may escape unharmed any future troubles
coming from this land. But you will not succeed.
Instead of that what you will get is this:
my vengeful ghost haunting your land forever
and for my sons this legacy from me,
as much of my own land as they will need
to lie on when they die, no more than that.   [790]
As far as Thebes' future is concerned,
Creon, am I not a wiser man than you?

πολλῷ γ᾽, ὅσῳπερ κἀκ σαφεστέρων κλύω,
Φοίβου τε καὐτοῦ Ζηνός, ὃς κείνου πατήρ.
τὸ σὸν δ᾽ ἀφῖκται δεῦρ᾽ ὑπόβλητον στόμα,
πολλὴν ἔχον στόμωσιν· ἐν δὲ τῷ λέγειν   795
κάκ᾽ ἂν λάβοις τὰ πλείον᾽ ἢ σωτήρια.
ἡμᾶς δ᾽ ἔα ζῆν ἐνθάδ᾽· οὐ γὰρ ἂν κακῶς
οὐδ᾽ ὧδ᾽ ἔχοντες ζῶμεν, εἰ τερποίμεθα.

ΚΡΕΩΝ

πότερα νομίζεις δυστυχεῖν ἔμ᾽ ἐς τὰ σά,   800
ἤ σ᾽ εἰς τὰ σαυτοῦ μᾶλλον, ἐς τῷ νῦν λόγῳ;

ΟΙΔΙΠΟΥΣ

ἐμοὶ μέν ἐσθ᾽ ἥδιστον, εἰ σὺ μήτ᾽ ἐμὲ
πείθειν οἷός τ᾽ εἶ μήτε τούσδε τοὺς πέλας.

ΚΡΕΩΝ

ὦ δύσμορ᾽, οὐδὲ τῷ χρόνῳ φύσας φανεῖ
φρένας ποτ᾽ ἀλλὰ λῦμα τῷ γήρᾳ τρέφει;   805

ΟΙΔΙΠΟΥΣ

γλώσσῃ σὺ δεινός· ἄνδρα δ᾽ οὐδέν᾽ οἶδ᾽ ἐγὼ
δίκαιον ὅστις ἐξ ἅπαντος εὖ λέγει.

ΚΡΕΩΝ

χωρὶς τό τ᾽ εἰπεῖν πολλὰ καὶ τὰ καίρια.

ΟΙΔΙΠΟΥΣ

ὡς δὴ σὺ βραχέα, ταῦτα δ᾽ ἐν καιρῷ λέγεις.

ΚΡΕΩΝ

οὐ δῆθ᾽ ὅτῳ γε νοῦς ἴσος καὶ σοὶ πάρα.   810

ΟΙΔΙΠΟΥΣ

ἄπελθ᾽, ἐρῶ γὰρ καὶ πρὸ τῶνδε, μηδέ με
φύλασσ᾽ ἐφορμῶν ἔνθα χρὴ ναίειν ἐμέ.

Yes, much wiser—since those I listen to
are the most knowledgeable ones of all,
Phoebus Apollo and his father Zeus.
You come here with that corrupt tongue of yours
honed sharp as hardened steel, but what you say
will bring you grief rather than salvation.
I know these words of mine will not convince you,
so you should leave. Let us keep living here.
To exist like this would not be difficult,
not if it brought enjoyment and content.

CREON

In this debate, which one of us do you think   [800]
has more to lose by what you are doing,
you or me?

OEDIPUS

                    For me the sweetest outcome
will be when you fail to win me over
or to convince the people standing here.

CREON

You poor man! Will you make a public show
of how in all these years you have learned nothing?
Will you keep on disgracing your old age?

OEDIPUS

You have a glib tongue, but I do not know
any righteous man who can argue well
and in support of every point of view.

CREON

One can say a lot and yet avoid the issue.

OEDIPUS

As if your speech was short and to the point!

CREON

That is not possible with minds like yours.   [810]

OEDIPUS

Go away! I speak for these men here, as well.
And do not try to set up a blockade
and spy on me where I am meant to live.

ΚΡΕΩΝ

μαρτύρομαι τούσδ᾽, οὐ σέ· πρὸς δὲ τοὺς φίλους
οἷ᾽ ἀνταμείβει ῥήματ᾽, ἤν σ᾽ ἕλω ποτέ—

ΟΙΔΙΠΟΥΣ

τίς δ᾽ ἄν με τῶνδε συμμάχων ἕλοι βίᾳ;   815

ΚΡΕΩΝ

ἦ μὴν σὺ κἄνευ τοῦδε λυπηθεὶς ἔσει.

ΟΙΔΙΠΟΥΣ

ποίῳ σὺν ἔργῳ τοῦτ᾽ ἀπειλήσας ἔχεις;

ΚΡΕΩΝ

παίδοιν δυοῖν σοι τὴν μὲν ἀρτίως ἐγὼ
ξυναρπάσας ἔπεμψα, τὴν δ᾽ ἄξω τάχα.

ΟΙΔΙΠΟΥΣ

οἴμοι.

ΚΡΕΩΝ

τάχ᾽ ἕξεις μᾶλλον οἰμώζειν τάδε.   820

ΟΙΔΙΠΟΥΣ

τὴν παῖδ᾽ ἔχεις μου;

ΚΡΕΩΝ

τήνδε τ᾽ οὐ μακροῦ χρόνου.

ΟΙΔΙΠΟΥΣ

ἰὼ ξένοι, τί δράσετ᾽; ἦ προδώσετε,
κοὐκ ἐξελᾶτε τὸν ἀσεβῆ τῆσδε χθονός;

ΧΟΡΟΣ

χώρει, ξέν᾽, ἔξω θᾶσσον. οὔτε γὰρ τὰ νῦν
δίκαια πράσσεις οὔθ᾽ ἃ πρόσθεν εἴργασαι.   825

ΚΡΕΩΝ

ὑμῖν ἂν εἴη τήνδε καιρὸς ἐξάγειν
ἄκουσαν, εἰ θέλουσα μὴ πορεύεται.

CREON

    I call on these men—not on you—to witness
the way you answer your own family friends.
If I ever capture you . . . ³⁵

OEDIPUS

                     Who could seize me
if these men, my allies, are unwilling?

CREON

    Even without that you will still suffer!

OEDIPUS

    You are threatening me? What will you do?

CREON

    I have just seized one of your two daughters
and sent her away. Soon I'll take the other.

OEDIPUS

    No!

CREON

          Before long you'll have more to cry about.   [820]

OEDIPUS

    You have taken my daughter?

CREON

                     Yes I have.
And soon enough I'll have this other one.

OEDIPUS

    Alas, strangers, what are you going to do?
Will you abandon me? Will you not drive
this sacrilegious man away from here?

CHORUS *[to Creon]*

    You must leave here, stranger—without delay!
What you have just done and are doing now
is not acceptable.

CREON *[to his escort]*

                If this young girl
does not wish to come with us, it's now time
for you to take her into custody
against her will.

ΑΝΤΙΓΟΝΗ
οἴμοι τάλαινα, ποῖ φύγω; ποίαν λάβω
θεῶν ἄρηξιν ἢ βροτῶν;

ΧΟΡΟΣ
τί δρᾷς, ξένε;

ΚΡΕΩΝ
οὐχ ἅψομαι τοῦδ᾽ ἀνδρός, ἀλλὰ τῆς ἐμῆς.   830

ΟΙΔΙΠΟΥΣ
ὦ γῆς ἄνακτες.

ΧΟΡΟΣ
ὦ ξέν᾽, οὐ δίκαια δρᾷς.

ΚΡΕΩΝ
δίκαια.

ΧΟΡΟΣ
πῶς δίκαια;

ΚΡΕΩΝ
τοὺς ἐμοὺς ἄγω.

ΟΙΔΙΠΟΥΣ
ἰὼ πόλις.

ΧΟΡΟΣ
τί δρᾷς, ὦ ξέν᾽; οὐκ ἀφήσεις; τάχ᾽ εἰς βάσανον εἶ
χερῶν.   835

ΚΡΕΩΝ
εἴργου.

ΧΟΡΟΣ
σοῦ μὲν οὔ, τάδε γε μωμένου.

ΚΡΕΩΝ
πόλει μαχεῖ γάρ, εἴ τι πημανεῖς ἐμέ.

ANTIGONE

      This is insufferable!
Where can I run to? Who will help me now,
what gods or men?

CHORUS *[to Creon]*
     Stranger, what are you doing?

CREON *[to the Chorus Leader]*
 I will not lay a finger on this man here,   [830]
but I will take her. She belongs to me.

[CREON and his ESCORT move to apprehend ANTIGONE]

OEDIPUS
 O you who rule this land!

CHORUS
       These acts of yours,
 stranger, are not just.

CREON
        They are quite legal.

CHORUS
 How are they legal?

CREON
     I am taking what is mine.

OEDIPUS
 Help us, Athens!

CHORUS
     Stranger, what are you doing?
 Leave her alone—or else you'll quickly face
a test where we resolve this in a fight.

CREON
 Stay back!

CHORUS
    Not if you keep acting in this way.

CREON
 If you harm me, you'll be at war with Thebes.

ΟΙΔΙΠΟΥΣ
οὐκ ἠγόρευον ταῦτ᾽ ἐγώ;

ΧΟΡΟΣ
μέθες χεροῖν
τὴν παῖδα θᾶσσον.

ΚΡΕΩΝ
μὴ ᾽πίτασσ᾽ ἃ μὴ κρατεῖς.

ΧΟΡΟΣ
χαλᾶν λέγω σοι.   840

ΚΡΕΩΝ
σοὶ δ᾽ ἔγωγ᾽ ὁδοιπορεῖν.

ΧΟΡΟΣ
πρόβαθ᾽ ὧδε, βᾶτε βᾶτ᾽, ἔντοποι·
πόλις ἐναίρεται, πόλις ἐμά, σθένει· πρόβαθ᾽ ὧδέ μοι.

ΑΝΤΙΓΟΝΗ
ἀφέλκομαι δύστηνος, ὦ ξένοι ξένοι.

ΟΙΔΙΠΟΥΣ
ποῦ, τέκνον, εἶ μοι;   845

ΑΝΤΙΓΟΝΗ
πρὸς βίαν πορεύομαι.

ΟΙΔΙΠΟΥΣ
ὄρεξον, ὦ παῖ, χεῖρας.

ΑΝΤΙΓΟΝΗ
ἀλλ᾽ οὐδὲν σθένω.

ΚΡΕΩΝ
οὐκ ἄξεθ᾽ ὑμεῖς;

ΟΙΔΙΠΟΥΣ
ὦ τάλας ἐγώ, τάλας.

OEDIPUS
Is that not just what I predicted?

[Members of CREON'S ESCORT seize ANTIGONE]

CHORUS
Let go!
Take your hands off that girl immediately!

CREON
Do not give orders to those you do not rule.

CHORUS
I'm telling you to let that young girl go.

CREON *[to one of his soldiers holding Antigone]*
And I am ordering you to take her off.

[The ESCORT starts to drag ANTIGONE away]

CHORUS
Come here, you citizens of Colonus!
Come here and help! The city—our city—
is being violently attacked! Help us!

ANTIGONE
It's over for me—I'm being dragged away!
O you strangers, you are our hosts and friends . . .

OEDIPUS
Where are you, my child?

ANTIGONE
They're forcing me to go.

OEDIPUS
Give me your hand!

ANTIGONE
I can't—I haven't got the strength.

CREON
You men, take her away!

OEDIPUS
Alas, I'm finished!

ΚΡΕΩΝ

οὔκουν ποτ' ἐκ τούτοιν γε μὴ σκήπτροιν ἔτι
ὁδοιπορήσῃς· ἀλλ' ἐπεὶ νικᾶν θέλεις
πατρίδα τε τὴν σὴν καὶ φίλους, ὑφ' ὧν ἐγὼ   850
ταχθεὶς τάδ' ἔρδω, καὶ τύραννος ὢν ὅμως,
νίκα. χρόνῳ γάρ, οἶδ' ἐγώ, γνώσει τάδε,
ὁθούνεκ' αὐτὸς αὑτὸν οὔτε νῦν καλὰ
δρᾷς οὔτε πρόσθεν εἰργάσω βίᾳ φίλων,
ὀργῇ χάριν δούς, ἥ σ' ἀεὶ λυμαίνεται.   855

ΧΟΡΟΣ

ἐπίσχες αὐτοῦ, ξεῖνε.

ΚΡΕΩΝ

        μὴ ψαύειν λέγω.

ΧΟΡΟΣ

οὔτοι σ' ἀφήσω, τῶνδέ γ' ἐστερημένος.

ΚΡΕΩΝ

καὶ μεῖζον ἆρα ῥύσιον πόλει τάχα
θήσεις· ἐφάψομαι γὰρ οὐ ταύταιν μόναιν.

ΧΟΡΟΣ

ἀλλ' ἐς τί τρέψει;   860

ΚΡΕΩΝ

        τόνδ' ἀπάξομαι λαβών.

ΧΟΡΟΣ

δεινὸν λέγοις ἄν.

ΚΡΕΩΝ

        τοῦτο νῦν πεπράξεται.

ΧΟΡΟΣ

ἢν μή σ' ὁ κραίνων τῆσδε γῆς ἀπειργάθῃ.

ΟΙΔΙΠΟΥΣ

ὦ φθέγμ' ἀναιδές, ἦ σὺ γὰρ ψαύσεις ἐμοῦ;

[Creon's SOLDIERS take ANTIGONE away]

CREON
>   You will not be stumbling around again
>   using these two young girls as your support.
>   But since you wish to win a victory
>   over your native country and your friends,   [850]
>   on whose behalf I undertook these acts,
>   though I am their king, enjoy your triumph.
>   I know in time to come you'll recognize
>   how in all your actions, now and in the past,
>   you have not acted well by giving in,
>   despite your friends, to your own temper.
>   That has always led you to disaster.³⁶

[The CHORUS moves to block CREON from leaving.]

CHORUS
>   Stop there, stranger!

CREON
>   I warn you: do not touch me!

CHORUS
>   If those young girls are taken away from here,
>   I will not let you leave.

CREON
>   If you do that,
>   you'll soon be giving Thebes a greater prize—
>   for I'll be taking more than these two girls.   [860]

CHORUS
>   What do you mean to do?

CREON *[pointing to Oedipus]*
>   I'll seize that man
>   and carry him away.

CHORUS
>   That's a bold threat.

CREON
>   One that will be made good without delay,
>   unless this country's ruler intervenes.

OEDIPUS
>   You glib talker! Would you lay hands on me?

265

ΚΡΕΩΝ

  αὐδῶ σιωπᾶν.

ΟΙΔΙΠΟΥΣ

         μὴ γὰρ αἴδε δαίμονες
  θεῖέν μ' ἄφωνον τῆσδε τῆς ἀρᾶς ἔτι,   865
  ὅς μ', ὦ κάκιστε, ψιλὸν ὄμμ' ἀποσπάσας
  πρὸς ὄμμασιν τοῖς πρόσθεν ἐξοίχει βίᾳ.
  τοιγὰρ σέ τ' αὐτὸν καὶ γένος τὸ σὸν θεῶν
  ὁ πάντα λεύσσων Ἥλιος δοίη βίον
  τοιοῦτον οἷον κἀμὲ γηρᾶναί ποτε.   870

ΚΡΕΩΝ

  ὁρᾶτε ταῦτα, τῆσδε γῆς ἐγχώριοι;

ΟΙΔΙΠΟΥΣ

  ὁρῶσι κἀμὲ καὶ σέ, καὶ φρονοῦσ' ὅτι
  ἔργοις πεπονθὼς ῥήμασίν σ' ἀμύνομαι.

ΚΡΕΩΝ

  οὔτοι καθέξω θυμόν, ἀλλ' ἄξω βίᾳ
  κεἰ μοῦνός εἰμι τόνδε καὶ χρόνῳ βραδύς.   875

ΟΙΔΙΠΟΥΣ

  ἰὼ τάλας.

ΧΟΡΟΣ

  ὅσον λῆμ' ἔχων ἀφίκου, ξέν', εἰ τάδε δοκεῖς τελεῖν.

ΚΡΕΩΝ

  δοκῶ.

ΧΟΡΟΣ

    τάνδ' ἄρ' οὐκέτι νεμῶ πόλιν.

ΚΡΕΩΝ

  τοῖς τοι δικαίοις χὠ βραχὺς νικᾷ μέγαν.   880

ΟΙΔΙΠΟΥΣ

  ἀκούεθ' οἷα φθέγγεται;

CREON
Do as I tell you and keep quiet!

OEDIPUS

No!

May the spirits here permit me to call down
one more curse against you, you worst of men,
since you have hauled away that helpless girl
and taken by force my one remaining eye.
May all-seeing Helios, god of the sun,
grant you and your entire family
a life like mine when you are growing old.   [870]

CREON
Do you see this, you men of Colonus?

OEDIPUS
They are observing you and me—they see
that when hostile actions make me suffer,
I defend myself with words.

CREON

I'll not check
the anger in my heart one moment more—
though I'm alone and age has slowed me down,
I'll seize this man and lead him off by force!

[CREON moves to take OEDIPUS away by himself.]

OEDIPUS *[struggling with Creon]*
Help me! Help!

CHORUS

How insolent you are, stranger,
if you believe you can accomplish this!

CREON
That is my intention.

CHORUS

If you succeed,
then I will say our city is no more.

CREON
With justice on its side, weakness conquers might.   [880]

OEDIPUS *[still struggling with Creon]*
You hear the sort of words he splutters?

Sophocles

ΧΟΡΟΣ

τά γ᾽ οὐ τελεῖ.

[ἴστω μέγας Ζεύς.]

ΚΡΕΩΝ

Ζεύς γ᾽ ἂν εἰδείη, σὺ δ᾽ οὔ.

ΧΟΡΟΣ

ἆρ᾽ οὐχ ὕβρις τάδ᾽;

ΚΡΕΩΝ

ὕβρις, ἀλλ᾽ ἀνεκτέα.

ΧΟΡΟΣ

ἰὼ πᾶς λεώς, ἰὼ γᾶς πρόμοι,
μόλετε σὺν τάχει, μόλετ᾽, ἐπεὶ πέραν περῶσ᾽
    οἵδε δή.   885

ΘΗΣΕΥΣ

τίς ποθ᾽ ἡ βοή; τί τοὔργον; ἐκ τίνος φόβου ποτὲ
βουθυτοῦντά μ᾽ ἀμφὶ βωμὸν ἔσχετ᾽ ἐναλίῳ θεῷ
τοῦδ᾽ ἐπιστάτῃ Κολωνοῦ; λέξαθ᾽, ὡς εἰδῶ τὸ πᾶν,
οὗ χάριν δεῦρ᾽ ᾖξα θᾶσσον ἢ καθ᾽ ἡδονὴν ποδός.   890

ΟΙΔΙΠΟΥΣ

ὦ φίλτατ᾽, ἔγνων γὰρ τὸ προσφώνημά σου,
πέπονθα δεινὰ τοῦδ᾽ ὑπ᾽ ἀνδρὸς ἀρτίως.

ΘΗΣΕΥΣ

τὰ ποῖα ταῦτα, τίς δ᾽ ὁ πημήνας; λέγε.

ΟΙΔΙΠΟΥΣ

Κρέων ὅδ᾽, ὃν δέδορκας, οἴχεται τέκνων
ἀποσπάσας μου τὴν μόνην ξυνωρίδα.   895

ΘΗΣΕΥΣ

πῶς εἶπας;

268

CHORUS

But great Zeus knows that he will not succeed
in doing what he says.

CREON

                             Zeus may well know,
but you do not.

CHORUS

                              Your actions are outrageous!

CREON

An outrage? Yes, but one you must endure!

CHORUS

All those of you who rule this land, help! Help!
Come here on the run! Come on! These Thebans
are on the move back across the border!

[THESEUS enters with a few ATTENDANTS]

THESEUS

Why all this shouting? What's happening here?
What are you afraid of? Why did you stop
my sacrifice at the altar to Poseidon,
god of the sea and lord of Colonus?
Explain all this so that I understand
why I had to hurry here more quickly   [890]
than was convenient.

OEDIPUS

                              I know that voice!
My dearest friend, I have just been suffering
dreadful things from this creature here.

THESEUS

                           What things?
Who has mistreated you? Tell me.

OEDIPUS

                            Creon has—
the man you see here. He took my children,
the only two I have.

THESEUS

                        What are you saying?

269

Sophocles

ΟΙΔΙΠΟΥΣ

     οἷά περ πέπονθ' ἀκήκοας.

ΘΗΣΕΥΣ

οὔκουν τις ὡς τάχιστα προσπόλων μολὼν
πρὸς τούσδε βωμούς, πάντ' ἀναγκάσει λεὼν
ἄνιππον ἱππότην τε θυμάτων ἄπο
σπεύδειν ἀπὸ ῥυτῆρος, ἔνθα δίστομοι   900
μάλιστα συμβάλλουσιν ἐμπόρων ὁδοί,
ὡς μὴ παρέλθωσ' αἱ κόραι, γέλως δ' ἐγὼ
ξένῳ γένωμαι τῷδε, χειρωθεὶς βίᾳ.
ἴθ', ὡς ἄνωγα, σὺν τάχει. τοῦτον δ' ἐγώ,
εἰ μὲν δι' ὀργῆς ἧκον, ἧς ὅδ' ἄξιος,   905
ἄτρωτον οὐ μεθῆκ' ἂν ἐξ ἐμῆς χερός.
νῦν δ' οὕσπερ αὐτὸς τοὺς νόμους εἰσῆλθ' ἔχων,
τούτοισι κοὐκ ἄλλοισιν ἁρμοσθήσεται.
οὐ γάρ ποτ' ἔξει τῆσδε τῆς χώρας, πρὶν ἂν
κείνας ἐναργεῖς δεῦρό μοι στήσῃς ἄγων·   910
ἐπεὶ δέδρακας οὔτ' ἐμοῦ καταξίως
οὔθ' ὧν πέφυκας αὐτὸς οὔτε σῆς χθονός·
ὅστις δίκαι' ἀσκοῦσαν εἰσελθὼν πόλιν
κἄνευ νόμου κραίνουσαν οὐδέν, εἶτ' ἀφεὶς
τὰ τῆσδε τῆς γῆς κύρι', ὧδ' ἐπεισπεσὼν   915
ἄγεις θ' ἃ χρῄζεις καὶ παρίστασαι βίᾳ,
καί μοι πόλιν κένανδρον ἢ δούλην τινὰ
ἔδοξας εἶναι κἄμ' ἴσον τῷ μηδενί.
καίτοι σε Θῆβαί γ' οὐκ ἐπαίδευσαν κακόν·
οὐ γὰρ φιλοῦσιν ἄνδρας ἐκδίκους τρέφειν,   920
οὐδ' ἄν σ' ἐπαινέσειαν, εἰ πυθοίατο
συλῶντα τἀμὰ καὶ τὰ τῶν θεῶν, βίᾳ
ἄγοντα φωτῶν ἀθλίων ἱκτήρια.
οὔκουν ἔγωγ' ἂν σῆς ἐπεμβαίνων χθονός,
οὐδ' εἰ τὰ πάντων εἶχον ἐνδικώτατα,   925
ἄνευ γε τοῦ κραίνοντος, ὅστις ἦν, χθονὸς
οὔθ' εἷλκον οὔτ' ἂν ἦγον, ἀλλ' ἠπιστάμην

OEDIPUS
I've told you what I have had to suffer.

THESEUS *[to his ATTENDANTS]*
One of you men, go as fast as you can
to those altars. Tell all the people there
to leave the sacrifice and move full speed—   [900]
both on foot and horseback—to that junction
where two highroads meet, so those young girls
do not pass by the place and I become
an object to be laughed at by this stranger
because his power got the better of me.
Go now! Do as I say—and quickly!

[One of the attendants accompanying Theseus runs off. THESEUS turns his attention to CREON]

As for this man, if my anger judged him
as he deserves, he would not escape my hand
without some injury. But now those laws
he himself brought with him when he came here
will render judgment—we need no others.
You will not leave this land until you bring
those young girls back and set them in plain view   [910]
right here in front of me. What you have done
is a disgrace to me, to your parents,
and to your native land. You marched in here,
to a city state that honours justice
and never condones acts outside the law,
and brushed aside this land's authorities,
bursting in like this and seizing prisoners,
using force to take whatever you desired.
You seem to think this city has no men
or Is full of slaves and I am nothing.
It was not Thebes who taught you to be bad.
That state does not like raising lawless men   [920]
and would not praise your actions if it learned
that you were stealing from me and the gods,
forcefully abducting their poor suppliants.
If I were to move into your country,
even with the most righteous of all claims,
I would not seize someone or lead them off
without permission of the ruling power,
whoever he might be. I would know how

ξένον παρ' ἀστοῖς ὡς διαιτᾶσθαι χρεών.
σὺ δ' ἀξίαν οὐκ οὖσαν αἰσχύνεις πόλιν
τὴν αὐτὸς αὐτοῦ, καί σ' ὁ πληθύων χρόνος   930
γέρονθ' ὁμοῦ τίθησι καὶ τοῦ νοῦ κενόν.
εἶπον μὲν οὖν καὶ πρόσθεν, ἐννέπω δὲ νῦν,
τὰς παῖδας ὡς τάχιστα δεῦρ' ἄγειν τινά,
εἰ μὴ μέτοικος τῆσδε τῆς χώρας θέλεις
εἶναι βίᾳ τε κοὐχ ἑκών· καὶ ταῦτά σοι   935
τῷ νῷ θ' ὁμοίως κἀπὸ τῆς γλώσσης λέγω.

ΧΟΡΟΣ

όρᾷς ἵν' ἥκεις, ὦ ξέν'; ὡς ἀφ' ὧν μὲν εἶ
φαίνει δίκαιος, δρῶν δ' ἐφευρίσκει κακά.

ΚΡΕΩΝ

ἐγὼ οὔτ' ἄνανδρον τήνδε τὴν πόλιν νέμων,
ὦ τέκνον Αἰγέως, οὔτ' ἄβουλον, ὡς σὺ φής,   940
τοὔργον τόδ' ἐξέπραξα, γιγνώσκων δ' ὅτι
οὐδείς ποτ' αὐτοὺς τῶν ἐμῶν ἂν ἐμπέσοι
ζῆλος ξυναίμων, ὥστ' ἐμοῦ τρέφειν βίᾳ.
ἤδη δ' ὁθούνεκ' ἄνδρα καὶ πατροκτόνον
κἄναγνον οὐ δεξοίατ', οὐδ' ὅτῳ γάμοι   945
ξυνόντες ηὑρέθησαν ἀνόσιοι τέκνων.
τοιοῦτον αὐτοῖς Ἄρεος εὔβουλον πάγον
ἐγὼ ξυνῄδη χθόνιον ὄνθ', ὃς οὐκ ἐᾷ
τοιούσδ' ἀλήτας τῇδ' ὁμοῦ ναίειν πόλει·
ᾧ πίστιν ἴσχων τήνδ' ἐχειρούμην ἄγραν.   950
καὶ ταῦτ' ἂν οὐκ ἔπρασσον, εἰ μή μοι πικρὰς
αὐτῷ τ' ἀρὰς ἠρᾶτο καὶ τὠμῷ γένει·
ἀνθ' ὧν πεπονθὼς ἠξίουν τάδ' ἀντιδρᾶν.
θυμοῦ γὰρ οὐδὲν γῆράς ἐστιν ἄλλο πλὴν
θανεῖν· θανόντων δ' οὐδὲν ἄλγος ἅπτεται.   955
πρὸς ταῦτα πράξεις οἷον ἂν θέλῃς· ἐπεὶ
ἐρημία με, κεἰ δίκαι', ὅμως λέγω,
σμικρὸν τίθησι· πρὸς δὲ τὰς πράξεις ὅμως,
καὶ τηλικόσδ' ὤν, ἀντιδρᾶν πειράσομαι.

a stranger ought to act with citizens.
But you are a disgrace to your own city.
Thebes does not deserve that. Advancing years   [930]
have made you old and robbed you of all sense.
So I tell you now what I said before—
have those girls brought here as quickly as you can,
unless you wish to be held here by force,
a resident of this land against your will.
What my tongue utters, I intend to do.

CHORUS *[to Creon]*

You see the situation you are in, stranger?
From your origins you seem a righteous man,
but your actions show you are dishonest.

CREON

Son of Aegeus, I have not done these things
because I thought Athens was devoid of men,   [940]
as you have claimed. No. I had sound reasons.
But I did not believe your citizens
would be so devoted to my relatives
that they would keep them here against my will.
And I was sure people would not welcome
a polluted man, who killed his father
and whose unholy marriage was exposed,
a mother wedded to her son. For I knew
such wise restrictions were traditional
with the Council on the Hill of Ares,
which never would permit such vagrant types
to settle in the Athenian state.[37]
Trusting that knowledge, I chased down my prey.   [950]
But I would not have acted in this fashion,
if he had not called down stinging curses
on my family and me. In my view,
what he made me suffer entitled me
to take revenge. Anger never grows old
until death comes, for dead men feel no pain.
You will deal with this however you wish.
What I say is right, but I am alone
and therefore feeble. Still, though I am old,
I will seek to pay you back for what you do.

ΟΙΔΙΠΟΥΣ

ὦ λῆμ᾽ ἀναιδές, τοῦ καθυβρίζειν δοκεῖς,　　　　960
πότερον ἐμοῦ γέροντος ἢ σαυτοῦ, τόδε;
ὅστις φόνους μοι καὶ γάμους καὶ συμφορὰς
τοῦ σοῦ διῆκας στόματος, ἃς ἐγὼ τάλας
ἤνεγκον ἄκων· θεοῖς γὰρ ἦν οὕτω φίλον,
τάχ᾽ ἄν τι μηνίουσιν εἰς γένος πάλαι.　　　　965
ἐπεὶ καθ᾽ αὑτόν γ᾽ οὐκ ἂν ἐξεύροις ἐμοὶ
ἁμαρτίας ὄνειδος οὐδέν, ἀνθ᾽ ὅτου
τάδ᾽ εἰς ἐμαυτὸν τοὺς ἐμούς θ᾽ ἡμάρτανον.
ἐπεὶ δίδαξον, εἴ τι θέσφατον πατρὶ
χρησμοῖσιν ἱκνεῖθ᾽ ὥστε πρὸς παίδων θανεῖν,　　970
πῶς ἂν δικαίως τοῦτ᾽ ὀνειδίζοις ἐμοί,
ὃς οὔτε βλάστας πω γενεθλίους πατρός,
οὐ μητρὸς εἶχον, ἀλλ᾽ ἀγέννητος τότ᾽ ἦ;
εἰ δ᾽ αὖ φανεὶς δύστηνος, ὡς ἐγὼ ᾽φάνην,
ἐς χεῖρας ἦλθον πατρὶ καὶ κατέκτανον,　　　　975
μηδὲν ξυνιεὶς ὧν ἔδρων εἰς οὕς τ᾽ ἔδρων,
πῶς ἂν τό γ᾽ ἄκον πρᾶγμ᾽ ἂν εἰκότως ψέγοις;
μητρὸς δέ, τλῆμον, οὐκ ἐπαισχύνει γάμους
οὔσης ὁμαίμου σῆς μ᾽ ἀναγκάζων λέγειν,
οἵους ἐρῶ τάχ᾽· οὐ γὰρ οὖν σιγήσομαι,　　　　980
σοῦ γ᾽ εἰς τόδ᾽ ἐξελθόντος ἀνόσιον στόμα.
ἔτικτε γάρ μ᾽ ἔτικτεν, ὤμοι μοι κακῶν,
οὐκ εἰδότ᾽ οὐκ εἰδυῖα, καὶ τεκοῦσά με,
αὑτῆς ὄνειδος παῖδας ἐξέφυσέ μοι.
ἀλλ᾽ ἓν γὰρ οὖν ἔξοιδα, σὲ μὲν ἑκόντ᾽ ἐμὲ
κείνην τε ταῦτα δυσστομεῖν· ἐγὼ δέ νιν　　　　985
ἄκων ἔγημα φθέγγομαί τ᾽ ἄκων τάδε.
ἀλλ᾽ οὐ γὰρ οὔτ᾽ ἐν τοῖσδ᾽ ἁλώσομαι κακὸς
γάμοισιν οὔθ᾽ οὓς αἰὲν ἐμφορεῖς σύ μοι
φόνους πατρῴους ἐξονειδίζων πικρῶς.　　　　990

Oedipus

What blatant arrogance! For whose old age   [960]
do you think this abuse is more degrading,
yours or mine? Against me that mouth of yours
spits out words like murder, incest, misery—
sufferings I, in my wretchedness, endured
through no fault of my own. All these events
were pleasing to the gods—perhaps because
my family long ago offended them.
For looking at my life, you could not find
a single reason to blame me for mistakes
for which I needed to pay retribution
with destructive acts injuring myself
and my own kindred. Explain this to me:
if some divine voice in an oracle
told my father he was going to die
at the hand of his own son, how can you   [970]
justly blame me for it. I was not born.
No father's seed had yet begotten me,
nor had any mother's womb conceived me.
I did not exist! And if I was born,
as I was, to a life of wretchedness,
had a lethal fight with my own father,
and killed him, with no idea who he was
or what I had done, are you justified
in disparaging me for what I did
without intending to? As for my mother,
you disgraceful brute, are you not ashamed
to force me to speak about her marriage,
when she was your sister? Well then, I shall.
I will not stay silent about the details,
when you have gone to such great lengths to talk   [980]
of sacrilegious things. She gave birth to me—
yes, alas for me, she was my mother.
But I did not know that, and nor did she.
And she had children with the son she bore,
to her great shame. But this one thing I know—
you freely choose to heap insults on us,
but I did not freely choose to marry her,
nor do I ever choose to mention it.
No, I will not be called an evil man
because I married her and killed my father,
that death you keep on hurling in my teeth,
always abusing me with bitter insults.   [990]

ἓν γάρ μ' ἄμειψαι μοῦνον ὧν σ' ἀνιστορῶ.
εἴ τις σὲ τὸν δίκαιον αὐτίκ' ἐνθάδε
κτείνοι παραστάς, πότερα πυνθάνοι' ἂν εἰ
πατήρ σ' ὁ καίνων ἢ τίνοι' ἂν εὐθέως;
δοκῶ μέν, εἴπερ ζῆν φιλεῖς, τὸν αἴτιον   995
τίνοι' ἂν οὐδὲ τοὔνδικον περιβλέποις.
τοιαῦτα μέντοι καὐτὸς εἰσέβην κακά,
θεῶν ἀγόντων· οἷς ἐγὼ οὐδὲ τὴν πατρὸς
ψυχὴν ἂν οἶμαι ζῶσαν ἀντειπεῖν ἐμοί.
σὺ δ', εἶ γὰρ οὐ δίκαιος, ἀλλ' ἅπαν καλὸν   1000
λέγειν νομίζων ῥητὸν ἄρρητόν τ' ἔπος,
τοιαῦτ' ὀνειδίζεις με τῶνδ' ἐναντίον.
καί σοι τὸ Θησέως ὄνομα θωπεῦσαι καλόν,
καὶ τὰς Ἀθήνας, ὡς κατῴκηνται καλῶς·
κᾆθ' ὧδ' ἐπαινῶν πολλὰ τοῦδ' ἐκλανθάνει,   1005
ὁθούνεκ' εἴ τις γῇ θεοὺς ἐπίσταται
τιμαῖς σεβίζειν, ἥδε τοῦθ' ὑπερφέρει·
ἀφ' ἧς σὺ κλέψας τὸν ἱκέτην γέροντ' ἐμὲ
αὐτόν τ' ἐχειροῦ τὰς κόρας τ' οἴχει λαβών.
ἀνθ' ὧν ἐγὼ νῦν τάσδε τὰς θεὰς ἐμοὶ   1010
καλῶν ἱκνοῦμαι καὶ κατασκήπτω λιταῖς
ἐλθεῖν ἀρωγοὺς ξυμμάχους θ', ἵν' ἐκμάθῃς
οἵων ὑπ' ἀνδρῶν ἥδε φρουρεῖται πόλις.

ΧΟΡΟΣ
    ὁ ξεῖνος, ὦναξ, χρηστός· αἱ δὲ συμφοραὶ
    αὐτοῦ πανώλεις, ἄξιαι δ' ἀμυναθεῖν.   1015

ΘΗΣΕΥΣ
    ἅλις λόγων, ὡς οἱ μὲν ἐξειργασμένοι
    σπεύδουσιν, ἡμεῖς δ' οἱ παθόντες ἔσταμεν.

Here is a question. How would you answer?
If someone were to march in here right now
and attempt to kill you, you righteous man,
would your first response be to ask the killer,
"Are you my father?" or to fight him back?
It seems to me that, if you love your life,
you would fight back against the murderer,
not search for what was legally correct.
That is how I was led on by the gods
and embarked upon a life of evils.
I do not think my father's ghostly shade,
if it came back to life, would contradict me.
But because you are not a righteous man,   [1000]
you think you can say anything at all,
without considering if what you speak
is suitable or should not be mentioned.
And so in front of all these people here
you keep hurling accusations at me.
You think it serves your purposes to flatter
the great name of Theseus and Athens
as a well-governed state. But when you praise,
you forget that if there is one city
that understands how to respect the gods
that place is Athens—she excels in that.
Yet it is from here you wished to steal me,
an old man and a suppliant, as well.
You laid hands on me, tried to drag me off,
after having hauled away my daughters.
So now I call upon these goddesses,   [1010]
I appeal to them, and with my prayers
I beseech them to come to my aid here,
to fight on my behalf, so you may learn
the quality of those who guard this city.

CHORUS
My lord, this stranger is a worthy man.
His misfortunes have been devastating,
but he deserves our help.

THESEUS
                We have talked enough!
Those who took the girls are hurrying off,
while we, the ones they robbed, are standing still.

277

Sophocles

ΚΡΕΩΝ

τί δῆτ᾽ ἀμαυρῷ φωτὶ προστάσσεις ποεῖν;

ΘΗΣΕΥΣ

 ὁδοῦ κατάρχειν τῆς ἐκεῖ, πομπὸν δέ με
χωρεῖν, ἵν᾽, εἰ μὲν ἐν τόποισι τοῖσδ᾽ ἔχεις   1020
τὰς παῖδας ἡμῖν αὐτὸς ἐκδείξῃς ἐμοί·
εἰ δ᾽ ἐγκρατεῖς φεύγουσιν, οὐδὲν δεῖ πονεῖν.
ἄλλοι γὰρ οἱ σπεύδοντες, οὓς οὐ μή ποτε
χώρας φυγόντες τῆσδ᾽ ἐπεύξωνται θεοῖς.
ἀλλ᾽ ἐξυφηγοῦ· γνῶθι δ᾽ ὡς ἔχων ἔχει   1025
καί σ᾽ εἷλε θηρῶνθ᾽ ἡ τύχη· τὰ γὰρ δόλῳ
τῷ μὴ δικαίῳ κτήματ᾽ οὐχὶ σῴζεται.
κοὐκ ἄλλον ἕξεις εἰς τάδ᾽· ὡς ἔξοιδά σε
οὐ ψιλὸν οὐδ᾽ ἄσκευον ἐς τοσήνδ᾽ ὕβριν
ἥκοντα τόλμης τῆς παρεστώσης τανῦν,   1030
ἀλλ᾽ ἔσθ᾽ ὅτῳ σὺ πιστὸς ὢν ἔδρας τάδε.
ἃ δεῖ μ᾽ ἀθρῆσαι, μηδὲ τήνδε τὴν πόλιν
ἑνὸς ποῆσαι φωτὸς ἀσθενεστέραν.
νοεῖς τι τούτων, ἢ μάτην τὰ νῦν τέ σοι
δοκεῖ λελέχθαι χὦτε ταῦτ᾽ ἐμηχανῶ;   1035

ΚΡΕΩΝ

 οὐδὲν σὺ μεμπτὸν ἐνθάδ᾽ ὢν ἐρεῖς ἐμοί·
οἴκοι δὲ χἠμεῖς εἰσόμεσθ᾽ ἃ χρὴ ποεῖν.

ΘΗΣΕΥΣ

 χωρῶν ἀπείλει νῦν· σὺ δ᾽ ἡμίν, Οἰδίπους,
ἔκηλος αὐτοῦ μίμνε, πιστωθεὶς ὅτι,
ἢν μὴ θάνω ᾽γὼ πρόσθεν, οὐχὶ παύσομαι   1040
πρὶν ἄν σε τῶν σῶν κύριον στήσω τέκνων.

CREON

> I am a weak man. What would you have me do?

THESEUS

> I want you to lead us on the pathway
> to those girls, while I serve as your escort,
> so if you are keeping those two children   [1020]
> in this place, you will personally show me
> where they are. But if those who have seized them
> are on the run, there is nothing we need do,
> for other men are chasing after them,
> from whom they never will escape and leave
> this land to give thank offerings to the gods.
> Come, then, lead on. And you might ponder this—
> the hunter has been hunted down, and Fate
> has seized you while you were stalking others.
> What people gain unjustly with a trick
> they do not keep, and no one else involved
> will help you in this matter. For I know
> you would not reach such heights of insolence
> and act so recklessly as you do now   [1030]
> all on your own, without accomplices.
> You were relying on someone else's help
> when you resolved to carry out this act.[38]
> I need to think further on this matter—
> one man must not prove stronger than the state.
> Do these words of warning make any sense,
> or do they now seem as meaningless to you
> as what you heard when you were planning this?

CREON

> Here in Athens, you can say what you wish.
> I will not object. But when I am home,
> I, too, will realize what must be done.

THESEUS

> Make your threats, but move. And you, Oedipus,
> stay here, and do not worry. Trust this pledge—
> unless I die beforehand, I will not rest   [1040]
> until I have restored your children to you.

[CREON, THESEUS, and the ATTENDANTS leave]

ΟΙΔΙΠΟΥΣ

   ὄναιο, Θησεῦ, τοῦ τε γενναίου χάριν
   καὶ τῆς πρὸς ἡμᾶς ἐνδίκου προμηθίας.

ΧΟΡΟΣ

   εἴην ὅθι δαΐων
   ἀνδρῶν τάχ᾽ ἐπιστροφαὶ   1045
   τὸν χαλκοβόαν Ἄρη
   μείξουσιν, ἢ πρὸς Πυθίαις
   ἢ λαμπάσιν ἀκταῖς,
   οὗ πότνιαι σεμνὰ τιθηνοῦνται τέλη   1050
   θνατοῖσιν, ὧν καὶ χρυσέα
   κλῇς ἐπὶ γλώσσᾳ βέβακε
   προσπόλων Εὐμολπιδᾶν·
   ἔνθ᾽ οἶμαι τὸν ἐγρεμάχαν
   Θησέα καὶ τὰς διστόλους   1055
   ἀδμῆτας ἀδελφὰς
   αὐτάρκει τάχ᾽ ἐμμίξειν βοᾷ
   τούσδ᾽ ἀνὰ χώρους·

   ἤ που τὸν ἐφεσπέρου
   πέτρας νιφάδος πελῶσ᾽   1060
   Οἰάτιδος εἰς νόμον,
   πώλοισιν ἢ ῥιμφαρμάτοις
   φεύγοντες ἀμίλλαις.
   ἁλώσεται· δεινὸς ὁ προσχώρων Ἄρης,   1065
   δεινὰ δὲ Θησειδᾶν ἀκμά.
   πᾶς γὰρ ἀστράπτει χαλινός,
   πᾶσα δ᾽ ὁρμᾶται καθεῖσ᾽
   ἀμπυκτήρια στομίων
   ἄμβασις, οἳ τὰν ἱππίαν   1070
   τιμῶσιν Ἀθάναν
   καὶ τὸν πόντιον γαιάοχον
   Ῥέας φίλον υἱόν.

   ἔρδουσ᾽ ἢ μέλλουσιν; ὡς
   προμνᾶταί τί μοι   1075
   γνώμα τάχ᾽ ἀντάσειν
   τᾶν δεινὰ τλασᾶν, δεινὰ δ᾽ εὑρουσᾶν πρὸς αὐθαίμων πάθη.

OEDIPUS *[calling after Theseus]*
    Bless you, Theseus, for your noble heart
    and for your righteous care on my behalf!

CHORUS
    O how I wish I could be there,
    where the enemy wheels to fight
    and quickly joins the battle clash,
    the clamour of Ares' brazen spears,
    hard by the Phythian shore—
    or else beside the torch-lit strand
    where those two goddesses perform   [1050]
    their sacred rites for mortal men
    whose tongues their holy ministers,
    the Eumolpidae, have silenced
    by placing there a seal of gold.[39]
    There, I think, our warlike Theseus
    and those two unmarried girls
    will soon meet in this land of ours,
    amid the cries of our brave fighting men.

    Or else they may be closing in
    on pastures west of Oea's snowy peak,   [1060]
    racing ahead on youthful horses,
    their chariots careening at full speed.
    Now Creon will be overthrown!
    Our men are terrifying in war,
    and Theseus' troops are battle strong.
    Every bit and bridle glitters,
    as all our horsemen charge the foe,
    in honour of equestrian Athena   [1070]
    and the god encircling the earth,
    lord of the sea, Rhea's beloved son.[40]

    Have they already come to blows,
    or are our men about to fight?
    My mind is telling me to hope
    we soon will meet those two young girls,
    whose suffering has been intense,
    afflictions they have undergone
    at the blood-linked hands of their own kin.

τελεῖ τελεῖ Ζεύς τι κατ᾽ ἆμαρ
μάντις εἴμ᾽ ἐσθλῶν ἀγώνων.
εἴθ᾽ ἀελλαία ταχύρρωστος πελειὰς
αἰθερίας νεφέλας κύρσαιμ᾽ ἄνωθ᾽ ἀγώνων   1080
αἰωρήσασα τοὐμὸν ὄμμα.

ἰὼ θεῶν πάνταρχε, παντ-   1085
όπτα Ζεῦ, πόροις
γᾶς τᾶσδε δαμούχοις
σθένει 'πινικείῳ τὸν εὔαγρον τελειῶσαι λόχον,
σεμνά τε παῖς Παλλὰς Ἀθάνα.   1090
καὶ τὸν ἀγρευτὰν Ἀπόλλω
καὶ κασιγνήταν πυκνοστίκτων ὀπαδὸν
ὠκυπόδων ἐλάφων στέργω διπλᾶς ἀρωγὰς
μολεῖν γᾷ τᾷδε καὶ πολίταις.

— ὦ ξεῖν᾽ ἀλῆτα, τῷ σκοπῷ μὲν οὐκ ἐρεῖς   1095
ὡς ψευδόμαντις· τὰς κόρας γὰρ εἰσορῶ
τάσδ᾽ ἆσσον αὖθις ὧδε προσπολουμένας.

ΟΙΔΙΠΟΥΣ
   ποῦ ποῦ; τί φής; πῶς εἶπας;

ΑΝΤΙΓΟΝΗ
                                 ὦ πάτερ πάτερ,
   τίς ἂν θεῶν σοι τόνδ᾽ ἄριστον ἄνδρ᾽ ἰδεῖν   1100
   δοίη, τὸν ἡμᾶς δεῦρο προσπέμψαντά σοι;

ΟΙΔΙΠΟΥΣ
   ὦ τέκνον, ἦ πάρεστον;

ΑΝΤΙΓΟΝΗ
                                 αἵδε γὰρ χέρες
   Θησέως ἔσωσαν φιλτάτων τ᾽ ὀπαόνων.

Today Zeus brings some great event
to its fulfilment, its final end.
I can foresee a glorious fight!
O to be a dove on the wing,
as strong and swift as a storming wind,
to soar up high in the upper air   [1080]
and gaze from a cloud on the battle below!

O Zeus, who watches everything,
almighty king of all the gods,
grant to defenders of this land
the strength to win a victory,
to catch the enemy unaware
and end the chase successfully!
And I pray that Pallas Athena
your revered daughter, grants that, too,   [1090]
as well as Apollo, the hunter god,
and with him his sister Artemis,
who tracks swift-moving speckled deer—
O may they bring their two-fold help,
assisting our citizens and Athens.

[Enter THESEUS, ANTIGONE, ISMENE, and ATTENDANTS]

CHORUS *[to OEDIPUS]*
Well, my wandering friend, you cannot say
those watching out for you are lying prophets—
I see your daughters being escorted back.

OEDIPUS
What? Where are they? What are you talking about?

ANTIGONE
O father, father, I wish one of the gods   [1100]
would let you see this very best of men,
who brought us here and led us back to y0u.

OEDIPUS
My child, are you really here, both of you?

ANTIGONE
Yes—saved by the strong hands of Theseus
and his most loyal comrades.

283

ΟΙΔΙΠΟΥΣ

προσέλθετ᾽ ὦ παῖ, πατρὶ καὶ τὸ μηδαμὰ
ἐλπισθὲν ἥξειν σῶμα βαστάσαι δότε.　　　　　1105

ΑΝΤΙΓΟΝΗ

αἰτεῖς ἃ τεύξει· σὺν πόθῳ γὰρ ἡ χάρις.

ΟΙΔΙΠΟΥΣ

ποῦ δῆτα, ποῦ 'στόν;

ΑΝΤΙΓΟΝΗ

αἵδ᾽ ὁμοῦ πελάζομεν.

ΟΙΔΙΠΟΥΣ

ὦ φίλτατ᾽ ἔρνη.

ΑΝΤΙΓΟΝΗ

τῷ τεκόντι πᾶν φίλον.

ΟΙΔΙΠΟΥΣ

ὦ σκῆπτρα φωτός.

ΑΝΤΙΓΟΝΗ

δυσμόρου γε δύσμορα.

ΟΙΔΙΠΟΥΣ

ἔχω τὰ φίλτατ᾽, οὐδ᾽ ἔτ᾽ ἂν πανάθλιος　　　　　1110
θανὼν ἂν εἴην σφῷν παρεστώσαιν ἐμοί.
ἐρείσατ᾽, ὦ παῖ, πλευρὸν ἀμφιδέξιον
ἐμφύντε τῷ φύσαντι, κἀναπαύσατον
τοῦ πρόσθ᾽ ἐρήμου τοῦδε δυστήνου πλάνου.
καί μοι τὰ πραχθέντ᾽ εἴπαθ᾽ ὡς βράχιστ᾽, ἐπεὶ　　　　　1115
ταῖς τηλικαῖσδε σμικρὸς ἐξαρκεῖ λόγος.

ΑΝΤΙΓΟΝΗ

ὅδ᾽ ἔσθ᾽ ὁ σώσας· τοῦδε χρὴ κλύειν, πάτερ,
οὗ κἄστι τοὔργον· τοὐμὸν ὧδ᾽ ἔσται βραχύ.

OEDIPUS

O children,
come to your father and let me hold you.
I was losing hope you would be coming back.

ANTIGONE

You will get your wish. That embrace you want
is what we long for.

OEDIPUS

Where are the two of you?

ANTIGONE

We're coming—both of us together.

[ANTIGONE, ISMENE, and OEDIPUS embrace]

OEDIPUS

My dearest children!

ANTIGONE

To any father
every child is dear.

OEDIPUS

An old man's support . . .

ANTIGONE

With a destiny as wretched as his own.

OEDIPUS

I am now holding those I love the most.   [1110]
If I should die with you two beside me,
I could not be entirely unhappy.
O children, hold me close—one on each side—
cling to your father, help him recover
from his past days of lonely wandering,
a life of misery. And now tell us
what you went through, but keep the speeches short—
from girls like you a brief word is enough.

ANTIGONE

Father, the one who rescued us is here.
He is the one you should be listening to,
the man who did it. What I have to say
will not be much.

ΟΙΔΙΠΟΥΣ

ὦ ξεῖνε, μὴ θαύμαζε, πρὸς τὸ λιπαρὲς
τέκν᾽ εἰ φανέντ᾽ ἄελπτα μηκύνω λόγον.   1120
ἐπίσταμαι γὰρ τήνδε τὴν ἐς τάσδε μοι
τέρψιν παρ᾽ ἄλλου μηδενὸς πεφασμένην·
σὺ γάρ νιν ἐξέσωσας, οὐκ ἄλλος βροτῶν.
καί σοι θεοὶ πόροιεν ὡς ἐγὼ θέλω,
αὐτῷ τε καὶ γῇ τῇδ᾽, ἐπεὶ τό γ᾽ εὐσεβὲς   1125
μόνοις παρ᾽ ὑμῖν ηὗρον ἀνθρώπων ἐγὼ
καὶ τοὐπιεικὲς καὶ τὸ μὴ ψευδοστομεῖν.
εἰδὼς δ᾽ ἀμύνω τοῖσδε τοῖς λόγοις τάδε·
ἔχω γὰρ ἅχω διὰ σὲ κοὐκ ἄλλον βροτῶν·
καί μοι χέρ᾽, ὦναξ, δεξιὰν ὄρεξον, ὡς   1130
ψαύσω φιλήσω τ᾽, εἰ θέμις, τὸ σὸν κάρα.
καίτοι τί φωνῶ; πῶς σ᾽ ἂν ἄθλιος γεγὼς
θιγεῖν θελήσαιμ᾽ ἀνδρός, ᾧ τίς οὐκ ἔνι
κηλὶς κακῶν ξύνοικος; οὐκ ἔγωγέ σε,
οὐδ᾽ οὖν ἐάσω· τοῖς γὰρ ἐμπείροις βροτῶν   1135
μόνοις οἷόν τε συνταλαιπωρεῖν τάδε.
σὺ δ᾽ αὐτόθεν μοι χαῖρε καὶ τὰ λοιπά μου
μέλου δικαίως, ὥσπερ ἐς τόδ᾽ ἡμέρας.

ΘΗΣΕΥΣ

οὔτ᾽ εἴ τι μῆκος τῶν λόγων ἔθου πλέον,
τέκνοισι τερφθεὶς τοῖσδε, θαυμάσας ἔχω,   1140
οὔτ᾽ εἰ πρὸ τοὐμοῦ προύλαβες τὰ τῶνδ᾽ ἔπη.
βάρος γὰρ ἡμᾶς οὐδὲν ἐκ τούτων ἔχει.
οὐ γὰρ λόγοισι τὸν βίον σπουδάζομεν
λαμπρὸν ποεῖσθαι μᾶλλον ἢ τοῖς δρωμένοις.
δείκνυμι δ᾽· ὧν γὰρ ὤμοσ᾽ οὐκ ἐψευσάμην   1145
οὐδέν σε, πρέσβυ· τάσδε γὰρ πάρειμ᾽ ἄγων
ζώσας, ἀκραιφνεῖς τῶν κατηπειλημένων.

OEDIPUS *[to THESEUS]*
                    You must not be amazed,
my friend, that I keep talking for so long   [1120]
to these children, so suddenly restored.
For I know that my present joy in them
I owe entirely to you. You saved them—
you and no one else. And may gods grant
to you and to this land what I would wish,
for among all those living on the earth
only here with you have I encountered
men of piety and just character
who tell no lies. I know that about you,
and I pay tribute to your qualities
with these words of mine. Everything I have
I have because of you and no one else.
O royal king, hold your right hand out to me,   [1130]
so I can touch it. If it is lawful,
let me be permitted to kiss your cheek.
But what am I saying? A wretch like me,
how could I want you to touch a man
in whom every form of defiling stain
has found a home? No, I will not touch you.
That is an action I cannot permit,
not even if you yourself were willing.
Only those mortals who have been with me
in my misfortunes can share my suffering.[41]
So from where you stand accept my gratitude,
and, as you have done up to this moment,
deal with me justly in the days to come.

THESEUS
Given your delight in these two children,
I am not surprised your conversation   [1140]
has taken some time or that you prefer
to talk to them before you talk to me.
I can find no offence to me in that.
I do not wish to add lustre to my life
through the words I speak, but by what I do.
And I have demonstrated that to you,
old man, for my word has not proven false
in any of those promises I made.
I am here, having brought back your daughters
alive and unharmed by the threats they faced.

287

χὤπως μὲν ἀγὼν ᾑρέθη, τί δεῖ μάτην
κομπεῖν, ἅ γ᾽ εἴσει καὐτὸς ἐκ ταύταιν ξυνών;
λόγος δ᾽ ὃς ἐμπέπτωκεν ἀρτίως ἐμοὶ   1150
στείχοντι δεῦρο, συμβαλοῦ γνώμην, ἐπεὶ
σμικρὸς μὲν εἰπεῖν, ἄξιος δὲ θαυμάσαι·
πρᾶγος δ᾽ ἀτίζειν οὐδὲν ἄνθρωπον χρεών.

ΟΙΔΙΠΟΥΣ

τί δ᾽ ἔστι, τέκνον Αἰγέως; δίδασκέ με
ὡς μὴ εἰδότ᾽ αὐτὸν μηδὲν ὧν σὺ πυνθάνει.   1155

ΘΗΣΕΥΣ

φασίν τιν᾽ ἡμῖν ἄνδρα, σοὶ μὲν ἔμπολιν
οὐκ ὄντα, συγγενῆ δέ, προσπεσόντα πως
βωμῷ καθῆσθαι τῷ Ποσειδῶνος, παρ᾽ ᾧ
θύων ἔκυρον, ἡνίχ᾽ ὡρμώμην ἐγώ.

ΟΙΔΙΠΟΥΣ

ποδαπόν; τί προσχρῄζοντα τῷ θακήματι·   1160

ΘΗΣΕΥΣ

οὐκ οἶδα πλὴν ἕν· σοῦ γάρ, ὡς λέγουσί μοι,
βραχύν τιν᾽ αἰτεῖ μῦθον οὐκ ὄγκου πλέων.

ΟΙΔΙΠΟΥΣ

ποῖόν τιν᾽; οὐ γὰρ ἥδ᾽ ἕδρα σμικροῦ λόγου.

ΘΗΣΕΥΣ

σοὶ φασὶν αὐτὸν ἐς λόγους ἐλθεῖν μόνον
αἰτεῖν ἀπελθεῖν τ᾽ ἀσφαλῶς τῆς δεῦρ᾽ ὁδοῦ.   1165

ΟΙΔΙΠΟΥΣ

τίς δῆτ᾽ ἂν εἴη τήνδ᾽ ὁ προσθακῶν ἕδραν;

As for how we triumphed in that struggle,
why should I vainly boast about a fight
whose details you will hear from these two girls
when you get to spend some time together.
But a moment ago, on my way here,   [1150]
I heard an odd report, and I would like
to learn what you advise. It was quite short,
but very strange and worth attending to,
for men should never overlook anything
that might be of concern.

OEDIPUS
                    What did it say,
son of Aegeus? Describe it to me.
Otherwise I have no idea at all
what you wish to know.

THESEUS
                    People say a man,
someone who is a relative of yours
but not from Thebes, has somehow made his way
to Poseidon's altar and is sitting there,
where I was offering a sacrifice
the first time I was summoned here.

OEDIPUS
                    Where is he from?   [1160]
If he's a suppliant, what does he want?

THESEUS
From what people tell me, I only know
he wishes to have a brief word with you
about some minor matter.

OEDIPUS
                    What about?
If he's there sitting as a suppliant,
the issue is not trivial.

THESEUS
                    They say
he only wants to have a talk with you
and then safe passage to return from here.

OEDIPUS
Who would sit there praying for such things?

ΘΗΣΕΥΣ

　　ὅρα κατ᾽ Ἄργος εἴ τις ὑμὶν ἐγγενὴς
　　ἔσθ᾽, ὅστις ἄν σου τοῦτο προσχρῄζοι τυχεῖν.

ΟΙΔΙΠΟΥΣ

　　ὦ φίλτατε, σχὲς οὗπερ εἶ.

ΘΗΣΕΥΣ

　　　　　　　　τί δ᾽ ἔστι σοι;

ΟΙΔΙΠΟΥΣ

　　μή μου δεηθῇς.　　　　　　　　　　　　　1170

ΘΗΣΕΥΣ

　　　　　　　πράγματος ποίου; λέγε.

ΟΙΔΙΠΟΥΣ

　　ἔξοιδ᾽ ἀκούων τῶνδ᾽ ὅς ἐσθ᾽ ὁ προστάτης.

ΘΗΣΕΥΣ

　　καὶ τίς ποτ᾽ ἐστὶν ὅν γ᾽ ἐγὼ ψέξαιμί τι;

ΟΙΔΙΠΟΥΣ

　　παῖς οὑμός, ὦναξ, στυγνός, οὗ λόγων ἐγὼ
　　ἄλγιστ᾽ ἂν ἀνδρῶν ἐξανασχοίμην κλύων.

ΘΗΣΕΥΣ

　　τί δ᾽; οὐκ ἀκούειν ἔστι καὶ μὴ δρᾶν ἃ μὴ　　1175
　　χρῄζεις; τί σοι τοῦτ᾽ ἐστὶ λυπηρὸν κλύειν;

ΟΙΔΙΠΟΥΣ

　　ἔχθιστον, ὦναξ, φθέγμα τοῦθ᾽ ἥκει πατρί·
　　καὶ μή μ᾽ ἀνάγκῃ προσβάλῃς τάδ᾽ εἰκαθεῖν.

ΘΗΣΕΥΣ

　　ἀλλ᾽ εἰ τὸ θάκημ᾽ ἐξαναγκάζει, σκόπει
　　μή σοι πρόνοι᾽ ᾖ τοῦ θεοῦ φυλακτέα.　　　1180

THESEUS

    Could it be a member of your family,
    someone from Argos, who might be asking
    a favour from you?

OEDIPUS

                    Stop there, my dear friend!

THESEUS

    What's troubling you?

OEDIPUS

                  You must not ask me to . . .

THESEUS

    Do what? Tell me.   [1170]

OEDIPUS

                  From what you said just now,
    I know the suppliant.

THESEUS

                      Who is he?
    And why should I find him offensive?

OEDIPUS

    My lord, he is a son of mine, a person
    I detest. What he has to say would pain me
    more than words from any other man.

THESEUS

    What? Could you not just listen to him speak
    and then not do what you don't wish to do?
    Is there any harm in merely listening?

OEDIPUS

    My lord, his voice has become abhorrent
    to me, his father. Do not compel me
    to yield to his request.

THESEUS

                But consider this—
    does not the fact that he's a suppliant
    force your hand? What about the reverence
    you owe the god?   [1180]

Sophocles

ΑΝΤΙΓΟΝΗ

πάτερ, πιθοῦ μοι, κεἰ νέα παραινέσω.
τὸν ἄνδρ᾽ ἔασον τόνδε τῇ θ᾽ αὑτοῦ φρενὶ
χάριν παρασχεῖν τῷ θεῷ θ᾽ ἃ βούλεται,
καὶ νῷν ὕπεικε τὸν κασίγνητον μολεῖν.   1185
οὐ γάρ σε, θάρσει, πρὸς βίαν παρασπάσει
γνώμης, ἃ μή σοι συμφέροντα λέξεται.
λόγων δ᾽ ἀκοῦσαι τίς βλάβη; τά τοι κακῶς
ηὑρημέν᾽ ἔργα τῷ λόγῳ μηνύεται.
ἔφυσας αὐτόν· ὥστε μηδὲ δρῶντά σε   1190
τὰ τῶν κακίστων δυσσεβέστατ᾽, ὦ πάτερ,
θέμις σέ γ᾽ εἶναι κεῖνον ἀντιδρᾶν κακῶς.
ἀλλ᾽ ἔασον· εἰσὶ χἀτέροις γοναὶ κακαὶ
καὶ θυμὸς ὀξύς, ἀλλὰ νουθετούμενοι
φίλων ἐπῳδαῖς ἐξεπάδονται φύσιν.   1195
σὺ δ᾽ εἰς ἐκεῖνα, μὴ τὰ νῦν, ἀποσκόπει
πατρῷα καὶ μητρῷα πήμαθ᾽ ἅπαθες·
κἂν κεῖνα λεύσσῃς, οἶδ᾽ ἐγώ, γνώσει κακοῦ
θυμοῦ τελευτὴν ὡς κακὴ προσγίγνεται.
ἔχεις γὰρ οὐχὶ βαιὰ τἀνθυμήματα,   1200
τῶν σῶν ἀδέρκτων ὀμμάτων τητώμενος.
ἀλλ᾽ ἡμὶν εἶκε· λιπαρεῖν γὰρ οὐ καλὸν
δίκαια προσχρήζουσιν, οὐδ᾽ αὐτὸν μὲν εὖ
πάσχειν, παθόντα δ᾽ οὐκ ἐπίστασθαι τίνειν.

ΟΙΔΙΠΟΥΣ

τέκνον, βαρεῖαν ἡδονὴν νικᾶτέ με   1205
λέγοντες· ἔστω δ᾽ οὖν ὅπως ὑμῖν φίλον.
μόνον, ξέν᾽, εἴπερ κεῖνος ὧδ᾽ ἐλεύσεται,
μηδεὶς κρατείτω τῆς ἐμῆς ψυχῆς ποτε.

ANTIGONE

                                  Father, listen to me.
Though I am young, I'll offer my advice.
Permit the king to act as his own heart
and the god dictate and do what he desires.
And for the sake of your two daughters,
let our brother come here. You need not fear.
His words cannot force you to change your mind,
if what he says is not for your own good.
What harm is there in listening to him?
As you know, a conversation can expose
malicious acts someone intends to do.
Besides, he is your son, and even if   [1190]
he harmed you with the most immoral act,
for you to take revenge by hurting him,
father, would not be right. So let him come.
Other men have evil sons who make them
intensely angry, but when they listen
to advice from friends, then, as if spellbound,
their mood softens and they are pacified.
Set aside the present—think of the past,
the sufferings your parents made you bear.
If you consider that, then I am sure
you'll recognize how an evil temper
can lead to catastrophic consequences.
This is a serious matter, and you   [1200]
have every reason to reflect on it—
you have no eyes and can no longer see.[42]
Do what we ask. For it is not proper
that those pleading on behalf of justice
should have to persist with their entreaties,
nor is it appropriate that someone
who has been treated kindly does not know
how to show such kindness in return.

OEDIPUS

                                 My child,
what you desire is difficult for me.
However, your speech has won me over.
We will do as you wish. But still, my friend,
if that man does come here, I only pray
that no one will end up controlling me.

293

Sophocles

ΘΗΣΕΥΣ

   ἅπαξ τὰ τοιαῦτ᾽, οὐχὶ δὶς χρῄζω κλύειν,
   ὦ πρέσβυ. κομπεῖν δ᾽ οὐχὶ βούλομαι· σὺ δ᾽ ὢν
   σῶς ἴσθ᾽, ἐάν περ κἀμέ τις σῴζῃ θεῶν.   1210

ΧΟΡΟΣ

   ὅστις τοῦ πλέονος μέρους χρῄζει τοῦ μετρίου παρεὶς
   ζώειν, σκαιοσύναν φυλάσσων ἐν ἐμοὶ κατάδηλος
      ἔσται.
   ἐπεὶ πολλὰ μὲν αἱ μακραὶ ἁμέραι κατέθεντο δὴ   1215
   λύπας ἐγγυτέρω, τὰ τέρποντα δ᾽ οὐκ ἂν ἴδοις ὅπου,
   ὅταν τις ἐς πλέον πέσῃ
   τοῦ δέοντος· ὁ δ᾽ ἐπίκουρος ἰσοτέλεστος,   1220
   Ἄιδος ὅτε μοῖρ᾽ ἀνυμέναιος
   ἄλυρος ἄχορος ἀναπέφηνε,
   θάνατος ἐς τελευτάν.

   μὴ φῦναι τὸν ἅπαντα νικᾷ λόγον· τὸ δ᾽, ἐπεὶ φανῇ,   1225
   βῆναι κεῖθεν ὅθεν περ ἥκει, πολὺ δεύτερον, ὡς
      τάχιστα.
   ὡς εὖτ᾽ ἂν τὸ νέον παρῇ κούφας ἀφροσύνας φέρον,   1230
   τίς πλαγὰ πολύμοχθος ἔξω; τίς οὐ καμάτων ἔνι;
   φθόνος, στάσεις, ἔρις, μάχαι
   καὶ φόνοι· τό τε κατάμεμπτον ἐπιλέλογχε   1235
   πύματον ἀκρατὲς ἀπροσόμιλον
   γῆρας ἄφιλον, ἵνα πρόπαντα
   κακὰ κακῶν ξυνοικεῖ.

   ἐν ᾧ τλάμων ὅδ᾽, οὐκ ἐγὼ μόνος,
   πάντοθεν βόρειος ὥς τις   1240
   ἀκτὰ κυματοπλὴξ χειμερία κλονεῖται,
   ὣς καὶ τόνδε κατ᾽ ἄκρας
   δειναὶ κυματοαγεῖς
   ἆται κλονέουσιν ἀεὶ ξυνοῦσαι,
   αἱ μὲν ἀπ᾽ ἀελίου δυσμᾶν,   1245
   αἱ δ᾽ ἀνατέλλοντος·
   αἱ δ᾽ ἀνὰ μέσσαν ἀκτῖν᾽,
   αἱ δ᾽ ἐννυχιᾶν ἀπὸ Ῥιπᾶν.

THESEUS
> I do not need to hear you say that twice.
> Once is enough. I do not wish to boast,
> old man, but you should surely understand
> you are quite safe, if gods keep me alive.   [1210]

[THESEUS and his ATTENDANTS leave]

CHORUS
> A man desperate for many years of life,
> not content to live a moderate span,
> is, in my judgment, obviously a fool.
> For many feelings stored by lengthy years
> evoke more pain than joy, and when we live
> beyond those years that are appropriate,
> then our delights are nowhere to be found.
> The same Deliverer visits all of us,   [1220]
> and when our fate from Hades comes at last,
> there is no music, dance, or wedding song—
> no—only the finality of Death.

> The finest of all possibilities
> is never to be born, but if a man
> sees the light of day, the next best thing by far
> is to return as quickly as he can,
> to go back to the place from which he came.
> For once the careless follies of his youth   [1230]
> have passed, what harsh affliction is he spared,
> what suffering does he not undergo?
> Envy and quarrels, murder, strife and war,
> until at last he reaches his old age,
> rejected and alone, unloved and weak,
> a state where every form of sadness dwells.

> That is where I live, but not alone,
> for suffering Oedipus is there as well—
> like some north-facing cliff beside the sea   [1240]
> lashed on every side by winter blasts,
> beaten constantly by breaking waves
> of violent disaster, storms which come
> from western regions of the setting sun,
> or eastern countries where it rises,
> or southern realms of noontime heat,
> or northern mountains, dark as night.

ΑΝΤΙΓΟΝΗ

    καὶ μὴν ὅδ' ἡμῖν, ὡς ἔοικεν, ὁ ξένος

    ἀνδρῶν γε μοῦνος, ὦ πάτερ, δι' ὄμματος   1250

    ἀστακτὶ λείβων δάκρυον ὧδ' ὁδοιπορεῖ.

ΟΙΔΙΠΟΥΣ

    τίς οὗτος;

ΑΝΤΙΓΟΝΗ

        ὅνπερ καὶ πάλαι κατείχομεν

    γνώμῃ, πάρεστι δεῦρο Πολυνείκης ὅδε.

ΠΟΛΥΝΕΙΚΗΣ

    οἴμοι, τί δράσω; πότερα τἀμαυτοῦ κακὰ

    πρόσθεν δακρύσω, παῖδες, ἢ τὰ τοῦδ' ὁρῶν   1255

    πατρὸς γέροντος; ὃς ξένης ἐπὶ χθονὸς

    σὺν σφῷν ἐφηύρηκ' ἐνθάδ' ἐκβεβλημένον

    ἐσθῆτι σὺν τοιᾷδε, τῆς ὁ δυσφιλὴς

    γέρων γέροντι συγκατῴκηκεν πίνος

    πλευρὰν μαραίνων, κρατὶ δ' ὀμματοστερεῖ   1260

    κόμη δι' αὔρας ἀκτένιστος ᾄσσεται·

    ἀδελφὰ δ', ὡς ἔοικε, τούτοισιν φορεῖ

    τὰ τῆς ταλαίνης νηδύος θρεπτήρια.

    ἀγὼ πανώλης ὄψ' ἄγαν ἐκμανθάνω·

    καὶ μαρτυρῶ κάκιστος ἀνθρώπων τροφαῖς   1265

    ταῖς σαῖσιν ἥκειν· τἀμὰ μὴ 'ξ ἄλλων πύθῃ.

    ἀλλ' ἔστι γὰρ καὶ Ζηνὶ σύνθακος θρόνων

    Αἰδὼς ἐπ' ἔργοις πᾶσι, καὶ πρὸς σοί, πάτερ,

    παρασταθήτω· τῶν γὰρ ἡμαρτημένων

    ἄκη μέν ἐστι, προσφορὰ δ' οὐκ ἔστ' ἔτι.   1270

    τί σιγᾷς;

    φώνησον, ὦ πάτερ, τι· μή μ' ἀποστραφῇς.

    οὐδ' ἀνταμείβει μ' οὐδέν, ἀλλ' ἀτιμάσας

    πέμψεις ἄναυδος, οὐδ' ἃ μηνίεις φράσας;

ANTIGONE

> Look there! It appears as if the stranger
> is coming here alone, without an escort.   [1250]
> Father, he has tears streaming from his eyes.

OEDIPUS

> Who is he?

ANTIGONE

>   The one we talked about just now—
> it's Polyneices. He's coming closer!

[Enter POLYNEICES. He greets ANTIGONE and ISMENE first.]

POLYNEICES

> Alas, my sisters, how should I begin?
> Should I lament my own misfortunes first
> or my father's troubles? I see him here,
> an old man, and I find him with you
> cast out in a foreign land, an exile,
> dressed in such disgusting clothes—so filthy
> the grime from years ago is now engrained
> in his old flesh, putrefying his skin.   [1260]
> Above those empty sockets in his face
> his wild dishevelled hair blows in the wind,
> and I suppose the food he has with him
> is just the same, scraps for his poor belly.
> I am a wretch to learn of this too late!

[POLYNEICES turns his attention to OEDIPUS.]

> I admit that in the care I've shown for you
> I've proved myself the very worst of men—
> and I'm the one confessing this to you!
> But since in all he does Zeus shares his throne
> with divine Compassion, let that goddess
> inspire you, father. For the wrongs I did
> can be made good—I cannot make them worse.   [1270]
> Why are you silent? Say something, father.
> Do not turn aside! Will you not answer me?
> Will you dishonour me—send me away
> without uttering a word or telling me
> why you are so angry?

Sophocles

ὦ σπέρματ᾽ ἀνδρὸς τοῦδ᾽, ἐμαὶ δ᾽ ὁμαίμονες,   1275
πειράσατ᾽ ἀλλ᾽ ὑμεῖς γε κινῆσαι πατρὸς
τὸ δυσπρόσοιστον κἀπροσήγορον στόμα,
ὡς μή μ᾽ ἄτιμον, τοῦ θεοῦ γε προστάτην,
οὕτως ἀφῇ με μηδὲν ἀντειπὼν ἔπος.

ΑΝΤΙΓΟΝΗ

λέγ᾽, ὦ ταλαίπωρ᾽, αὐτὸς ὢν χρείᾳ πάρει·   1280
τὰ πολλὰ γάρ τοι ῥήματ᾽ ἢ τέρψαντά τι,
ἢ δυσχεράναντ᾽ ἢ κατοικτίσαντά πως,
παρέσχε φωνὴν τοῖς ἀφωνήτοις τινά.

ΠΟΛΥΝΕΙΚΗΣ

ἀλλ᾽ ἐξερῶ· καλῶς γὰρ ἐξηγεῖ σύ μοι·
πρῶτον μὲν αὐτὸν τὸν θεὸν ποιούμενος   1285
ἀρωγόν, ἔνθεν μ᾽ ὧδ᾽ ἀνέστησεν μολεῖν
ὁ τῆσδε τῆς γῆς κοίρανος, διδοὺς ἐμοὶ
λέξαι τ᾽ ἀκοῦσαί τ᾽ ἀσφαλεῖ σὺν ἐξόδῳ.
καὶ ταῦτ᾽ ἀφ᾽ ὑμῶν, ὦ ξένοι, βουλήσομαι
καὶ ταῖνδ᾽ ἀδελφαῖν καὶ πατρὸς κυρεῖν ἐμοί.   1290
ἃ δ᾽ ἦλθον, ἤδη σοι θέλω λέξαι, πάτερ.
γῆς ἐκ πατρῴας ἐξελήλαμαι φυγάς,
τοῖς σοῖς πανάρχοις οὕνεκ᾽ ἐνθακεῖν θρόνοις
γονῇ πεφυκὼς ἠξίουν γεραίτερος.
ἀνθ᾽ ὧν μ᾽ Ἐτεοκλῆς, ὢν φύσει νεώτερος,   1295
γῆς ἐξέωσεν, οὔτε νικήσας λόγῳ
οὔτ᾽ εἰς ἔλεγχον χειρὸς οὐδ᾽ ἔργου μολών,
πόλιν δὲ πείσας. ὧν ἐγὼ μάλιστα μὲν
τὴν σὴν ἐρινὺν αἰτίαν εἶναι λέγω.
ἔπειτα κἀπὸ μάντεων ταύτῃ κλύω.   1300
ἐπεὶ γὰρ ἦλθον Ἄργος ἐς τὸ Δωρικόν,
λαβὼν Ἄδραστον πενθερόν, ξυνωμότας
ἔστησ᾽ ἐμαυτῷ γῆς ὅσοιπερ Ἀπίας
πρῶτοι καλοῦνται καὶ τετίμηνται δόρει,

[OEDIPUS refuses to acknowledge POLYNEICES]

                              Come, my sisters,
you are this man's daughters. You, above all,
should try to ease that stubborn tongue Of his
which makes him so difficult to talk to.
Otherwise he will never speak to me
and will dismiss me in disgrace from here,
where I stand a suppliant to the gods.

ANTIGONE
   You poor unfortunate, tell him yourself   [1280]
   the reason you came here. A moving speech
   may well awaken pleasure, rage, or pity
   and rouse a silent listener to speak.

POLYNEICES
   You have advised me well. I will speak out.
   And to begin with, I appeal for help
   to lord Poseidon, for at his altar
   the king of Athens told me to stand up
   and come here, giving me assurances
   I could listen and speak and leave unharmed.
   I trust these promises will be observed,
   strangers, by you, by both my sisters here,
   and by my father, too. And now, father,   [1290]
   I want to tell you the reason I am here.
   I have been driven from my native land
   into exile because, as your elder son,
   I thought the right to sit upon your throne
   and wield your royal power belonged to me.
   But then Eteocles, my younger brother,
   forced me out of Thebes, not by prevailing
   with legal arguments or trial by combat,
   but by persuading Thebes to back his side.
   The most important cause of this, in my view,
   is that old curse placed on your family,
   an opinion I have heard from prophets, too.   [1300]
   And so I went to Dorian Argos,
   made king Adrastus my father-in-law,
   and bound to me as sworn companions
   all the most celebrated warriors
   in Apian lands, so that with these allies

ὅπως τὸν ἑπτάλογχον ἐς Θήβας στόλον   1305
ξὺν τοῖσδ' ἀγείρας ἢ θάνοιμι πανδίκως
ἢ τοὺς τάδ' ἐκπράξαντας ἐκβάλοιμι γῆς.
εἶεν· τί δῆτα νῦν ἀφιγμένος κυρῶ;
σοὶ προστροπαίους, ὦ πάτερ, λιτὰς ἔχων
αὐτός τ' ἐμαυτοῦ ξυμμάχων τε τῶν ἐμῶν,   1310
οἳ νῦν σὺν ἑπτὰ τάξεσιν σὺν ἑπτά τε
λόγχαις τὸ Θήβης πέδιον ἀμφεστᾶσι πᾶν·
οἷος δορυσσοῦς Ἀμφιάρεως, τὰ πρῶτα μὲν
δόρει κρατύνων, πρῶτα δ' οἰωνῶν ὁδοῖς·
ὁ δεύτερος δ' Αἰτωλὸς Οἰνέως τόκος   1315
Τυδεύς. τρίτος δ' Ἐτέοκλος, Ἀργεῖος γεγώς·
τέταρτον Ἱππομέδοντ' ἀπέστειλεν πατὴρ
Ταλαός· ὁ πέμπτος δ' εὔχεται κατασκαφῇ
Καπανεὺς τὸ Θήβης ἄστυ δῃώσειν πυρί·
ἕκτος δὲ Παρθενοπαῖος Ἀρκὰς ὄρνυται,   1320
ἐπώνυμος τῆς πρόσθεν ἀδμήτης χρόνῳ
μητρὸς λοχευθείς, πιστὸς Ἀταλάντης γόνος·
ἐγὼ δὲ σός, κεἰ μὴ σός, ἀλλὰ τοῦ κακοῦ
πότμου φυτευθείς, σός γέ τοι καλούμενος,
ἄγω τὸν Ἄργους ἄφοβον ἐς Θήβας στρατόν.   1325
οἵ σ' ἀντὶ παίδων τῶνδε καὶ ψυχῆς, πάτερ,
ἱκετεύομεν ξύμπαντες ἐξαιτούμενοι
μῆνιν βαρεῖαν εἰκαθεῖν ὁρμωμένῳ
τῷδ' ἀνδρὶ τοὐμοῦ πρὸς κασιγνήτου τίσιν,
ὅς μ' ἐξέωσε κἀπεσύλησεν πάτρας.   1330
εἰ γάρ τι πιστόν ἐστιν ἐκ χρηστηρίων,
οἷς ἂν σὺ προσθῇ, τοῖσδ' ἔφασκ' εἶναι κράτος.
πρὸς νῦν σε κρηνῶν καὶ θεῶν ὁμογνίων
αἰτῶ πιθέσθαι καὶ παρεικαθεῖν, ἐπεὶ
πτωχοὶ μὲν ἡμεῖς καὶ ξένοι, ξένος δὲ σύ.   1335

I might levy an armed force of spearmen
in seven companies to march on Thebes
and die in a just cause or else drive out
the people who had treated me this way.43
What then do I now seek by coming here?
Father, I have come to you in person
pleading for your help—with prayers from me
and from my comrades, those seven spearmen,
who with their seven armies now surround
the entire Theban plain. Of those leaders,
one is spear-hurling Amphiaraus,
an expert warrior and preeminent
in reading omens in the flights of birds.
The second chieftain there is Tydeus,
from Aetolia, son of Oeneus.
The third is Argive-born Eteoclus;
the fourth is Hippomedon, sent to Thebes
by Talaos, his father. The fifth of them,
Capaneus, boasts he will burn Thebes
and utterly obliterate the city.
The sixth, Arcadian Parthenopaeus,   [1320]
is eager for the fight. He gets his name
from Atalanta, who was his mother.
She remained a virgin for many years
before she married and gave birth to him.44
I am the seventh of them, your own son,
or if not yours, a child of evil fate,
although I may be yours in name.45 I've brought
to Thebes a valiant force of Argives.
Each and every one of us implores you,
as you love your daughters and your life,
pleading with you, father, to put aside
that oppressive rage you feel against me,
as I set out to pay my brother back.
He forced me into exile and robbed me   [1330]
of my native land. For if we can trust
in prophecy, then those allied with you,
so say the oracles, will win the day.
So by our fountains and our family gods,
I'm begging you to listen and relent.
For I am a stranger and a beggar
on foreign soil, and so are you, as well.

ἄλλους δὲ θωπεύοντες οἰκοῦμεν σύ τε
κἀγώ, τὸν αὐτὸν δαίμον' ἐξειληχότες.
ὁ δ' ἐν δόμοις τύραννος, ὦ τάλας ἐγώ,
κοινῇ καθ' ἡμῶν ἐγγελῶν ἁβρύνεται·
ὅν, εἰ σὺ τῇμῇ ξυμπαραστήσει φρενί,   1340
βραχεῖ σὺν ὄγκῳ καὶ χρόνῳ διασκεδῶ.
ὥστ' ἐν δόμοισι τοῖσι σοῖς στήσω σ' ἄγων.
στήσω δ' ἐμαυτόν, κεῖνον ἐκβαλὼν βίᾳ.
καὶ ταῦτα σοῦ μὲν ξυνθέλοντος ἔστι μοι
κομπεῖν, ἄνευ σοῦ δ' οὐδὲ σωθῆναι σθένω.   1345

Χορος

τὸν ἄνδρα τοῦ πέμψαντος οὕνεκ', Οἰδίπους
εἰπὼν ὁποῖα ξύμφορ' ἔκπεμψαι πάλιν.

Οιδιπους

ἀλλ' εἰ μέν, ἄνδρες, τῆσδε δημοῦχοι χθονός
μὴ 'τύγχαν' αὐτὸν δεῦρο προσπέμψας ἐμοὶ
Θησεύς, δικαιῶν ὥστ' ἐμοῦ κλύειν λόγους,   1350
οὔ τἄν ποτ' ὀμφῆς τῆς ἐμῆς ἐπῄσθετο·
νῦν δ' ἀξιωθεὶς εἶσι κἀκούσας γ' ἐμοῦ
τοιαῦθ' ἃ τὸν τοῦδ' οὔ ποτ' εὐφρανεῖ βίον·
ὅς γ', ὦ κάκιστε, σκῆπτρα καὶ θρόνους ἔχων,
ἃ νῦν ὁ σὸς ξύναιμος ἐν Θήβαις ἔχει,   1355
τὸν αὐτὸς αὑτοῦ πατέρα τόνδ' ἀπήλασας
κἄθηκας ἄπολιν καὶ στολὰς ταύτας φορεῖν,
ἃς νῦν δακρύεις εἰσορῶν, ὅτ' ἐν πόνῳ
ταὐτῷ βεβηκὼς τυγχάνεις κακῶν ἐμοί.
οὐ κλαυστὰ δ' ἐστίν, ἀλλ' ἐμοὶ μὲν οἰστέα   1360
τάδ', ἕωσπερ ἂν ζῶ, σοῦ φονέως μεμνημένος·
σὺ γάρ με μόχθῳ τῷδ' ἔθηκας ἔντροφον,

You and I both share a similar fate—
we get a place to live by flattery,
paying court to others, while my brother,
unhappily for me, lives in the palace,
an arrogant tyrant mocking both of us.
If you become our ally in this fight,   [1340]
I'll scatter his armed forces to the winds—
that won't be difficult or take much time—
and then I'll bring you back and set you up
in your own home and me in mine and drive
Eteocles away by force. All this
I promise to achieve with your support.
Without you, I shall not return alive.

CHORUS

For the sake of the king who sent him here,
Oedipus, make a suitable response
before you send him on his way.

OEDIPUS *[to the CHORUS]*

                          You men,
guardians of this land, if Theseus
were not the one who sent this man to me,
thinking it right that I should speak to him,   [1350]
then he would never hear me say a word.
But since you all insist he ought to have
an audience with me before he leaves,
let him hear what I have to say—my words
will never bring his life the slightest joy.

[OEDIPUS turns his attention to POLYNEICES]

You there, you most despicable of men,
when you were on the throne and held the sceptre,
the power your brother now wields in Thebes,
you hounded me, your father, from the land,
pushed me into exile, and made me wear
these garments which, when you look at them now,
bring tears into your eyes, because you find
your life is just as miserable as mine![46]
For me there is no point in shedding tears—   [1360]
while I am still alive, I must endure it,
remembering that you're my murderer.
You forced me to live in this wretched state!

303

σύ μ' ἐξέωσας, ἐκ σέθεν δ' ἀλώμενος
ἄλλους ἐπαιτῶ τὸν καθ' ἡμέραν βίον.
εἰ δ' ἐξέφυσα τάσδε μὴ 'μαυτῷ τροφοὺς   1365
τὰς παῖδας, ἦ τἂν οὐκ ἂν ἦ, τὸ σὸν μέρος·
νῦν δ' αἵδε μ' ἐκσῴζουσιν, αἵδ' ἐμαὶ τροφοί,
αἵδ' ἄνδρες, οὐ γυναῖκες, εἰς τὸ συμπονεῖν·
ὑμεῖς δ' ἀπ' ἄλλου κοὐκ ἐμοῦ πεφύκατον.
τοιγάρ σ' ὁ δαίμων εἰσορᾷ μὲν οὔ τί πω   1370
ὡς αὐτίκ', εἴπερ οἵδε κινοῦνται λόχοι
πρὸς ἄστυ Θήβης. οὐ γὰρ ἔσθ' ὅπως πόλιν
κείνην ἐρείψεις, ἀλλὰ πρόσθεν αἵματι
πεσεῖ μιανθεὶς χὠ σύναιμος ἐξ ἴσου.
τοιάσδ' ἀρὰς σφῶν πρόσθε τ' ἐξανῆκ' ἐγὼ   1375
νῦν τ' ἀνακαλοῦμαι ξυμμάχους ἐλθεῖν ἐμοί,
ἵν' ἀξιῶτον τοὺς φυτεύσαντας σέβειν
καὶ μὴ 'ξατιμάζητον, εἰ τυφλοῦ πατρὸς
τοιώδ' ἐφύτην· αἵδε γὰρ τάδ' οὐκ ἔδρων.
τοιγὰρ τὸ σὸν θάκημα καὶ τοὺς σοὺς θρόνους   1380
κρατοῦσιν, εἴπερ ἐστὶν ἡ παλαίφατος
Δίκη ξύνεδρος Ζηνὸς ἀρχαίοις νόμοις.
σὺ δ' ἔρρ' ἀπόπτυστός τε κἀπάτωρ ἐμοῦ,
κακῶν κάκιστε, τάσδε συλλαβὼν ἀράς,
ἅς σοι καλοῦμαι, μήτε γῆς ἐμφυλίου   1385
δόρει κρατῆσαι μήτε νοστῆσαί ποτε
τὸ κοῖλον Ἄργος, ἀλλὰ συγγενεῖ χερὶ
θανεῖν κτανεῖν θ' ὑφ' οὗπερ ἐξελήλασαι.
τοιαῦτ' ἀρῶμαι καὶ καλῶ τὸ Ταρτάρου
στυγνὸν πατρῷον ἔρεβος, ὥς σ' ἀποικίσῃ,   1390
καλῶ δὲ τάσδε δαίμονας, καλῶ δ' Ἄρη
τὸν σφῷν τὸ δεινὸν μῖσος ἐμβεβληκότα.

You two banished me, and because of you,
I am a vagrant, begging every day
for bread from strangers. If I had not fathered
these two daughters, who serve as my support,
I would have died for lack of help from you.
But now these girls are looking after me—
they provide for me and share my suffering.
They are like men, not women. But you two,
you are both bastards, born from someone else,
no sons of mine! And so the eye of god   [1370]
is watching you—but not as it will soon,
if your armies mean to march on Thebes.
For you will never overwhelm that city.
Before that happens, you and your brother
will fall, polluted by each other's blood.
And now I summon those very curses
I called down earlier against you both.
I cry to them to come to my assistance,
so that the two of you will understand
those who bore you are worthy of respect.47
It is not right to treat them with contempt,
because a father who had sons like you
has lost his eyes. These girls did not do that.
And so if Justice established long ago   [1380]
and sanctioned by our ancient laws still sits
alongside Zeus, these curses I call down
will overpower your suppliant prayers
and all claims to the throne.48 Get out of here!
I spit you out! You are no son of mine!
You most contemptible of evil men!
Take with you these prayers I make on your behalf—
may your armies never overwhelm that land
where you were born, may you never return
to the land of Argos, but rather die
at the hand of the one of your own kinsmen,
and kill the man who drove you out of Thebes!
That is what I pray for. And I call on
the dreadful paternal dark of Tartarus   [1390]
to deliver you to your new dwelling place.49
I invoke the spirits here, the Furies,
and summon Ares, god of war, who set
such lethal hatred in the two of you!

καὶ ταῦτ' ἀκούσας στεῖχε, κἀξάγγελλ' ἰὼν
καὶ πᾶσι Καδμείοισι τοῖς σαυτοῦ θ' ἅμα
πιστοῖσι συμμάχοισιν, οὕνεκ' Οἰδίπους   1395
τοιαῦτ' ἔνειμε παισὶ τοῖς αὐτοῦ γέρα.

ΧΟΡΟΣ
Πολύνεικες, οὔτε ταῖς παρελθούσαις ὁδοῖς
ξυνήδομαί σοι, νῦν τ' ἴθ' ὡς τάχος πάλιν.

ΠΟΛΥΝΕΙΚΗΣ
οἴμοι κελεύθου τῆς τ' ἐμῆς δυσπραξίας,
οἴμοι δ' ἑταίρων· οἷον ἆρ' ὁδοῦ τέλος   1400
Ἄργους ἀφωρμήθημεν, ὦ τάλας ἐγώ,
τοιοῦτον οἷον οὐδὲ φωνῆσαί τινι
ἔξεσθ' ἑταίρων, οὐδ' ἀποστρέψαι πάλιν,
ἀλλ' ὄντ' ἄναυδον τῇδε συγκῦρσαι τύχῃ.
ὦ τοῦδ' ὅμαιμοι παῖδες, ἀλλ' ὑμεῖς, ἐπεὶ   1405
τὰ σκληρὰ πατρὸς κλύετε ταῦτ' ἀρωμένου,
μή τοί με πρὸς θεῶν σφώ γ', ἐὰν αἱ τοῦδ' ἀραὶ
πατρὸς τελῶνται καί τις ὑμῖν ἐς δόμους
νόστος γένηται, μή μ' ἀτιμάσητέ γε,
ἀλλ' ἐν τάφοισι θέσθε κἀν κτερίσμασιν.   1410
καὶ σφῷν ὁ νῦν ἔπαινος, ὃν κομίζετον
τοῦδ', ἀνδρὸς οἷς πονεῖτον, οὐκ ἐλάσσονα
ἔτ' ἄλλον οἴσει τῆς ἐμῆς ὑπουργίας.

ΑΝΤΙΓΟΝΗ
Πολύνεικες, ἱκετεύω σε πεισθῆναί τί μοι.

ΠΟΛΥΝΕΙΚΗΣ
ὦ φιλτάτη, τὸ ποῖον, Ἀντιγόνη; λέγε.   1415

ΑΝΤΙΓΟΝΗ
στρέψαι στράτευμ' ἐς Ἄργος ὡς τάχιστά γε,
καὶ μὴ σέ τ' αὐτὸν καὶ πόλιν διεργάσῃ.

ΠΟΛΥΝΕΙΚΗΣ
ἀλλ' οὐχ οἷόν τε· πῶς γὰρ αὖθις ἂν πάλιν
στράτευμ' ἄγοιμι ταὐτόν. εἰσάπαξ τρέσας;

You have heard what I have spoken. Now leave.
Proclaim to all the citizens of Thebes
and to your loyal confederates, as well,
that Oedipus has handed out these gifts
as royal bequests to his two sons.

CHORUS

                                   Polyneices,
the journey you have made brings me no joy—
and now you must return without delay.

POLYNEICES

So much for my trip here—it's a disaster.
Alas for my companions! This is the end   [1400]
of the road we marched when we left Argos—
unhappily for me! I cannot speak of this
to any of my friends or turn them back.
I must stay silent and confront my fate.
But you, my sisters, daughters of this man,
you have heard our father's brutal curses.
If what he is praying for is fulfilled
and you get back to Thebes, then I beg you,
by all the gods, do not leave my body
to be dishonored. Set me in a tomb,
and have me buried with full funeral rites.   [1410]
If you do that, the praises you both earn
from this man for the help you two provide
will be increased by no less generous praise
you will receive for looking after me.

ANTIGONE

Polyneices, listen to me, I beg you!

POLYNEICES

Dearest Antigone, what is it? Speak out.

ANTIGONE

Turn your forces back—and do it quickly.
Return to Argos. Do not ravage Thebes
and destroy yourself.

POLYNEICES

                     That is not possible.
Once I turn back because I am afraid,
how could I ever lead that force again?

Sophocles

ΑΝΤΙΓΟΝΗ

τί δ' αὖθις, ὦ παῖ, δεῖ σε θυμοῦσθαι; τί σοι   1420
πάτραν κατασκάψαντι κέρδος ἔρχεται;

ΠΟΛΥΝΕΙΚΗΣ

αἰσχρὸν τὸ φεύγειν καὶ τὸ πρεσβεύοντ' ἐμὲ
οὕτω γελᾶσθαι τοῦ κασιγνήτου πάρα.

ΑΝΤΙΓΟΝΗ

ὁρᾷς τὰ τοῦδ' οὖν ὡς ἐς ὀρθὸν ἐκφέρει
μαντεύμαθ', ὃς σφῷν θάνατον ἐξ ἀμφοῖν θροεῖ;   1425

ΠΟΛΥΝΕΙΚΗΣ

χρῄζει γάρ· ἡμῖν δ' οὐχὶ συγχωρητέα.

ΑΝΤΙΓΟΝΗ

οἴμοι τάλαινα· τίς δὲ τολμήσει κλύων
τὰ τοῦδ' ἕπεσθαι τἀνδρός, οἷ' ἐθέσπισεν;

ΠΟΛΥΝΕΙΚΗΣ

οὐκ ἀγγελοῦμεν φλαῦρ'· ἐπεὶ στρατηλάτου
χρηστοῦ τὰ κρείσσω μηδὲ τἀνδεᾶ λέγειν.   1430

ΑΝΤΙΓΟΝΗ

οὕτως ἄρ', ὦ παῖ, ταῦτά σοι δεδογμένα;

ΠΟΛΥΝΕΙΚΗΣ

καὶ μή μ' ἐπίσχῃς γ'· ἀλλ' ἐμοὶ μὲν ἥδ' ὁδὸς
ἔσται μέλουσα δύσποτμός τε καὶ κακὴ
πρὸς τοῦδε πατρὸς τῶν τε τοῦδ' ἐρινύων·
σφῷν δ' εὖ διδοίη Ζεύς, τάδ' εἰ θανόντι μοι   1435
τελεῖτ', ἐπεὶ οὔ μοι ζῶντί γ' αὖθις ἕξετον.
μέθεσθε δ' ἤδη χαίρετόν τ'· οὐ γάρ μ' ἔτι
βλέποντ' ἐσόψεσθ' αὖθις.

308

ANTIGONE

   Again? Why, brother, would you ever again   [1420]
   get so angry? How do you benefit
   from destroying the city of your birth?

POLYNEICES

   It is dishonourable to live in exile
   and to be made a laughing stock like this,
   when I'm the elder son.

ANTIGONE

                    But don't you see
   you will be confirming the prophecies
   our father uttered? They are predicting
   you and Eteocles will kill each other.

POLYNEICES

   That's what he wants. But I cannot give up.

ANTIGONE

   Alas, that is insufferable for me!
   But who will follow you once he has heard
   what has been prophesied?

POLYNEICES

                I will not tell them
   such a grim prediction. A proper leader
   conveys good things and hides unwelcome news.   [1430]

ANTIGONE

   Are you resolved to do this, my brother?

POLYNEICES

   I am. Do not attempt to hold me back.
   This ill-fated, catastrophic path is now
   the one destined for me, thanks to my father
   and his avenging Furies. But for you two,
   my sisters, may Zeus provide rich favours,
   if you will carry out full burial rites
   for me when I am dead. There's nothing more
   you can perform for me while I still live.
   So let me set out on my way. Farewell.
   You will not see me in this life again.

ΑΝΤΙΓΟΝΗ

ὦ τάλαιν᾽ ἐγώ.

ΠΟΛΥΝΕΙΚΗΣ

μή τοί μ᾽ ὀδύρου.

ΑΝΤΙΓΟΝΗ

καὶ τίς ἄν σ᾽ ὁρμώμενον
εἰς προῦπτον Ἅιδην οὐ καταστένοι, κάσι;   1440

ΠΟΛΥΝΕΙΚΗΣ

εἰ χρή, θανοῦμαι.

ΑΝΤΙΓΟΝΗ

μὴ σύ γ᾽, ἀλλ᾽ ἐμοὶ πιθοῦ.

ΠΟΛΥΝΕΙΚΗΣ

μὴ πεῖθ᾽ ἃ μὴ δεῖ.

ΑΝΤΙΓΟΝΗ

δυστάλαινά τἄρ᾽ ἐγώ,
εἴ σου στερηθῶ.

ΠΟΛΥΝΕΙΚΗΣ

ταῦτα δ᾽ ἐν τῷ δαίμονι
καὶ τῇδε φῦναι χἀτέρᾳ. σφὼ δ᾽ οὖν ἐγὼ
θεοῖς ἀρῶμαι μή ποτ᾽ ἀντῆσαι κακῶν·   1445
ἀνάξιαι γὰρ πᾶσίν ἐστε δυστυχεῖν.

ΧΟΡΟΣ

νέα τάδε νεόθεν ἦλθέ μοι
κακὰ βαρύποτμα παρ᾽ ἀλαοῦ ξένου,
εἴ τι μοῖρα μὴ κιγχάνει.   1450
μάταν γὰρ οὐδὲν ἀξίωμα δαιμόνων ἔχω φράσαι.
ὁρᾷ ὁρᾷ ταῦτ᾽ ἀεὶ χρόνος, τρέχων μὲν ἕτερα,
τὰ δὲ παρ᾽ ἦμαρ αὖθις αὔξων ἄνω.   1455
ἔκτυπεν αἰθήρ, ὦ Ζεῦ.

ANTIGONE
I am so wretched!

POLYNEICES
Do not feel sad for me.

ANTIGONE
Who would not feel sad for you, my brother,
when you are marching off to certain death?   [1440]

POLYNEICES
If it is my fate, then I shall die.

Antigone
No!
Listen to me instead!

POLYNEICES
Do not keep pleading
for what will never happen.

ANTIGONE
If I lose you,
my life will have no joy.

POLYNEICES
Fate will decide
one way or the other. As for you both,
may gods grant you never meet disaster,
for all men know you two do not deserve
a life of suffering and misery.

[POLYNEICES leaves. There is a rumble of thunder in the distance.]

CHORUS
I sense the approach of fresh misfortune,
a new load of grief from this blind stranger,
unless Fate is now perhaps approaching   [1450]
its predestined end, for I cannot say
decisions of the gods stay unfulfilled.
Time keeps watch and always sees these things—
one day it casts some down, and on the next
it raises others up once more.

[There is another peal of thunder, this time much closer than before.]

O Zeus,
your heavenly skies reverberate!

ΟΙΔΙΠΟΥΣ

 ὦ τέκνα τέκνα, πῶς ἄν, εἴ τις ἔντοπος,
 τὸν πάντ᾽ ἄριστον δεῦρο Θησέα πόροι;

ΑΝΤΙΓΟΝΗ

 πάτερ, τί δ᾽ ἐστὶ τἀξίωμ᾽ ἐφ᾽ ᾧ καλεῖς;

ΟΙΔΙΠΟΥΣ

 Διὸς πτερωτὸς ἥδε μ᾽ αὐτίκ᾽ ἄξεται   1460
 βροντὴ πρὸς Ἅιδην· ἀλλὰ πέμψαθ᾽ ὡς τάχος.

ΧΟΡΟΣ

 μέγας, ἴδε, μάλ᾽ ὅδ᾽ ἐρείπεται
 κτύπος ἄφατος διόβολος· ἐς δ᾽ ἄκραν
 δεῖμ᾽ ὑπῆλθε κρατὸς φόβαν.   1465
 ἔπτηξα θυμόν· οὐρανία γὰρ ἀστραπὴ φλέγει πάλιν.
 τί μὰν ἀφήσει τέλος; δέδοικα δ᾽· οὐ γὰρ ἅλιον
 ἀφορμᾷ ποτ᾽, οὐκ ἄνευ ξυμφορᾶς.   1470
 ὦ μέγας αἰθήρ, ὦ Ζεῦ.

ΟΙΔΙΠΟΥΣ

 ὦ παῖδες, ἥκει τῷδ᾽ ἐπ᾽ ἀνδρὶ θέσφατος
 βίου τελευτὴ κοὐκέτ᾽ ἔστ᾽ ἀποστροφή.

ΑΝΤΙΓΟΝΗ

 πῶς οἶσθα; τῷ δὲ τοῦτο συμβαλὼν ἔχεις;

ΟΙΔΙΠΟΥΣ

 καλῶς κάτοιδ᾽· ἀλλ᾽ ὡς τάχιστά μοι μολὼν   1475
 ἄνακτα χώρας τῆσδέ τις πορευσάτω.

ΧΟΡΟΣ

 ἔα ἔα, ἰδοὺ μάλ᾽ αὖθις ἀμφίσταται διαπρύσιος ὄτοβος.

OEDIPUS

My children, if there is anyone here,
tell him to summon Theseus back,
that finest of all men.

ANTIGONE

                              Why, father?
Why do you want us to send for Theseus?

OEDIPUS

Zeus' winged thunder will soon lead me   [1460]
on to Hades. Send someone now—and quickly!

[Thunder peals again, sounding very close, and lightning flashes.]

CHORUS

Listen! The crash of an immense thunderbolt
hurled down by Zeus—my scalp bristles,
overwhelmed with fear, my heart recoils!

Lightning blazes once more through the sky!
What final purposes are being revealed?

I am afraid. Such fire from Zeus
never flashes down in vain, not without   [1470]
some great calamity.

[Another peal of thunder breaks above them.]

                  O mighty heavens! O Zeus!

OEDIPUS

My children, for me the destined end of life
is drawing near. There is no turning back.

Antigone

How do you know? What signs have you received?

OEDIPUS

I sense it clearly. Get someone to go
and fetch the king as quickly as he can.

[More peals of thunder and flashes of lightning.]

CHORUS

Listen! Listen to that! The piercing noise
is all around us once again!

ἵλαος, ὦ δαίμων, ἵλαος εἴ τι γᾷ   1480

ματέρι τυγχάνεις ἀφεγγὲς φέρων.

ἐναισίου δὲ σοῦ τύχοιμι, μηδ' ἄλαστον ἄνδρ' ἰδὼν

ἀκερδῆ χάριν μετάσχοιμί πως. Ζεῦ ἄνα σοὶ φωνῶ.

ΟΙΔΙΠΟΥΣ

ἆρ' ἐγγὺς ἀνήρ; ἆρ' ἔτ' ἐμψύχου, τέκνα,   1486

κιχήσεταί μου καὶ κατορθοῦντος φρένα;

ΑΝΤΙΓΟΝΗ

τί δ' ἂν θέλοις τὸ πιστὸν ἐμφῦναι φρενί;

ΟΙΔΙΠΟΥΣ

ἀνθ' ὧν ἔπασχον εὖ, τελεσφόρον χάριν

δοῦναί σφιν, ἥνπερ τυγχάνων ὑπεσχόμην.   1490

ΧΟΡΟΣ

ἰὼ ἰὼ παῖ, βᾶθι βᾶθ', εἴτ' ἄκρα,

περὶ γύαλ' ἐναλίῳ Ποσειδωνίῳ θεῷ, τυγχάνεις

βούθυτον ἑστίαν ἁγίζων, ἱκοῦ.

ὁ γὰρ ξένος σε καὶ πόλισμα καὶ φίλους ἐπαξιοῖ

δικαίαν χάριν παρασχεῖν παθών.

[σπεῦσον] ἄϊσσ', ὦναξ.

ΘΗΣΕΥΣ

τίς αὖ παρ' ὑμῶν κοινὸς ἠχεῖται κτύπος,   1500

σαφὴς μὲν ἀστῶν, ἐμφανὴς δὲ τοῦ ξένου;

O god,

be gracious to us—show us your mercy,   [1480]
if you are bringing some catastrophe
to Athens, our maternal home.

                    May I find you
generous to us—if I have looked upon
a man polluted by his acts, do not,
I beg you, somehow let me share his curse
or favours that bring no benefit to me!⁵⁰
O Zeus on high, I cry out to you!

OEDIPUS

My children, is lord Theseus nearby?
When he gets here will I still be alive
with my mind intact?

ANTIGONE

                    What trustworthy pledge
do you wish to plant within his heart?

OEDIPUS

In return for the goodwill I received,
I will do him a favour by fulfilling   [1490]
everything I promised earlier.⁵¹

CHORUS

Come, my son, come here to us!
If you by chance are at the altar
in the deepest corner of the grove
offering an ox to god Poseidon,
lord of the sea, then come to us.
This stranger thinks it only just
that you, your city, and your friends
receive a favour for those benefits
you have so graciously conferred on him.
My lord, make haste! Come quickly!

[THESEUS enters.]

THESEUS

What is this noise? Why are you once again   [1500]
all making such a din—it's clearly coming
from you citizens and from the stranger, too.

μή τις Διὸς κεραυνὸς ἢ τις ὀμβρία
χάλαζ' ἐπιρράξασα; πάντα γὰρ θεοῦ
τοιαῦτα χειμάζοντος εἰκάσαι πάρα.

ΟΙΔΙΠΟΥΣ

ἄναξ, ποθοῦντι προυφάνης, καί σοι θεῶν   1505
τύχην τις ἐσθλὴν τῆσδ' ἔθηκε τῆς ὁδοῦ.

ΘΗΣΕΥΣ

τί δ' ἐστίν, ὦ παῖ Λαΐου, νέορτον αὖ;

ΟΙΔΙΠΟΥΣ

ῥοπὴ βίου μοι· καί σ' ἅπερ ξυνῄνεσα
θέλω πόλιν τε τήνδε μὴ ψεύσας θανεῖν.

ΘΗΣΕΥΣ

τῷ δ' ἐκπέπεισαι τοῦ μόρου τεκμηρίῳ;   1510

ΟΙΔΙΠΟΥΣ

αὐτοὶ θεοὶ κήρυκες ἀγγέλλουσί μοι,
ψεύδοντες οὐδὲν σῆμα τῶν προκειμένων.

ΘΗΣΕΥΣ

πῶς εἶπας, ὦ γεραιέ, δηλοῦσθαι τάδε;

ΟΙΔΙΠΟΥΣ

αἱ πολλὰ βρονταὶ διατελεῖς τὰ πολλά τε
στράψαντα χειρὸς τῆς ἀνικήτου βέλη.   1515

ΘΗΣΕΥΣ

πείθεις με· πολλὰ γάρ σε θεσπίζονθ' ὁρῶ
κοὐ ψευδόφημα· χὤ τι χρὴ ποιεῖν λέγε.

ΟΙΔΙΠΟΥΣ

ἐγὼ διδάξω, τέκνον Αἰγέως, ἅ σοι
γήρως ἄλυπα τῇδε κείσεται πόλει.
χῶρον μὲν αὐτὸς αὐτίκ' ἐξηγήσομαι,   1520
ἄθικτος ἡγητῆρος, οὗ με χρὴ θανεῖν.

Were you frightened by a thunderbolt from Zeus
or driving showers of hail? When a god
unleashes a ferocious storm like this,
it can presage all sorts of things to come.

OEDIPUS

My lord, I have been hoping you were here—
some god has seen to it that you arrive
at a propitious time.

THESEUS

                         Son of Laius,
What is going on? Is it something new?

OEDIPUS

For me life moves beyond its tipping point.
I do not wish to die without confirming
the promises I made to you and Athens.

THESEUS

What omens tell you that your death is near?   [1510]

OEDIPUS

The messengers who announced the news to me
are the gods themselves. They have not proven false,
for they have shown me the appointed signs.

THESEUS

What are these fatal signs, old man? Tell me.

OEDIPUS

All those frequent rolling peals of thunder
and many lightning flashes hurtling down
from an invincible hand.

THESEUS

                     You have convinced me.
From your many prophecies I have learned
you do not lie. Tell me what I must do.

OEDIPUS

Son of Aegeus, I will set out for you
the glories that lie in store for Athens
and that never will diminish with old age.
In a moment I myself will lead the way   [1520]
to the place where I must die. I will need

317

τοῦτον δὲ φράζε μή ποτ' ἀνθρώπων τινί,
μήθ' οὖ κέκευθε μήτ' ἐν οἷς κεῖται τόποις·
ὡς σοι πρὸ πολλῶν ἀσπίδων ἀλκὴν ὅδε
δορός τ' ἐπακτοῦ γειτόνων ἀεὶ τιθῇ.   1525
ἃ δ' ἐξάγιστα μηδὲ κινεῖται λόγῳ,
αὐτὸς μαθήσει, κεῖσ' ὅταν μόλῃς μόνος·
ὡς οὔτ' ἂν ἀστῶν τῶνδ' ἂν ἐξείποιμί τῳ
οὔτ' ἂν τέκνοισι τοῖς ἐμοῖς, στέργων ὅμως.
ἀλλ' αὐτὸς αἰεὶ σῷζε, χὤταν εἰς τέλος   1530
τοῦ ζῆν ἀφικνῇ, τῷ προφερτάτῳ μόνῳ
σήμαιν', ὁ δ' αἰεὶ τὠπιόντι δεικνύτω.
χοὕτως ἀδῇον τήνδ' ἐνοικήσεις πόλιν
σπαρτῶν ἀπ' ἀνδρῶν· αἱ δὲ μυρίαι πόλεις,
κἂν εὖ τις οἰκῇ, ῥᾳδίως καθύβρισαν.   1535
θεοὶ γὰρ εὖ μέν, ὀψὲ δ' εἰσορῶσ', ὅταν
τὰ θεῖ' ἀφείς τις εἰς τὸ μαίνεσθαι τραπῇ·
ὃ μὴ σύ, τέκνον Αἰγέως, βούλου παθεῖν.
τὰ μὲν τοιαῦτ' οὖν εἰδότ' ἐκδιδάσκομεν.
χῶρον δ', ἐπείγει γάρ με τοὐκ θεοῦ παρόν,   1540
στείχωμεν ἤδη μηδ' ἔτ' ἐντρεπώμεθα.
ὦ παῖδες, ὧδ' ἕπεσθ'· ἐγὼ γὰρ ἡγεμὼν
σφῷν αὖ πέφασμαι καινός, ὥσπερ σφὼ πατρί.
χωρεῖτε καὶ μὴ ψαύετ', ἀλλ' ἐᾶτέ με
αὐτὸν τὸν ἱερὸν τύμβον ἐξευρεῖν, ἵνα   1545
μοῖρ' ἀνδρὶ τῷδε τῇδε κρυφθῆναι χθονί.
τῇδ' ὧδε, τῇδε βᾶτε· τῇδε γάρ μ' ἄγει
Ἑρμῆς ὁ πομπὸς ἥ τε νερτέρα θεός.
ὦ φῶς ἀφεγγές, πρόσθε πού ποτ' ἦσθ' ἐμόν,
νῦν δ' ἔσχατόν σου τοὐμὸν ἅπτεται δέμας.   1550

no hand to guide me. You must not ever
divulge this place to any mortal man
by revealing its concealed location
or the general area where it lies,
so that for all time it may protect you
more effectively than shields and spears
or many foreign allies. You yourself
will learn, once you enter that place alone,
forbidden things of which no one may speak.
I would not talk of them to any citizen
or to my children, although I love them.
You must always keep these matters secret,   [1530]
and when your life is coming to an end,
reveal them to your most important heir—
to him alone. He must always pass them on
to his successor. If you keep doing this,
then life in Athens will never be disrupted
by citizens born from the dragon's teeth.[52]
Even if in countless cities men live well,
they find it all too easy to commit
outrageous crimes, for gods are slow to act,
although they clearly intervene when men
abandon piety and turn to madness.[53]
Son of Aegeus, do not let that happen.
But I am stating what you know already.
But since what comes from god urges me on,   [1540]
let us set off for the designated place
and hesitate no longer.

[OEDIPUS turns his attention to ANTIGONE and ISMENE.]

My children,
follow me, for though it seems new and strange,
I will once more show both of you the way,
just as you two used to guide your father.
So move on. Do not lay a hand on me.
Let me find the sacred burial ground myself,
where Fate has ordained I will lie hidden
here in Athens. This way—follow my lead.
Hermes the Guide and the goddess of the dead,
Persephone, are showing me the path.
O light, that is no light to me, though once,
in earlier days, my eyes could see you,
now for the last time you caress my body.   [1550]

319

ἤδη γὰρ ἔρπω τὸν τελευταῖον βίον
κρύψων παρ' Ἅιδην. ἀλλά, φίλτατε ξένων,
αὐτός τε χώρα θ' ἥδε πρόσπολοί τε σοὶ
εὐδαίμονες γένοισθε, κἀπ' εὐπραξίᾳ
μέμνησθέ μου θανόντος εὐτυχεῖς ἀεί.   1555

ΧΟΡΟΣ
εἰ θέμις ἐστί μοι τὰν ἀφανῆ θεὸν
καὶ σὲ λιταῖς σεβίζειν,
ἐννυχίων ἄναξ,
Αἰδωνεῦ Αἰδωνεῦ, λίσσωμαι   1560
ἄπονα μήτ' ἐπὶ βαρυαχεῖ
ξένον ἐξανύσαι
μόρῳ τὰν παγκευθῆ κάτω
νεκρῶν πλάκα καὶ Στύγιον δόμον.
πολλῶν γὰρ ἂν καὶ μάταν   1565
πημάτων ἱκνουμένων
πάλιν σφε δαίμων δίκαιος αὔξοι.

ὦ χθόνιαι θεαὶ σῶμά τ' ἀνικάτου
θηρός, ὃν ἐν πύλαισι
ταῖσι πολυξένοις   1570
εὐνᾶσθαι κνυζεῖσθαί τ' ἐξ ἄντρων
ἀδάματον φύλακα παρ' Ἅιδᾳ
λόγος αἰὲν ἔχει·
τόν, ὦ Γᾶς παῖ καὶ Ταρτάρου,
κατεύχομαι ἐν καθαρῷ βῆναι   1575
ὁρμωμένῳ νερτέρας
τῷ ξένῳ νεκρῶν πλάκας·
σέ τοι κικλήσκω τὸν αἰένυπνον.

ΑΓΓΕΛΟΣ
ἄνδρες πολῖται, ξυντομωτάτως, μὲν ἂν
τύχοιμι λέξας Οἰδίπουν ὀλωλότα·   1580
ἃ δ' ἦν τὰ πραχθέντ', οὔθ' ὁ μῦθος ἐν βραχεῖ
φράσαι πάρεστιν οὔτε τἄργ' ὅσ' ἦν ἐκεῖ.

For already I am shuffling on my way
to hide the final portion of my life
in Hades.

[OEDIPUS stops to address THESEUS.]

But you, most cherished stranger,
may you, your followers, and your land
fare well, and may you, in your prosperity,
remember me, as I move to my death,
and may you have good fortune evermore.

[OEDIPUS, ANTIGONE, ISMENE, and THESEUS move off together.]

CHORUS
    If by our traditions it is right
    for me to worship with my prayers
    the unseen goddess, as well as you,
    lord of the dead, then Aidoneus,
    O Aidoneus, I entreat you—   [1560]
    may the stranger move on free of pain
    or heavy grieving for his fate
    to the all-concealing fields of dead
    and the chamber of the Styx below.⁵⁴
    Through no fault of his own he met
    great torments, but may a righteous god
    restore his splendour once again.

    O goddesses of the lower world
    and you, the unconquerable beast,
    whose body lies, so people say,
    beside the gate of countless guests,   [1570]
    snarling at the entry to your cave,
    invincible guardian of Hades,
    O child of Earth and Tartarus,
    I pray the path the stranger treads
    may be left clear, as he moves on
    to fields of the dead below.
    I cry to you, lord of eternal sleep.⁵⁵

[A MESSENGER enters]

MESSENGER
    Citizens, the news I will report is brief—
    Oedipus is dead. But I cannot provide   [1580]
    details of his death in a short report,
    since what went on there lasted for some time.

ΧΟΡΟΣ

ὄλωλε γὰρ δύστηνος;

ΑΓΓΕΛΟΣ

ὡς λελοιπότα
κεῖνον τὸν ἀεὶ βίοτον ἐξεπίστασο.

ΧΟΡΟΣ

πῶς; ἆρα θείᾳ κἀπόνῳ τάλας τύχῃ;   1585

ΑΓΓΕΛΟΣ

ταῦτ᾽ ἐστὶν ἤδη κἀποθαυμάσαι πρέπον.
ὡς μὲν γὰρ ἐνθένδ᾽ εἷρπε, καὶ σύ που παρὼν
ἔξοισθ᾽, ὑφηγητῆρος οὐδενὸς φίλων,
ἀλλ᾽ αὐτὸς ἡμῖν πᾶσιν ἐξηγούμενος.
ἐπεὶ δ᾽ ἀφῖκτο τὸν καταρράκτην ὁδὸν   1590
χαλκοῖς βάθροισι γῆθεν ἐρριζωμένον,
ἔστη κελεύθων ἐν πολυσχίστων μιᾷ,
κοίλου πέλας κρατῆρος, οὗ τὰ Θησέως
Περίθου τε κεῖται πίστ᾽ ἀεὶ ξυνθήματα.
ἀφ᾽ οὗ μέσος στὰς τοῦ τε Θορικίου πέτρου   1595
κοίλης τ᾽ ἀχέρδου κἀπὸ λαΐνου τάφου,
καθέζετ᾽· εἶτ᾽ ἔλυσε δυσπινεῖς στολάς.
κἄπειτ᾽ ἀΰσας παῖδας ἠνώγει ῥυτῶν
ὑδάτων ἐνεγκεῖν λουτρὰ καὶ χοάς ποθεν·
τὼ δ᾽ εὐχλόου Δήμητρος εἰς προσόψιον   1600
πάγον μολοῦσαι τάσδ᾽ ἐπιστολὰς πατρὶ
ταχεῖ ᾽πόρευσαν σὺν χρόνῳ, λουτροῖς τέ νιν
ἐσθῆτί τ᾽ ἐξήσκησαν ᾗ νομίζεται.
ἐπεὶ δὲ παντὸς εἶχε δρῶντος ἡδονὴν
κοὐκ ἦν ἔτ᾽ οὐδὲν ἀργὸν ὧν ἐφίετο,   1605
κτύπησε μὲν Ζεὺς χθόνιος αἱ δὲ παρθένοι
ῥίγησαν, ὡς ἤκουσαν· ἐς δὲ γούνατα
πατρὸς πεσοῦσαι ᾽κλαιον οὐδ᾽ ἀνίεσαν
στέρνων ἀραγμοὺς οὐδὲ παμμήκεις γόους.

CHORUS

   Has the unlucky man died at last?

MESSENGER

   You can rest assured—he has left this life.

CHORUS

   How did the poor man die? Was his passing
   divinely ordered and free of pain?

MESSENGER

                    To tell the truth,
   his death inspired wonder. How he left here
   you already know, since you were present.
   None of his loved ones led him on his way.
   Instead, he acted as a guide for all of us.
   When he came to the steep cleft that plunges   [1590]
   down the bronze stairway rooted deep in earth,
   he stopped near one of the many pathways
   which converge by a hollow in the rock
   where Theseus and Peirithous set up
   the lasting pledge of their eternal bond.
   He stood halfway between the basin there
   and the Thorician rock, with the stone tomb
   and the hollow pear tree on either side.[56]
   There he sat down, took off his filthy clothes,
   and, after calling for his daughters, asked them
   to bring him water from a flowing stream,
   so he could wash and offer a libation.
   The two of them went up the rocky hill
   of fresh, green Demeter, which we could see,   [1600]
   soon came back with what their father wanted,
   and then, following our usual customs,
   washed and dressed him.[57] When they were finished
   and had done all that Oedipus requested,
   without ignoring any of his wishes,
   at that moment Zeus of the Underworld
   produced a peal of thunder.[58] The young girls
   heard the noise and trembled. Then they collapsed,
   falling at their father's knees and weeping.
   They kept on striking their breasts and wailing,
   voicing their pain with loud and bitter cries.

ὁ δ' ὡς ἀκούει φθόγγον ἐξαίφνης πικρόν,   1610
πτύξας ἐπ' αὐταῖς χεῖρας εἶπεν· ὦ τέκνα,
οὐκ ἔστ' ἔθ' ὑμῖν τῇδ' ἐν ἡμέρᾳ πατήρ.
ὄλωλε γὰρ δὴ πάντα τἀμά, κοὐκέτι
τὴν δυσπόνητον ἕξετ' ἀμφ' ἐμοὶ τροφήν·
σκληρὰν μέν, οἶδα, παῖδες· ἀλλ' ἓν γὰρ μόνον   1615
τὰ πάντα λύει ταῦτ' ἔπος μοχθήματα.
τὸ γὰρ φιλεῖν οὐκ ἔστιν ἐξ ὅτου πλέον
ἢ τοῦδε τἀνδρὸς ἔσχεθ', οὗ τητώμεναι
τὸ λοιπὸν ἤδη τὸν βίον διάζετον.
τοιαῦτ' ἐπ' ἀλλήλοισιν ἀμφικείμενοι   1620
λύγδην ἔκλαιον πάντες. ὡς δὲ πρὸς τέλος
γόων ἀφίκοντ' οὐδ' ἔτ' ὠρώρει βοή,
ἦν μὲν σιωπή· φθέγμα δ' ἐξαίφνης τινὸς
θώϋξεν αὐτόν, ὥστε πάντας ὀρθίας
στῆσαι φόβῳ δείσαντας ἐξαίφνης τρίχας,   1625
καλεῖ γὰρ αὐτὸν πολλὰ πολλαχῇ θεός·
ὦ οὗτος οὗτος, Οἰδίπους, τί μέλλομεν
χωρεῖν; πάλαι δὴ τἀπὸ σοῦ βραδύνεται.
ὁ δ' ὡς ἐπῄσθετ' ἐκ θεοῦ καλούμενος,
αὐδᾷ μολεῖν οἱ γῆς ἄνακτα Θησέα.   1630
κἀπεὶ προσῆλθεν, εἶπεν· ὦ φίλον κάρα,
δός μοι χερὸς σῆς πίστιν ὁρκίαν τέκνοις,
ὑμεῖς τε, παῖδες, τῷδε· καὶ καταίνεσον
μήποτε προδώσειν τάσδ' ἑκών, τελεῖν δ' ὅσ' ἂν
μέλλῃς φρονῶν εὖ ξυμφέροντ' αὐτοῖς ἀεί.   1635
ὁ δ', ὡς ἀνὴρ γενναῖος, οὐκ οἴκτου μέτα
κατῄνεσεν τάδ' ὅρκιος δράσειν ξένῳ.
ὅπως δὲ ταῦτ' ἔδρασεν, εὐθὺς Οἰδίπους
ψαύσας ἀμαυραῖς χερσὶν ὧν παίδων λέγει·
'ὦ παῖδε, τλάσας χρὴ τὸ γενναῖον φρενὶ   1640
χωρεῖν τόπων ἐκ τῶνδε, μηδ' ἃ μὴ θέμις

When he heard these sudden howls of sorrow, [1610]
Oedipus held them in his arms and said,
"Children, today your father is no more.
Everything I was has perished, and you two
will no longer share the heavy burden
of looking after me. Children, I know
that task was difficult, but a single word
makes up for all your labours, for never
will you find anyone whose love for you
is greater than the love you both received
from the man who was your father. And now,
for all the days remaining in your lives,
you will not have him with you anymore."
They remained like this, holding one another, [1620]
all of them distraught with grief and sobbing.
Then they paused and stopped their mournful wailing.
They made no sound, and everything was still.
Suddenly a voice called out to Oedipus.
It made the hairs on all our heads stand up—
we were so terrified! Again and again
the god cried out to him in different ways,
"You there, you, Oedipus, why this delay
in our departure? You have been lingering
for far too long." Once he became aware
the god was summoning him, Oedipus
asked lord Theseus to come up to him, [1630]
and when the king did so, Oedipus said,
"My dear friend, give me the time-honoured pledge
of your right hand for my children, and you,
my daughters, give him your sworn pledge, as well.
My lord, promise you will not betray them
of your own free will but will always do
whatever you believe is best for them."
Since Theseus is an honorable king,
he showed no sign of sorrow and agreed
to fulfil that promise for the stranger.
Once Theseus had sworn he would do this,
Oedipus suddenly clutched his daughters
with his blind hands and said to them, "Children,
you must bear my death with a noble heart [1640]
and leave this place. For you cannot believe

λεύσσειν δικαιοῦν μηδὲ φωνούντων κλύειν,
ἀλλ᾽ ἕρπεθ᾽ ὡς τάχιστα· πλὴν ὁ κύριος
Θησεὺς παρέστω μανθάνων τὰ δρώμενα.᾽
τοσαῦτα φωνήσαντος εἰσηκούσαμεν   1645
ξύμπαντες· ἀστακτὶ δὲ σὺν ταῖς παρθένοις
στένοντες ὡμαρτοῦμεν. ὡς δ᾽ ἀπήλθομεν,
χρόνῳ βραχεῖ στραφέντες ἐξαπείδομεν
τὸν ἄνδρα τὸν μὲν οὐδαμοῦ παρόντ᾽ ἔτι,
ἄνακτα δ᾽ αὐτὸν ὀμμάτων ἐπίσκιον   1650
χεῖρ᾽ ἀντέχοντα κρατός, ὡς δεινοῦ τινος
φόβου φανέντος οὐδ᾽ ἀνασχετοῦ βλέπειν.
ἔπειτα μέντοι βαιὸν οὐδὲ σὺν χρόνῳ
ὁρῶμεν αὐτὸν γῆν τε προσκυνοῦνθ᾽ ἅμα
καὶ τὸν θεῶν Ὄλυμπον ἐν ταὐτῷ λόγῳ.   1655
μόρῳ δ᾽ ὁποίῳ κεῖνος ὤλετ᾽, οὐδ᾽ ἂν εἷς
θνητῶν φράσειε, πλὴν τὸ Θησέως κάρα.
οὐ γάρ τις αὐτὸν οὔτε πυρφόρος θεοῦ
κεραυνὸς ἐξέπραξεν οὔτε ποντία
θύελλα κινηθεῖσα τῷ τότ᾽ ἐν χρόνῳ,   1660
ἀλλ᾽ ἤ τις ἐκ θεῶν πομπὸς ἢ τὸ νερτέρων
εὔνουν διαστὰν γῆς ἀλύπητον βάθρον.
ἀνὴρ γὰρ οὐ στενακτὸς οὐδὲ σὺν νόσοις
ἀλγεινὸς ἐξεπέμπετ᾽, ἀλλ᾽ εἴ τις βροτῶν
θαυμαστός. εἰ δὲ μὴ δοκῶ φρονῶν λέγειν,   1665
οὐκ ἂν παρείμην οἷσι μὴ δοκῶ φρονεῖν.

ΧΟΡΟΣ
    ποῦ δ᾽ αἵ τε παῖδες χοἱ προπέμψαντες φίλων;

ΑΓΓΕΛΟΣ
    αἵδ᾽ οὐχ ἑκάς· γόων γὰρ οὐκ ἀσήμονες
    φθόγγοι σφε σημαίνουσι δεῦρ᾽ ὁρμωμένας.

326

it is appropriate to view those acts
which our traditions say should not be seen
or listen to things said you should not hear.
You must go now—and quickly. Let Theseus,
the sovereign king, stay and learn what happens."
All of us heard him say these words and then,
full of sorrow, with our eyes streaming tears,
we followed the young girls and left the place.
Once we moved off, after a few moments
we looked back from a distance and noticed
Oedipus was no longer to be seen.
Theseus was alone, holding his hands up   [1650]
right before his face to protect his eyes,
as if he had just seen something fearful
that no human being could bear to see.
And then, after that, a short time later,
we saw Theseus offering a single prayer,
worshipping divine Olympus and the Earth.
How Oedipus met his fate and perished
no mortal knows, other than Theseus.
It was no fiery lightning bolt from god
that took him away, nor was he carried off
by some momentary whirlwind rising   [1660]
out at sea. No—some escort from the gods
came for him or else, in an act of kindness,
the rock-hard world of the dead split open
so he would feel no pain. He passed away
without a groan or symptom of disease.
If any mortal man has ever died
in a miraculous way, then he did.
If someone thinks I talk just like a fool,
I will not try to teach him otherwise,
since he believes my words do not make sense.

CHORUS
      Where are the ones who went away with him—
      his daughters and their friends?

MESSENGER
      Not far away. The sound of their laments
      is getter closer—they are almost here.

[ANTIGONE and ISMENE enter]

327

Sophocles

ΑΝΤΙΓΟΝΗ

αἰαῖ, φεῦ, ἔστιν ἔστι νῷν δὴ   1670
οὐ τὸ μέν, ἄλλο δὲ μή, πατρὸς ἔμφυτον
ἄλαστον αἷμα δυσμόροιν στενάζειν,
ᾧτινι τὸν πολὺν
ἄλλοτε μὲν πόνον ἔμπεδον εἴχομεν,
ἐν πυμάτῳ δ' ἀλόγιστα παροίσομεν   1675
ἰδόντε καὶ παθόντε.

ΧΟΡΟΣ

τί δ' ἔστιν;

ΑΝΤΙΓΟΝΗ

ἔστιν μὲν εἰκάσαι, φίλοι.

ΧΟΡΟΣ

βέβηκεν;

ΑΝΤΙΓΟΝΗ

ὡς μάλιστ' ἂν ἐν πόθῳ λάβοις.
τί γάρ, ὅτῳ μήτ' Ἄρης
μήτε πόντος ἀντέκυρσεν,   1680
ἄσκοποι δὲ πλάκες ἔμαρψαν
ἐν ἀφανεῖ τινι μόρῳ φερόμενον.
τάλαινα· νῷν δ' ὀλεθρία
νὺξ ἐπ' ὄμμασιν βέβακε. πῶς γὰρ ἤ τιν' ἀπίαν   1685
γᾶν ἢ πόντιον κλύδων' ἀλώμεναι, βίου
δύσοιστον ἕξομεν τροφάν;

ΙΣΜΗΝΗ

οὐ κάτοιδα. κατά με φόνιος Ἀΐδας ἕλοι
πατρὶ ξυνθανεῖν γεραιῷ   1690
τάλαιναν, ὡς ἔμοιγ' ὁ μέλλων βίος οὐ βιωτός.

ΧΟΡΟΣ

ὦ διδύμα τέκνων ἀρίστα, τὸ φέρον ἐκ θεοῦ φέρειν,
μηδὲν ἄγαν φλέγεσθον· οὔ τοι κατάμεμπτ' ἔβητον.   1695

328

ANTIGONE

    Alas! This is so sad! Now the two of us,   [1670]
    both subject to an abject destiny,
    will spend every moment grieving
    the family curse we carry in our blood,
    inherited from our father. For him
    before today we laboured long and hard.
    Now he is dead, and we are left to speak
    of what we saw and went through at the end,
    events that baffle reason.

CHORUS

                      What happened?

ANTIGONE

    One can only guess, my friends.

CHORUS

    Has Oedipus truly gone?

ANTIGONE

                 He has gone
    exactly as one might have wished—
    not seized by Ares, god of war,
    or by the sea, but snatched away   [1680]
    by unseen fate and carried off
    to the hidden fields of death.
    I feel so sad! A death-filled night
    now shrouds our eyes. How do we find
    daily nourishment in a harsh life
    of wandering some distant land
    or roaming waves of the sea?

ISMENE

                 I do not know.
    Things are desperate! How I wish
    Hades the killer would seize me too
    and let me share death with my old father!
    For the life I face is not worth living.   [1690]

CHORUS

    You two most excellent of daughters
    must bear whatever gods provide.
    Do not let your hearts burn up
    in flames of excess passion—
    for what has happened to you here
    gives you no reason to complain.

Sophocles

ΑΝΤΙΓΟΝΗ

πόθος τοι καὶ κακῶν ἄρ' ἦν τις.
καὶ γὰρ ὃ μηδαμὰ δὴ φίλον ἦν φίλον,   1700
ὁπότε γε καὶ τὸν ἐν χεροῖν κατεῖχον.
ὦ πάτερ, ὦ φίλος,
ὦ τὸν ἀεὶ κατὰ γᾶς σκότον εἱμένος·
οὐδέ γ' ἔνερθ' ἀφίλητος ἐμοί ποτε
καὶ τᾷδε μὴ κυρήσῃς.   1705

ΧΟΡΟΣ

ἔπραξεν;

ΑΝΤΙΓΟΝΗ

ἔπραξεν οἷον ἤθελεν.

ΧΟΡΟΣ

τὸ ποῖον;

ΑΝΤΙΓΟΝΗ

ἃς ἔχρῃζε γᾶς ἐπὶ ξένας
ἔθανε· κοίταν δ' ἔχει
νέρθεν εὐσκίαστον αἰέν,
οὐδὲ πένθος ἔλιπ' ἄκλαυτον.
ἀνὰ γὰρ ὄμμα σε τόδ', ὦ πάτερ, ἐμὸν
στένει δακρῦον, οὐδ' ἔχω   1710
πῶς με χρὴ τὸ σὸν τάλαιναν ἀφανίσαι τοσόνδ' ἄχος.
ὤμοι, γᾶς ἐπὶ ξένας θανεῖν ἔχρῃζες ἀλλ'
ἔρημος ἔθανες ὧδέ μοι.

ΙΣΜΗΝΗ

ὦ τάλαινα, τίς ἄρα με πότμος αὖθις ὧδ'   1715
< . . . >
ἐπαμμένει σέ τ', ὦ φίλα, τὰς πατρὸς ὧδ' ἐρήμας;   1719

ΧΟΡΟΣ

ἀλλ' ἐπεὶ ὀλβίως γ' ἔλυσεν τὸ τέλος, ὦ φίλαι, βίου,   1720
λήγετε τοῦδ' ἄχους· κακῶν γὰρ δυσάλωτος οὐδείς.

330

ANTIGONE

> One laments the loss of even painful things.
> That life for which I felt no love at all   [1700]
> I did love when I held him in my arms.
> O my beloved father, now wrapped
> in the underworld's eternal darkness,
> even though you are no longer here,
> my sister and I will love you always.

CHORUS

> He ended . . .

ANTIGONE

>   He had the end he wished for.

CHORUS

> In what way?

ANTIGONE

>   He perished in a foreign land,
> as he desired, and is eternally at rest
> beneath the ground in a well-shaded place.
> He did not leave us without being mourned.
> With tear-filled eyes I still grieve for you,
> my father, and in my unhappy state
> I do not know how I should relieve   [1710]
> the grief I feel with such intensity.
> Alas! You wished to die in a strange land,
> but when you died I was not with you!

ISMENE

> I feel so desperate! What fate awaits us,
> my dear sister, now we have no father?[59]

CHORUS

> Friends, since the ending of his life was blessed,   [1720]
> you should cease this grieving. No mortal
> has a life immune from great misfortune.

ΑΝΤΙΓΟΝΗ
πάλιν, φίλα, συθῶμεν.

ΙΣΜΗΝΗ
ὡς τί ῥέξομεν;

ΑΝΤΙΓΟΝΗ
ἵμερος ἔχει με.

ΙΣΜΗΝΗ
τίς;

ΑΝΤΙΓΟΝΗ
τὰν χθόνιον ἑστίαν ἰδεῖν   1725

ΙΣΜΗΝΗ
τίνος;

ΑΝΤΙΓΟΝΗ
πατρός, τάλαιν᾽ ἐγώ.

ΙΣΜΗΝΗ
θέμις δὲ πῶς τάδ᾽ ἐστί; μῶν
οὐχ ὁρᾷς;   1730

ΑΝΤΙΓΟΝΗ
τί τόδε ἐπέπληξας;

ΙΣΜΗΝΗ
καὶ τόδ᾽, ὡς

ΑΝΤΙΓΟΝΗ
τί τόδε μάλ᾽ αὖθις;

ΙΣΜΗΝΗ
ἄταφος ἔπιτνε δίχα τε παντός.

ΑΝΤΙΓΟΝΗ
ἄγε με, καὶ τότ᾽ ἐπενάριξον.

ΙΣΜΗΝΗ
αἰαῖ, δυστάλαινα, ποῦ δῆτ᾽
αὖθις ὧδ᾽ ἔρημος ἄπορος   1735
αἰῶνα τλάμον᾽ ἕξω;

ANTGONE
Dear sister, we must hurry back.

ISMENE
But why?
What do we have to do?

ANTIGONE
I need to see it!

ISMENE
See what?

ANTIGONE
That earthly resting place.

ISMENE
Whose resting place?

ANTIGONE
I cannot bear this grief—
I have to see our father's burial ground!

ISMENE
But how does such a wish not break our laws?   [1730]
Don't you see that?

ANTIGONE
Why do you disapprove?

ISMENE
And then there is also this . . .

ANTIGONE
What other things
are you complaining of?

ISMENE
Our father perished
without a grave—and no one else was there.

ANTIGONE
Lead me there, and then slaughter me, as well.[60]

ISMENE
Alas for me, in my miserable state!
Where am I now to spend this wretched life,
with no support and totally abandoned!

ΧΟΡΟΣ
φίλαι, τρέσητε μηδέν.

ΑΝΤΙΓΟΝΗ
              ἀλλὰ ποῖ φύγω;

ΧΟΡΟΣ
καὶ πάρος ἀπέφυγε

ΑΝΤΙΓΟΝΗ
       τί;

ΧΟΡΟΣ
τὰ σφῷν τὸ μὴ πίτνειν κακῶς.   1740

ΑΝΤΙΓΟΝΗ
φρονῶ.

ΧΟΡΟΣ
     τί δῆθ' ὅπερ νοεῖς;

ΑΝΤΙΓΟΝΗ
ὅπως μολούμεθ' ἐς δόμους
οὐκ ἔχω.

ΧΟΡΟΣ
     μηδέ γε μάτευε.

ΑΝΤΙΓΟΝΗ
μόγος ἔχει.

ΧΟΡΟΣ
     καὶ πάρος ἐπεῖχε.

ΑΝΤΙΓΟΝΗ
τοτὲ μὲν ἄπορα, τοτὲ δ' ὕπερθεν.   1745

ΧΟΡΟΣ
μέγ' ἄρα πέλαγος ἐλάχετόν τι.

ΑΝΤΙΓΟΝΗ
ναὶ ναί.

ΧΟΡΟΣ
     ξύμφημι καὐτός.

CHORUS
Do not fear, my friends.

ANTIGONE
            But where do I take refuge?[61]

CHORUS
You have already found a place for that.

ANTIGONE
What are you saying?

CHORUS
                You two have reached
a place where you are safe from harm.   [1740]

ANTIGONE
Yes, I understand that.

CHORUS
                        What else is there?
What are you thinking?

ANTIGONE
                        I have no idea
how we get home to Thebes.

CHORUS
                    Don't even think of that!

ANTIGONE
This present trouble has us in its grip!

CHORUS
The evils you faced before were harsh enough.

ANTIGONE
Back then we had no hope. Now things are worse.

CHORUS
You have been destined for a sea of troubles.

ANTIGONE
Yes, that is true.

CHORUS
                That's what it seems to me.

Sophocles

ΑΝΤΙΓΟΝΗ
αἰαῖ, ποῖ μόλωμεν, ὦ Ζεῦ;
ἐλπίδων γὰρ ἐς τίν' ἔτι με
δαίμων τανῦν γ' ἐλαύνει; 1750

ΘΗΣΕΥΣ
παύετε θρήνων, παῖδες· ἐν οἷς γὰρ
χάρις ἡ χθονία ξύν' ἀπόκειται,
πενθεῖν οὐ χρή· νέμεσις γάρ.

ΑΝΤΙΓΟΝΗ
ὦ τέκνον Αἰγέως, προσπίτνομέν σοι. 1755

ΘΗΣΕΥΣ
τίνος, ὦ παῖδες, χρείας ἀνύσαι;

ΑΝΤΙΓΟΝΗ
τύμβον θέλομεν προσιδεῖν αὐταὶ
πατρὸς ἡμετέρου.

ΘΗΣΕΥΣ
        ἀλλ' οὐ θεμιτόν.

ΑΝΤΙΓΟΝΗ
πῶς εἶπας, ἄναξ, κοίραν' Ἀθηνῶν;

ΘΗΣΕΥΣ
ὦ παῖδες, ἀπεῖπεν ἐμοὶ κεῖνος 1765
μήτε πελάζειν ἐς τούσδε τόπους
μήτ' ἐπιφωνεῖν μηδένα θνητῶν
θήκην ἱεράν, ἣν κεῖνος ἔχει.
καὶ ταῦτά μ' ἔφη πράσσοντα καλῶς
χώραν ἕξειν αἰὲν ἄλυπον.
ταῦτ' οὖν ἔκλυεν δαίμων ἡμῶν
χὠ πάντ' ἀΐων Διὸς Ὅρκος.

ΑΝΤΙΓΟΝΗ
ἀλλ' εἰ τάδ' ἔχει κατὰ νοῦν κείνῳ,
ταῦτ' ἂν ἀπαρκοῖ· Θήβας δ' ἡμᾶς

336

ANTIGONE
    Alas! Alas! O Zeus, where do we go?
    Where is our destiny now driving us—
    towards what last remaining hope?   [1750]

[Enter THESEUS]

THESEUS
    Stop these laments, children! When gods below
    store up public favours for the dead,
    we must feel no sorrow—for if we do
    then retribution follows.[62]

ANTIGONE
                    Son of Aegeus,
    we beg one request from you.

THESEUS
                      What is it,
    my children. What do you desire?

ANTIGONE
                          We wish
    to see our father's grave with our own eyes.

THESEUS
    To go there is forbidden by our laws.

ANTIGONE
    O lord and ruler of Athenians,
    what do you mean?

THESEUS
                Children, your father told me   [1760]
    that no living person should come near the place
    or speak any words beside the sacred ground
    where he is buried. And he promised me,
    if I made sure of that, then I would keep
    the land of Athens free of pain forever.
    The god there heard me swear that I would do it,
    and so did Horkos, too, Zeus' servant,
    who witnesses all oaths and makes them strong.[63]

ANTIGONE
    If this is what my father has in mind,
    then we must comply. Send us on our way

Sophocles

τὰς ὠγυγίους πέμψον, ἐάν πως   1770
διακωλύσωμεν ἰόντα φόνον
τοῖσιν ὁμαίμοις.

ΘΗΣΕΥΣ

δράσω καὶ τάδε καὶ πάνθ᾽ ὁπόσ᾽ ἂν
μέλλω πράσσειν πρόσφορά θ᾽ ὑμῖν
καὶ τῷ κατὰ γῆς, ὃς νέον ἔρρει,   1775
πρὸς χάριν· οὐ δεῖ μ᾽ ἀποκάμνειν.

ΧΟΡΟΣ

ἀλλ᾽ ἀποπαύετε μηδ᾽ ἐπὶ πλείω
θρῆνον ἐγείρετε·
πάντως γὰρ ἔχει τάδε κῦρος.

to ancient Thebes, to see if we somehow [1770]
can stop the coming slaughter of our brothers.

THESEUS

I will do that and perform whatever else
may be a service to you and to the man
who has just died and lies beneath the earth.
On his behalf I must spare no effort,
for Oedipus has earned my gratitude.

CHORUS

So let us cease with our laments,
and chant our funeral songs no more.
For these events have all been preordained.

NOTES

1. The Eumenides (Kindly Ones) is another name for the Furies, the goddesses of blood revenge, especially within the family. The Greeks sometimes liked to give particularly fearful things euphemistic names (e.g., calling the Black Sea the Euxine or "Hospitable" Sea).

2. As we learn shortly, Apollo has told Oedipus that when he reaches a holy shrine his wanderings will end. See line 106 ff. below.

3. The Titans, descendants of Earth and Sky, were divine figures of the generation before the Olympians. Prometheus, son of the Titan Iapetus, stole fire from heaven and gave it to human beings.

4. Jebb explains that near this sacred grove was a steep channel in the rock, where someone had constructed some bronze steps. It was called the "threshold of Hades." Hence the whole area was called "the bronze threshold" and was considered an important element in the safety of Athens.

5. Some commentators have suggested that there may well be a statue of Colonus somewhere on the stage. If so, this line would presumably be a reference to it.

6. Libations to the Furies were made, not with wine, but with water.

7. As Jebb points out, this remark is bitterly ironic. Oedipus is, in effect, saying: "I have suffered more than any other living person, but perhaps I have not yet suffered enough to win a concession from the gods."

8. In the religious rituals libations of water and of water mixed with honey were poured separately.

9. At this point there is a gap in the manuscript of three or four lines.

10. Laius was Oedipus' father; Labdacus was the father of Laius. They were both kings of Thebes.

11. Earlier the Chorus promised Oedipus he would not be removed from refuge against his will.

12. The argument here is that Oedipus earlier deceived the Chorus by not revealing who he was before they made their promise to him. Therefore, they are justified in setting that promise aside.

13. Oedipus is arguing that in his actions he was responding to the treatment he received from his parents (who had tried to kill him as an infant by exposing him on Mount Cithaeron, outside Thebes). And in attacking his father, Oedipus was reacting to the latter's hostile actions. Hence, even if he had known that his opponent was his father, Oedipus states, one could not consider him evil for defending himself.

14. This is almost certainly a reference to the way his parents tried to kill the infant Oedipus by pinning his feet together and abandoning him on the mountain. They were driven to do that by a prophecy that said the newborn child would grow up to kill his father.

15. Ismene presumably enters on foot, having dismounted from her horse.

16. The curse on the family of Laius, Oedipus' father, originated in Laius' abduction and rape of Chrysippus, a young son of Pelops, king of Pisa (in the Peloponnese) and Pelops' host. As a result of this crime, Chrysippus committed suicide, and Pelops laid a curse on Laius and his descendants. A profane act by a member of the family could bring religious pollution to an entire community.

17. Sophocles here makes Polyneices the elder of the two brothers. In some other versions of the story, Eteocles is the firstborn son. This change makes each brother a wrongdoer: Eteocles for usurping his elder brother, and Polyneices for seeking a foreign army to fight against his homeland.

18. Polyneices married Argeia, daughter of Adrastus, king of Argos, as part of his strategy to raise an army and attack Thebes.

19. This sentence is rather ambiguous in the Greek. If Argos defeats Thebes, Polyneices and his friends will win honour. The alternative is that Argos will sing someone's praises to the skies. Jebb suggests that Argos will be singing the praises of Thebes for having won the battle. Another possibility is that Argos will be exalting Polyneices and his friends for having taken a great risk, fought the battle, and behaved heroically, even though they did not succeed. The latter seems to me more probable, given that it is the sort of idea young men bent on a dangerous expedition would come up with. Cadmean land is a reference to Thebes: Cadmus was the one who founded the city.

20. Oedipus' anger at his sons is not primarily rage at their foolish conduct for quarrelling over the throne but rather fury because, although the sons know about the prophecy that the security of Thebes is to depend upon the way Thebans treat Oedipus and his tomb, they are not working to get him accepted back at Thebes and perhaps even restored to the throne. Instead they are concentrating on trying to become king themselves. His concern is the injury he thinks has been done to him. What the latest prophecy is saying is that if Oedipus is buried in Athenian lands then, at some point in the future the Thebans will invade those lands but will be defeated by the Athenians at Oedipus' grave. In other words, Oedipus' anger will eventually work against them. The only way of averting that is to get control of Oedipus now, to make sure he cannot be buried in Athens.

21. It is not clear how long a period of time passed between Oedipus' self-mutilation and his exile from Thebes. During this period the city was ruled by Creon, who presumably made the decision to exile Oedipus.

22. Oedipus has spoken earlier about a prophecy he received from Apollo many years before that he would finally find rest (see line 106 above). He is now combining that oracular utterance with what Ismene has told him about recent prophecies concerning him.

23. As Jebb observes, the Chorus' shock here suggests that they are just finding out that Jocasta was not only Oedipus' wife and mother, but also the mother of his children. In some versions of the story of Oedipus, he had no children with Jocasta, and his children were from a second wife, Euryganeia.

24. Thebes had been plagued by a monster, the Sphinx, which could only be conquered by someone who answered a riddle correctly. Oedipus solved the riddle and saved the city. He was made king for his services and married Jocasta, the wife of king Laius (who had been murdered some years before).

25. Oedipus killed his father, Laius when the two encountered each other in a place where three roads meet. Laius and his escort shoved Oedipus aside and assaulted him. Thinking his life in danger, Oedipus killed them all, not knowing who they were.

26. Theseus, one of the most famous legendary heroes of Athens, was the son of Aethra, daughter of king Pittheus of Troezen. His father was Aegeus, king of Athens. After Theseus was conceived in Troezen, his father returned to Athens, but he left behind evidence of his identity

for his son to discover when he was old enough. Theseus grew up in Troezen and learned about his father as a young man. He set off for Athens and after a series of famous adventures was eventually reunited with Aegeus, his father.

27. Theseus seems surprised by Oedipus' remarks, since he is probably assuming Oedipus will request protection during his lifetime. Oedipus, however, is concerned only about where he will be buried; hence, he does not care about what happens to him between now and his death, so long as he is confident his grave will be in Athens. As we soon learn, Oedipus' request to be buried in Athens implicitly includes a demand that the Athenians will not hand him over to anyone else, because if he is taken away, then Theseus will be unable to fulfil his pledge to bury Oedipus at Athens.

28. The nymphs of Mount Nysa were given the infant god Dionysus to raise after he was born from Zeus' thigh. They later became the first of those who joined him in his revels (the Bacchantes).

29. The two great goddesses are Demeter and her daughter Persephone. Persephone was gathering a narcissus when she was abducted by Hades, god of the underworld.

30. The "great Dorian isle of Pelops" is a reference to the Peloponnese, that area of mainland Greece south of the Isthmus of Corinth (it is almost an island). Jebb notes that Sophocles does not mean that the olive tree does not grow elsewhere, but rather that the olive does not flourish in other places the way it does in Athens, where it enjoys divine protection. The tree was, according to Athenian legends, a gift from the goddess Athena, who made the first one spring spontaneously from the soil of the city (hence human beings did not plant it in Athens).

31. Zeus here is called "morios," is a word referring to the sacred olive trees in Athens, of which Zeus was the divine guardian. Hence, the title Zeus Morios.

32. Nereus, a sea god in Greek mythology, was a son of Pontus and Gaia (the Sea and the Earth) and the father of the fifty Nereids, nymphs who lived in the sea. This last stanza is a tribute to the importance of Poseidon at Athens. According to legend he introduced horses in Athens and helped to make Athenians expert sailors.

33. Creon was the brother of Oedipus' wife and mother, Jocasta.

34. The word "justly" here refers to the law. Creon is reminding those listening that Thebes has a better legal claim to Oedipus than Athens does, because of the time Oedipus spent there and his family connection with Creon.

35. Creon's appeal for the Chorus to witness Oedipus's conduct is a continuation of his legal thinking. Oedipus wishes to associate himself with Colonus and Athens. Creon has been making the point that, given Oedipus' history and family ties, Thebes has a better legal right to have Oedipus back. At this point, seeing that neither Oedipus nor the Chorus is accepting the legal argument, Creon resorts to threats and violence.

36. The "triumph" Creon refers to is Oedipus' "victory" in not returning to Thebes with him. Creon is claiming here that he has been acting in the best interests of Thebes and of Oedipus' family, although, as absolute ruler of the city, he has no need to defer to their wishes. He is also pointing out that Oedipus' temper has always led to consequences injurious to his family (e.g., his own self-mutilation and expulsion from Thebes, the suicide of Jocasta, his mother-wife and Creon's sister, and the harsh life of his two daughters).

37. The Hill of Ares is a rocky outcrop near the entrance to the Acropolis in Athens. The Council there, the Areopagus, was a court dealing with criminal and civil cases and general moral censorship in the earlier days of Athenian democracy.

38. Theseus is apparently assuming that Creon has entered into a secret agreement with some unspecified Athenian conspirators before challenging Theseus' royal authority by entering his territory. There is no mention of that elsewhere in the play or in other versions of the story.

39. The Chorus is here imagining the impending clash between Theseus and Creon, which, in their view, may take place either on the bay of Eleusis ("the Pythian shores") or else at Eleusis, the centre of a major religious festival dedicated to the goddess Demeter ("beside the torch-lit shore"). In the next section they consider a third possibility. Ares is the god of war, and the goddesses referred to are Demeter and her daughter Persephone. The Eumolpidae were the priests of the religious rituals, responsible for ensuring the secrets of the divine mysteries.

40. This tribute to the two main deities of Athens, Athena and Poseidon, identifies the former with the epithet *hippeia* ("of the horse," "equestrian"), an association linked to her as the inventor of the

chariot, and the latter by a common epithet "encircling the earth" and by a reference to his mother, Rhea, also the mother of the gods Zeus and Hades.

41. These lines indicate that Oedipus still feels he is suffering from religious pollution. Hence, anyone who shows him affection (e.g., by touching) runs the risk of being contaminated. Those who have been with him throughout his suffering run no such risk, since they have long been in frequent physical contact with him.

42. Antigone's obvious point here is that in his past actions Oedipus has let his explosive temper take control of his actions, with disastrous effect. The most obvious evidence for that is his self-inflicted blindness.

43. The words *Dorian* and *Apian* in these lines both refer to the Peloponnese. The word *Argos* by itself can refer to a number of different places in ancient Hellas.

44. Eteoclus, the Argive leader in the force Polyneices has assembled, should obviously not be confused with Eteocles, Polyneices' brother. The name Parthenopaeus means "child of the maiden" or "child of the virgin."

45. Polyneices words mean, in effect, "I am your son, but if I am not (because you have disowned me), then I am the child of fate, even if among the general public I am still considered your child."

46. This detail seems to contradict the chronology of events concerning the governance of Thebes. According to lines 400 ff. above, after Oedipus blinded himself, his sons deferred to the authority of Creon, who ruled as regent, and it seems they began their fight after Oedipus went into exile. Creon himself speaks as if he has sole regal authority in Thebes, but we are told (by Polyneices and Oedipus) that Eteocles is now the ruling king. There has been no suggestion up to this point that Polyneices was ever *de facto* king of Thebes, although, as he says, he is the elder son and therefore, in his eyes, the rightful heir.

47. Jebb offers the useful note that curses, once uttered, become divine agents of vengeance. Oedipus is therefore calling for the agents created by his earlier curses against his two sons to come to his assistance now.

48. Oedipus is claiming here that his curse on Polyneices will defeat any legal claims Polyneices may have to justify his attack on Thebes (both as a suppliant and as the elder son) because ancient natural Justice demands that children respect their parents, a law that is more powerful than any Polyneices can appeal to.

49. Tartarus is a deep pit in Hades, usually associated with punishment and imprisonment. The word "paternal" may refer to the idea that darkness the father of everything or that Polyneices will be going to a place as dark as the world of his father, Oedipus.

50. These lines from the Chorus refer once again to the notion that contact with a polluted person (i.e., someone cursed by the gods) can bring the anger of the gods down on those who have had dealings with him.

51. For details of what Oedipus has promised Theseus, see lines 723 ff. above.

52. The founder of Thebes, Cadmus, killed a dragon living at the site of the future city. When he sowed the monster's teeth across the earth, armed men sprang up and began fighting and killing each other, until only a few were left. These men were the first Thebans. Oedipus is, in effect, promising that Athens will never suffer from civil disturbances, if Athenians remember his instructions.

53. The point here is that even well-governed cities will suffer from the hubristic ambitions of some citizens because, although the gods will eventually punish evil citizens, such divine retribution is slow and therefore the troublemakers will have time to disrupt civic life.

54. Aidoneus is another name for Hades, god of the underworld. The "unseen goddess" is Persephone, wife of Hades. The name "Styx" refers to the river separating the earth and the underworld. The word also often designates the underworld generally.

55. The "goddesses in the lower world" are probably the Furies, the divine agents of blood revenge, and the "beast" is a reference to Cerberus, a dog with several heads (the number varies from one account to another) who is a resident of Hades, with a lair near the entrance to the underworld. It is not clear to whom the phrase "child of Earth and Tartarus" refers, since it does not describe the parentage of Cerberus (perhaps it is a general reference to Death, the "lord of eternal sleep").

56. For an explanation of the "bronze stairway" as the threshold of the descent to Hades, see Endnote 4 above. Peirithous was king of the Lapiths and a close friend of Theseus. In a famous heroic exploit, the two men together went down to Hades, were captured by Hades, and then rescued by Hercules. The "lasting pledge" is some sort of memorial to their friendship. Thoricus was a town in Attica. Jebb notes that in a legendary story Thoricus was a place where a mortal called Cephalus

was taken up to the gods and that the "hollow pear tree" may mark the spot where Persephone was abducted by Hades and taken down to the underworld (i.e., they are references to places where the gods took some mortal being away).

57. Demeter was a goddess protecting crops. She was worshipped in various manifestations (Black Demeter, Green Demeter, Yellow Demeter—symbolizing the different stages of the crop cycle—black earth, the first appearance of a young crop, and harvest time).

58. Zeus is traditionally a god associated with the sky and heaven, but some Greek cities worshipped Zeus as a god of earth or of under the earth.

59. Some lines have been apparently been lost from this speech.

60. Ismene's objections to Antigone's desire to visit Oedipus' resting place are that it opposes Oedipus' express wishes (and is therefore not lawful) and that no one knows where the burial site is.

61. Jebb questions whether in this exchange (up to the arrival of Theseus) there might be some confusion in the way speeches have traditionally been assigned, since Antigone's sudden and urgent concern about where she is to go now does not seem to fit her obviously strong preoccupation with visiting her father's burial place as soon as possible. The speeches given to Antigone here seem much more appropriate coming from Ismene, who is clearly wondering about where she is to find a home now that Oedipus is dead. I have made no changes to the traditional arrangement, but I find Jebb's observations quite attractive (and I would probably try them out if I were mounting a production of the play).

62. Since with the death of Oedipus in Athens, the gods have seen to it that he gets what he most desires and that the Athenians obtain a guarantee of political security, there is no reason to feel sad. To do so would be to go against what the gods have established (and thus invite their angry punishment).

63. The "god there" is (one assumes) the divine spirit who took Oedipus away. Horkos (meaning Oath) is a god who serves Zeus by witnessing oaths and punishing perjury. I have added a line in English to clarify his function.

ΑΝΤΙΓΟΝΗ

ANTIGONE

ΤΑ ΤΟΥ ΔΡΑΜΑΤΟΣ ΠΡΟΣΩΠΑ

ΑΝΤΙΓΟΝΗ

ΙΣΜΗΝΗ

ΧΟΡΟΣ

ΚΡΕΩΝ

ΦΥΛΑΞ

ΑΙΜΩΝ

ΤΕΙΡΕΣΙΑΣ

ΑΓΓΕΛΟΣ

ΕΥΡΥΔΙΚΗ

ΕΞΑΓΓΕΛΟΣ

DRAMATIS PERSONAE

ANTIGONE: daughter of Oedipus

ISMENE: daughter of Oedipus, sister of Antigone

CREON: king of Thebes

EURYDICE: wife of Creon

HAEMON: son of Creon and Euridice, engaged to Antigone.

TEIRESIAS: an old blind prophet

BOY: a young lad guiding Teiresias

GUARD: a soldier serving Creon

MESSENGER

CHORUS: Theban Elders

ATTENDANTS.

Ἀντιγόνη

ΑΝΤΙΓΟΝΗ

 ὦ κοινὸν αὐτάδελφον Ἰσμήνης κάρα,
 ἆρ᾽ οἶσθ᾽ ὅ τι Ζεὺς τῶν ἀπ᾽ Οἰδίπου κακῶν
 ὁποῖον οὐχὶ νῷν ἔτι ζώσαιν τελεῖ;
 οὐδὲν γὰρ οὔτ᾽ ἀλγεινὸν οὔτ᾽ ἄτης ἄτερ
 οὔτ᾽ αἰσχρὸν οὔτ᾽ ἄτιμόν ἐσθ᾽, ὁποῖον οὐ   5
 τῶν σῶν τε κἀμῶν οὐκ ὄπωπ᾽ ἐγὼ κακῶν.
 καὶ νῦν τί τοῦτ᾽ αὖ φασι πανδήμῳ πόλει
 κήρυγμα θεῖναι τὸν στρατηγὸν ἀρτίως;
 ἔχεις τι κεἰσήκουσας; ἤ σε λανθάνει
 πρὸς τοὺς φίλους στείχοντα τῶν ἐχθρῶν κακά;   10

ΙΣΜΗΝΗ

 ἐμοὶ μὲν οὐδεὶς μῦθος, Ἀντιγόνη φίλων
 οὔθ᾽ ἡδὺς οὔτ᾽ ἀλγεινὸς ἵκετ᾽ ἐξ ὅτου
 δυοῖν ἀδελφοῖν ἐστερήθημεν δύο,
 μιᾷ θανόντοιν ἡμέρᾳ διπλῇ χερί·
 ἐπεὶ δὲ φροῦδός ἐστιν Ἀργείων στρατὸς   15
 ἐν νυκτὶ τῇ νῦν, οὐδὲν οἶδ᾽ ὑπέρτερον,
 οὔτ᾽ εὐτυχοῦσα μᾶλλον οὔτ᾽ ἀτωμένη.

ΑΝΤΙΓΟΝΗ

 ᾔδη καλῶς, καί σ᾽ ἐκτὸς αὐλείων πυλῶν
 τοῦδ᾽ οὕνεκ᾽ ἐξέπεμπον, ὡς μόνη κλύοις.

ΙΣΜΗΝΗ

 τί δ᾽ ἔστι; δηλοῖς γάρ τι καλχαίνουσ᾽ ἔπος.   20

Antigone

[*In Thebes, directly in front of the royal palace, which stands in the background, its main doors facing the audience. Enter Antigone leading Ismene away from the palace*]

ANTIGONE

    Now, dear Ismene, my own blood sister,
    do you have any sense of all the troubles
    Zeus keeps bringing on the two of us,
    as long as we're alive? All that misery
    which stems from Oedipus? There's no suffering,
    no shame, no ruin—not one dishonour—
    which I have not seen in all the troubles
    you and I go through. What's this they're saying now,
    something our general has had proclaimed
    throughout the city? Do you know of it?
    Have you heard? Or have you just missed the news?
    Dishonours which better fit our enemies
    are now being piled up on the ones we love.   [10]

ISMENE

    I've had no word at all, Antigone,
    nothing good or bad about our family,
    not since we two lost both our brothers,
    killed on the same day by a double blow.
    And since the Argive army, just last night,
    has gone away, I don't know any more
    if I've been lucky or face total ruin.

ANTIGONE

    I know that. That's why I brought you here,
    outside the gates, so only you can hear.

ISMENE

    What is it? The way you look makes it seem   [20]
    you're thinking of some dark and gloomy news.

Sophocles

ΑΝΤΙΓΟΝΗ

οὐ γὰρ τάφου νῷν τὼ κασιγνήτω Κρέων
τὸν μὲν προτίσας, τὸν δ' ἀτιμάσας ἔχει;
Ἐτεοκλέα μέν, ὡς λέγουσι, σὺν δίκης
χρήσει δικαίᾳ καὶ νόμου κατὰ χθονὸς
ἔκρυψε τοῖς ἔνερθεν ἔντιμον νεκροῖς·   25
τὸν δ' ἀθλίως θανόντα Πολυνείκους νέκυν
ἀστοῖσί φασιν ἐκκεκηρῦχθαι τὸ μὴ
τάφῳ καλύψαι μηδὲ κωκῦσαί τινα,
ἐᾶν δ' ἄκλαυτον, ἄταφον, οἰωνοῖς γλυκὺν
θησαυρὸν εἰσορῶσι πρὸς χάριν βορᾶς.   30
τοιαῦτά φασι τὸν ἀγαθὸν Κρέοντα σοὶ
κἀμοί, λέγω γὰρ κἀμέ, κηρύξαντ' ἔχειν,
καὶ δεῦρο νεῖσθαι ταῦτα τοῖσι μὴ εἰδόσιν
σαφῆ προκηρύξοντα, καὶ τὸ πρᾶγμ' ἄγειν
οὐχ ὡς παρ' οὐδέν, ἀλλ' ὃς ἂν τούτων τι δρᾷ,   35
φόνον προκεῖσθαι δημόλευστον ἐν πόλει.
οὕτως ἔχει σοι ταῦτα, καὶ δείξεις τάχα
εἴτ' εὐγενὴς πέφυκας εἴτ' ἐσθλῶν κακή.

ΙΣΜΗΝΗ

τί δ', ὦ ταλαῖφρον, εἰ τάδ' ἐν τούτοις, ἐγὼ
λύουσ' ἂν ἢ 'φάπτουσα προσθείμην πλέον;   40

ΑΝΤΙΓΟΝΗ

εἰ ξυμπονήσεις καὶ ξυνεργάσει σκόπει.

ΙΣΜΗΝΗ

ποῖόν τι κινδύνευμα; ποῦ γνώμης ποτ' εἶ;

ΑΝΤΙΓΟΝΗ

εἰ τὸν νεκρὸν ξὺν τῇδε κουφιεῖς χερί.

ΙΣΜΗΝΗ

ἦ γὰρ νοεῖς θάπτειν σφ', ἀπόρρητον πόλει;

ANTIGONE

    Look—what's Creon doing with our two brothers?
    He's honouring one with a full funeral
    and treating the other one disgracefully!
    Eteocles, they say, has had his burial
    according to our customary rites,
    to win him honour with the dead below.
    But as for Polyneices, who perished
    so miserably, an order has gone out
    throughout the city—that's what people say.
    He's to have no funeral or lament,
    but to be left unburied and unwept,
    a sweet treasure for the birds to look at,
    for them to feed on to their heart's content.   [30]
    That's what people say the noble Creon
    has announced to you and me—I mean to me—
    and now he's coming to proclaim the fact,
    to state it clearly to those who have not heard.
    For Creon this matter's really serious.
    Anyone who acts against the order
    will be stoned to death before the city.
    Now you know, and you'll quickly demonstrate
    whether you are nobly born, or else
    a girl unworthy of her splendid ancestors.

ISMENE

    O my poor sister, if that's what's happening,
    what can I say that would be any help
    to ease the situation or resolve it?   [40]

ANTIGONE

    Think whether you will work with me in this
    and act together.

ISMENE

                In what kind of work?
    What do you mean?

ANTIGONE

                Will you help these hands
    take up Polyneices' corpse and bury it?

ISMENE

    What? You're going to bury Polyneices,
    when that's been made a crime for all in Thebes?

Sophocles

ΑΝΤΙΓΟΝΗ

τὸν γοῦν ἐμὸν καὶ τὸν σόν ἢν σὺ μὴ θέλῃς   45
ἀδελφόν· οὐ γὰρ δὴ προδοῦσ' ἁλώσομαι.

ΙΣΜΗΝΗ

ὦ σχετλία, Κρέοντος ἀντειρηκότος;

ΑΝΤΙΓΟΝΗ

ἀλλ' οὐδὲν αὐτῷ τῶν ἐμῶν μ' εἴργειν μέτα.

ΙΣΜΗΝΗ

οἴμοι. φρόνησον, ὦ κασιγνήτη, πατὴρ
ὡς νῷν ἀπεχθὴς δυσκλεής τ' ἀπώλετο,   50
πρὸς αὐτοφώρων ἀμπλακημάτων διπλᾶς
ὄψεις ἀράξας αὐτὸς αὐτουργῷ χερί.
ἔπειτα μήτηρ καὶ γυνή, διπλοῦν ἔπος,
πλεκταῖσιν ἀρτάναισι λωβᾶται βίον·
τρίτον δ' ἀδελφὼ δύο μίαν καθ' ἡμέραν   55
αὐτοκτονοῦντε τὼ ταλαιπώρω μόρον
κοινὸν κατειργάσαντ' ἐπαλλήλοιν χεροῖν.
νῦν δ' αὖ μόνα δὴ νὼ λελειμμένα σκόπει
ὅσῳ κάκιστ' ὀλούμεθ', εἰ νόμου βίᾳ
ψῆφον τυράννων ἢ κράτη παρέξιμεν.   60
ἀλλ' ἐννοεῖν χρὴ τοῦτο μὲν γυναῖχ' ὅτι
ἔφυμεν, ὡς πρὸς ἄνδρας οὐ μαχουμένα.
ἔπειτα δ' οὕνεκ' ἀρχόμεσθ' ἐκ κρεισσόνων,
καὶ ταῦτ' ἀκούειν κἄτι τῶνδ' ἀλγίονα.
ἐγὼ μὲν οὖν αἰτοῦσα τοὺς ὑπὸ χθονὸς   65
ξύγγνοιαν ἴσχειν, ὡς βιάζομαι τάδε,
τοῖς ἐν τέλει βεβῶσι πείσομαι· τὸ γὰρ
περισσὰ πράσσειν οὐκ ἔχει νοῦν οὐδένα.

ΑΝΤΙΓΟΝΗ

οὔτ' ἂν κελεύσαιμ' οὔτ' ἄν, εἰ θέλοις ἔτι
πράσσειν, ἐμοῦ γ' ἂν ἡδέως δρῴης μέτα.   70
ἀλλ' ἴσθ' ὁποῖά σοι δοκεῖ, κεῖνον δ' ἐγὼ
θάψω· καλόν μοι τοῦτο ποιούσῃ θανεῖν.

358

ANTIGONE

    Yes. I'll do my duty to my brother—
    and yours as well, if you're not prepared to.
    I won't be caught betraying him.

ISMENE

                        You're too rash.
    Has Creon not expressly banned that act?

ANTIGONE

    Yes. But he's no right to keep me from what's mine.

ISMENE

    O dear. Think, Antigone. Consider
    how our father died, hated and disgraced, [50]
    when those mistakes which his own search revealed
    forced him to turn his hand against himself
    and stab out both his eyes. Then that woman,
    his mother and his wife—her double role—
    destroyed her own life in a twisted noose.
    Then there's our own two brothers, both butchered
    in a single day—that ill-fated pair
    with their own hands slaughtered one another
    and brought about their common doom.
    Now, the two of us are left here quite alone.
    Think how we'll die far worse than all the rest,
    if we defy the law and move against [60]
    the king's decree, against his royal power.
    We must remember that by birth we're women,
    and, as such, we shouldn't fight with men.
    Since those who rule are much more powerful,
    we must obey in this and in events
    which bring us even harsher agonies.
    So I'll ask those underground for pardon—
    since I'm being compelled, I will obey
    those in control. That's what I'm forced to do.
    It makes no sense to try to do too much.

ANTIGONE

    I wouldn't urge you to. No. Not even
    if you were keen to act. Doing this with you
    would bring me no joy. So be what you want. [70]
    I'll still bury him. It would be fine to die

Sophocles

φίλη μετ᾽ αὐτοῦ κείσομαι, φίλου μέτα,
ὅσια πανουργήσασ᾽. ἐπεὶ πλείων χρόνος
ὃν δεῖ μ᾽ ἀρέσκειν τοῖς κάτω τῶν ἐνθάδε.   75
ἐκεῖ γὰρ αἰεὶ κείσομαι· σοὶ δ᾽, εἰ δοκεῖ,
τὰ τῶν θεῶν ἔντιμ᾽ ἀτιμάσασ᾽ ἔχε.

ΙΣΜΗΝΗ
ἐγὼ μὲν οὐκ ἄτιμα ποιοῦμαι, τὸ δὲ
βίᾳ πολιτῶν δρᾶν ἔφυν ἀμήχανος.

ΑΝΤΙΓΟΝΗ
σὺ μὲν τάδ᾽ ἂν προὔχοι᾽· ἐγὼ δὲ δὴ τάφον   80
χώσουσ᾽ ἀδελφῷ φιλτάτῳ πορεύσομαι.

ΙΣΜΗΝΗ
οἴμοι ταλαίνης, ὡς ὑπερδέδοικά σου.

ΑΝΤΙΓΟΝΗ
μὴ ᾽μοῦ προτάρβει· τὸν σὸν ἐξόρθου πότμον.

ΙΣΜΗΝΗ
ἀλλ᾽ οὖν προμηνύσῃς γε τοῦτο μηδενὶ
τοὔργον, κρυφῇ δὲ κεῦθε, σὺν δ᾽ αὔτως ἐγώ.   85

ΑΝΤΙΓΟΝΗ
οἴμοι, καταύδα· πολλὸν ἐχθίων ἔσει
σιγῶσ᾽, ἐὰν μὴ πᾶσι κηρύξῃς τάδε.

ΙΣΜΗΝΗ
θερμὴν ἐπὶ ψυχροῖσι καρδίαν ἔχεις.

ΑΝΤΙΓΟΝΗ
ἀλλ᾽ οἶδ᾽ ἀρέσκουσ᾽ οἷς μάλισθ᾽ ἀδεῖν με χρή.

ΙΣΜΗΝΗ
εἰ καὶ δυνήσει γ᾽· ἀλλ᾽ ἀμηχάνων ἐρᾷς.   90

ΑΝΤΙΓΟΝΗ
οὐκοῦν, ὅταν δὴ μὴ σθένω, πεπαύσομαι.

while doing that. I'll lie there with him,
with a man I love, pure and innocent,
for all my crime. My honours for the dead
must last much longer than for those up here.
I'll lie down there forever. As for you,
well, if you wish, you can show contempt
for those laws the gods all hold in honour.

ISMENE

I'm not disrespecting them. But I can't act
against the state. That's not in my nature.

ANTIGONE

Let that be your excuse. I'm going now   [80]
to make a burial mound for my dear brother.

ISMENE

Oh poor Antigone, I'm so afraid for you.

ANTIGONE

Don't fear for me. Set your own fate in order.

ISMENE

Make sure you don't reveal to anyone
what you intend. Keep it closely hidden.
I'll do the same.

ANTIGONE

          No, no. Announce the fact—
if you don't let everybody know,
I'll despise your silence even more.

ISMENE

Your heart is hot to do cold deeds.

ANTIGONE

                But I know
I'll please the ones I'm duty bound to please.

ISMENE

Yes, if you can. But you're after something   [90]
which you're incapable of carrying out.

ANTIGONE

Well, when my strength is gone, then I'll give up.

ΙΣΜΗΝΗ

ἀρχὴν δὲ θηρᾶν οὐ πρέπει τἀμήχανα.

ΑΝΤΙΓΟΝΗ

εἰ ταῦτα λέξεις, ἐχθαρεῖ μὲν ἐξ ἐμοῦ,
ἐχθρὰ δὲ τῷ θανόντι προσκείσει δίκη.
ἀλλ' ἔα με καὶ τὴν ἐξ ἐμοῦ δυσβουλίαν   95
παθεῖν τὸ δεινὸν τοῦτο· πείσομαι γὰρ οὐ
τοσοῦτον οὐδὲν ὥστε μὴ οὐ καλῶς θανεῖν.

ΙΣΜΗΝΗ

ἀλλ' εἰ δοκεῖ σοι, στεῖχε· τοῦτο δ' ἴσθ' ὅτι
ἄνους μὲν ἔρχει, τοῖς φίλοις δ' ὀρθῶς φίλη.

ΧΟΡΟΣ

ἀκτὶς ἀελίου, τὸ κάλλιστον ἑπταπύλῳ φανὲν   100
Θήβᾳ τῶν προτέρων φάος,
ἐφάνθης ποτ', ὦ χρυσέας
ἀμέρας βλέφαρον,
Διρκαίων ὑπὲρ ῥεέθρων μολοῦσα,   105
τὸν λεύκασπιν Ἀργόθεν ἐκβάντα φῶτα πανσαγίᾳ
φυγάδα πρόδρομον ὀξυτέρῳ κινήσασα χαλινῷ·

— ὃς ἐφ' ἡμετέρᾳ γᾷ Πολυνείκους   110
ἀρθεὶς νεικέων ἐξ ἀμφιλόγων
ὀξέα κλάζων
ἀετὸς εἰς γᾶν ὣς ὑπερέπτα,
λευκῆς χιόνος πτέρυγι στεγανός,
πολλῶν μεθ' ὅπλων   115
ξύν θ' ἱπποκόμοις κορύθεσσιν.

— στὰς δ' ὑπὲρ μελάθρων φονώσαισιν ἀμφιχανὼν κύκλῳ
λόγχαις ἑπτάπυλον στόμα

ISMENE

    A vain attempt should not be made at all.

ANTIGONE

    I'll hate you if you're going to talk that way.
    And you'll rightly earn the loathing of the dead.
    So leave me and my foolishness alone—
    we'll get through this fearful thing. I won't suffer
    anything as bad as a disgraceful death.

ISMENE

    All right then, go, if that's what you think right.
    But remember this—even though your mission
    makes no sense, your friends do truly love you.

[Exit Antigone away from the palace. Ismene watches her go and then turns slowly into the palace. Enter the Chorus of Theban elders]

CHORUS

    O ray of sunlight,   [100]
    most beautiful that ever shone
    on Thebes, city of the seven gates,
    you've appeared at last,
    you glowing eye of golden day,
    moving above the streams of Dirce,
    driving into headlong flight
    the white-shield warrior from Argos,
    who marched here fully armed,
    now forced back by your sharper power.[1]

CHORUS LEADER

    Against our land he marched,   [110]
    sent here by the warring claims
    of Polyneices, with piercing screams,
    an eagle flying above our land,
    covered wings as white as snow,
    and hordes of warriors in arms,
    helmets topped with horsehair crests.

CHORUS

    Standing above our homes,
    he ranged around our seven gates,
    with threats to swallow us
    and spears thirsting to kill.

ἔβα, πρίν ποθ' ἁμετέρων
αἱμάτων γένυσιν πλησθῆναί τε καὶ στεφάνωμα
    πύργων   120
πευκάενθ' Ἥφαιστον ἑλεῖν. τοῖος ἀμφὶ νῶτ' ἐτάθη
πάταγος Ἄρεος, ἀντιπάλῳ δυσχείρωμα δράκοντος.   125

— Ζεὺς γὰρ μεγάλης γλώσσης κόμπους
ὑπερεχθαίρει, καὶ σφας ἐσιδὼν
πολλῷ ῥεύματι προσνισσομένους
χρυσοῦ καναχῆς ὑπεροπλίαις,   130
παλτῷ ῥιπτεῖ πυρὶ βαλβίδων
ἐπ' ἄκρων ἤδη
νίκην ὁρμῶντ' ἀλαλάξαι.

— ἀντιτύπᾳ δ' ἐπὶ γᾷ πέσε τανταλωθεὶς
πυρφόρος, ὃς τότε μαινομένᾳ ξὺν ὁρμᾷ   135
βακχεύων ἐπέπνει
ῥιπαῖς ἐχθίστων ἀνέμων.
εἶχε δ' ἄλλᾳ τὰ μέν,
ἄλλα δ' ἐπ' ἄλλοις ἐπενώμα στυφελίζων μέγας Ἄρης
δεξιόσειρος.   140

— ἑπτὰ λοχαγοὶ γὰρ ἐφ' ἑπτὰ πύλαις
ταχθέντες ἴσοι πρὸς ἴσους ἔλιπον
Ζηνὶ τροπαίῳ πάγχαλκα τέλη,
πλὴν τοῖν στυγεροῖν, ὣ πατρὸς ἑνὸς
μητρός τε μιᾶς φύντε καθ' αὑτοῖν   145
δικρατεῖς λόγχας στήσαντ' ἔχετον
κοινοῦ θανάτου μέρος ἄμφω.

— ἀλλὰ γὰρ ἁ μεγαλώνυμος ἦλθε Νίκα
τᾷ πολυαρμάτῳ ἀντιχαρεῖσα Θήβᾳ,

Before his jaws had had their fill [120]
and gorged themselves on Theban blood,
before Hephaistos' pine-torch flames
had seized our towers, our fortress crown,
he went back, driven in retreat.[2]
Behind him rings the din of war—
his enemy, the Theban dragon-snake,
too difficult for him to overcome.

CHORUS LEADER

Zeus hates an arrogant boasting tongue.
Seeing them march here in a mighty stream,
in all their clanging golden pride, [130]
he hurled his fire and struck the man,
up there, on our battlements, as he began
to scream aloud his victory.

CHORUS

The man swung down, torch still in hand,
and smashed into unyielding earth—
the one who not so long ago attacked,
who launched his furious, enraged assault,
to blast us, breathing raging storms.
But things turned out not as he'd hoped.
Great war god Ares assisted us—
he smashed them down and doomed them all [140]
to a very different fate.

CHORUS LEADER

Seven captains at seven gates
matched against seven equal warriors
paid Zeus their full bronze tribute,
the god who turns the battle tide,
all but that pair of wretched men,
born of one father and one mother, too—
who set their conquering spears against each other
and then both shared a common death.

CHORUS

Now victory with her glorious name
has come, bringing joy to well-armed Thebes.

Sophocles

ἐκ μὲν δὴ πολέμων   150
τῶν νῦν θέσθαι λησμοσύναν,
θεῶν δὲ ναοὺς χοροῖς
παννυχίοις πάντας ἐπέλθωμεν, ὁ Θήβας δ' ἐλελίχθων
Βάκχιος ἄρχοι.

— ἀλλ' ὅδε γὰρ δὴ βασιλεὺς χώρας,   155
Κρέων ὁ Μενοικέως [ἄρχων] νεοχμὸς
νεαραῖσι θεῶν ἐπὶ συντυχίαις
χωρεῖ, τίνα δὴ μῆτιν ἐρέσσων,
ὅτι σύγκλητον τήνδε γερόντων   160
προὔθετο λέσχην,
κοινῷ κηρύγματι πέμψας;

ΚΡΕΩΝ
ἄνδρες, τὰ μὲν δὴ πόλεος ἀσφαλῶς θεοὶ
πολλῷ σάλῳ σείσαντες ὤρθωσαν πάλιν.
ὑμᾶς δ' ἐγὼ πομποῖσιν ἐκ πάντων δίχα
ἔστειλ' ἱκέσθαι τοῦτο μὲν τὰ Λαΐου   165
σέβοντας εἰδὼς εὖ θρόνων ἀεὶ κράτη,
τοῦτ' αὖθις, ἡνίκ' Οἰδίπους ὤρθου πόλιν,
κἀπεὶ διώλετ', ἀμφὶ τοὺς κείνων ἔτι
παῖδας μένοντας ἐμπέδοις φρονήμασιν.
ὅτ' οὖν ἐκεῖνοι πρὸς διπλῆς μοίρας μίαν   170
καθ' ἡμέραν ὤλοντο παίσαντές τε καὶ
πληγέντες αὐτόχειρι σὺν μιάσματι,
ἐγὼ κράτη δὴ πάντα καὶ θρόνους ἔχω
γένους κατ' ἀγχιστεῖα τῶν ὀλωλότων.
ἀμήχανον δὲ παντὸς ἀνδρὸς ἐκμαθεῖν   175
ψυχήν τε καὶ φρόνημα καὶ γνώμην, πρὶν ἂν
ἀρχαῖς τε καὶ νόμοισιν ἐντριβὴς φανῇ.
ἐμοὶ γὰρ ὅστις πᾶσαν εὐθύνων πόλιν
μὴ τῶν ἀρίστων ἅπτεται βουλευμάτων
ἀλλ' ἐκ φόβου του γλῶσσαν ἐγκλῄσας ἔχει   180
κάκιστος εἶναι νῦν τε καὶ πάλαι δοκεῖ·
καὶ μεῖζον ὅστις ἀντὶ τῆς αὑτοῦ πάτρας
φίλον νομίζει, τοῦτον οὐδαμοῦ λέγω.
ἐγὼ γάρ, ἴστω Ζεὺς ὁ πάνθ' ὁρῶν ἀεί,
οὔτ' ἂν σιωπήσαιμι τὴν ἄτην ὁρῶν   185

The battle's done—let's strive now to forget   [150]
with songs and dancing all night long,
with Bacchus leading us to make Thebes shake.

[The palace doors are thrown open and guards appear at the doors]

CHORUS LEADER
But here comes Creon, new king of our land,
son of Menoikeos. Thanks to the gods,
who've brought about our new good fortune.
What plan of action does he have in mind?
What's made him hold this special meeting,   [160]
with elders summoned by a general call?

[Enter Creon from the palace. He addresses the assembled elders]

CREON
Men, after much tossing of our ship of state,
the gods have safely set things right again.
Of all the citizens I've summoned you,
because I know how well you showed respect
for the eternal power of the throne,
first with Laius and again with Oedipus,
once he restored our city.³ When he died,
you stood by his children, firm in loyalty.
Now his sons have perished in a single day,
killing each other with their own two hands,
a double slaughter, stained with brother's blood.   [170]
And so I have the throne, all royal power,
for I'm the one most closely linked by blood
to those who have been killed. It's impossible
to really know a man, to know his soul,
his mind and will, before one witnesses
his skill in governing and making laws.
For me, a man who rules the entire state
and does not take the best advice there is,
but through fear keeps his mouth forever shut,   [180]
such a man is the very worst of men—
and always will be. And a man who thinks
more highly of a friend than of his country,
well, he means nothing to me. Let Zeus know,
the god who always watches everything,
I would not stay silent if I saw disaster

στείχουσαν ἀστοῖς ἀντὶ τῆς σωτηρίας,
οὔτ' ἂν φίλον ποτ' ἄνδρα δυσμενῆ χθονὸς
θείμην ἐμαυτῷ, τοῦτο γιγνώσκων ὅτι
ἥδ' ἐστὶν ἡ σῴζουσα καὶ ταύτης ἔπι
πλέοντες ὀρθῆς τοὺς φίλους ποιούμεθα.   190
τοιοῖσδ' ἐγὼ νόμοισι τήνδ' αὔξω πόλιν,
καὶ νῦν ἀδελφὰ τῶνδε κηρύξας ἔχω
ἀστοῖσι παίδων τῶν ἀπ' Οἰδίπου πέρι·
Ἐτεοκλέα μέν, ὃς πόλεως ὑπερμαχῶν
ὄλωλε τῆσδε, πάντ' ἀριστεύσας δόρει,   195
τάφῳ τε κρύψαι καὶ τὰ πάντ' ἀφαγνίσαι
ἃ τοῖς ἀρίστοις ἔρχεται κάτω νεκροῖς.
τὸν δ' αὖ ξύναιμον τοῦδε, Πολυνείκη λέγω,
ὃς γῆν πατρῴαν καὶ θεοὺς τοὺς ἐγγενεῖς
φυγὰς κατελθὼν ἠθέλησε μὲν πυρὶ   200
πρῆσαι κατ' ἄκρας, ἠθέλησε δ' αἵματος
κοινοῦ πάσασθαι, τοὺς δὲ δουλώσας ἄγειν,
τοῦτον πόλει τῇδ' ἐκκεκήρυκται τάφῳ
μήτε κτερίζειν μήτε κωκῦσαί τινα,
ἐᾶν δ' ἄθαπτον καὶ πρὸς οἰωνῶν δέμας   205
καὶ πρὸς κυνῶν ἐδεστὸν αἰκισθέν τ' ἰδεῖν.
τοιόνδ' ἐμὸν φρόνημα, κοὔποτ' ἔκ γ' ἐμοῦ
τιμὴν προέξουσ' οἱ κακοὶ τῶν ἐνδίκων·
ἀλλ' ὅστις εὔνους τῇδε τῇ πόλει, θανὼν
καὶ ζῶν ὁμοίως ἐξ ἐμοῦ τιμήσεται.   210

ΧΟΡΟΣ
    σοὶ ταῦτ' ἀρέσκει, παῖ Μενοικέως Κρέον,
    τὸν τῇδε δύσνουν κὰς τὸν εὐμενῆ πόλει·
    νόμῳ δὲ χρῆσθαι παντί που πάρεστί σοι
    καὶ τῶν θανόντων χὠπόσοι ζῶμεν πέρι.

ΚΡΕΩΝ
    ὡς ἂν σκοποὶ νῦν εἴτε τῶν εἰρημένων.   215

368

moving here against the citizens,
a threat to their security. For anyone
who acts against the state, its enemy,
I'd never make my friend. For I know well
our country is a ship which keeps us safe,
and only when it sails its proper course   [190]
do we make friends. These are the principles
I'll use in order to protect our state.
That's why I've announced to all citizens
my orders for the sons of Oedipus—
Eteocles, who perished in the fight
to save our city, the best and bravest
of our spearmen, will have his burial,
with all those purifying rituals
which accompany the noblest corpses,
as they move below. As for his brother—
that Polyneices, who returned from exile,
eager to wipe out in all-consuming fire   [200]
his ancestral city and its native gods,
keen to seize upon his family's blood
and lead men into slavery—for him,
the proclamation in the state declares
he'll have no burial mound, no funeral rites,
and no lament. He'll be left unburied,
his body there for birds and dogs to eat,
a clear reminder of his shameful fate.
That's my decision. For I'll never act
to respect an evil man with honours
in preference to a man who's acted well.
Anyone who's well disposed towards our state,
alive or dead, that man I will respect.   [210]

CHORUS LEADER
        Son of Menoikeos, if that's your will
        for this city's friends and enemies,
        it seems to me you now control all laws
        concerning those who've died and us as well—
        the ones who are still living.

CREON
                                See to it then,
        and act as guardians of what's been proclaimed.

ΧΟΡΟΣ

νεωτέρῳ τῳ τοῦτο βαστάζειν πρόθες.

ΚΡΕΩΝ

ἀλλ᾽ εἴσ᾽ ἕτοιμοι τοῦ νεκροῦ γ᾽ ἐπίσκοποι.

ΧΟΡΟΣ

τί δῆτ᾽ ἂν ἄλλο τοῦτ᾽ ἐπεντέλλοις ἔτι;

ΚΡΕΩΝ

τὸ μὴ 'πιχωρεῖν τοῖς ἀπιστοῦσιν τάδε.

ΧΟΡΟΣ

οὐκ ἔστιν οὕτω μῶρος ὃς θανεῖν ἐρᾷ.　　　　　　　　220

ΚΡΕΩΝ

καὶ μὴν ὁ μισθός γ᾽, οὗτος· ἀλλ᾽ ὑπ᾽ ἐλπίδων
ἄνδρας τὸ κέρδος πολλάκις διώλεσεν.

ΦΥΛΑΞ

ἄναξ, ἐρῶ μὲν οὐχ ὅπως τάχους ὕπο
δύσπνους ἱκάνω κοῦφον ἐξάρας πόδα.
πολλὰς γὰρ ἔσχον φροντίδων ἐπιστάσεις,　　　　　　225
ὁδοῖς κυκλῶν ἐμαυτὸν εἰς ἀναστροφήν·
ψυχὴ γὰρ ηὔδα πολλά μοι μυθουμένη·
τάλας, τί χωρεῖς οἷ μολὼν δώσεις δίκην;
τλήμων, μενεῖς αὖ; κεἰ τάδ᾽ εἴσεται Κρέων
ἄλλου παρ᾽ ἀνδρός; πῶς σὺ δῆτ᾽ οὐκ ἀλγύνει;　　230
τοιαῦθ᾽ ἑλίσσων ἤνυτον σχολῇ βραδύς.
χοὕτως ὁδὸς βραχεῖα γίγνεται μακρά.
τέλος γε μέντοι δεῦρ᾽ ἐνίκησεν μολεῖν
σοί. κεἰ τὸ μηδὲν ἐξερῶ, φράσω δ᾽ ὅμως·
τῆς ἐλπίδος γὰρ ἔρχομαι δεδραγμένος,　　　　　　235
τὸ μὴ παθεῖν ἂν ἄλλο πλὴν τὸ μόρσιμον.

ΚΡΕΩΝ

τί δ᾽ ἐστὶν ἀνθ᾽ οὗ τήνδ᾽ ἔχεις ἀθυμίαν;

CHORUS
Give that task to younger men to deal with.

CREON
There are men assigned to oversee the corpse.

CHORUS LEADER
Then what remains that you would have us do?

CREON
Don't yield to those who contravene my orders.

CHORUS LEADER
No one is such a fool that he loves death. [220]

CREON
Yes, that will be his full reward, indeed.
And yet men have often been destroyed
because they hoped to profit in some way.

[Enter a guard, coming towards the palace]

GUARD
My lord, I can't say I've come out of breath
by running here, making my feet move fast.
Many times I stopped to think things over—
and then I'd turn around, retrace my steps.
My mind was saying many things to me,
"You fool, why go to where you know for sure
your punishment awaits?"—"And now, poor man,
why are you hesitating yet again?
If Creon finds this out from someone else, [230]
how will you escape being hurt?" Such matters
kept my mind preoccupied. And so I went,
slowly and reluctantly, and thus made
a short road turn into a lengthy one.
But then the view that I should come to you
won out. If what I have to say is nothing,
I'll say it nonetheless. For I've come here
clinging to the hope that I'll not suffer
anything that's not part of my destiny.

CREON
What's happening that's made you so upset?

Sophocles

ΦΥΛΑΞ

φράσαι θέλω σοι πρῶτα τἀμαυτοῦ· τὸ γὰρ
πρᾶγμ' οὔτ' ἔδρασ' οὔτ' εἶδον ὅστις ἦν ὁ δρῶν,
οὐδ' ἂν δικαίως ἐς κακὸν πέσοιμί τι.   240

ΚΡΕΩΝ

εὖ γε στοχάζει κἀποφάργνυσαι κύκλῳ
τὸ πρᾶγμα· δηλοῖς δ' ὥς τι σημανῶν νέον.

ΦΥΛΑΞ

τὰ δεινὰ γάρ τοι προστίθησ' ὄκνον πολύν.

ΚΡΕΩΝ

οὔκουν ἐρεῖς ποτ', εἶτ' ἀπαλλαχθεὶς ἄπει;

ΦΥΛΑΞ

καὶ δὴ λέγω σοι. τὸν νεκρόν τις ἀρτίως   245
θάψας βέβηκε κἀπὶ χρωτὶ διψίαν
κόνιν παλύνας κἀφαγιστεύσας ἃ χρή·

ΚΡΕΩΝ

τί φής; τίς ἀνδρῶν ἦν ὁ τολμήσας τάδε;

ΦΥΛΑΞ

οὐκ οἶδ'· ἐκεῖ γὰρ οὔτε του γενῇδος ἦν
πλῆγμ', οὐ δικέλλης ἐκβολή. στύφλος δὲ γῆ   250
καὶ χέρσος, ἀρρὼξ οὐδ' ἐπημαξευμένη
τροχοῖσιν, ἀλλ' ἄσημος οὑργάτης τις ἦν.
ὅπως δ' ὁ πρῶτος ἡμὶν ἡμεροσκόπος
δείκνυσι, πᾶσι θαῦμα δυσχερὲς παρῆν.
ὁ μὲν γὰρ ἠφάνιστο, τυμβήρης μὲν οὔ,   255
λεπτὴ δ', ἄγος φεύγοντος ὥς, ἐπῆν κόνις·
σημεῖα δ' οὔτε θηρὸς οὔτε του κυνῶν
ἐλθόντος, οὐ σπάσαντος ἐξεφαίνετο.
λόγοι δ' ἐν ἀλλήλοισιν ἐρρόθουν κακοί,
φύλαξ ἐλέγχων φύλακα, κἂν ἐγίγνετο   260
πληγὴ τελευτῶσ', οὐδ' ὁ κωλύσων παρῆν.
εἷς γάρ τις ἦν ἕκαστος οὑξειργασμένος,
κοὐδεὶς ἐναργής, ἀλλ' ἔφευγε μὴ εἰδέναι.

372

GUARD

> I want to tell you first about myself.
> I did not do it. And I didn't see
> the one who did. So it would be unjust
> if I should come to grief. [240]

CREON

> You hedge so much.
> Clearly you have news of something ominous.

GUARD

> Yes. Strange things that make me pause a lot.

CREON

> Why not say it and then go—just leave.

GUARD

> All right, I'll tell you. It's about the corpse.
> Someone has buried it and disappeared,
> after spreading thirsty dust onto the flesh
> and undertaking all appropriate rites.

CREON

> What are you saying? What man would dare this?

GUARD

> I don't know. There was no sign of digging,
> no marks of any pick axe or a mattock. [250]
> The ground was dry and hard and very smooth,
> without a wheel track. Whoever did it
> left no trace. When the first man on day watch
> revealed it to us, we were all amazed.
> The corpse was hidden, but not in a tomb.
> It was lightly covered up with dirt,
> as if someone wanted to avert a curse.
> There was no trace of a wild animal
> or dogs who'd come to rip the corpse apart.
> Then the words flew round among us all,
> with every guard accusing someone else. [260]
> We were about to fight, to come to blows—
> no one was there to put a stop to it.
> Every one of us was responsible,
> but none of us was clearly in the wrong.
> In our defence we pleaded ignorance.

ἦμεν δ' ἕτοιμοι καὶ μύδρους αἴρειν χεροῖν
καὶ πῦρ διέρπειν καὶ θεοὺς ὁρκωμοτεῖν, 265
τὸ μήτε δρᾶσαι μήτε τῳ ξυνειδέναι
τὸ πρᾶγμα βουλεύσαντι μηδ' εἰργασμένῳ.
τέλος δ' ὅτ' οὐδὲν ἦν ἐρευνῶσιν πλέον,
λέγει τις εἷς, ὃ πάντας ἐς πέδον κάρα
νεῦσαι φόβῳ προὔτρεψεν· οὐ γὰρ εἴχομεν 270
οὔτ' ἀντιφωνεῖν οὔθ' ὅπως δρῶντες καλῶς
πράξαιμεν. ἦν δ' ὁ μῦθος ὡς ἀνοιστέον
σοὶ τοὔργον εἴη τοῦτο κοὐχὶ κρυπτέον.
καὶ ταῦτ' ἐνίκα, κἀμὲ τὸν δυσδαίμονα
πάλος καθαιρεῖ τοῦτο τἀγαθὸν λαβεῖν. 275
πάρειμι δ' ἄκων οὐχ ἑκοῦσιν, οἶδ' ὅτι·
στέργει γὰρ οὐδεὶς ἄγγελον κακῶν ἐπῶν.

ΧΟΡΟΣ
ἄναξ, ἐμοί τοί, μή τι καὶ θεήλατον
τοὔργον τόδ', ἡ ξύννοια βουλεύει πάλαι

ΚΡΕΩΝ
παῦσαι, πρὶν ὀργῆς καί 'μὲ μεστῶσαι λέγων, 280
μὴ 'φευρεθῇς ἄνους τε καὶ γέρων ἅμα.
λέγεις γὰρ οὐκ ἀνεκτὰ δαίμονας λέγων
πρόνοιαν ἴσχειν τοῦδε τοῦ νεκροῦ πέρι.
πότερον ὑπερτιμῶντες ὡς εὐεργέτην
ἔκρυπτον αὐτόν, ὅστις ἀμφικίονας 285
ναοὺς πυρώσων ἦλθε κἀναθήματα
καὶ γῆν ἐκείνων καὶ νόμους διασκεδῶν;
ἦ τοὺς κακοὺς τιμῶντας εἰσορᾷς θεούς;
οὔκ ἔστιν. ἀλλὰ ταῦτα καὶ πάλαι πόλεως
ἄνδρες μόλις φέροντες ἐρρόθουν ἐμοί, 290
κρυφῇ κάρα σείοντες, οὐδ' ὑπὸ ζυγῷ
λόφον δικαίως εἶχον, ὡς στέργειν ἐμέ.
ἐκ τῶνδε τούτους ἐξεπίσταμαι καλῶς
παρηγμένους μισθοῖσιν εἰργάσθαι τάδε.

Then we each stated we were quite prepared
to pick up red-hot iron, walk through flames,
or swear by all the gods that we'd not done it,
we'd no idea how the act was planned,
or how it had been carried out. At last,
when all our searching had proved useless,
one man spoke up, and his words forced us all
to drop our faces to the ground in fear.   [270]
We couldn't see things working out for us,
whether we agreed or disagreed with him.
He said we must report this act to you—
we must not hide it. And his view prevailed.
I was the unlucky man who won the prize,
the luck of the draw. That's why I'm now here,
not of my own free will or by your choice.
I know that—for no one likes a messenger
who comes bearing unwelcome news with him.

CHORUS LEADER
My lord, I've been wondering for some time now—
could this act not be something from the gods?

CREON
Stop now—before what you're about to say   [280]
enrages me completely and reveals
that you're not only old but stupid, too.
No one can tolerate what you've just said,
when you claim gods might care about this corpse.
Would they pay extraordinary honours
and bury as a man who'd served them well
someone who came to burn their offerings,
their pillared temples, to torch their lands
and scatter all its laws? Or do you see
gods paying respect to evil men? No, no.
For quite a while some people in the town
have secretly been muttering against me.   [290]
They don't agree with what I have decreed.
They shake their heads and have not kept their necks
under my yoke, as they are duty bound to do
if they were men who are content with me.
I well know that these guards were led astray—
such men urged them to carry out this act
for money. To foster evil actions,

375

οὐδὲν γὰρ ἀνθρώποισιν οἷον ἄργυρος   295
κακὸν νόμισμ' ἔβλαστε. τοῦτο καὶ πόλεις
πορθεῖ, τόδ' ἄνδρας ἐξανίστησιν δόμων·
τόδ' ἐκδιδάσκει καὶ παραλλάσσει φρένας
χρηστὰς πρὸς αἰσχρὰ πράγματ' ἵστασθαι βροτῶν·
πανουργίας δ' ἔδειξεν ἀνθρώποις ἔχειν   300
καὶ παντὸς ἔργου δυσσέβειαν εἰδέναι.
ὅσοι δὲ μισθαρνοῦντες ἤνυσαν τάδε,
χρόνῳ ποτ' ἐξέπραξαν ὡς δοῦναι δίκην.
ἀλλ' εἴπερ ἴσχει Ζεὺς ἔτ' ἐξ ἐμοῦ σέβας,
εὖ τοῦτ' ἐπίστασ', ὅρκιος δέ σοι λέγω·   305
εἰ μὴ τὸν αὐτόχειρα τοῦδε τοῦ τάφου
εὑρόντες ἐκφανεῖτ' ἐς ὀφθαλμοὺς ἐμούς,
οὐχ ὑμῖν Ἅιδης μοῦνος ἀρκέσει, πρὶν ἂν
ζῶντες κρεμαστοὶ τήνδε δηλώσηθ' ὕβριν,
ἵν' εἰδότες τὸ κέρδος ἔνθεν οἰστέον   310
τὸ λοιπὸν ἁρπάζητε, καὶ μάθηθ' ὅτι
οὐκ ἐξ ἅπαντος δεῖ τὸ κερδαίνειν φιλεῖν.
ἐκ τῶν γὰρ αἰσχρῶν λημμάτων τοὺς πλείονας
ἀτωμένους ἴδοις ἂν ἢ σεσωσμένους.

ΦΥΛΑΞ
    εἰπεῖν τι δώσεις ἢ στραφεὶς οὕτως ἴω;   315

ΚΡΕΩΝ
    οὐκ οἶσθα καὶ νῦν ὡς ἀνιαρῶς λέγεις;

ΦΥΛΑΞ
    ἐν τοῖσιν ὠσὶν ἢ 'πὶ τῇ ψυχῇ δάκνει;

ΚΡΕΩΝ
    τί δὲ ῥυθμίζεις τὴν ἐμὴν λύπην ὅπου;

ΦΥΛΑΞ
    ὁ δρῶν σ' ἀνιᾷ τὰς φρένας, τὰ δ' ὦτ' ἐγώ.

ΚΡΕΩΝ
    οἴμ' ὡς λάλημα δῆλον ἐκπεφυκὸς εἶ.   320

to make them commonplace among all men,
nothing is as powerful as money.
It destroys cities, driving men from home.
Money trains and twists the minds in worthy men,
so they then undertake disgraceful acts.
Money teaches men to live as scoundrels,   [300]
familiar with every profane enterprise.
But those who carry out such acts for cash
sooner or later see how for their crimes
they pay the penalty. For if great Zeus
still has my respect, then understand this—
I swear to you on oath—unless you find
the one whose hands really buried him,
unless you bring him here before my eyes,
then death for you will never be enough.
No, not before you're hung up still alive
and you confess to this gross, violent act.
That way you'll understand in future days,   [310]
when there's a profit to be gained from theft,
you'll learn that it's not good to be in love
with every kind of monetary gain.
You'll know more men are ruined than are saved
when they earn profits from dishonest schemes.

GUARD
    Do I have your permission to speak now,
    or do I just turn around and go away?

CREON
    But I find your voice so irritating—
    don't you realize that?

GUARD
               Where does it hurt?
    Is it in your ears or in your mind?

CREON
    Why try to question where I feel my pain?

GUARD
    The man who did it—he upsets your mind.
    I offend your ears.

CREON
          My, my, it's clear to see
    it's natural for you to chatter on.   [320]

ΦΥΛΑΞ

οὔκουν τό γ᾽ ἔργον τοῦτο ποιήσας ποτέ.

ΚΡΕΩΝ

καὶ ταῦτ᾽ ἐπ᾽ ἀργύρῳ γε τὴν ψυχὴν προδούς.

ΦΥΛΑΞ

φεῦ·
ἦ δεινὸν ᾧ δοκῇ γε καὶ ψευδῆ δοκεῖν.

ΚΡΕΩΝ

κόμψευέ νυν τὴν δόξαν· εἰ δὲ ταῦτα μὴ
φανεῖτέ μοι τοὺς δρῶντας, ἐξερεῖθ᾽ ὅτι   325
τὰ δειλὰ κέρδη πημονὰς ἐργάζεται.

ΦΥΛΑΞ

ἀλλ᾽ εὑρεθείη μὲν μάλιστ᾽· ἐὰν δέ τοι
ληφθῇ τε καὶ μή, τοῦτο γὰρ τύχη κρινεῖ,
οὐκ ἔσθ᾽ ὅπως ὄψει σὺ δεῦρ᾽ ἐλθόντα με·
καὶ νῦν γὰρ ἐκτὸς ἐλπίδος γνώμης τ᾽ ἐμῆς   330
σωθεὶς ὀφείλω τοῖς θεοῖς πολλὴν χάριν.

ΧΟΡΟΣ

πολλὰ τὰ δεινὰ κοὐδὲν ἀνθρώπου δεινότερον πέλει.
τοῦτο καὶ πολιοῦ πέραν πόντου χειμερίῳ νότῳ   335
χωρεῖ, περιβρυχίοισιν
περῶν ὑπ᾽ οἴδμασιν.
θεῶν τε τὰν ὑπερτάταν, Γᾶν
ἄφθιτον, ἀκαμάταν, ἀποτρύεται
ἰλλομένων ἀρότρων ἔτος εἰς ἔτος
ἱππείῳ γένει πολεύων.   340

κουφονόων τε φῦλον ὀρνίθων ἀμφιβαλὼν ἄγει
καὶ θηρῶν ἀγρίων ἔθνη πόντου τ᾽ εἰναλίαν φύσιν   345
σπείραισι δικτυοκλώστοις,
περιφραδὴς ἀνήρ·
κρατεῖ δὲ μηχαναῖς ἀγραύλου
θηρὸς ὀρεσσιβάτα, λασιαύχενά θ᾽   350
ἵππον ὀχμάζεται ἀμφὶ λόφον ζυγῶν
οὔρειόν τ᾽ ἀκμῆτα ταῦρον.

GUARD
  Perhaps. But I never did this.

CREON
                This and more—
  you sold your life for silver.

GUARD
                How strange and sad
  when the one who sorts this out gets it all wrong.

CREON
  Well, enjoy your sophisticated views.
  But if you don't reveal to me who did this,
  you'll just confirm how much your treasonous gains
  have made you suffer.

[Exit Creon back into the palace. The doors close behind him]

GUARD
                Well, I hope he's found.
  That would be best. But whether caught or not—
  and that's something sheer chance will bring about—
  you won't see me coming here again.
  This time, against all hope and expectation,   [330]
  I'm still unhurt. I owe the gods great thanks.

[Exit the Guard away from the palace]

CHORUS
  There are many strange and wonderful things,
  but nothing more strangely wonderful than man.
  He moves across the white-capped ocean seas
  blasted by winter storms, carving his way
  under the surging waves engulfing him.
  With his teams of horses he wears down
  the unwearied and immortal earth,
  the oldest of the gods, harassing her,
  as year by year his ploughs move back and forth.   [340]

  He snares the light-winged flocks of birds,
  herds of wild beasts, creatures from deep seas,
  trapped in the fine mesh of his hunting nets.
  O resourceful man, whose skill can overcome
  ferocious beasts roaming mountain heights.   [350]
  He curbs the rough-haired horses with his bit
  and tames the inexhaustible mountain bulls,
  setting their savage necks beneath his yoke.

καὶ φθέγμα καὶ ἀνεμόεν φρόνημα καὶ ἀστυνόμους   355
ὀργὰς ἐδιδάξατο καὶ δυσαύλων
πάγων ὑπαίθρεια καὶ δύσομβρα φεύγειν βέλη
παντοπόρος· ἄπορος ἐπ' οὐδὲν ἔρχεται
τὸ μέλλον· Ἅιδα μόνον φεῦξιν οὐκ ἐπάξεται·   360
νόσων δ' ἀμηχάνων φυγὰς ξυμπέφρασται.

σοφόν τι τὸ μηχανόεν τέχνας ὑπὲρ ἐλπίδ' ἔχων   365
τοτὲ μὲν κακόν, ἄλλοτ' ἐπ' ἐσθλὸν ἕρπει,
νόμους γεραίρων χθονὸς θεῶν τ' ἔνορκον δίκαν,
ὑψίπολις· ἄπολις ὅτῳ τὸ μὴ καλὸν   370
ξύνεστι τόλμας χάριν. μήτ' ἐμοὶ παρέστιος
γένοιτο μήτ' ἴσον φρονῶν ὃς τάδ' ἔρδει.   375

— ἐς δαιμόνιον τέρας ἀμφινοῶ
τόδε· πῶς εἰδὼς ἀντιλογήσω
τήνδ' οὐκ εἶναι παῖδ' Ἀντιγόνην.
ὦ δύστηνος
καὶ δυστήνου πατρὸς Οἰδιπόδα,   380
τί ποτ'; οὐ δή που σέ γ' ἀπιστοῦσαν
τοῖς βασιλείοισιν ἄγουσι νόμοις
καὶ ἐν ἀφροσύνῃ καθελόντες;

ΦΥΛΑΞ

ἥδ' ἔστ' ἐκείνη τοὔργον ἡ 'ξειργασμένη·
τήνδ' εἵλομεν θάπτουσαν. ἀλλὰ ποῦ Κρέων;   385

ΧΟΡΟΣ

ὅδ' ἐκ δόμων ἄψορρος εἰς δέον περᾷ.

He's taught himself speech and wind-swift thought,
trained his feelings for communal civic life,
learning to escape the icy shafts of frost,
volleys of pelting rain in winter storms,
the harsh life lived under the open sky.
That's man—so resourceful in all he does.   [360]
There's no event his skill cannot confront—
other than death—that alone he cannot shun,
although for many baffling sicknesses
he has discovered his own remedies.

The qualities of his inventive skills
bring arts beyond his dreams and lead him on,
sometimes to evil and sometimes to good.
If he treats his country's laws with due respect
and honours justice by swearing on the gods,
he wins high honours in his city.
But when he grows bold and turns to evil,   [370]
then he has no city. A man like that—
let him not share my home or know my mind.

[Enter the Guard, bringing Antigone with him. She is not resisting]

CHORUS LEADER
What this? I fear some omen from the gods.
I can't deny what I see here so clearly—
that young girl there—it's Antigone.
O you poor girl, daughter of Oedipus,
child of a such a father, so unfortunate,
what's going on? Surely they've not brought you here
because you've disobeyed the royal laws,
because they've caught you acting foolishly?   [380]

GUARD
This here's the one who carried out the act.
We caught her as she was burying the corpse.
Where's Creon?

[The palace doors open. Enter Creon with attendants]

CHORUS LEADER
                    He's coming from the house—
and just in time.

381

ΚΡΕΩΝ

τί δ' ἔστι; ποία ξύμμετρος προὔβην τύχῃ;

ΦΥΛΑΞ

ἄναξ, βροτοῖσιν οὐδέν ἔστ' ἀπώμοτον.
ψεύδει γὰρ ἡ 'πίνοια τὴν γνώμην· ἐπεὶ
σχολῇ ποθ' ἥξειν δεῦρ' ἂν ἐξηύχουν ἐγὼ   390
ταῖς σαῖς ἀπειλαῖς αἷς ἐχειμάσθην τότε
ἀλλ' ἡ γὰρ ἐκτὸς καὶ παρ' ἐλπίδας χαρὰ
ἔοικεν ἄλλῃ μῆκος οὐδὲν ἡδονῇ,
ἥκω, δι' ὅρκων καίπερ ὢν ἀπώμοτος,
κόρην ἄγων τήνδ', ἣ καθῃρέθη τάφον   395
κοσμοῦσα. κλῆρος ἐνθάδ' οὐκ ἐπάλλετο,
ἀλλ' ἔστ' ἐμὸν θοὔρμαιον, οὐκ ἄλλου, τόδε.
καὶ νῦν, ἄναξ, τήνδ' αὐτός, ὡς θέλεις, λαβὼν
καὶ κρῖνε κἀξέλεγχ'· ἐγὼ δ' ἐλεύθερος
δίκαιός εἰμι τῶνδ' ἀπηλλάχθαι κακῶν.   400

ΚΡΕΩΝ

ἄγεις δὲ τήνδε τῷ τρόπῳ πόθεν λαβών;

ΦΥΛΑΞ

αὕτη τὸν ἄνδρ' ἔθαπτε· πάντ' ἐπίστασαι.

ΚΡΕΩΝ

ἦ καὶ ξυνίης καὶ λέγεις ὀρθῶς ἃ φῄς;

ΦΥΛΑΞ

ταύτην γ' ἰδὼν θάπτουσαν ὃν σὺ τὸν νεκρὸν
ἀπεῖπας. ἆρ' ἔνδηλα καὶ σαφῆ λέγω;   405

ΚΡΕΩΝ

καὶ πῶς ὁρᾶται κἀπίληπτος ᾑρέθη;

ΦΥΛΑΞ

τοιοῦτον ἦν τὸ πρᾶγμ'. ὅπως γὰρ ἥκομεν,
πρὸς σοῦ τὰ δείν' ἐκεῖν' ἐπηπειλημένοι,
πᾶσαν κόνιν σήραντες, ἣ κατεῖχε τὸν
νέκυν, μυδῶν τε σῶμα γυμνώσαντες εὖ,   410

CREON

                 Why have I come "just in time"?
What's happening? What is it?

GUARD

                         My lord,
human beings should never take an oath
there's something they'll not do—for later thoughts
contradict what they first meant. I'd have sworn   [390]
I'd not soon venture here again. Back then,
the threats you made brought me a lot of grief.
But there's no joy as great as what we pray for
against all hope. And so I have come back,
breaking that oath I swore. I bring this girl,
captured while she was honouring the grave.
This time we did not draw lots. No. This time
I was the lucky man, not someone else.
And now, my lord, take her for questioning.
Convict her. Do as you wish. As for me,
by rights I'm free and clear of all this trouble.   [400]

CREON

    This girl here—how did you catch her? And where?

GUARD

    She was burying that man. Now you know
all there is to know.

CREON

                      Do you understand
just what you're saying? Are your words the truth?

GUARD

    We saw this girl giving that dead man's corpse
full burial rites—an act you'd made illegal.
Is what I say simple and clear enough?

CREON

    How did you see her, catch her in the act?

GUARD

    It happened this way. When we got there,
after hearing those awful threats from you,
we swept off all the dust covering the corpse,
so the damp body was completely bare.   [410]

Sophocles

καθήμεθ' ἄκρων ἐκ πάγων ὑπήνεμοι,
ὀσμὴν ἀπ' αὐτοῦ μὴ βάλοι πεφευγότες,
ἐγερτὶ κινῶν ἄνδρ' ἀνὴρ ἐπιρρόθοις
κακοῖσιν, εἴ τις τοῦδ' ἀκηδήσοι πόνου.
χρόνον τάδ' ἦν τοσοῦτον, ἔστ' ἐν αἰθέρι   415
μέσῳ κατέστη λαμπρὸς ἡλίου κύκλος
καὶ καῦμ' ἔθαλπε· καὶ τότ' ἐξαίφνης χθονὸς
τυφὼς ἀείρας σκηπτόν οὐράνιον ἄχος,
πίμπλησι πεδίον, πᾶσαν αἰκίζων φόβην
ὕλης πεδιάδος, ἐν δ' ἐμεστώθη μέγας   420
αἰθήρ· μύσαντες δ' εἴχομεν θείαν νόσον.
καὶ τοῦδ' ἀπαλλαγέντος ἐν χρόνῳ μακρῷ,
ἡ παῖς ὁρᾶται, κἀνακωκύει πικρᾶς
ὄρνιθος ὀξὺν φθόγγον, ἐς ὅταν κενῆς
εὐνῆς νεοσσῶν ὀρφανὸν βλέψῃ λέχος.   425
οὕτω δὲ χαὕτη, ψιλὸν ὡς ὁρᾷ νέκυν,
γόοισιν ἐξώμωξεν, ἐκ δ' ἀρὰς κακὰς
ἠρᾶτο τοῖσι τοὔργον ἐξειργασμένοις.
καὶ χερσὶν εὐθὺς διψίαν φέρει κόνιν,
ἔκ τ' εὐκροτήτου χαλκέας ἄρδην πρόχου   430
χοαῖσι τρισπόνδοισι τὸν νέκυν στέφει.
χἠμεῖς ἰδόντες ἱέμεσθα, σὺν δέ νιν
θηρώμεθ' εὐθὺς οὐδὲν ἐκπεπληγμένην,
καὶ τάς τε πρόσθεν τάς τε νῦν ἠλέγχομεν
πράξεις· ἄπαρνος δ' οὐδενὸς καθίστατο,   435
ἅμ' ἡδέως ἔμοιγε κἀλγεινῶς ἅμα.
τὸ μὲν γὰρ αὐτὸν ἐκ κακῶν πεφευγέναι
ἥδιστον, ἐς κακὸν δὲ τοὺς φίλους ἄγειν
ἀλγεινόν· ἀλλὰ πάντα ταῦθ' ἥσσω λαβεῖν
ἐμοὶ πέφυκε τῆς ἐμῆς σωτηρίας.   440

ΚΡΕΩΝ

σὲ δή, σὲ τὴν νεύουσαν εἰς πέδον κάρα,
φὴς ἢ καταρνεῖ μὴ δεδρακέναι τάδε·

ΑΝΤΙΓΟΝΗ

καὶ φημὶ δρᾶσαι κοὐκ ἀπαρνοῦμαι τὸ μή.

Then we sat down on rising ground up wind,
to escape the body's putrid rotting stench.
We traded insults just to stay awake,
in case someone was careless on the job.
That's how we spent the time right up 'til noon,
when the sun's bright circle in the sky
had moved half way and it was burning hot.
Then suddenly a swirling windstorm came,
whipping clouds of dust up from the ground,
filling the plain—some heaven-sent trouble.
In that level place the dirt storm damaged
all the forest growth, and the air around   [420]
was filled with dust for miles. We shut our mouths
and just endured this scourge sent from the gods.
A long time passed. The storm came to an end.
That's when we saw the girl. She was shrieking—
a distressing painful cry, just like a bird
who's seen an empty nest, its fledglings gone.
That's how she was when she saw the naked corpse.
She screamed out a lament, and then she swore,
calling evil curses down upon the ones
who'd done this. Then right away her hands
threw on the thirsty dust. She lifted up
a finely made bronze jug and then three times   [430]
poured out her tributes to the dead.
When we saw that, we rushed up right away
and grabbed her. She was not afraid at all.
We charged her with her previous offence
as well as this one. She just kept standing there,
denying nothing. That made me happy—
though it was painful, too. For it's a joy
escaping troubles which affect oneself,
but painful to bring evil on one's friends.
But all that is of less concern to me
than my own safety.   [440]

CREON

                  You there—you with your face
bent down towards the ground, what do you say?
Do you deny you did this or admit it?

ANTIGONE

    I admit I did it. I won't deny that.

385

ΚΡΕΩΝ

σὺ μὲν κομίζοις ἂν σεαυτὸν ἧ θέλεις
ἔξω βαρείας αἰτίας ἐλεύθερον· 445
σὺ δ᾽ εἰπέ μοι μὴ μῆκος, ἀλλὰ συντόμως,
ἤδησθα κηρυχθέντα μὴ πράσσειν τάδε;

ΑΝΤΙΓΟΝΗ

ἤδη· τί δ᾽ οὐκ ἔμελλον; ἐμφανῆ γὰρ ἦν.

ΚΡΕΩΝ

καὶ δῆτ᾽ ἐτόλμας τούσδ᾽ ὑπερβαίνειν νόμους;

ΑΝΤΙΓΟΝΗ

οὐ γάρ τί μοι Ζεὺς ἦν ὁ κηρύξας τάδε, 450
οὐδ᾽ ἡ ξύνοικος τῶν κάτω θεῶν Δίκη
τοιούσδ᾽ ἐν ἀνθρώποισιν ὥρισεν νόμους.
οὐδὲ σθένειν τοσοῦτον ᾠόμην τὰ σὰ
κηρύγμαθ᾽, ὥστ᾽ ἄγραπτα κἀσφαλῆ θεῶν
νόμιμα δύνασθαι θνητὸν ὄνθ᾽ ὑπερδραμεῖν. 455
οὐ γάρ τι νῦν γε κἀχθές, ἀλλ᾽ ἀεί ποτε
ζῇ ταῦτα, κοὐδεὶς οἶδεν ἐξ ὅτου ᾽φάνη.
τούτων ἐγὼ οὐκ ἔμελλον, ἀνδρὸς οὐδενὸς
φρόνημα δείσασ᾽, ἐν θεοῖσι τὴν δίκην
δώσειν· θανουμένη γὰρ ἐξῄδη, τί δ᾽ οὔ; 460
κεἰ μὴ σὺ προὐκήρυξας. εἰ δὲ τοῦ χρόνου
πρόσθεν θανοῦμαι, κέρδος αὔτ᾽ ἐγὼ λέγω.
ὅστις γὰρ ἐν πολλοῖσιν ἐς ἐγὼ κακοῖς
ζῇ, πῶς ὅδ᾽ οὐχὶ κατθανὼν κέρδος φέρει;
οὕτως ἔμοιγε τοῦδε τοῦ μόρου τυχεῖν 465
παρ᾽ οὐδὲν ἄλγος· ἀλλ᾽ ἄν, εἰ τὸν ἐξ ἐμῆς
μητρὸς θανόντ᾽ ἄθαπτον ἠνσχόμην νέκυν,
κείνοις ἂν ἤλγουν· τοῖσδε δ᾽ οὐκ ἀλγύνομαι.
σοὶ δ᾽ εἰ δοκῶ νῦν μῶρα δρῶσα τυγχάνειν,
σχεδόν τι μώρῳ μωρίαν ὀφλισκάνω. 470

CREON *[to the Guard]*
    You're dismissed—go where you want. You're free—
    no serious charges made against you.

[Exit the Guard. Creon turns to interrogate Antigone]

    Tell me briefly—not in some lengthy speech—
    were you aware there was a proclamation
    forbidding what you did?

ANTIGONE
                    I'd heard of it.
    How could I not? It was public knowledge.

CREON
    And yet you dared to break those very laws?

ANTIGONE
    Yes. Zeus did not announce those laws to me. [450]
    And Justice living with the gods below
    sent no such laws for men. I did not think
    anything which you proclaimed strong enough
    to let a mortal override the gods
    and their unwritten and unchanging laws.
    They're not just for today or yesterday,
    but exist forever, and no one knows
    where they first appeared. So I did not mean
    to let a fear of any human will
    lead to my punishment among the gods.
    I know all too well I'm going to die— [460]
    how could I not?—it makes no difference
    what you decree. And if I have to die
    before my time, well, I count that a gain.
    When someone has to live the way I do,
    surrounded by so many evil things,
    how can she fail to find a benefit
    in death? And so for me meeting this fate
    won't bring any pain. But if I'd allowed
    my own mother's dead son to just lie there,
    an unburied corpse, then I'd feel distress.
    What's going on here does not hurt me at all.
    If you think what I'm doing now is stupid,
    perhaps I'm being charged with foolishness [470]
    by someone who's a fool.

Sophocles

ΧΟΡΟΣ

δηλοῖ τὸ γέννημ' ὠμὸν ἐξ ὠμοῦ πατρὸς
τῆς παιδός. εἴκειν δ' οὐκ ἐπίσταται κακοῖς.

ΚΡΕΩΝ

ἀλλ' ἴσθι τοι τὰ σκλήρ' ἄγαν φρονήματα
πίπτειν μάλιστα, καὶ τὸν ἐγκρατέστατον
σίδηρον ὀπτὸν ἐκ πυρὸς περισκελῆ   475
θραυσθέντα καὶ ῥαγέντα πλεῖστ' ἂν εἰσίδοις·
σμικρῷ χαλινῷ δ' οἶδα τοὺς θυμουμένους
ἵππους καταρτυθέντας· οὐ γὰρ ἐκπέλει
φρονεῖν μέγ' ὅστις δοῦλός ἐστι τῶν πέλας.
αὕτη δ' ὑβρίζειν μὲν τότ' ἐξηπίστατο,   480
νόμους ὑπερβαίνουσα τοὺς προκειμένους·
ὕβρις δ', ἐπεὶ δέδρακεν, ἥδε δευτέρα,
τούτοις ἐπαυχεῖν καὶ δεδρακυῖαν γελᾶν.
ἦ νῦν ἐγὼ μὲν οὐκ ἀνήρ, αὕτη δ' ἀνήρ,
εἰ ταῦτ' ἀνατὶ τῇδε κείσεται κράτη.   485
ἀλλ' εἴτ' ἀδελφῆς εἴθ' ὁμαιμονεστέρα
τοῦ παντὸς ἡμῖν Ζηνὸς ἑρκείου κυρεῖ,
αὐτή τε χἠ ξύναιμος οὐκ ἀλύξετον
μόρου κακίστου· καὶ γὰρ οὖν κείνην ἴσον
ἐπαιτιῶμαι τοῦδε βουλεῦσαι τάφου.   490
καί νιν καλεῖτ'· ἔσω γὰρ εἶδον ἀρτίως
λυσσῶσαν αὐτὴν οὐδ' ἐπήβολον φρενῶν.
φιλεῖ δ' ὁ θυμὸς πρόσθεν, ᾑρῆσθαι κλοπεὺς
τῶν μηδὲν ὀρθῶς ἐν σκότῳ τεχνωμένων·
μισῶ γε μέντοι χὤταν ἐν κακοῖσί τις   495
ἁλοὺς ἔπειτα τοῦτο καλλύνειν θέλῃ.

ΑΝΤΙΓΟΝΗ

θέλεις τι μεῖζον ἢ κατακτεῖναί μ' ἑλών;

ΚΡΕΩΝ

ἐγὼ μὲν οὐδέν· τοῦτ' ἔχων ἅπαντ' ἔχω.

388

CHORUS LEADER
                    It's clear enough
    the spirit in this girl is passionate—
    her father was the same. She has no sense
    of compromise in times of trouble.

CREON *[to the Chorus Leader]*
    But you should know the most obdurate wills
    are those most prone to break. The strongest iron
    tempered in the fire to make it really hard—
    that's the kind you see most often shatter.
    I'm well aware the most tempestuous horses
    are tamed by one small bit. Pride has no place
    in anyone who is his neighbour's slave.
    This girl here was already very insolent   [480]
    in contravening laws we had proclaimed.
    Here she again displays her proud contempt—
    having done the act, she now boasts of it.
    She laughs at what she's done. Well, in this case,
    if she gets her way and goes unpunished,
    then she's the man here, not me. No. She may be
    my sister's child, closer to me by blood
    than anyone belonging to my house
    who worships Zeus Herkeios in my home,
    but she'll not escape my harshest punishment—
    her sister, too, whom I accuse as well.4
    She had an equal part in all their plans   [490]
    to do this burial. Go summon her here.
    I saw her just now inside the palace,
    her mind out of control, some kind of fit.

[Exit attendants into the palace to fetch Ismene]

    When people hatch their mischief in the dark
    their minds often convict them in advance,
    betraying their treachery. How I despise
    a person caught committing evil acts
    who then desires to glorify the crime.

ANTIGONE
    Take me and kill me—what more do you want?

CREON
    Me? Nothing. With that I have everything.

ΑΝΤΙΓΟΝΗ

τί δῆτα μέλλεις; ὡς ἐμοὶ τῶν σῶν λόγων
ἀρεστὸν οὐδὲν μηδ' ἀρεσθείη ποτέ· 500
οὕτω δὲ καὶ σοὶ τἄμ' ἀφανδάνοντ' ἔφυ.
καίτοι πόθεν κλέος γ' ἂν εὐκλεέστερον
κατέσχον ἢ τὸν αὐτάδελφον ἐν τάφῳ
τιθεῖσα; τούτοις τοῦτο πᾶσιν ἁνδάνειν
λέγοιτ' ἄν, εἰ μὴ γλῶσσαν ἐγκλῄοι φόβος. 505
ἀλλ' ἡ τυραννὶς πολλά τ' ἄλλ' εὐδαιμονεῖ
κἄξεστιν αὐτῇ δρᾶν λέγειν θ' ἃ βούλεται.

ΚΡΕΩΝ

σὺ τοῦτο μούνη τῶνδε Καδμείων ὁρᾷς.

ΑΝΤΙΓΟΝΗ

ὁρῶσι χοὗτοι, σοὶ δ' ὑπίλλουσιν στόμα.

ΚΡΕΩΝ

σὺ δ' οὐκ ἐπαιδεῖ, τῶνδε χωρὶς εἰ φρονεῖς; 510

ΑΝΤΙΓΟΝΗ

οὐδὲν γὰρ αἰσχρὸν τοὺς ὁμοσπλάγχνους σέβειν.

ΚΡΕΩΝ

οὔκουν ὅμαιμος χὠ καταντίον θανών;

ΑΝΤΙΓΟΝΗ

ὅμαιμος ἐκ μιᾶς τε καὶ ταὐτοῦ πατρός.

ΚΡΕΩΝ

πῶς δῆτ' ἐκείνῳ δυσσεβῆ τιμᾷς χάριν;

ΑΝΤΙΓΟΝΗ

οὐ μαρτυρήσει ταῦθ' ὁ κατθανὼν νέκυς. 515

ΚΡΕΩΝ

εἴ τοί σφε τιμᾷς ἐξ ἴσου τῷ δυσσεβεῖ.

ANTIGONE

    Then why delay? There's nothing in your words
    that I enjoy—may that always be the case!   [500]
    And what I say displeases you as much.
    But where could I gain greater glory
    than setting my own brother in his grave?
    All those here would confirm this pleases them
    if their lips weren't sealed by fear—being king,
    which offers all sorts of various benefits,
    means you can talk and act just as you wish.

CREON

    In all of Thebes, you're the only one
    who looks at things that way.

ANTIGONE

                  They share my views,
    but they keep their mouths shut just for you.

CREON

    These views of yours—so different from the rest—
    don't they bring you any sense of shame?   [510]

ANTIGONE

    No—there's nothing shameful in honouring
    my mother's children.

CREON

              You had a brother
    killed fighting for the other side.

ANTIGONE

    Yes—from the same mother and father, too.

CREON

    Why then give tributes which insult his name?

ANTIGONE

    But his dead corpse won't back up what you say.

CREON

    Yes, he will, if you give equal honours
    to a wicked man.

Sophocles

ΑΝΤΙΓΟΝΗ

οὐ γάρ τι δοῦλος, ἀλλ᾽ ἀδελφὸς ὤλετο.

ΚΡΕΩΝ

πορθῶν δὲ τήνδε γῆν· ὁ δ᾽ ἀντιστὰς ὕπερ.

ΑΝΤΙΓΟΝΗ

ὁμῶς ὅ γ᾽ Ἅιδης τοὺς νόμους τούτους ποθεῖ.

ΚΡΕΩΝ

ἀλλ᾽ οὐχ ὁ χρηστὸς τῷ κακῷ λαχεῖν ἴσος.   520

ΑΝΤΙΓΟΝΗ

τίς οἶδεν εἰ κάτωθεν εὐαγῆ τάδε;

ΚΡΕΩΝ

οὔτοι ποθ᾽ οὑχθρός, οὐδ᾽ ὅταν θάνῃ, φίλος.

ΑΝΤΙΓΟΝΗ

οὔτοι συνέχθειν, ἀλλὰ συμφιλεῖν ἔφυν.

ΚΡΕΩΝ

κάτω νυν ἐλθοῦσ᾽, εἰ φιλητέον, φίλει
κείνους· ἐμοῦ δὲ ζῶντος οὐκ ἄρξει γυνή.   525

ΧΟΡΟΣ

καὶ μὴν πρὸ πυλῶν ἥδ᾽ Ἰσμήνη,
φιλάδελφα κάτω δάκρυ᾽ εἰβομένη·
νεφέλη δ᾽ ὀφρύων ὕπερ αἱματόεν
ῥέθος αἰσχύνει,
τέγγουσ᾽ εὐῶπα παρειάν.   530

ΚΡΕΩΝ

σὺ δ᾽, ἣ κατ᾽ οἴκους ὡς ἔχιδν᾽ ὑφειμένη
λήθουσά μ᾽ ἐξέπινες, οὐδ᾽ ἐμάνθανον
τρέφων δύ᾽ ἄτα κἀπαναστάσεις θρόνων,

392

ANTIGONE

But the one who died
was not some slave—it was his own brother.

CREON

Who was destroying this country—the other one
went to his death defending it.

ANTIGONE

That may be,
but Hades still desires equal rites for both.⁵

CREON

A good man does not wish what we give him   [520]
to be the same an evil man receives.

ANTIGONE

Who knows? In the world below perhaps
such actions are no crime.

CREON

An enemy
can never be a friend, not even in death.

ANTIGONE

But my nature is to love. I cannot hate.

CREON

Then go down to the dead. If you must love,
love them. No woman's going to govern me—
no, no—not while I'm still alive.

[Enter two attendants from the house bringing Ismene to Creon]

CHORUS LEADER

Ismene's coming. There—right by the door.
She's crying. How she must love her sister!
From her forehead a cloud casts its shadow
down across her darkly flushing face—
and drops its rain onto her lovely cheeks.   [530]

CREON

You there—you snake lurking in my house,
sucking out my life's blood so secretly.
I'd no idea I was nurturing two pests,
who aimed to rise against my throne. Come here.

φέρ᾽, εἰπὲ δή μοι, καὶ σὺ τοῦδε τοῦ τάφου
φήσεις μετασχεῖν, ἢ ᾽ξομεῖ τὸ μὴ εἰδέναι;   535

ΙΣΜΗΝΗ

δέδρακα τοὔργον, εἴπερ ἥδ᾽ ὁμορροθεῖ
καὶ ξυμμετίσχω καὶ φέρω τῆς αἰτίας.

ΑΝΤΙΓΟΝΗ

ἀλλ᾽ οὐκ ἐάσει τοῦτό γ᾽ ἡ δίκη σ᾽, ἐπεὶ
οὔτ᾽ ἠθέλησας οὔτ᾽ ἐγὼ ᾽κοινωσάμην.

ΙΣΜΗΝΗ

ἀλλ᾽ ἐν κακοῖς τοῖς σοῖσιν οὐκ αἰσχύνομαι   540
ξύμπλουν ἐμαυτὴν τοῦ πάθους ποιουμένη.

ΑΝΤΙΓΟΝΗ

ὧν τοὔργον, Ἅιδης χοἰ κάτω ξυνίστορες·
λόγοις δ᾽ ἐγὼ φιλοῦσαν οὐ στέργω φίλην.

ΙΣΜΗΝΗ

μήτοι, κασιγνήτη, μ᾽ ἀτιμάσῃς τὸ μὴ οὐ
θανεῖν τε σὺν σοὶ τὸν θανόντα θ᾽ ἁγνίσαι.   545

ΑΝΤΙΓΟΝΗ

μή μοι θάνῃς σὺ κοινὰ μηδ᾽ ἃ μὴ ᾽θιγες
ποιοῦ σεαυτῆς. ἀρκέσω θνῄσκουσ᾽ ἐγώ.

ΙΣΜΗΝΗ

καὶ τίς βίος μοι σοῦ λελειμμένῃ φίλος;

ΑΝΤΙΓΟΝΗ

Κρέοντ᾽ ἐρώτα· τοῦδε γὰρ σὺ κηδεμών.

ΙΣΜΗΝΗ

τί ταῦτ᾽ ἀνιᾷς μ᾽, οὐδὲν ὠφελουμένη;   550

ΑΝΤΙΓΟΝΗ

ἀλγοῦσα μὲν δῆτ᾽ εἰ γελῶ γ᾽ ἐν σοὶ γελῶ.

ΙΣΜΗΝΗ

τί δῆτ᾽ ἂν ἀλλὰ νῦν σ᾽ ἔτ᾽ ὠφελοῖμ᾽ ἐγώ;

Tell me this—do you admit you played your part
in this burial, or will you swear an oath
you had no knowledge of it?

ISMENE

                    I did it—
I admit it, and she'll back me up.
So I bear the guilt as well.

ANTIGONE

                    No, no—
justice will not allow you to say that.
You didn't want to. I didn't work with you.

ISMENE

But now you're in trouble, I'm not ashamed   [540]
of suffering, too, as your companion.

ANTIGONE

Hades and the dead can say who did it—
I don't love a friend whose love is only words.

ISMENE

You're my sister. Don't dishonour me.
Let me respect the dead and die with you.

ANTIGONE

Don't try to share my death or make a claim
to actions which you did not do. I'll die—
and that will be enough.

ISMENE

                    But if you're gone,
what is there in life for me to love?

ANTIGONE

Ask Creon. He's the one you care about.

ISMENE

Why hurt me like this? It doesn't help you.   [550]

ANTIGONE

If I am mocking you, it pains me, too.

ISMENE

Even now is there some way I can help?

ΑΝΤΙΓΟΝΗ

σῶσον σεαυτήν· οὐ φθονῶ σ' ὑπεκφυγεῖν.

ΙΣΜΗΝΗ

οἴμοι τάλαινα, κἀμπλάκω τοῦ σοῦ μόρου;

ΑΝΤΙΓΟΝΗ

σὺ μὲν γὰρ εἵλου ζῆν, ἐγὼ δὲ κατθανεῖν.   555

ΙΣΜΗΝΗ

ἀλλ' οὐκ ἐπ' ἀρρήτοις γε τοῖς ἐμοῖς λόγοις.

ΑΝΤΙΓΟΝΗ

καλῶς σὺ μὲν τοῖς, τοῖς δ' ἐγὼ 'δόκουν φρονεῖν.

ΙΣΜΗΝΗ

καὶ μὴν ἴση νῷν ἐστιν ἡ 'ξαμαρτία.

ΑΝΤΙΓΟΝΗ

θάρσει· σὺ μὲν ζῇς, ἡ δ' ἐμὴ ψυχὴ πάλαι
τέθνηκεν, ὥστε τοῖς θανοῦσιν ὠφελεῖν.   560

ΚΡΕΩΝ

τὼ παῖδε φημὶ τώδε τὴν μὲν ἀρτίως
ἄνουν πεφάνθαι, τὴν δ' ἀφ' οὗ τὰ πρῶτ' ἔφυ.

ΙΣΜΗΝΗ

οὐ γάρ ποτ', ὦναξ, οὐδ' ὃς ἂν βλάστῃ μένει
νοῦς τοῖς κακῶς πράσσουσιν, ἀλλ' ἐξίσταται.

ΚΡΕΩΝ

σοὶ γοῦν, ὅθ' εἵλου σὺν κακοῖς πράσσειν κακά.   565

ΙΣΜΗΝΗ

τί γὰρ μόνῃ μοι τῆσδ' ἄτερ βιώσιμον;

ΚΡΕΩΝ

ἀλλ' ἥδε μέντοι μὴ λέγ'· οὐ γὰρ ἔστ' ἔτι.

ΙΣΜΗΝΗ

ἀλλὰ κτενεῖς νυμφεῖα τοῦ σαυτοῦ τέκνου;

ANTIGONE

>Save yourself. I won't envy your escape.

ISMENE

>I feel so wretched leaving you to die.

ANTIGONE

>But you chose life—it was my choice to die.

ISMENE

>But not before I'd said those words just now.

ANTIGONE

>Some people may approve of how you think—
>others will believe my judgment's good.

ISMENE

>But the mistake's the same for both of us.

ANTIGONE

>Be brave. You're alive. But my spirit died
>some time ago so I might help the dead   [560]

CREON

>I'd say one of these girls has just revealed
>how mad she is—the other's been that way
>since she was born.

ISMENE

>   My lord, whatever good sense
>people have by birth no longer stays with them
>once their lives go wrong—it abandons them.

CREON

>In your case, that's true, once you made your choice
>to act in evil ways with wicked people.

ISMENE

>How could I live alone, without her here?

CREON

>Don't speak of her being here. Her life is over.

ISMENE

>You're going to kill your own son's bride?

ΚΡΕΩΝ

ἀρώσιμοι γὰρ χἀτέρων εἰσὶν γύαι.

ΙΣΜΗΝΗ

οὐχ ὥς γ' ἐκείνῳ τῇδέ τ' ἦν ἡρμοσμένα.   570

ΚΡΕΩΝ

κακὰς ἐγὼ γυναῖκας υἱέσι στυγῶ.

ΑΝΤΙΓΟΝΗ

ὦ φίλταθ' Αἷμον, ὥς σ' ἀτιμάζει πατήρ.

ΚΡΕΩΝ

ἄγαν γε λυπεῖς καὶ σὺ καὶ τὸ σὸν λέχος.

ΧΟΡΟΣ

ἦ γὰρ στερήσεις τῆσδε τὸν σαυτοῦ γόνον;

ΚΡΕΩΝ

Ἅιδης ὁ παύσων τούσδε τοὺς γάμους ἔφυ.   575

ΧΟΡΟΣ

δεδογμέν', ὡς ἔοικε, τήνδε κατθανεῖν.

ΚΡΕΩΝ

καὶ σοί γε κἀμοί. μὴ τριβὰς ἔτ', ἀλλά νιν
κομίζετ' εἴσω, δμῶες· ἐκ δὲ τοῦδε χρὴ
γυναῖκας εἶναι τάσδε μηδ' ἀνειμένας.
φεύγουσι γάρ τοι χοἰ θρασεῖς, ὅταν πέλας   580
ἤδη τὸν, Ἅιδην εἰσορῶσι τοῦ βίου.

ΧΟΡΟΣ

εὐδαίμονες οἷσι κακῶν ἄγευστος αἰών.
οἷς γὰρ ἂν σεισθῇ θεόθεν δόμος, ἄτας
οὐδὲν ἐλλείπει γενεᾶς ἐπὶ πλῆθος ἕρπον·   585

398

CREON
Why not? There are other fields for him to plough.

ISMENE
No one will make him a more loving wife
than she will.   [570]

CREON
                              I have no desire my son
should have an evil wife.

ANTIGONE
                              Dearest Haemon,
how your father wrongs you.

CREON
                              I've had enough of this—
you and your marriage.

ISMENE
                              You really want that?
You're going to take her from him?

CREON
                                        No, not me.
Hades is the one who'll stop the marriage.

CHORUS LEADER
So she must die—that seems decided on.

CREON
Yes—for you and me the matter's closed.

[Creon turns to address his attendants]

No more delay. You slaves, take them inside.
From this point on they must act like women
and have no liberty to wander off.
Even bold men run when they see Hades   [580]
coming close to them to snatch their lives.

[The attendants take Antigone and Ismene into the palace, leaving Creon and the Chorus on stage]

CHORUS
Those who live without tasting evil
have happy lives—for when the gods
shake a house to its foundations,
then inevitable disasters strike,
falling upon whole families,

ὅμοιον ὥστε ποντίαις οἶδμα δυσπνόοις ὅταν
Θρήσσαισιν ἔρεβος ὕφαλον ἐπιδράμῃ πνοαῖς,
κυλίνδει βυσσόθεν κελαινὰν θῖνα καὶ   590
δυσάνεμοι, στόνῳ βρέμουσι δ᾽ ἀντιπλῆγες ἀκταί.

ἀρχαῖα τὰ Λαβδακιδᾶν οἴκων ὁρῶμαι
πήματα φθιτῶν ἐπὶ πήμασι πίπτοντ᾽,   595
οὐδ᾽ ἀπαλλάσσει γενεὰν γένος, ἀλλ᾽ ἐρείπει
θεῶν τις, οὐδ᾽ ἔχει λύσιν. νῦν γὰρ ἐσχάτας ὕπερ
ῥίζας ὃ τέτατο φάος ἐν Οἰδίπου δόμοις,   600
κατ᾽ αὖ νιν φοινία θεῶν τῶν νερτέρων
ἀμᾷ κόνις λόγου τ᾽ ἄνοια καὶ φρενῶν ἐρινύς.

τεάν, Ζεῦ, δύνασιν τίς ἀνδρῶν ὑπερβασία κατάσχοι; 605
τὰν οὔθ᾽ ὕπνος αἱρεῖ ποθ᾽ ὁ πάντ᾽ ἀγρεύων,
οὔτε θεῶν ἄκματοι μῆνες, ἀγήρῳ δὲ χρόνῳ
δυνάστας κατέχεις Ὀλύμπου μαρμαρόεσσαν αἴγλαν. 610
τό τ᾽ ἔπειτα καὶ τὸ μέλλον
καὶ τὸ πρὶν ἐπαρκέσει
νόμος ὅδ᾽, οὐδὲν ἕρπει
θνατῶν βιότῳ πάμπολύ γ᾽ ἐκτὸς ἄτας.

ἁ γὰρ δὴ πολύπλαγκτος ἐλπὶς πολλοῖς μὲν ὄνασις
    ἀνδρῶν,   615
πολλοῖς δ᾽ ἀπάτα κουφονόων ἐρώτων·
εἰδότι δ᾽ οὐδὲν ἕρπει, πρὶν πυρὶ θερμῷ πόδα τις
προσαύσῃ. σοφίᾳ γὰρ ἔκ του κλεινὸν ἔπος πέφανται. 620
τὸ κακὸν δοκεῖν ποτ᾽ ἐσθλὸν
τῷδ᾽ ἔμμεν ὅτῳ φρένας
θεὸς ἄγει πρὸς ἄταν·
πράσσει δ᾽ ὀλίγιστον χρόνον ἐκτὸς ἄτας.   625

just as a surging ocean swell
running before cruel Thracian winds
across the dark trench of the sea
churns up the deep black sand   [590]
and crashes headlong on the cliffs,
which scream in pain against the wind.

I see this house's age-old sorrows,
the house of Labdakos' children,
sorrows falling on the sorrows of the dead,
one generation bringing no relief
to generations after it—some god
strikes at them—on and on without an end.
For now the light which has been shining
over the last roots of Oedipus' house   [600]
is being cut down with a bloody knife
belonging to the gods below—
for foolish talk and frenzy in the soul.[6]

O Zeus, what human trespasses
can check your power? Even Sleep,
who casts his nets on everything,
cannot master that—nor can the months,
the tireless months the gods control.
A sovereign who cannot grow old,
you hold Olympus as your own,
in all its glittering magnificence.[7]   [610]
From now on into all future time,
as in the past, your law holds firm.
It never enters lives of human beings
in its full force without disaster.

Hope ranging far and wide brings comfort
to many men—but then hope can deceive,
delusions born of volatile desire.
It comes upon the man who's ignorant
until his foot is seared in burning fire.
Someone's wisdom has revealed to us   [620]
this famous saying—sometimes the gods
lure a man's mind forward to disaster,
and he thinks evil's something good.
But then he lives only the briefest time
free of catastrophe.

— ὅδε μὴν Αἵμων, παίδων τῶν σῶν
νέατον γέννημ᾽· ἆρ᾽ ἀχνύμενος
τάλιδος ἥκει μόρον Ἀντιγόνης,
ἀπάτης λεχέων ὑπεραλγῶν;   630

ΚΡΕΩΝ

    τάχ᾽ εἰσόμεσθα μάντεων ὑπέρτερον.
    ὦ παῖ, τελείαν ψῆφον ἆρα μὴ κλύων
    τῆς μελλονύμφου πατρὶ λυσσαίνων πάρει;
    ἢ σοὶ μὲν ἡμεῖς πανταχῇ, δρῶντες φίλοι;

ΑΙΜΩΝ

    πάτερ, σός εἰμι, καὶ σύ μοι γνώμας ἔχων   635
    χρηστὰς ἀπορθοῖς, αἷς ἔγωγ᾽ ἐφέψομαι.
    ἐμοὶ γὰρ οὐδεὶς ἀξιώσεται γάμος
    μείζων φέρεσθαι σοῦ καλῶς ἡγουμένου.

ΚΡΕΩΝ

    οὕτω γάρ, ὦ παῖ, χρὴ διὰ στέρνων ἔχειν,
    γνώμης πατρῴας πάντ᾽ ὄπισθεν ἑστάναι.   640
    τούτου γὰρ οὕνεκ᾽ ἄνδρες εὔχονται γονὰς
    κατηκόους φύσαντες ἐν δόμοις ἔχειν,
    ὡς καὶ τὸν ἐχθρὸν ἀνταμύνωνται κακοῖς
    καὶ τὸν φίλον τιμῶσιν ἐξ ἴσου πατρί.
    ὅστις δ᾽ ἀνωφέλητα φιτύει τέκνα,   645
    τί τόνδ᾽ ἂν εἴποις ἄλλο πλὴν αὑτῷ πόνους
    φῦσαι, πολὺν δὲ τοῖσιν ἐχθροῖσιν γέλων;
    μή νύν ποτ᾽, ὦ παῖ, τὰς φρένας ὑφ᾽ ἡδονῆς
    γυναικὸς οὕνεκ᾽ ἐκβάλῃς, εἰδὼς ὅτι
    ψυχρὸν παραγκάλισμα τοῦτο γίγνεται,   650
    γυνὴ κακὴ ξύνευνος ἐν δόμοις. τί γὰρ
    γένοιτ᾽ ἂν ἕλκος μεῖζον ἢ φίλος κακός;

[The palace doors open]

CHORUS LEADER
               Here comes Haemon,
  your only living son. Is he grieving
  the fate of Antigone, his bride,
  bitter that his marriage hopes are gone?   [630]

CREON
  We'll soon find out—more accurately
  than any prophet here could indicate.

[Enter Haemon from the palace]

  My son, have you heard the sentence that's been passed
  upon your bride? And have you now come here
  angry at your father? Or are you loyal to me,
  on my side no matter what I do?

HAEMON
  Father, I'm yours. For me your judgments
  and the ways you act on them are good—
  I shall follow them. I'll not consider
  any marriage a greater benefit
  than your fine leadership.

CREON
                          Indeed, my son,
  that's how your heart should always be resolved,
  to stand behind your father's judgment   [640]
  on every issue. That's what men pray for—
  obedient children growing up at home
  who will pay back their father's enemies,
  evil to them for evil done to him,
  while honouring his friends as much as he does.
  A man who fathers useless children—
  what can one say of him except he's bred
  troubles for himself, and much to laugh at
  for those who fight against him? So, my son,
  don't ever throw good sense aside for pleasure,
  for some woman's sake. You understand
  how such embraces can turn freezing cold   [650]
  when an evil woman shares your life at home.
  What greater wound is there than a false friend?

Sophocles

ἀλλὰ πτύσας ὡσεί τε δυσμενῆ μέθες
τὴν παῖδ᾽ ἐν Ἅιδου τήνδε νυμφεύειν τινί.
ἐπεὶ γὰρ αὐτὴν εἷλον ἐμφανῶς ἐγὼ   655
πόλεως ἀπιστήσασαν ἐκ πάσης μόνην,
ψευδῆ γ᾽ ἐμαυτὸν οὐ καταστήσω πόλει,
ἀλλὰ κτενῶ. πρὸς ταῦτ᾽ ἐφυμνείτω Δία
ξύναιμον. εἰ γὰρ δὴ τά γ᾽ ἐγγενῆ φύσει
ἄκοσμα θρέψω, κάρτα τοὺς ἔξω γένους   660
ἐν τοῖς γὰρ οἰκείοισιν ὅστις ἔστ᾽ ἀνὴρ
χρηστός, φανεῖται κἀν πόλει δίκαιος ὤν.
καὶ τοῦτον ἂν τὸν ἄνδρα θαρσοίην ἐγὼ   668
καλῶς μὲν ἄρχειν, εὖ δ᾽ ἂν ἄρχεσθαι θέλειν,
δορός τ᾽ ἂν ἐν χειμῶνι προστεταγμένον   670
μένειν δίκαιον κἀγαθὸν παραστάτην.   671
ὅστις δ᾽ ὑπερβὰς ἢ νόμους βιάζεται   663
ἢ τοὐπιτάσσειν τοῖς κρατύνουσιν νοεῖ,   664
οὐκ ἔστ᾽ ἐπαίνου τοῦτον ἐξ ἐμοῦ τυχεῖν.   665
ἀλλ᾽ ὃν πόλις στήσειε τοῦδε χρὴ κλύειν   666
καὶ σμικρὰ καὶ δίκαια καὶ τἀναντία.   667
ἀναρχίας δὲ μεῖζον οὐκ ἔστιν κακόν.   672
αὕτη πόλεις ὄλλυσιν, ἥδ᾽ ἀναστάτους
οἴκους τίθησιν, ἥδε συμμάχου δορὸς
τροπὰς καταρρήγνυσι· τῶν δ᾽ ὀρθουμένων   675
σῴζει τὰ πολλὰ σώμαθ᾽ ἡ πειθαρχία.
οὕτως ἀμυντέ᾽ ἐστὶ τοῖς κοσμουμένοις,
κοὔτοι γυναικὸς οὐδαμῶς ἡσσητέα.
κρεῖσσον γάρ, εἴπερ δεῖ, πρὸς ἀνδρὸς ἐκπεσεῖν,
κοὐκ ἂν γυναικῶν ἥσσονες καλοίμεθ᾽ ἄν.   680

ΧΟΡΟΣ
ἡμῖν μέν, εἰ μὴ τῷ χρόνῳ κεκλέμμεθα,
λέγειν φρονούντως ὧν λέγεις δοκεῖς πέρι.

ΑΙΜΩΝ
πάτερ, θεοὶ φύουσιν ἀνθρώποις φρένας,
πάντων ὅσ᾽ ἐστὶ κτημάτων ὑπέρτατον.
ἐγὼ δ᾽ ὅπως σὺ μὴ λέγεις ὀρθῶς τάδε,   685
οὔτ᾽ ἂν δυναίμην μήτ᾽ ἐπισταίμην λέγειν.

404

So spit this girl out—she's your enemy.
Let her marry someone else in Hades.
Since I caught her clearly disobeying,
the only culprit in the entire city,
I won't perjure myself before the state.
No—I'll kill her. And so let her appeal
to Zeus, the god of blood relationships.
If I foster any lack of full respect
in my own family, I surely do the same
with those who are not linked to me by blood.   [660]
The man who acts well with his household
will be found a just man in the city.[8]
I'd trust such a man to govern wisely
or to be content with someone ruling him.
And in the thick of battle at his post   [670]
he'll stand firm beside his fellow soldier,
a loyal, brave man. But anyone who's proud
and violates our laws or thinks he'll tell
our leaders what to do, a man like that
wins no praise from me. No. We must obey
whatever man the city puts in charge,
no matter what the issue—great or small,
just or unjust. For there's no greater evil
than a lack of leadership. That destroys
whole cities, turns households into ruins,
and in war makes soldiers break and run away.
When men succeed, what keeps their lives secure
in almost every case is their obedience.
That's why they must support those in control,
and never let some woman beat us down.
If we must fall from power, let that come
at some man's hand—at least, we won't be called
inferior to any woman.   [680]

CHORUS LEADER
    Unless we're being deceived by our old age,
    what you've just said seems reasonable to us.

HAEMON
    Father, the gods instill good sense in men—
    the greatest of all the things which we possess.
    I could not find your words somehow not right—
    I hope that's something I never learn to do.

Sophocles

γένοιτο μεντἂν χἀτέρῳ καλῶς ἔχον.
σοῦ δ' οὖν πέφυκα πάντα προσκοπεῖν ὅσα
λέγει τις ἢ πράσσει τις ἢ ψέγειν ἔχει.
τὸ γὰρ σὸν ὄμμα δεινὸν, ἀνδρὶ δημότῃ   690
λόγοις τοιούτοις, οἷς σὺ μὴ τέρψει κλύων·
ἐμοὶ δ' ἀκούειν ἔσθ' ὑπὸ σκότου τάδε,
τὴν παῖδα ταύτην οἷ', ὀδύρεται πόλις,
πασῶν γυναικῶν ὡς ἀναξιωτάτη
κάκιστ' ἀπ' ἔργων εὐκλεεστάτων φθίνει.   695
ἥτις τὸν αὑτῆς αὐτάδελφον ἐν φοναῖς
πεπτῶτ' ἄθαπτον μήθ' ὑπ' ὠμηστῶν κυνῶν
εἴασ' ὀλέσθαι μήθ' ὑπ' οἰωνῶν τινος.
οὐχ ἥδε χρυσῆς ἀξία τιμῆς λαχεῖν;
τοιάδ' ἐρεμνὴ σῖγ' ἐπέρχεται φάτις.   700
ἐμοὶ δὲ σοῦ πράσσοντος εὐτυχῶς, πάτερ,
οὐκ ἔστιν οὐδὲν κτῆμα τιμιώτερον,
τί γὰρ πατρὸς θάλλοντος εὐκλείας τέκνοις
ἄγαλμα μεῖζον, ἢ τί πρὸς παίδων πατρί;
μή νυν ἓν ἦθος μοῦνον ἐν σαυτῷ φόρει,   705
ὡς φῂς σύ, κοὐδὲν ἄλλο, τοῦτ' ὀρθῶς ἔχειν.
ὅστις γὰρ αὐτὸς ἢ φρονεῖν μόνος δοκεῖ,
ἢ γλῶσσαν, ἣν οὐκ ἄλλος, ἢ ψυχὴν ἔχειν,
οὗτοι διαπτυχθέντες ὤφθησαν κενοί.
ἀλλ' ἄνδρα, κεἴ τις ᾖ σοφός, τὸ μανθάνειν   710
πόλλ', αἰσχρὸν οὐδὲν καὶ τὸ μὴ τείνειν ἄγαν.
ὁρᾷς παρὰ ῥείθροισι χειμάρροις ὅσα
δένδρων ὑπείκει, κλῶνας ὡς ἐκσῴζεται,
τὰ δ' ἀντιτείνοντ' αὐτόπρεμν' ἀπόλλυται.
αὔτως δὲ ναὸς ὅστις ἐγκρατῆ πόδα   715
τείνας ὑπείκει μηδέν, ὑπτίοις κάτω
στρέψας τὸ λοιπὸν σέλμασιν ναυτίλλεται.
ἀλλ' εἶκε καὶ θυμῷ μετάστασιν δίδου.
γνώμῃ γὰρ εἴ τις κἀπ' ἐμοῦ νεωτέρου
πρόσεστι, φήμ' ἔγωγε πρεσβεύειν πολὺ   720
φῦναι τὸν ἄνδρα πάντ' ἐπιστήμης πλέων·
εἰ δ' οὖν, φιλεῖ γὰρ τοῦτο μὴ ταύτῃ ῥέπειν,
καὶ τῶν λεγόντων εὖ καλὸν τὸ μανθάνειν.

But other words might be good, as well.
Because of who you are, you can't perceive
all the things men say or do—or their complaints.
Your gaze makes citizens afraid—they can't   [690]
say anything you would not like to hear.
But in the darkness I can hear them talk—
the city is upset about the girl.
They say of all women here she's least deserves
the worst of deaths for her most glorious act.
When in the slaughter her own brother died,
she did not just leave him there unburied,
to be ripped apart by carrion dogs or birds.
Surely she deserves some golden honour?
That's the dark secret rumour people speak.   [700]
For me, father, nothing is more valuable
than your well being. For any children,
what could be a greater honour to them
than their father's thriving reputation?
A father feels the same about his sons.
So don't let your mind dwell on just one thought,
that what you say is right and nothing else.
A man who thinks that only he is wise,
that he can speak and think like no one else,
when such men are exposed, then all can see
their emptiness inside. For any man,   [710]
even if he's wise, there's nothing shameful
in learning many things, staying flexible.
You notice how in winter floods the trees
which bend before the storm preserve their twigs.
The ones who stand against it are destroyed,
root and branch. In the same way, those sailors
who keep their sails stretched tight, never easing off,
make their ship capsize—and from that point on
sail with their rowing benches all submerged.
So end your anger. Permit yourself to change.
For if I, as a younger man, may state
my views, I'd say it would be for the best   [720]
if men by nature understood all things—
if not, and that is usually the case,
when men speak well, it good to learn from them.

ΧΟΡΟΣ

ἄναξ, σέ τ᾽ εἰκός, εἴ τι καίριον λέγει,
μαθεῖν, σέ τ᾽ αὖ τοῦδ᾽· εὖ γὰρ εἴρηται διπλῇ.　　725

ΚΡΕΩΝ

οἱ τηλικοίδε καὶ διδαξόμεσθα δὴ
φρονεῖν ὑπ᾽ ἀνδρὸς τηλικοῦδε τὴν φύσιν;

ΑΙΜΩΝ

μηδὲν τὸ μὴ δίκαιον· εἰ δ᾽ ἐγὼ νέος,
οὐ τὸν χρόνον χρὴ μᾶλλον ἢ τἄργα σκοπεῖν.

ΚΡΕΩΝ

ἔργον γάρ ἐστι τοὺς ἀκοσμοῦντας σέβειν;　　730

ΑΙΜΩΝ

οὐδ᾽ ἂν κελεύσαιμ᾽, εὐσεβεῖν εἰς τοὺς κακούς.

ΚΡΕΩΝ

οὐχ ἥδε γὰρ τοιᾷδ᾽ ἐπείληπται νόσῳ;

ΑΙΜΩΝ

οὔ φησι Θήβης τῆσδ᾽ ὁμόπτολις λεώς.

ΚΡΕΩΝ

πόλις γὰρ ἡμῖν ἁμὲ χρὴ τάσσειν ἐρεῖ;

ΑΙΜΩΝ

ὁρᾷς τόδ᾽ ὡς εἴρηκας ὡς ἄγαν νέος;　　735

ΚΡΕΩΝ

ἄλλῳ γὰρ ἢ 'μοὶ χρή με τῆσδ᾽ ἄρχειν χθονός;

ΑΙΜΩΝ

πόλις γὰρ οὐκ ἔσθ᾽ ἥτις ἀνδρός ἐσθ᾽ ἑνός.

CHORUS LEADER
My lord, if what he's said is relevant,
it seems appropriate to learn from him,
and you too, Haemon, listen to the king.
The things which you both said were excellent.

CREON
And men my age—are we then going to school
to learn what's wise from men as young as him?

HAEMON
There's nothing wrong in that. And if I'm young,
don't think about my age—look at what I do.

CREON
And what you do—does that include this,   [730]
honouring those who act against our laws?

HAEMON
I would not encourage anyone
to show respect to evil men.

CREON
                                              And her—
is she not suffering from the same disease?

HAEMON
The people here in Thebes all say the same—
they deny she is.

CREON
                                   So the city now
will instruct me how I am to govern?

HAEMON
Now you're talking like someone far too young.
Don't you see that?

CREON
                                   Am I to rule this land
at someone else's whim or by myself?

HAEMON
A city which belongs to just one man
is no true city.

Sophocles

ΚΡΕΩΝ

οὐ τοῦ κρατοῦντος ἡ πόλις νομίζεται;

ΑΙΜΩΝ

καλῶς γ' ἐρήμης ἂν σὺ γῆς ἄρχοις μόνος.

ΚΡΕΩΝ

ὅδ', ὡς ἔοικε, τῇ γυναικὶ συμμαχεῖ.   740

ΑΙΜΩΝ

εἴπερ γυνὴ σύ. σοῦ γὰρ οὖν προκήδομαι.

ΚΡΕΩΝ

ὦ παγκάκιστε, διὰ δίκης ἰὼν πατρί;

ΑΙΜΩΝ

οὐ γὰρ δίκαιά σ' ἐξαμαρτάνονθ' ὁρῶ.

ΚΡΕΩΝ

ἁμαρτάνω γὰρ τὰς ἐμὰς ἀρχὰς σέβων;

ΑΙΜΩΝ

οὐ γὰρ σέβεις τιμάς γε τὰς θεῶν πατῶν.   745

ΚΡΕΩΝ

ὦ μιαρὸν ἦθος καὶ γυναικὸς ὕστερον.

ΑΙΜΩΝ

οὔ τἂν ἕλοις ἥσσω γε τῶν αἰσχρῶν ἐμέ.

ΚΡΕΩΝ

ὁ γοῦν λόγος σοι πᾶς ὑπὲρ κείνης ὅδε.

CREON
                According to our laws,
does not the ruler own the city?

HAEMON
By yourself you'd make an excellent king
but in a desert.

CREON
                It seems as if this boy   [740]
is fighting on the woman's side.

HAEMON
                    That's true—
if you're the woman. I'm concerned for you.

CREON
You're the worst there is—you set your judgment up
against your father.

HAEMON
                No, not when I see
you making a mistake and being unjust.

CREON
Is it a mistake to honour my own rule?

HAEMON
You're not honouring that by trampling on
the gods' prerogatives.

CREON
                You foul creature—
you're worse than any woman.

HAEMON
                You'll not catch me
giving way to some disgrace.

CREON
                But your words
all speak on her behalf.

HAEMON
                And yours and mine—
and for the gods below.

CREON
                You woman's slave—
don't try to win me over.

ΑΙΜΩΝ

καὶ σοῦ γε κἀμοῦ, καὶ θεῶν τῶν νερτέρων.

ΚΡΕΩΝ

ταύτην ποτ᾽ οὐκ ἔσθ᾽ ὡς ἔτι ζῶσαν γαμεῖς.　　750

ΑΙΜΩΝ

γυναικὸς ὢν δούλευμα μὴ κώτιλλέ με.　　756

ΚΡΕΩΝ

βούλει λέγειν τι καὶ λέγων μηδὲν κλύειν;　　757

ΑΙΜΩΝ

ἦ δ᾽ οὖν θανεῖται καὶ θανοῦσ᾽ ὀλεῖ τινα.　　751

ΚΡΕΩΝ

ἦ κἀπαπειλῶν ὧδ᾽ ἐπεξέρχει θρασύς;

ΑΙΜΩΝ

τίς δ᾽ ἔστ᾽ ἀπειλὴ πρὸς κενὰς γνώμας λέγειν;

ΚΡΕΩΝ

κλαίων φρενώσεις, ὢν φρενῶν αὐτὸς κενός.

ΑΙΜΩΝ

εἰ μὴ πατὴρ ἦσθ᾽, εἶπον ἄν σ᾽ οὐκ εὖ φρονεῖν.　　755

ΚΡΕΩΝ

ἄληθες; ἀλλ᾽ οὐ τόνδ᾽ Ὄλυμπον, ἴσθ᾽ ὅτι,　　758
χαίρων ἐπὶ ψόγοισι δεννάσεις ἐμέ.
ἄγαγε τὸ μῖσος ὡς κατ᾽ ὄμματ᾽ αὐτίκα　　760
παρόντι θνήσκῃ πλησία τῷ νυμφίῳ.

ΑΙΜΩΝ

οὐ δῆτ᾽ ἔμοιγε, τοῦτο μὴ δόξῃς ποτέ,
οὔθ᾽ ἥδ᾽ ὀλεῖται πλησία, σύ τ᾽ οὐδαμὰ
τοὐμὸν προσόψει κρᾶτ᾽ ἐν ὀφθαλμοῖς ὁρῶν,
ὡς τοῖς θέλουσι τῶν φίλων μαίνῃ συνών.　　765

HAEMON

                         What do you want—
to speak and never hear someone reply?9

CREON

You'll never marry her while she's alive.   [750]

HAEMON

Then she'll die—and in her death kill someone else.

CREON

Are you so insolent you threaten me?

HAEMON

Where's the threat in challenging a bad decree?

CREON

You'll regret parading what you think like this—
you—a person with an empty brain!

HAEMON

If you were not my father, I might say
you were not thinking straight.

CREON

                          Would you, indeed?
Well, then, by Olympus, I'll have you know
you'll be sorry for demeaning me
with all these insults.

[Creon turns to his attendants]

                          Go bring her out—   [760]
that hateful creature, so she can die right here,
with him present, before her bridegroom's eyes.

HAEMON

No. Don't ever hope for that. She'll not die
with me just standing there. And as for you—
your eyes will never see my face again.
So let your rage charge on among your friends
who want to stand by you in this.

[Exit Haemon, running back into the palace]

413

Sophocles

ΧΟΡΟΣ

ἀνήρ, ἄναξ, βέβηκεν ἐξ ὀργῆς ταχύς·
νοῦς δ' ἐστὶ τηλικοῦτος ἀλγήσας βαρύς.

ΚΡΕΩΝ

δράτω· φρονείτω μεῖζον ἢ κατ' ἄνδρ' ἰών·
τὼ δ' οὖν κόρα τώδ' οὐκ ἀπαλλάξει μόρου.

ΧΟΡΟΣ

ἄμφω γὰρ αὐτὼ καὶ κατακτεῖναι νοεῖς;   770

ΚΡΕΩΝ

οὐ τήν γε μὴ θιγοῦσαν· εὖ γὰρ οὖν λέγεις.

ΧΟΡΟΣ

μόρῳ δὲ ποίῳ καί σφε βουλεύει κτανεῖν;

ΚΡΕΩΝ

ἄγων ἔρημος ἔνθ' ἂν ᾖ βροτῶν στίβος
κρύψω πετρώδει ζῶσαν ἐν κατώρυχι,
φορβῆς τοσοῦτον ὡς ἄγος μόνον προθείς,   775
ὅπως μίασμα πᾶσ' ὑπεκφύγῃ πόλις.
κἀκεῖ τὸν Ἅιδην, ὃν μόνον σέβει θεῶν,
αἰτουμένη που τεύξεται τὸ μὴ θανεῖν,
ἢ γνώσεται γοῦν ἀλλὰ τηνικαῦθ' ὅτι
πόνος περισσός ἐστι τὰν Ἅιδου σέβειν.   780

ΧΟΡΟΣ

Ἔρως ἀνίκατε μάχαν, Ἔρως, ὃς ἐν κτήνεσι πίπτεις,
ὃς ἐν μαλακαῖς παρειαῖς νεάνιδος ἐννυχεύεις,
φοιτᾷς δ' ὑπερπόντιος ἔν τ' ἀγρονόμοις αὐλαῖς·   785
καί σ' οὔτ' ἀθανάτων φύξιμος οὐδεὶς
οὔθ' ἁμερίων σέ γ' ἀνθρώπων. ὁ δ' ἔχων μέμηνεν.   790
σὺ καὶ δικαίων ἀδίκους φρένας παρασπᾷς ἐπὶ λώβᾳ,
σὺ καὶ τόδε νεῖκος ἀνδρῶν ξύναιμον ἔχεις ταράξας·

414

CHORUS LEADER
  My lord, Haemon left in such a hurry.
  He's angry—in a young man at his age
  the mind turns bitter when he's feeling hurt.

CREON
  Let him dream up or carry out great deeds
  beyond the power of man, he'll not save these girls—
  their fate is sealed.

CHORUS LEADER
                    Are you going to kill them both?   [770]

CREON
  No—not the one whose hands are clean. You're right.

CHORUS LEADER
  How do you plan to kill Antigone?

CREON
  I'll take her on a path no people use,
  and hide her in a cavern in the rocks,
  while still alive. I'll set out provisions,
  as much as piety requires, to make sure
  the city is not totally corrupted.[10]
  Then she can speak her prayers to Hades,
  the only god she worships, for success
  avoiding death—or else, at least, she'll learn,
  although too late, how it's a waste of time
  to work to honour those whom Hades holds.   [780]

CHORUS
  O Eros, the conqueror in every fight,
  Eros, who squanders all men's wealth,
  who sleeps at night on girls' soft cheeks,
  and roams across the ocean seas
  and through the shepherd's hut—
  no immortal god escapes from you,
  nor any man, who lives but for a day.[11]
  And the one whom you possess goes mad.   [790]
  Even in good men you twist their minds,
  perverting them to their own ruin.
  You provoke these men to family strife.

Sophocles

νικᾷ δ' ἐναργὴς βλεφάρων ἵμερος εὐλέκτρου   795
νύμφας, τῶν μεγάλων πάρεδρος ἐν ἀρχαῖς
θεσμῶν. ἄμαχος γὰρ ἐμπαίζει θεὸς, Ἀφροδίτα.   800

— νῦν δ' ἤδη 'γὼ καὐτὸς θεσμῶν
ἔξω φέρομαι τάδ' ὁρῶν ἴσχειν δ'
οὐκέτι πηγὰς δύναμαι δάκρυ
τὸν παγκοίτην ὅθ' ὁρῶ θάλαμον
τήνδ' Ἀντιγόνην ἀνύτουσαν.   805

ΑΝΤΙΓΟΝΗ

ὁρᾶτ' ἔμ', ὦ γᾶς πατρίας πολῖται, τὰν νεάταν ὁδὸν
στείχουσαν, νέατον δὲ φέγγος λεύσσουσαν ἀελίου,
κοὔποτ' αὖθις. ἀλλά μ' ὁ παγκοίτας Ἅιδας ζῶσαν ἄγει
τὰν Ἀχέροντος   812
ἀκτάν, οὔθ' ὑμεναίων ἔγκληρον, οὔτ' ἐπινύμφειός
πώ μέ τις ὕμνος ὕμνησεν, ἀλλ' Ἀχέροντι νυμφεύσω. 815

ΧΟΡΟΣ

οὐκοῦν κλεινὴ καὶ ἔπαινον ἔχουσ'
ἐς τόδ' ἀπέρχει κεῦθος νεκύων,
οὔτε φθινάσιν πληγεῖσα νόσοις
οὔτε ξιφέων ἐπίχειρα λαχοῦσ',   820
ἀλλ' αὐτόνομος ζῶσα μόνη δὴ
θνητῶν Ἅιδην καταβήσει.

ΑΝΤΙΓΟΝΗ

ἤκουσα δὴ λυγρότατον ὀλέσθαι τὰν Φρυγίαν ξέναν
Ταντάλου Σιπύλῳ πρὸς ἄκρῳ, τὰν κισσὸς ὡς ἀτενὴς 825
πετραία βλάστα δάμασεν, καί νιν ὄμβροι τακομέναν,
ὡς φάτις ἀνδρῶν,

416

The bride's desire seen glittering in her eyes—
that conquers everything, its power
enthroned beside eternal laws, for there
the goddess Aphrodite works her will,   [800]
whose ways are irresistible.[12]

[Antigone enters from the palace with attendants who are taking her away to her execution]

CHORAL LEADER

    When I look at her I forget my place.
    I lose restraint and can't hold back my tears—
    Antigone going to her bridal room
    where all are laid to rest in death.

ANTIGONE

    Look at me, my native citizens,
    as I go on my final journey,
    as I gaze upon the sunlight one last time,
    which I'll never see again—for Hades,
    who brings all people to their final sleep,
    leads me on, while I'm still living,   [810]
    down to the shores of Acheron.[13]
    I've not yet had my bridal chant,
    nor has any wedding song been sung—
    for my marriage is to Acheron.

CHORUS

    Surely you carry fame with you and praise,
    as you move to the deep home of the dead.
    You were not stricken by lethal disease
    or paid your wages with a sword.`   [820]
    No. You were in charge of your own fate.
    So of all living human beings, you alone
    make your way down to Hades still alive.

ANTIGONE

    I've heard about a guest of ours,
    daughter of Tantalus, from Phrygia—
    she went to an excruciating death
    in Sipylus, right on the mountain peak.
    The stone there, just like clinging ivy,
    wore her down, and now, so people say,

χιών τ᾽ οὐδαμὰ λείπει, τέγγει δ᾽ ὑπ᾽ ὀφρύσι
παγκλαύτοις   830
δειράδας· με δαίμων ὁμοιοτάταν κατευνάζει.

ΧΟΡΟΣ
ἀλλὰ θεός τοι καὶ θεογεννής,
ἡμεῖς δὲ βροτοὶ καὶ θνητογενεῖς.   835
καίτοι φθιμένῃ μέγα κἀκοῦσαι
τοῖς ἰσοθέοις σύγκληρα λαχεῖν.
ζῶσαν καὶ ἔπειτα θανοῦσαν.

ΑΝΤΙΓΟΝΗ
οἴμοι γελῶμαι. τί με, πρὸς θεῶν πατρῴων.
οὐκ οἰχομέναν ὑβρίζεις, ἀλλ᾽ ἐπίφαντον;   840
ὦ πόλις, ὦ πόλεως πολυκτήμονες ἄνδρες·
ἰὼ Διρκαῖαι κρῆναι
Θήβας τ᾽ εὐαρμάτου ἄλσος, ἔμπας ξυμμάρτυρας ὔμμ᾽
ἐπικτῶμαι,   845
οἷα φίλων ἄκλαυτος, οἵοις νόμοις
πρὸς ἔργμα τυμβόχωστον ἔρχομαι τάφου ποταινίου·
ἰὼ δύστανος, βροτοῖς οὔτε νεκροῖς κυροῦσα   850
μέτοικος οὐ ζῶσιν, οὐ θανοῦσιν.

ΧΟΡΟΣ
προβᾶσ᾽ ἐπ᾽ ἔσχατον θράσους
ὑψηλὸν ἐς Δίκας βάθρον
προσέπεσες, ὦ τέκνον, πολύ·   855
πατρῷον δ᾽ ἐκτίνεις τιν᾽ ἆθλον.

ΑΝΤΙΓΟΝΗ
ἔψαυσας ἀλγεινοτάτας ἐμοὶ μερίμνας,
πατρὸς τριπόλιστον οἶκτον τοῦ τε πρόπαντος
ἁμετέρου πότμου κλεινοῖς Λαβδακίδαισιν.   860
ἰὼ ματρῷαι λέκτρων
ἆται κοιμήματά τ᾽ αὐτογέννητ᾽ ἐμῷ πατρὶ δυσμόρου
ματρός,   865

the snow and rain never leave her there,   [830]
as she laments. Below her weeping eyes
her neck is wet with tears. God brings me
to a final rest which most resembles hers.

CHORUS

But Niobe was a goddess, born divine—
and we are human beings, a race which dies.
But still, it's a fine thing for a woman,
once she's dead, to have it said she shared,
in life and death, the fate of demi-gods.[14]

ANTIGONE

Oh, you are mocking me! Why me—
by our fathers' gods—why do you all,
my own city and the richest men of Thebes,
insult me now right to my face,
without waiting for my death?
Well at least I have Dirce's springs,
the holy grounds of Thebes,
a city full of splendid chariots,
to witness how no friends lament for me
as I move on—you see the laws
which lead me to my rock-bound prison,
a tomb made just for me. Alas!
In my wretchedness I have no home,   [850]
not with human beings or corpses,
not with the living or the dead.

CHORUS

You pushed your daring to the limit, my child,
and tripped against Justice's high altar—
perhaps your agonies are paying back
some compensation for your father.[15]

ANTIGONE

Now there you touch on my most painful thought—
my father's destiny—always on my mind,
along with that whole fate which sticks to us,   [860]
the splendid house of Labdakos—the curse
arising from a mother's marriage bed,
when she had sex with her own son, my father.

419

οἴων ἐγώ ποθ᾽ ἁ ταλαίφρων ἔφυν·
πρὸς οὓς ἀραῖος ἄγαμος ἅδ᾽ ἐγὼ μέτοικος ἔρχομαι.
ἰὼ δυσπότμων κασίγνητε γάμων κυρήσας,   870
θανὼν ἔτ᾽ οὖσαν κατήναρές με.

ΧΟΡΟΣ
σέβειν μὲν εὐσέβειά τις,
κράτος δ᾽, ὅτῳ κράτος μέλει
παραβατὸν οὐδαμᾷ πέλει·
σὲ δ᾽ αὐτόγνωτος ὤλεσ᾽ ὀργά.   875

ΑΝΤΙΓΟΝΗ
ἄκλαυτος, ἄφιλος, ἀνυμέναιος ταλαίφρων ἄγομαι
τὰν πυμάταν ὁδόν.
οὐκέτι μοι τόδε λαμπάδος ἱερὸν
ὄμμα θέμις ὁρᾶν ταλαίνᾳ·   880
τὸν δ᾽ ἐμὸν πότμον ἀδάκρυτον
οὐδεὶς φίλων στενάζει.

ΚΡΕΩΝ
ἆρ᾽ ἴστ᾽, ἀοιδὰς καὶ γόους πρὸ τοῦ θανεῖν
ὡς οὐδ᾽ ἂν εἷς παύσαιτ᾽ ἄν, εἰ χρείη λέγειν;
οὐκ ἄξεθ᾽ ὡς τάχιστα; καὶ κατηρεφεῖ   885
τύμβῳ περιπτύξαντες, ὡς εἴρηκ᾽ ἐγώ,
ἄφετε μόνην ἔρημον, εἴτε χρῇ θανεῖν
εἴτ᾽ ἐν τοιαύτῃ ζῶσα τυμβεύειν στέγῃ·
ἡμεῖς γὰρ ἁγνοὶ τοὐπὶ τήνδε τὴν κόρην
μετοικίας δ᾽ οὖν τῆς ἄνω στερήσεται.   890

ΑΝΤΙΓΟΝΗ
ὦ τύμβος, ὦ νυμφεῖον, ὦ κατασκαφὴς
οἴκησις ἀείφρουρος, οἷ πορεύομαι
πρὸς τοὺς ἐμαυτῆς, ὧν ἀριθμὸν ἐν νεκροῖς
πλεῖστον δέδεκται Φερσέφασσ᾽ ὀλωλότων·
ὧν λοισθία 'γὼ καὶ κάκιστα δὴ μακρῷ   895
κάτειμι, πρίν μοι μοῖραν ἐξήκειν βίου.
ἐλθοῦσα μέντοι κάρτ᾽ ἐν ἐλπίσιν τρέφω

From what kind of parents was I born,
their wretched daughter? I go to them,
unmarried and accursed, an outcast.
Alas, too, for my brother Polyneices,
who made a fatal marriage and then died—   [870]
and with that death killed me while still alive.[16]

CHORUS

To be piously devout shows reverence,
but powerful men, who in their persons
incorporate authority, cannot bear
anyone to break their rules. Hence, you die
because of your own selfish will.

ANTIGONE

Without lament, without a friend,
and with no marriage song, I'm being led
in this miserable state, along my final road.
So wretched that I no longer have the right   [880]
to look upon the sun, that sacred eye.
But my fate prompts no tears, and no friend mourns.

CREON

Don't you know that no one faced with death
would ever stop the singing and the groans,
if that would help? Take her and shut her up,
as I have ordered, in her tomb's embrace.
And get it done as quickly as you can.
Then leave her there alone, all by herself—
she can sort out whether she wants suicide
or remains alive, buried in a place like that.
As far as she's concerned, we bear no guilt.
But she's lost her place living here with us.[17]   [890]

ANTIGONE

Oh my tomb and bridal chamber—
my eternal hollow dwelling place,
where I go to join my people. Most of them
have perished—Persephone has welcomed them
among the dead.[18] I'm the last one, dying here
the most evil death by far, as I move down
before the time allotted for my life is done.
But I go nourishing the vital hope

φίλη μὲν ἥξειν πατρί, προσφιλὴς δὲ σοί,
μῆτερ, φίλη δὲ σοί, κασίγνητον κάρα·
ἐπεὶ θανόντας αὐτόχειρ ὑμᾶς ἐγὼ   900
ἔλουσα κἀκόσμησα κἀπιτυμβίους
χοὰς ἔδωκα. νῦν δέ Πολύνεικες, τὸ σὸν
δέμας περιστέλλουσα τοιάδ᾽ ἄρνυμαι.
καίτοι σ᾽ ἐγὼ ᾽τίμησα τοῖς φρονοῦσιν εὖ.
οὐ γάρ ποτ᾽ οὔτ᾽ ἄν, εἰ τέκνων μήτηρ ἔφυν,   905
οὔτ᾽ εἰ πόσις μοι κατθανὼν ἐτήκετο,
βίᾳ πολιτῶν τόνδ᾽ ἂν ᾐρόμην πόνον.
τίνος νόμου δὴ ταῦτα πρὸς χάριν λέγω;
πόσις μὲν ἄν μοι κατθανόντος ἄλλος ἦν,
καὶ παῖς ἀπ᾽ ἄλλου φωτός, εἰ τοῦδ᾽ ἤμπλακον,   910
μητρὸς δ᾽ ἐν Ἅιδου καὶ πατρὸς κεκευθότοιν
οὐκ ἔστ᾽ ἀδελφὸς ὅστις ἂν βλάστοι ποτέ.
τοιῷδε μέντοι σ᾽ ἐκπροτιμήσασ᾽ ἐγὼ
νόμῳ Κρέοντι ταῦτ᾽ ἔδοξ᾽ ἁμαρτάνειν
καὶ δεινὰ τολμᾶν, ὦ κασίγνητον κάρα.   915
καὶ νῦν ἄγει με διὰ χερῶν οὕτω λαβὼν
ἄλεκτρον, ἀνυμέναιον, οὔτε του γάμου
μέρος λαχοῦσαν οὔτε παιδείου τροφῆς,
ἀλλ᾽ ὧδ᾽ ἔρημος πρὸς φίλων ἡ δύσμορος
ζῶσ᾽ εἰς θανόντων ἔρχομαι κατασκαφάς.   920
ποίαν παρεξελθοῦσα δαιμόνων δίκην;
τί χρή με τὴν δύστηνον ἐς θεοὺς ἔτι
βλέπειν; τίν᾽ αὐδᾶν ξυμμάχων; ἐπεί γε δὴ
τὴν δυσσέβειαν εὐσεβοῦσ᾽, ἐκτησάμην.
ἀλλ᾽ εἰ μὲν οὖν τάδ᾽ ἐστὶν ἐν θεοῖς καλά,   925
παθόντες ἂν ξυγγνοῖμεν ἡμαρτηκότες·
εἰ δ᾽ οἵδ᾽ ἁμαρτάνουσι, μὴ πλείω κακὰ
πάθοιεν ἢ καὶ δρῶσιν ἐκδίκως ἐμέ.

ΧΟΡΟΣ
ἔτι τῶν αὐτῶν ἀνέμων αὐταὶ
ψυχῆς ῥιπαὶ τήνδε γ᾽ ἔχουσιν.   930

my father will be pleased to see me come,
and you, too, my mother, will welcome me,
as well as you, my own dear brother.
When you died, with my own hands I washed you.   [900]
I arranged your corpse and at the grave mound
poured out libations. But now, Polyneices,
this is my reward for covering your corpse.[19]
However, for wise people I was right
to honour you. I'd never have done it
for children of my own, not as their mother,
nor for a dead husband lying in decay—
no, not in defiance of the citizens.
What law do I appeal to, claiming this?
If my husband died, there'd be another one,
and if I were to lose a child of mine
I'd have another with some other man.   [910]
But since my father and my mother, too,
are hidden away in Hades' house,
I'll never have another living brother.
That was the law I used to honour you.
But Creon thought that I was in the wrong
and acting recklessly for you, my brother.
Now he seizes me by force and leads me here—
no wedding and no bridal song, no share
in married life or raising children.
Instead I go in sorrow to my grave,
without my friends, to die while still alive.   [920]
What holy justice have I violated?
In my wretchedness, why should I still look
up to the gods? Which one can I invoke
to bring me help, when for my reverence
they charge me with impiety? Well, then,
if this is something fine among the gods,
I'll come to recognize that I've done wrong.
But if these people here are being unjust
may they endure no greater punishment
than the injustices they're doing to me.

CHORUS LEADER
The same storm blasts continue to attack
the mind in this young girl.   [930]

ΚΡΕΩΝ

τοιγὰρ τούτων τοῖσιν ἄγουσιν
κλαύμαθ᾽ ὑπάρξει βραδυτῆτος ὕπερ.

ΑΝΤΙΓΟΝΗ

οἴμοι, θανάτου τοῦτ᾽ ἐγγυτάτω
τοὔπος ἀφῖκται.

ΧΟΡΟΣ

θαρσεῖν οὐδὲν παραμυθοῦμαι   935
μὴ οὐ τάδε ταύτῃ κατακυροῦσθαι.

ΑΝΤΙΓΟΝΗ

ὦ γῆς Θήβης ἄστυ πατρῷον
καὶ θεοὶ προγενεῖς,
ἄγομαι δὴ κοὐκέτι μέλλω.
λεύσσετε, Θήβης οἱ κοιρανίδαι   940
τὴν βασιλειδᾶν μούνην λοιπήν,
οἷα πρὸς οἵων ἀνδρῶν πάσχω,
τὴν εὐσεβίαν σεβίσασα.

ΧΟΡΟΣ

ἔτλα καὶ Δανάας οὐράνιον φῶς
ἀλλάξαι δέμας ἐν χαλκοδέτοις αὐλαῖς·   945
κρυπτομένα δ᾽ ἐν τυμβήρει θαλάμῳ κατεζεύχθη·
καίτοι καὶ γενεᾷ τίμιος, ὦ παῖ παῖ,
καὶ Ζηνὸς ταμιεύεσκε γονὰς χρυσορύτους.   950
ἀλλ᾽ ἁ μοιριδία τις δύνασις δεινά·
οὔτ᾽ ἄν νιν ὄλβος οὔτ᾽ Ἄρης, οὐ πύργος, οὐχ ἁλίκτυποι
κελαιναὶ νᾶες ἐκφύγοιεν.

ζεύχθη δ᾽ ὀξύχολος παῖς ὁ Δρύαντος,   955
Ἠδωνῶν βασιλεύς, κερτομίοις ὀργαῖς
ἐκ Διονύσου πετρώδει κατάφαρκτος ἐν δεσμῷ.
οὕτω τᾶς μανίας δεινὸν ἀποστάζει
ἀνθηρόν τε μένος. κεῖνος ἐπέγνω μανίαις   960
ψαύων τὸν θεὸν ἐν κερτομίοις γλώσσαις.

CREON

    Then those escorting her
    will be sorry they're so slow.

ANTIGONE

                        Alas, then,
    those words mean death is very near at hand.

CREON

    I won't encourage you or cheer you up,
    by saying the sentence won't be carried out.

ANTIGONE

    O city of my fathers
    in this land of Thebes—
    and my ancestral gods,
    I am being led away.
    No more delaying for me.
    Look on me, you lords of Thebes,   [940]
    the last survivor of your royal house,
    see what I have to undergo,
    the kind of men who do this to me,
    for paying reverence to true piety.

[Antigone is led away under escort]

CHORUS

    In her brass-bound room fair Danaë as well
    endured her separation from the heaven's light,
    a prisoner hidden in a chamber like a tomb,
    although she, too, came from a noble line.[20]
    And she, my child, had in her care
    the liquid streaming golden seed of Zeus.   [950]
    But the power of fate is full of mystery.
    There's no evading it, no, not with wealth,
    or war, or walls, or black sea-beaten ships.

    And the hot-tempered child of Dryas,
    king of the Edonians, was put in prison,
    closed up in the rocks by Dionysus,
    for his angry mocking of the god.[21]
    There the dreadful flower of his rage   [960]
    slowly withered, and he came to know
    the god who in his frenzy he had mocked
    with his own tongue. For he had tried

Sophocles

παύεσκε μὲν γὰρ ἐνθέους γυναῖκας εὐιόν τε πῦρ,
φιλαύλους τ᾽ ἠρέθιζε Μούσας.   965

παρὰ δὲ κυανεᾶν πελάγει διδύμας ἁλὸς
ἀκταὶ Βοσπόριαι ἤδ᾽ ὁ Θρῃκῶν ἄξενος
Σαλμυδησσός, ἵν᾽ ἀγχίπτολις Ἄρης   970
δισσοῖσι Φινείδαις
εἶδεν ἀρατὸν ἕλκος
τυφλωθὲν ἐξ ἀγρίας δάμαρτος
ἀλαὸν ἀλαστόροισιν ὀμμάτων κύκλοις
ἀραχθέντων, ὑφ᾽ αἱματηραῖς   975
χείρεσσι καὶ κερκίδων ἀκμαῖσιν.

κατὰ δὲ τακόμενοι μέλεοι μελέαν πάθαν
κλαῖον, ματρὸς ἔχοντες ἀνύμφευτον γονάν·   980
ἁ δὲ σπέρμα μὲν ἀρχαιογόνων
ἄντασ᾽ Ἐρεχθειδᾶν,
τηλεπόροις δ᾽ ἐν ἄντροις
τράφη θυέλλαισιν ἐν πατρῴαις
Βορεὰς ἄμιππος ὀρθόποδος ὑπὲρ πάγου   985
θεῶν παῖς. ἀλλὰ κἀπ᾽ ἐκείνᾳ
Μοῖραι μακραίωνες ἔσχον, ὦ παῖ.

ΤΕΙΡΕΣΙΑΣ
Θήβης ἄνακτες, ἥκομεν κοινὴν ὁδὸν
δύ᾽ ἐξ ἑνὸς βλέποντε· τοῖς τυφλοῖσι γὰρ
αὕτη κέλευθος ἐκ προηγητοῦ πέλει.   990

ΚΡΕΩΝ
τί δ᾽ ἔστιν, ὦ γεραιὲ Τειρεσία, νέον;

ΤΕΙΡΕΣΙΑΣ
ἐγὼ διδάξω, καὶ σὺ τῷ μάντει πιθοῦ.

ΚΡΕΩΝ
οὔκουν πάρος γε σῆς ἀπεστάτουν φρενός.

ΤΕΙΡΕΣΙΑΣ
τοιγὰρ δι᾽ ὀρθῆς τήνδ᾽ ἐναυκλήρεις πόλιν.

426

to hold in check women in that frenzy
inspired by the god, the Bacchanalian fire.
More than that—he'd made the Muses angry,
challenging the gods who love the flute.[22]

Beside the black rocks where the twin seas meet,
by Thracian Salmydessos at the Bosphorus,
close to the place where Ares dwells,   [970]
the war god witnessed the unholy wounds
which blinded the two sons of Phineus,
inflicted by his savage wife—the sightless holes
cried out for someone to avenge those blows
made with her sharpened comb in blood-stained hands.[23]

In their misery they wept, lamenting
their wretched suffering, sons of a mother
whose marriage had gone wrong. And yet,   [980]
she was an offspring of an ancient family,
the race of Erechtheus, raised far away,
in caves surrounded by her father's winds,
Boreas' child, a girl who raced with horses
across steep hills—child of the gods.
But she, too, my child, suffered much
from the immortal Fates.[24]

[Enter Teiresias, led by a young boy]

TEIRESIAS
    Lords of Thebes, we two have walked a common path,
    one person's vision serving both of us.
    The blind require a guide to find their way.   [990]

CREON
    What news do you have, old Teiresias?

TEIRESIAS
    I'll tell you—and you obey the prophet.

CREON
    I've not rejected your advice before.

TEIRESIAS
    That's the reason why you've steered the city
    on its proper course.

Sophocles

ΚΡΕΩΝ

ἔχω πεπονθὼς μαρτυρεῖν ὀνήσιμα.   995

ΤΕΙΡΕΣΙΑΣ

φρόνει βεβὼς αὖ νῦν ἐπὶ ξυροῦ τύχης.

ΚΡΕΩΝ

τί δ᾽ ἔστιν; ὡς ἐγὼ τὸ σὸν φρίσσω στόμα.

ΤΕΙΡΕΣΙΑΣ

γνώσει, τέχνης σημεῖα τῆς ἐμῆς κλύων.
εἰς γὰρ παλαιὸν θᾶκον ὀρνιθοσκόπον
ἵζων, ἵν᾽ ἦν μοι παντὸς οἰωνοῦ λιμήν,   1000
ἀγνῶτ᾽ ἀκούω φθόγγον ὀρνίθων, κακῷ
κλάζοντας οἴστρῳ καὶ βεβαρβαρωμένῳ.
καὶ σπῶντας ἐν χηλαῖσιν ἀλλήλους φοναῖς
ἔγνων· πτερῶν γὰρ ῥοῖβδος οὐκ ἄσημος ἦν.
εὐθὺς δὲ δείσας ἐμπύρων ἐγευόμην   1005
βωμοῖσι παμφλέκτοισιν· ἐκ δὲ θυμάτων
Ἥφαιστος οὐκ ἔλαμπεν, ἀλλ᾽ ἐπὶ σποδῷ
μυδῶσα κηκὶς μηρίων ἐτήκετο
κἄτυφε κἀνέπτυε, καὶ μετάρσιοι
χολαὶ διεσπείροντο, καὶ καταρρυεῖς   1010
μηροὶ καλυπτῆς ἐξέκειντο πιμελῆς.
τοιαῦτα παιδὸς τοῦδ᾽ ἐμάνθανον πάρα,
φθίνοντ᾽ ἀσήμων ὀργίων μαντεύματα.
ἐμοὶ γὰρ οὗτος ἡγεμών, ἄλλοις δ᾽ ἐγώ.
καὶ ταῦτα τῆς σῆς ἐκ φρενὸς νοσεῖ πόλις.   1015
βωμοὶ γὰρ ἡμῖν ἐσχάραι τε παντελεῖς
πλήρεις ὑπ᾽ οἰωνῶν τε καὶ κυνῶν βορᾶς
τοῦ δυσμόρου πεπτῶτος Οἰδίπου γόνου.
κᾆτ᾽ οὐ δέχονται θυστάδας λιτὰς ἔτι
θεοὶ παρ᾽ ἡμῶν οὐδὲ μηρίων φλόγα,   1020
οὐδ᾽ ὄρνις εὐσήμους ἀπορροιβδεῖ βοάς
ἀνδροφθόρου βεβρῶτες αἵματος λίπος.
ταῦτ᾽ οὖν, τέκνον, φρόνησον. ἀνθρώποισι γὰρ
τοῖς πᾶσι κοινόν ἐστι τοὐξαμαρτάνειν·

CREON
                        From my experience
I can confirm the help you give.

TEIRESIAS
                        Then know this—
your luck is once more on Fate's razor edge.

CREON
What? What you've just said makes me nervous.

TEIRESIAS
You'll know—once you hear the tokens of my art.
As I was sitting in my ancient place
receiving omens from the flights of birds
who all come there where I can hear them,   [1000]
I note among those birds an unknown cry—
evil, unintelligible, angry screaming.
I knew that they were tearing at each other
with murderous claws. The noisy wings
revealed that all too well. I was afraid.
So right away up on the blazing altar
I set up burnt offerings. But Hephaestus
failed to shine out from the sacrifice—
dark slime poured out onto the embers,
oozing from the thighs, which smoked and spat,
bile was sprayed high up into the air,   [1010]
and the melting thighs lost all the fat
which they'd been wrapped in. The rites had failed—
there was no prophecy revealed in them.
I learned that from this boy, who is my guide,
as I guide other men.25 Our state is sick—
your policies have done this. In the city
our altars and our hearths have been defiled,
all of them, with rotting flesh brought there
by birds and dogs from Oedipus' son,
who lies there miserably dead. The gods
no longer will accept our sacrifice,
our prayers, our thigh bones burned in fire.   [1020]
No bird will shriek out a clear sign to us,
for they have gorged themselves on fat and blood
from a man who's dead. Consider this, my son.
All men make mistakes—that's not uncommon.

ἐπεὶ δ' ἁμάρτῃ, κεῖνος οὐκέτ' ἔστ' ἀνὴρ   1025
ἄβουλος οὐδ' ἄνολβος, ὅστις ἐς κακὸν
πεσὼν ἀκῆται μηδ' ἀκίνητος πέλῃ.
αὐθαδία τοι σκαιότητ' ὀφλισκάνει.
ἀλλ' εἶκε τῷ θανόντι μηδ' ὀλωλότα
κέντει· τίς ἀλκὴ τὸν θανόντ' ἐπικτανεῖν;   1030
εὖ σοι φρονήσας εὖ λέγω. τὸ μανθάνειν δ'
ἥδιστον εὖ λέγοντος, εἰ κέρδος λέγοι.

ΚΡΕΩΝ

ὦ πρέσβυ, πάντες ὥστε τοξόται σκοποῦ
τοξεύετ' ἀνδρὸς τοῦδε, κοὐδὲ μαντικῆς
ἄπρακτος ὑμῖν εἰμι· τῶν δ' ὑπαὶ γένους   1035
ἐξημπόλημαι κἀμπεφόρτισμαι πάλαι.
κερδαίνετ', ἐμπολᾶτε τἀπὸ Σάρδεων
ἤλεκτρον, εἰ βούλεσθε, καὶ τὸν Ἰνδικὸν
χρυσόν· τάφῳ δ' ἐκεῖνον οὐχὶ κρύψετε,
οὐδ' εἰ θέλουσ', οἱ Ζηνὸς αἰετοὶ βορὰν   1040
φέρειν νιν ἁρπάζοντες ἐς Διὸς θρόνους,
οὐδ' ὡς μίασμα τοῦτο μὴ τρέσας ἐγὼ
θάπτειν παρήσω κεῖνον· εὖ γὰρ οἶδ' ὅτι
θεοὺς μιαίνειν οὔτις ἀνθρώπων σθένει.
πίπτουσι δ', ὦ γεραιὲ Τειρεσία, βροτῶν   1045
χοὶ πολλὰ δεινοὶ πτώματ' αἴσχρ', ὅταν λόγους
αἰσχροὺς καλῶς λέγωσι τοῦ κέρδους χάριν.

ΤΕΙΡΕΣΙΑΣ

φεῦ·
ἆρ' οἶδεν ἀνθρώπων τις, ἆρα φράζεται,

ΚΡΕΩΝ

τί χρῆμα; ποῖον τοῦτο πάγκοινον λέγεις;

ΤΕΙΡΕΣΙΑΣ

ὅσῳ κράτιστον κτημάτων εὐβουλία;   1050

But when they do, they're no longer foolish
or subject to bad luck if they try to fix
the evil into which they've fallen,
once they give up their intransigence.
Men who put their stubbornness on show
invite accusations of stupidity.
Make concessions to the dead—don't ever stab
a man who's just been killed. What's the glory
in killing a dead person one more time?   [1030]
I've been concerned for you. It's good advice.
Learning can be pleasant when a man speaks well,
especially when he seeks your benefit.

CREON
Old man, you're all like archers shooting at me—
For you all I've now become your target—
even prophets have been aiming at me.
I've long been bought and sold as merchandise
among that tribe. Well, go make your profits.
If it's what you want, then trade with Sardis
for their golden-silver alloy—or for gold
from India, but you'll never hide that corpse
in any grave. Even if Zeus' eagles   [1040]
should choose to seize his festering body
and take it up, right to the throne of Zeus,
not even then would I, in trembling fear
of some defilement, permit that corpse
a burial. For I know well that no man
has the power to pollute the gods.
But, old Teiresias, among human beings
the wisest suffer a disgraceful fall
when, to promote themselves, they use fine words
to spread around abusive insults.

TEIRESIAS
Alas, does any man know or think about . . .

Creon *[interrupting]*
Think what? What sort of pithy common thought
are you about to utter?

TEIRESIAS *[ignoring the interruption]*
                              . . . how good advice
is valuable—worth more than all possessions.   [1050]

431

ΚΡΕΩΝ

ὅσωπερ, οἶμαι, μὴ φρονεῖν πλείστη βλάβη.

ΤΕΙΡΕΣΙΑΣ

ταύτης σὺ μέντοι τῆς νόσου πλήρης ἔφυς.

ΚΡΕΩΝ

οὐ βούλομαι τὸν μάντιν ἀντειπεῖν κακῶς.

ΤΕΙΡΕΣΙΑΣ

καὶ μὴν λέγεις, ψευδῆ με θεσπίζειν λέγων.

ΚΡΕΩΝ

τὸ μαντικὸν γὰρ πᾶν φιλάργυρον γένος.   1055

ΤΕΙΡΕΣΙΑΣ

τὸ δ' ἐκ τυράννων αἰσχροκέρδειαν φιλεῖ.

ΚΡΕΩΝ

ἆρ' οἶσθα ταγοὺς ὄντας ἃν λέγῃς λέγων;

ΤΕΙΡΕΣΙΑΣ

οἶδ'· ἐξ ἐμοῦ γὰρ τήνδ' ἔχεις σώσας πόλιν.

ΚΡΕΩΝ

σοφὸς σὺ μάντις, ἀλλὰ τἀδικεῖν φιλῶν.

ΤΕΙΡΕΣΙΑΣ

ὄρσεις με τἀκίνητα διὰ φρενῶν φράσαι.   1060

ΚΡΕΩΝ

κίνει, μόνον δὲ μὴ 'πὶ κέρδεσιν λέγων.

ΤΕΙΡΕΣΙΑΣ

οὕτω γὰρ ἤδη καὶ δοκῶ τὸ σὸν μέρος.

CREON

    I think that's true, as much as foolishness
    is what harms us most.

TEIRESIAS

                Yet that's the sickness
    now infecting you.

CREON

                I have no desire
    to denigrate a prophet when I speak.

TEIRESIAS

    But that's what you are doing, when you claim
    my oracles are false.

CREON

              The tribe of prophets—
    all of them—are fond of money

TEIRESIAS

                And kings?
    Their tribe loves to benefit dishonestly.

CREON

    You know you're speaking of the man who rules you.

TEIRESIAS

    I know—thanks to me you saved the city
    and now are in control.[26]

CREON

           You're a wise prophet,
    but you love doing wrong.

TEIRESIAS

           You'll force me
    to speak of secrets locked inside my heart.   [1060]

CREON

    Do it—just don't speak to benefit yourself.

TEIRESIAS

    I don't think that I'll be doing that—
    not as far as you're concerned.

ΚΡΕΩΝ

ὡς μὴ 'μπολήσων ἴσθι τὴν ἐμὴν φρένα.

ΤΕΙΡΕΣΙΑΣ

ἀλλ' εὖ γέ τοι κάτισθι μὴ πολλοὺς ἔτι
τρόχους ἁμιλλητῆρας ἡλίου τελεῖν,   1065
ἐν οἷσι τῶν σῶν αὐτὸς ἐκ σπλάγχνων ἕνα
νέκυν νεκρῶν ἀμοιβὸν ἀντιδοὺς ἔσει,
ἀνθ' ὧν ἔχεις μὲν τῶν ἄνω βαλὼν κάτω
ψυχήν τ' ἀτίμως ἐν τάφῳ κατῴκισας,
ἔχεις δὲ τῶν κάτωθεν ἐνθάδ' αὖ θεῶν   1070
ἄμοιρον, ἀκτέριστον, ἀνόσιον νέκυν.
ὧν οὔτε σοὶ μέτεστιν οὔτε τοῖς ἄνω
θεοῖσιν, ἀλλ' ἐκ σοῦ βιάζονται τάδε.
τούτων σε λωβητῆρες ὑστεροφθόροι
λοχῶσιν Ἅιδου καὶ θεῶν Ἐρινύες,   1075
ἐν τοῖσιν αὐτοῖς τοῖσδε ληφθῆναι κακοῖς.
καὶ ταῦτ' ἄθρησον εἰ κατηργυρωμένος
λέγω· φανεῖ γὰρ οὐ μακροῦ χρόνου τριβὴ
ἀνδρῶν γυναικῶν σοῖς δόμοις κωκύματα.
ἐχθραὶ δὲ πᾶσαι συνταράσσονται πόλεις,   1080
ὅσων σπαράγματ' ἢ κύνες καθήγνισαν
ἢ θῆρες ἤ τις πτηνὸς οἰωνός, φέρων
ἀνόσιον ὀσμὴν ἑστιοῦχον ἐς πόλιν.
τοιαῦτά σου, λυπεῖς γάρ, ὥστε τοξότης
ἀφῆκα θυμῷ, καρδίας τοξεύματα   1085
βέβαια, τῶν σὺ θάλπος οὐχ ὑπεκδραμεῖ.
ὦ παῖ, σὺ δ' ἡμᾶς ἄπαγε πρὸς δόμους, ἵνα
τὸν θυμὸν οὗτος ἐς νεωτέρους ἀφῇ,
καὶ γνῷ τρέφειν τὴν γλῶσσαν ἡσυχαιτέραν
τὸν νοῦν τ' ἀμείνω τῶν φρενῶν ἢ νῦν φέρει.   1090

ΧΟΡΟΣ

ἀνήρ, ἄναξ, βέβηκε δεινὰ θεσπίσας·
ἐπιστάμεσθα δ', ἐξ ὅτου λευκὴν ἐγὼ
τήνδ' ἐκ μελαίνης ἀμφιβάλλομαι τρίχα,
μή πώ ποτ' αὐτὸν ψεῦδος ἐς πόλιν λακεῖν.

CREON

You can be sure

you won't change my mind to make yourself more rich.

TEIRESIAS

Then understand this well—you will not see
the sun race through its cycle many times
before you lose a child of your own loins,
a corpse in payment for these corpses.
You've thrown down to those below someone
from up above—in your arrogance
you've moved a living soul into a grave,
leaving here a body owned by gods below— [1070]
unburied, dispossessed, unsanctified.
That's no concern of yours or gods above.
In this you violate the ones below.
And so destroying avengers wait for you,
Furies of Hades and the gods, who'll see
you caught up in this very wickedness.
Now see if I speak as someone who's been bribed.
It won't be long before in your own house
the men and women all cry out in sorrow,
and cities rise in hate against you—all those [1080]
whose mangled soldiers have had burial rites
from dogs, wild animals, or flying birds
who carry the unholy stench back home,
to every city hearth.[27] Like an archer,
I shoot these arrows now into your heart
because you have provoked me. I'm angry—
so my aim is good. You'll not escape their pain.
Boy, lead us home so he can vent his rage
on younger men and keep a quieter tongue
and a more temperate mind than he has now. [1090]

[Exit Teiresias, led by the young boy]

CHORUS LEADER

My lord, my lord, such dreadful prophecies—
and now he's gone. Since my hair changed colour
from black to white, I know here in the city
he's never uttered a false prophecy.

435

ΚΡΕΩΝ

ἔγνωκα καὐτὸς καὶ ταράσσομαι φρένας.　　1095
τό τ᾽ εἰκαθεῖν γὰρ δεινόν, ἀντιστάντα δὲ
ἄτῃ πατάξαι θυμὸν ἐν δεινῷ πάρα.

ΧΟΡΟΣ

εὐβουλίας δεῖ, παῖ Μενοικέως, λαβεῖν.

ΚΡΕΩΝ

τί δῆτα χρὴ δρᾶν; φράζε. πείσομαι δ᾽ ἐγώ.

ΧΟΡΟΣ

ἐλθὼν κόρην μὲν ἐκ κατώρυχος στέγης　　1100
ἄνες, κτίσον δὲ τῷ προκειμένῳ, τάφον.

ΚΡΕΩΝ

καὶ ταῦτ᾽ ἐπαινεῖς καὶ δοκεῖς παρεικαθεῖν;

ΧΟΡΟΣ

ὅσον γ᾽, ἄναξ, τάχιστα· συντέμνουσι γὰρ
θεῶν ποδώκεις τοὺς κακόφρονας βλάβαι.

ΚΡΕΩΝ

οἴμοι· μόλις μέν, καρδίας δ᾽ ἐξίσταμαι　　1105
τὸ δρᾶν· ἀνάγκῃ δ᾽ οὐχὶ δυσμαχητέον.

ΧΟΡΟΣ

δρᾶ νυν τάδ᾽ ἐλθὼν μηδ᾽ ἐπ᾽ ἄλλοισιν τρέπε.

ΚΡΕΩΝ

ὧδ᾽ ὡς ἔχω στείχοιμ᾽ ἄν· ἴτ᾽ ἴτ᾽ ὀπάονες,
οἵ τ᾽ ὄντες οἵ τ᾽ ἀπόντες, ἀξίνας χεροῖν
ὁρμᾶσθ᾽ ἑλόντες εἰς ἐπόψιον τόπον.　　1110
ἐγὼ δ᾽, ἐπειδὴ δόξα τῇδ᾽ ἐπεστράφη,
αὐτός τ᾽ ἔδησα καὶ παρὼν ἐκλύσομαι.
δέδοικα γὰρ μὴ τοὺς καθεστῶτας νόμους
ἄριστον ᾖ σῴζοντα τὸν βίον τελεῖν.

CREON

    I know that, too—and it disturbs my mind.
    It's dreadful to give way, but to resist
    and let destruction hammer down my spirit—
    that's a fearful option, too.

CHORUS LEADER

                    Son of Menoikeos,
    you need to listen to some good advice.

CREON

    Tell me what to do. Speak up. I'll do it.

CHORUS LEADER

    Go and release the girl from her rock tomb.   [1100]
    Then prepare a grave for that unburied corpse.

CREON

    This is your advice? You think I should concede?

CHORUS LEADER

    Yes, my lord, as fast as possible.
    Swift footed injuries sent from the gods
    hack down those who act imprudently.

CREON

    Alas—it's difficult. But I'll give up.
    I'll not do what I'd set my heart upon.
    It's not right to fight against necessity.

CHORUS LEADER

    Go now and get this done. Don't give the work
    to other men to do.

CREON

                    I'll go just as I am.
    Come, you servants, each and every one of you.
    Come on. Bring axes with you. Go there quickly—
    up to the higher ground. I've changed my mind.   [1110]
    Since I'm the one who tied her up, I'll go
    and set her free myself. Now I'm afraid.
    Until one dies the best thing well may be
    to follow our established laws.

[Creon and his attendants hurry off stage]

Sophocles

ΧΟΡΟΣ
πολυώνυμε, Καδμείας νύμφας ἄγαλμα   1115
καὶ Διὸς βαρυβρεμέτα
γένος, κλυτὰν ὃς ἀμφέπεις
Ἰταλίαν, μέδεις δὲ
παγκοίνοις, Ἐλευσινίας
Δηοῦς ἐν κόλποις, Βακχεῦ Βακχᾶν   1120
ὁ ματρόπολιν Θήβαν
ναιετῶν παρ' ὑγρῶν
Ἰσμηνοῦ ῥείθρων ἀγρίου τ' ἐπὶ σπορᾷ δράκοντος·   1125

σὲ δ' ὑπὲρ διλόφου πέτρας στέροψ ὄπωπε
λιγνύς, ἔνθα Κωρύκιαι
στείχουσι νύμφαι Βακχίδες,
Κασταλίας τε νᾶμα.   1130
καί σε Νυσαίων ὀρέων
κισσήρεις ὄχθαι χλωρά τ' ἀκτὰ
πολυστάφυλος πέμπει,
ἀμβρότων ἐπέων
εὐαζόντων Θηβαΐας ἐπισκοποῦντ' ἀγυιάς·   1135

τὰν ἐκ πᾶσαι τιμᾷς ὑπερτάταν πόλεων
ματρὶ σὺν κεραυνίᾳ·
καὶ νῦν, ὡς βιαίας ἔχεται   1140
πάνδαμος πόλις ἐπὶ νόσου,
μολεῖν καθαρσίῳ ποδὶ Παρνασίαν ὑπὲρ κλιτὺν
ἢ στονόεντα πορθμόν.   1145

ἰὼ πῦρ πνειόντων χοράγ' ἄστρων, νυχίων
φθεγμάτων ἐπίσκοπε,
παῖ Διὸς γένεθλον, προφάνηθ'
ὦναξ, σαῖς ἅμα περιπόλοις   1150
Θυίαισιν, αἵ σε μαινόμεναι πάννυχοι χορεύουσι
τὸν ταμίαν Ἴακχον.

CHORUS
    O you with many names,
    you glory of that Theban bride,
    and child of thundering Zeus,
    you who cherish famous Italy,
    and rule the welcoming valley lands
    of Eleusianian Deo—
    O Bacchus—you who dwell
    in the bacchants' mother city Thebes,
    beside Ismenus' flowing streams,
    on land sown with the teeth
    of that fierce dragon.[28]

    Above the double mountain peaks,
    the torches flashing through the murky smoke
    have seen you where Corycian nymphs
    move on as they worship you
    by the Kastalian stream.   [1130]
    And from the ivy-covered slopes
    of Nysa's hills, from the green shore
    so rich in vines, you come to us,
    visiting our Theban ways,
    while deathless voices all cry out
    in honour of your name, "Evoë."[29]

    You honour Thebes, our city,
    above all others, you and your mother
    blasted by that lightning strike.[30]
    And now when all our people here   [1140]
    are captive to a foul disease,
    on your healing feet you come
    across the moaning strait
    or over the Parnassian hill.

    You who lead the dance,
    among the fire-breathing stars,
    who guard the voices in the night,
    child born of Zeus, oh my lord,   [1150]
    appear with your attendant Thyiads,
    who dance in frenzy all night long,
    for you their patron, Iacchus.[31]

[Enter a Messenger]

Sophocles

ΑΓΓΕΛΟΣ

Κάδμου πάροικοι καὶ δόμων Ἀμφίονος,   1155
οὐκ ἔσθ᾽ ὁποῖον στάντ᾽ ἂν ἀνθρώπου βίον
οὔτ᾽ αἰνέσαιμ᾽ ἂν οὔτε μεμψαίμην ποτέ.
τύχη γὰρ ὀρθοῖ καὶ τύχη καταρρέπει
τὸν εὐτυχοῦντα τόν τε δυστυχοῦντ᾽ ἀεί·
καὶ μάντις οὐδεὶς τῶν καθεστώτων βροτοῖς.   1160
Κρέων γὰρ ἦν ζηλωτός, ὡς ἐμοί, ποτέ,
σώσας μὲν ἐχθρῶν τήνδε Καδμείαν χθόνα
λαβών τε χώρας παντελῆ μοναρχίαν
ηὔθυνε, θάλλων εὐγενεῖ τέκνων σπορᾷ·
καὶ νῦν ἀφεῖται πάντα. τὰς γὰρ ἡδονὰς   1165
ὅταν προδῶσιν ἄνδρες, οὐ τίθημ᾽ ἐγὼ
ζῆν τοῦτον, ἀλλ᾽ ἔμψυχον ἡγοῦμαι νεκρόν.
πλούτει τε γὰρ κατ᾽ οἶκον, εἰ βούλει, μέγα
καὶ ζῆ τύραννον σχῆμ᾽ ἔχων· ἐὰν δ᾽ ἀπῇ
τούτων τὸ χαίρειν, τἄλλ᾽ ἐγὼ καπνοῦ σκιᾶς   1170
οὐκ ἂν πριαίμην ἀνδρὶ πρὸς τὴν ἡδονήν.

ΧΟΡΟΣ

τί δ᾽ αὖ τόδ᾽ ἄχθος βασιλέων ἥκεις φέρων;

ΑΓΓΕΛΟΣ

τεθνᾶσιν. οἱ δὲ ζῶντες αἴτιοι θανεῖν.

ΧΟΡΟΣ

καὶ τίς φονεύει; τίς δ᾽ ὁ κείμενος; λέγε.

ΑΓΓΕΛΟΣ

Αἵμων ὄλωλεν· αὐτόχειρ δ᾽ αἱμάσσεται.   1175

ΧΟΡΟΣ

πότερα πατρῴας ἢ πρὸς οἰκείας χερός;

MESSENGER

    All you here who live beside the home
    of Amphion and Cadmus—in human life
    there's no set place which I would praise or blame.[32]
    The lucky and unlucky rise or fall
    by chance day after day—and how these things
    are fixed for men no one can prophesy.   [1160]
    For Creon, in my view, was once a man
    we all looked up to. For he saved the state,
    this land of Cadmus, from its enemies.
    He took control and reigned as its sole king—
    and prospered with the birth of noble children.
    Now all is gone. For when a man has lost
    what gives him pleasure, I don't include him
    among the living—he's a breathing corpse.
    Pile up a massive fortune in your home,
    if that's what you want—live like a king.
    If there's no pleasure in it, I'd not give
    to any man a vapour's shadow for it,   [1170]
    not compared to human joy.

CHORUS LEADER

    Have you come with news of some fresh trouble
    in our house of kings?

MESSENGER

                    They're dead—
    and those alive bear the responsibility
    for those who've died.

CHORUS LEADER

              Who did the killing?
    Who's lying dead? Tell us.

MESSENGER

                Haemon has been killed.
    No stranger shed his blood.

CHORUS LEADER

             At his father's hand?
    Or did he kill himself?

ΑΓΓΕΛΟΣ

αὐτὸς πρὸς αὑτοῦ, πατρὶ μηνίσας φόνου.

ΧΟΡΟΣ

ὦ μάντι, τοὔπος ὡς ἄρ' ὀρθὸν ἤνυσας.

ΑΓΓΕΛΟΣ

ὡς ὧδ' ἐχόντων τἄλλα βουλεύειν πάρα.

ΧΟΡΟΣ

καὶ μὴν ὁρῶ τάλαιναν Εὐρυδίκην ὁμοῦ   1180
δάμαρτα τὴν Κρέοντος. ἐκ δὲ δωμάτων
ἤτοι κλύουσα παιδὸς ἢ τύχῃ πάρα.

ΕΥΡΥΔΙΚΗ

ὦ πάντες ἀστοί, τῶν λόγων ἐπῃσθόμην
πρὸς ἔξοδον στείχουσα, Παλλάδος θεᾶς
ὅπως ἱκοίμην εὐγμάτων προσήγορος.   1185
καὶ τυγχάνω τε κλῇθρ' ἀνασπαστοῦ πύλης
χαλῶσα καί με φθόγγος οἰκείου κακοῦ
βάλλει δι' ὤτων· ὑπτία δὲ κλίνομαι
δείσασα πρὸς δμωαῖσι κἀποπλήσσομαι
ἀλλ' ὅστις ἦν ὁ μῦθος αὖθις εἴπατε·   1190
κακῶν γὰρ οὐκ ἄπειρος οὖσ' ἀκούσομαι.

ΑΓΓΕΛΟΣ

ἐγώ, φίλη δέσποινα, καὶ παρὼν ἐρῶ
κοὐδὲν παρήσω τῆς ἀληθείας ἔπος.
τί γάρ σε μαλθάσσοιμ' ἂν ὧν ἐς ὕστερον
ψεῦσται φανούμεθ'; ὀρθὸν ἀλήθει' ἀεί.   1195
ἐγὼ δὲ σῷ ποδαγὸς ἑσπόμην πόσει
πεδίον ἐπ' ἄκρον, ἔνθ' ἔκειτο νηλεὲς
κυνοσπάρακτον σῶμα Πολυνείκους ἔτι·
καὶ τὸν μέν, αἰτήσαντες ἐνοδίαν θεὸν
Πλούτωνά τ' ὀργὰς εὐμενεῖς κατασχεθεῖν   1200
λούσαντες ἁγνὸν λουτρόν, ἐν νεοσπάσιν
θαλλοῖς ὃ δὴ λέλειπτο συγκατῄθομεν,
καὶ τύμβον ὀρθόκρανον οἰκείας χθονὸς
χώσαντες αὖθις πρὸς λιθόστρωτον κόρης
νυμφεῖον Ἅιδου κοῖλον εἰσεβαίνομεν.   1205

MESSENGER

                    By his own hand—
    angry at his father for the murder.

CHORUS LEADER
    Teiresias, how your words have proven true!

MESSENGER
    That's how things stand. Consider what comes next.

CHORUS LEADER
    I see Creon's wife, poor Eurydice—   [1180]
    she's coming from the house—either by chance,
    or else she's heard there's news about her son.

[Enter Eurydice from the palace with some attendants]

EURYDICE
    Citizens of Thebes, I heard you talking,
    as I was walking out, going off to pray,
    to ask for help from goddess Pallas.
    While I was unfastening the gate,
    I heard someone speaking of bad news
    about my family. I was terrified.
    I collapsed, fainting back into the arms
    of my attendants. So tell the news again—   [1190]
    I'll listen. I'm no stranger to misfortune.

MESSENGER
    Dear lady, I'll speak of what I saw,
    omitting not one detail of the truth.
    Why should I ease your mind with a report
    which turns out later to be incorrect?
    The truth is always best. I went to the plain,
    accompanying your husband as his guide.
    Polyneices' corpse, still unlamented,
    was lying there, the greatest distance off,
    torn apart by dogs. We prayed to Pluto
    and to Hecate, goddess of the road,
    for their good will and to restrain their rage.   [1200]
    We gave the corpse a ritual wash, and burned
    what was left of it on fresh-cut branches.
    We piled up a high tomb of his native earth.
    Then we moved to the young girl's rocky cave,
    the hollow cavern of that bride of death.

Sophocles

φωνῆς δ᾽ ἄπωθεν ὀρθίων κωκυμάτων
κλύει τις ἀκτέριστον ἀμφὶ παστάδα,
καὶ δεσπότῃ Κρέοντι σημαίνει μολών.
τῷ δ᾽ ἀθλίας ἄσημα περιβαίνει βοῆς
ἕρποντι μᾶλλον ἆσσον, οἰμώξας δ᾽ ἔπος   1210
ἵησι δυσθρήνητον· ᾽ὦ τάλας ἐγώ,
ἆρ᾽ εἰμὶ μάντις; ἆρα δυστυχεστάτην
κέλευθον ἕρπω τῶν παρελθουσῶν ὁδῶν;
παιδός με σαίνει φθόγγος. ἀλλὰ πρόσπολοι,
ἴτ᾽ ἆσσον ὠκεῖς καὶ παραστάντες τάφῳ   51215
ἀθρήσαθ᾽, ἁρμὸν χώματος λιθοσπαδῆ
δύντες πρὸς αὐτὸ στόμιον, εἰ τὸν Αἵμονος
φθόγγον συνίημ᾽ ἢ θεοῖσι κλέπτομαι.᾽
τάδ᾽ ἐξ ἀθύμου δεσπότου κελευσμάτων
ἠθροῦμεν· ἐν δὲ λοισθίῳ τυμβεύματι   1220
τὴν μὲν κρεμαστὴν αὐχένος κατείδομεν,
βρόχῳ μιτώδει σινδόνος καθημμένην,
τὸν δ᾽ ἀμφὶ μέσσῃ περιπετῆ προσκείμενον,
εὐνῆς ἀποιμώζοντα τῆς κάτω φθορὰν
καὶ πατρὸς ἔργα καὶ τὸ δύστηνον λέχος.   1225
ὁ δ᾽ ὡς ὁρᾷ σφε, στυγνὸν οἰμώξας ἔσω
χωρεῖ πρὸς αὐτὸν κἀνακωκύσας καλεῖ·
᾽ὦ τλῆμον, οἷον ἔργον εἴργασαι· τίνα
νοῦν ἔσχες; ἐν τῷ συμφορᾶς διεφθάρης;
ἔξελθε, τέκνον, ἱκέσιός σε λίσσομαι.᾽   1230
τὸν δ᾽ ἀγρίοις ὄσσοισι παπτήνας ὁ παῖς,
πτύσας προσώπῳ κοὐδὲν ἀντειπών, ξίφους
ἕλκει διπλοῦς κνώδοντας. ἐκ δ᾽ ὁρμωμένου
πατρὸς φυγαῖσιν ἤμπλακ᾽· εἶθ᾽ ὁ δύσμορος
αὑτῷ χολωθείς, ὥσπερ εἶχ᾽, ἐπενταθεὶς   1235
ἤρεισε πλευραῖς μέσσον ἔγχος, ἐς δ᾽ ὑγρὸν
ἀγκῶν᾽ ἔτ᾽ ἔμφρων παρθένῳ προσπτύσσεται.
καὶ φυσιῶν ὀξεῖαν ἐκβάλλει ῥοὴν
λευκῇ παρειᾷ φοινίου σταλάγματος.
κεῖται δὲ νεκρὸς περὶ νεκρῷ, τὰ νυμφικὰ   1240
τέλη λαχὼν δείλαιος εἰν Ἅιδου δόμοις,

444

From far away one man heard a voice
coming from the chamber where we'd put her
without a funeral—a piercing cry.
He went to tell our master Creon,
who, as he approached the place, heard the sound,
an unintelligible scream of sorrow.
He groaned and then spoke out these bitter words,   [1210]
"Has misery made me a prophet now?
And am I travelling along a road
that takes me to the worst of all disasters?
I've just heard the voice of my own son.
You servants, go ahead—get up there fast.
Remove the stones piled in the entrance way,
then stand beside the tomb and look in there
to see if that was Haemon's voice I heard,
or if the gods have been deceiving me."
Following what our desperate master asked,
we looked. In the furthest corner of the tomb   [1220]
we saw Antigone hanging by the neck,
held up in a noose—fine woven linen.
Haemon had his arms around her waist—
he was embracing her and crying out
in sorrow for the loss of his own bride,
now among the dead, his father's work,
and for his horrifying marriage bed.
Creon saw him, let out a fearful groan,
then went inside and called out anxiously,
"You unhappy boy, what have you done?
What are you thinking? Have you lost your mind?
Come out, my child—I'm begging you—please come."   [1230]
But the boy just stared at him with savage eyes,
spat in his face and, without saying a word,
drew his two-edged sword. Creon moved away,
so the boy's blow failed to strike his father.
Angry at himself, the ill-fated lad
right then and there leaned into his own sword,
driving half the blade between his ribs.
While still conscious he embraced the girl
in his weak arms, and, as he breathed his last,
he coughed up streams of blood on her fair cheek.
Now he lies there, corpse on corpse, his marriage   [1240]
has been fulfilled in chambers of the dead.

445

Sophocles

δείξας ἐν ἀνθρώποισι τὴν ἀβουλίαν
ὅσῳ μέγιστον ἀνδρὶ πρόσκειται κακόν.

ΧΟΡΟΣ

τί τοῦτ᾽ ἂν εἰκάσειας; ἡ γυνὴ πάλιν
φρούδη, πρὶν εἰπεῖν ἐσθλὸν ἢ κακὸν λόγον.   1245

ΑΓΓΕΛΟΣ

καὐτὸς τεθάμβηκ᾽· ἐλπίσιν δὲ βόσκομαι
ἄχη τέκνου κλύουσαν ἐς πόλιν γόους
οὐκ ἀξιώσειν, ἀλλ᾽ ὑπὸ στέγης ἔσω
δμωαῖς προθήσειν πένθος οἰκεῖον στένειν.
γνώμης γὰρ οὐκ ἄπειρος, ὥσθ᾽ ἁμαρτάνειν.   1250

ΧΟΡΟΣ

οὐκ οἶδ᾽· ἐμοὶ δ᾽ οὖν ἥ τ᾽ ἄγαν σιγὴ βαρὺ
δοκεῖ προσεῖναι χἠ μάτην πολλὴ βοή.

ΑΓΓΕΛΟΣ

ἀλλ᾽ εἰσόμεσθα, μή τι καὶ κατάσχετον
κρυφῇ καλύπτει καρδίᾳ θυμουμένῃ,
δόμους παραστείχοντες· εὖ γὰρ οὖν λέγεις,   1255
καὶ τῆς ἄγαν γάρ ἐστί που σιγῆς βάρος.

ΧΟΡΟΣ

καὶ μὴν ὅδ᾽ ἄναξ αὐτὸς ἐφήκει
μνῆμ᾽ ἐπίσημον διὰ χειρὸς ἔχων,
εἰ θέμις εἰπεῖν, οὐκ ἀλλοτρίαν
ἄτην, ἀλλ᾽ αὐτὸς ἁμαρτών.   1260

ΚΡΕΩΝ

ἰὼ
φρενῶν δυσφρόνων ἁμαρτήματα
στερεὰ θανατόεντ᾽,
ὦ κτανόντας τε καὶ
θανόντας βλέποντες ἐμφυλίους.

446

The unfortunate boy has shown all men
how, of all the evils which afflict mankind,
the most disastrous one is thoughtlessness.

[Eurydice turns and slowly returns into the palace]

CHORUS LEADER
What do you make of that? The queen's gone back.
She left without a word, good or bad.

MESSENGER
I'm surprised myself. It's about her son—
she heard that terrible report. I hope
she's gone because she doesn't think it right
to mourn for him in public. In the home,
surrounded by her servants, she'll arrange
a period of mourning for the house.
She's discreet and has experience—
she won't make mistakes.   [1250]

CHORUS LEADER
                              I'm not sure of that.
to me her staying silent was extreme—
it seems to point to something ominous,
just like a vain excess of grief.

MESSENGER
                              I'll go in.
We'll find out if she's hiding something secret,
deep within her passionate heart. You're right—
excessive silence can be dangerous.

[The Messenger goes up the stairs into the palace. Enter Creon from the side, with attendants. Creon is holding the body of Haemon]

CHORUS LEADER
Here comes the king in person—carrying
in his arms, if it's right to speak of this,
a clear reminder that this evil comes
not from some stranger, but his own mistakes.   [1260]

CREON
Aaiii—mistakes made by a foolish mind,
cruel mistakes that bring on death.
You see us here, all in one family—
the killer and the killed.

447

ὤμοι ἐμῶν ἄνολβα βουλευμάτων.　　　　1265
ἰὼ παῖ, νέος νέῳ ξὺν μόρῳ
αἰαῖ αἰαῖ,
ἔθανες, ἀπελύθης
ἐμαῖς οὐδὲ σαῖς δυσβουλίαις.

ΧΟΡΟΣ
οἴμ᾿ ὡς ἔοικας ὀψὲ τὴν δίκην ἰδεῖν.　　1270

ΚΡΕΩΝ
οἴμοι,
ἔχω μαθὼν δείλαιος· ἐν δ᾿ ἐμῷ κάρᾳ
θεὸς τότ᾿ ἄρα τότε μέγα βάρος μ᾿ ἔχων
ἔπαισεν, ἐν δ᾿ ἔσεισεν ἀγρίαις ὁδοῖς,
οἴμοι, λακπάτητον ἀντρέπων χαράν.　　1275
φεῦ φεῦ, ὦ πόνοι βροτῶν δύσπονοι.

ΕΞΑΓΓΕΛΟΣ
ὦ δέσποθ᾿, ὡς ἔχων τε καὶ κεκτημένος,
τὰ μὲν πρὸ χειρῶν τάδε φέρων, τὰ δ᾿ ἐν δόμοις
ἔοικας ἥκειν καὶ τάχ᾿ ὄψεσθαι κακά.　　1280

ΚΡΕΩΝ
τί δ᾿ ἔστιν αὖ κάκιον ἐκ κακῶν ἔτι;

ΕΞΑΓΓΕΛΟΣ
γυνὴ τέθνηκε, τοῦδε παμμήτωρ νεκροῦ,
δύστηνος, ἄρτι νεοτόμοισι πλήγμασιν.

ΚΡΕΩΝ
ἰώ.
ἰὼ δυσκάθαρτος Ἅιδου λιμήν,
τί μ᾿ ἄρα τί μ᾿ ὀλέκεις;　　　　　　　1285
ὦ κακάγγελτά μοι
προπέμψας ἄχη, τίνα θροεῖς λόγον;
αἰαῖ, ὀλωλότ᾿ ἄνδρ᾿ ἐπεξειργάσω.
τί φής, παῖ; τίν᾿ αὖ λέγεις μοι νέον,
αἰαῖ αἰαῖ,　　　　　　　　　　　　1290
σφάγιον ἐπ᾿ ὀλέθρῳ
γυναικεῖον ἀμφικεῖσθαι μόρον;

Oh the profanity of what I planned.
Alas, my son, you died so young—
a death before your time.
Aaiii . . . aaiii . . . you're dead . . . gone—
not your own foolishness but mine.

CHORUS LEADER
Alas, it seems you've learned to see what's right—
but far too late.   [1270]

CREON
Aaiiii . . . I've learned it in my pain.
Some god clutching a great weight struck my head,
then hurled me onto paths in wilderness,
throwing down and casting underfoot
what brought me joy.
So sad . . . so sad . . .
the wretched agony of human life.

[The Messenger reappears from the palace]

MESSENGER
My lord, you come like one who stores up evil,
what you hold in your arms and what you'll see
before too long inside the house.   [1280]

CREON
                                    What's that?
Is there something still more evil than all this?

MESSENGER
Your wife is dead—blood mother of that corpse—
slaughtered with a sword—her wounds are very new,
poor lady.

CREON
Aaiiii . . . . a gathering place for death . . .
no sacrifice can bring this to an end.
Why are you destroying me? You there—
you bringer of this dreadful news, this agony,
what are you saying now? Aaiii . . .
You kill a man then kill him once again.
What are you saying, boy? What news?
A slaughter heaped on slaughter—   [1290]
my wife, alas . . . she's dead?

449

ΧΟΡΟΣ

    ὁρᾶν πάρεστιν· οὐ γὰρ ἐν μυχοῖς ἔτι.

ΚΡΕΩΝ

    οἴμοι,
    κακὸν τόδ᾽ ἄλλο δεύτερον βλέπω τάλας.   1295
    τίς ἄρα, τίς με πότμος ἔτι περιμένει;
    ἔχω μὲν ἐν χείρεσσιν ἀρτίως τέκνον,
    τάλας, τὸν δ᾽ ἔναντα προσβλέπω νεκρόν.
    φεῦ φεῦ μᾶτερ ἀθλία, φεῦ τέκνον.   1300

ΕΞΑΓΓΕΛΟΣ

    ἡ δ᾽ ὀξυθήκτῳ βωμία περὶ ξίφει
    λύει κελαινὰ βλέφαρα, κωκύσασα μὲν
    τοῦ πρὶν θανόντος Μεγαρέως κλεινὸν λάχος,
    αὖθις δὲ τοῦδε, λοίσθιον δὲ σοὶ κακὰς
    πράξεις ἐφυμνήσασα τῷ παιδοκτόνῳ.   1305

ΚΡΕΩΝ

    αἰαῖ αἰαῖ,
    ἀνέπταν φόβῳ. τί μ᾽ οὐκ ἀνταίαν
    ἔπαισέν τις ἀμφιθήκτῳ ξίφει;
    δείλαιος ἐγώ, αἰαῖ,   1310
    δειλαίᾳ δὲ συγκέκραμαι δύᾳ.

ΕΞΑΓΓΕΛΟΣ

    ὡς αἰτίαν γε τῶνδε κἀκείνων ἔχων
    πρὸς τῆς θανούσης τῆσδ᾽ ἐπεσκήπτου μόρων

ΚΡΕΩΝ

    ποίῳ δὲ κἀπελύσατ᾽ ἐν φοναῖς τρόπῳ;

ΕΞΑΓΓΕΛΟΣ

    παίσας ὑφ᾽ ἧπαρ αὐτόχειρ αὑτήν, ὅπως   1315
    παιδὸς τόδ᾽ ᾔσθετ᾽ ὀξυκώκυτον πάθος.

ΚΡΕΩΝ

    ὤμοι μοι, τάδ᾽ οὐκ ἐπ᾽ ἄλλον βροτῶν
    ἐμᾶς ἁρμόσει ποτ᾽ ἐξ αἰτίας.

MESSENGER *[opening the palace doors, revealing the body of Eurydice]*
    Look here. No longer is she concealed inside.

CREON
    Alas, how miserable I feel—to look upon
    this second horror. What remains for me,
    what's fate still got in store? I've just held
    my own son in my arms, and now I see
    right here in front of me another corpse.
    Alas for this suffering mother.   [1300]
    Alas, my son.

MESSENGER
    Stabbed with a sharp sword at the altar,
    she let her darkening eyesight fail,
    once she had cried out in sorrow
    for the glorious fate of Megareos,
    who died some time ago, and then again
    for Haemon, and then, with her last breath,
    she called out evil things against you,
    the killer of your sons.[33]

CREON
    Aaaii . . . My fear now makes me tremble.
    Why won't someone now strike out at me,
    pierce my heart with a double bladed sword?
    How miserable I am . . . aaiii . . .   [1310]
    how full of misery and pain . . .

MESSENGER
    By this woman who lies dead you stand charged
    with the deaths of both your sons.

CREON
                      What about her?
    How did she die so violently?

MESSENGER
                      She killed herself,
    with her own hands she stabbed her belly,
    once she heard her son's unhappy fate.

CREON
    Alas for me . . . the guilt for all of this is mine—
    it can never be removed from me or passed
    to any other mortal man. I, and I alone . . .

ἐγὼ γάρ σ᾽ ἐγὼ ἔκανον, ὦ μέλεος,
ἐγώ, φάμ᾽ ἔτυμον. ἰὼ πρόσπολοι,   1320
ἄγετέ μ᾽ ὅτι τάχιστ᾽, ἄγετέ μ᾽ ἐκποδών,
τὸν οὐκ ὄντα μᾶλλον ἢ μηδένα.   1325

ΧΟΡΟΣ

κέρδη παραινεῖς, εἴ τι κέρδος ἐν κακοῖς.
βράχιστα γὰρ κράτιστα τὰν ποσὶν κακά.

ΚΡΕΩΝ

ἴτω ἴτω,
φανήτω μόρων ὁ κάλλιστ᾽ ἔχων
ἐμοὶ τερμίαν ἄγων ἁμέραν   1330
ὕπατος· ἴτω ἴτω,
ὅπως μηκέτ᾽ ἆμαρ ἄλλ᾽ εἰσίδω.

ΧΟΡΟΣ

μέλλοντα ταῦτα. τῶν προκειμένων τι χρὴ μέλειν
πράσσειν. μέλει γὰρ τῶνδ᾽ ὅτοισι χρὴ μέλειν   1335

ΚΡΕΩΝ

ἀλλ᾽ ὧν ἐρῶ, τοιαῦτα συγκατηυξάμην.

ΧΟΡΟΣ

μή νυν προσεύχου μηδέν· ὡς πεπρωμένης
οὐκ ἔστι θνητοῖς συμφορᾶς ἀπαλλαγή.

ΚΡΕΩΝ

ἄγοιτ᾽ ἂν μάταιον ἄνδρ᾽ ἐκποδών,
ὅς, ὦ παῖ, σέ τ᾽ οὐχ ἑκὼν κάκτανον   1340
σέ τ᾽ αὖ τάνδ᾽, ὤμοι μέλεος, οὐδ᾽ ἔχω
ὅπᾳ πρὸς πότερα κλιθῶ· πάντα γὰρ
λέχρια τὰν χεροῖν, τὰ δ᾽ ἐπὶ κρατί μοι   1345
πότμος δυσκόμιστος εἰσήλατο.

I murdered you . . . I speak the truth.
Servants—hurry and lead me off,   [1320]
get me away from here, for now
what I am in life is nothing.

CHORUS LEADER

What you advise is good—if good can come
with all these evils. When we face such things
the less we say the better.

CREON

Let that day come, O let it come,
the fairest of all destinies for me,
the one which brings on my last day.   [1330]
Oh, let it come, so that I never see
another dawn.

CHORUS LEADER

That's something for the times ahead.
Now we need to deal with what confronts us here.
What's yet to come is the concern of those
whose task it is to deal with it.

CREON

                                    In that prayer
I included everything I most desire.

CHORUS

                                    Pray for nothing.
There's no release for mortal human beings,
not from events which destiny has set.

CREON

Then take this foolish man away from here.
I killed you, my son, without intending to,   [1340]
and you, as well, my wife. How useless I am now.
I don't know where to look or find support.
Everything I touch goes wrong, and on my head
fate climbs up with its overwhelming load.

[The Attendants help Creon move up the stairs into the palace, taking Hae-mon's body with them]

Sophocles

ΧΟΡΟΣ
πολλῷ τὸ φρονεῖν εὐδαιμονίας
πρῶτον ὑπάρχει. χρὴ δὲ τά γ᾽ εἰς θεοὺς
μηδὲν ἀσεπτεῖν. μεγάλοι δὲ λόγοι   1350
μεγάλας πληγὰς τῶν ὑπεραύχων
ἀποτίσαντες
γήρᾳ τὸ φρονεῖν ἐδίδαξαν.

CHORUS

    The most important part of true success

    is wisdom—not to act impiously

    towards the gods, for boasts of arrogant men   [1350]

    bring on great blows of punishment—

    so in old age men can discover wisdom.

NOTES

1. Dirce is one of the rivers beside Thebes.

2. Hephaistos is god of fire.

3. Laius was king of Thebes and father of Oedipus. Oedipus killed him (not knowing who he was) and became the next king of Thebes by saving the city from the devastation of the Sphinx.

4. Zeus Herkeios refers to Zeus of the Courtyard, a patron god of worship within the home.

5. Hades, a brother of Zeus, is god of the underworld, lord of the dead.

6. Labdakos is the father of Laius and hence grandfather of Oedipus and great-grandfather of Antigone and Ismene.

7. Olympus is a mountain in northern Greece where, according to tradition, the major gods live.

8. Following common editorial practice, the lines of the Greek have been rearranged here, so that 663-7 come after 671, hence the apparently odd numbering of the lines.

9. Following the suggestion of Andrew Brown and others, I have moved lines 756-7 in the Greek text so that they come right after line 750.

10. The killing of a family member could bring on divine punishment in the form of a pollution involving the entire city (as in the case of Oedipus). Creon is, one assumes, taking refuge in the notion that he will not be executing Antigone directly.

11. Eros is the young god of erotic sexual passion.

12. Aphrodite was the goddess of sexual desire.

13. Acheron is one of the major rivers of the underworld.

14. The last two speeches refer to Niobe, daughter of Tantalus (a son of Zeus). Niobe had seven sons and seven daughters and boasted that she had more children than the goddess Leto. As punishment Artemis and Apollo, Leto's two children, destroyed all Niobe's children. Niobe turned

to stone in grief and was reportedly visible on Mount Sipylus (in Asia Minor). The Chorus' claim that Niobe was a goddess or semi-divine is odd here, since her story is almost always a tale of human presumption and divine punishment for human arrogance.

15. The Chorus here is offering the traditional suggestion that present afflictions can arise from a family curse originating in previous generations.

16. Polyneices married the daughter of Adrastus, an action which enabled him to acquire the army to attack Thebes.

17. Creon's logic seems to suggest that because he is not executing Antigone directly and is leaving her a choice between committing suicide and slowly starving to death in the cave, he has no moral responsibility for what happens.

18. Persephone is the wife of Hades and thus goddess of the underworld.

19. In these lines Antigone seems to be talking about both her brothers, first claiming she washed and dressed the body of Eteocles and then covered Polyneices. However, the pronoun references in the Greek are confusing. Lines 904 to 920 in the Greek text have prompted a great deal of critical debate, since they seem incompatible with Antigone's earlier motivation and do not make much sense in context (in addition most of them appear closely derived from Herodotus 3.119). Hence, some editors insist that the lines (or most of them) be removed. Brown provides a useful short summary of the arguments and some editorial options (Andrew Brown. *Sophocles: Antigone*. Warminster: Aris & Phillips, 1987. pp. 199-200).

20. Danaë was daughter of Acrisius, King of Argos. Because of a prophecy that he would be killed by a son born to Danaë, Acrisius imprisoned her. But Zeus made love to her in the form of a golden shower, and she gave birth to Perseus, who, once grown, killed Acrisius accidentally.

21. These lines refer to Lycurgus son of Dryas, a Thracian king. He attacked the god Dionysus and was punished with blinding or with being torn apart.

22. The anger of the Muses at a Thracian who boasted of his flute playing is not normally a part of the Lycurgus story but refers to another Thracian, Thamyras.

23. The black rocks were a famous hazard to shipping. They moved together to smash any ship moving between them. The Bosphorus is the strait

between the Black Sea and the Propontis (near the Hellespont). This verse and the next refer to the Thracian king Phineas, whose second wife blinded her two step sons (from Phineas' first wife Cleopatra) by stabbing out their eyes.

24. Cleopatra was the grand-daughter of Erechtheus, king of Athens. Boreas, father of Erechtheus, was god of the North Wind.

25. Teiresias' offering failed to catch fire. His interpretation is that it has been rejected by the gods, a very unfavourable omen.

26. This is the second reference to the fact that at some point earlier Teiresias has given important political help to Creon. It is not at all clear what this refers to.

27. Teiresias here is apparently accusing Creon of refusing burial to the dead allied soldiers Polyneices brought with him from other cities. There is no mention of this anywhere else in the play, although the detail is present in other versions of the story.

28. In these lines the Chorus celebrates Dionysus, the god born in Thebes to Semele, daughter of King Cadmus. The bacchants are those who worship Dionysus. Eleusis, a region on the coast near Athens, was famous for the its Eleusinian Mysteries, a secret ritual of worship. Deo is a reference to the goddess Demeter, who was worshipped at Eleusis. The Theban race sprang up from dragon's teeth sown in a field by Cadmus, founder of the city.

29. *Evoë* is a cry of celebration made by worshippers of Dionysus.

30. Semele, Dionysus' human mother, was destroyed by Zeus lightning bolt, because of the jealousy of Hera, Zeus' wife.

31. Thyiads were worshipers of Dionysus, and Iacchus was a divinity associated with Dionysus.

32. Amphion was legendary king of Thebes, husband of Niobe.

33. Megareos was Haemon's brother, who, we are to understand on the basis of this reference, died nobly some time before the play begins. It is not clear how Creon might have been responsible for his death. In another version of the story, Creon has a son Menoeceos, who kills himself in order to save the city.